Oracle Press™

Oracle Procure-to-Pay Guide

Melanie Anjele Cameron

New York   Chicago   San Francisco
Lisbon   London   Madrid   Mexico City   Milan
New Delhi   San Juan   Seoul   Singapore   Sydney   Toronto

The McGraw·Hill Companies

Cataloging-in-Publication Data is on file with the Library of Congress

McGraw-Hill books are available at special quantity discounts to use as premiums and sales promotions, or for use in corporate training programs. To contact a special sales representative, please visit the Contact Us page at www.mhprofessional.com.

Oracle Procure-to-Pay Guide

1234567890 DOC DOC 019

ISBN 978-0-07-162227-1
MHID   0-07-162227-6

Sponsoring Editor Lisa McClain	**Copy Editor** Robert Campbell	**Composition** Apollo Publishing
Editorial Supervisor Patty Mon	**Proofreader** Martin Benes	**Illustration** Apollo Publishing, Lyssa Wald
Project Editor LeeAnn Pickrell	**Indexer** James Minkin	**Art Director, Cover** Jeff Weeks
Acquisitions Coordinator Meghan Riley	**Production Supervisor** George Anderson	**Cover Designer** Pattie Lee
Technical Editor Lucas Belter		

For Mike. May you have found peace.

About the Author

Melanie Anjele Cameron has dedicated her career to improving business processes and business systems, especially in the areas of Finance and Accounting. Always strongly believing in sharing the knowledge about computer systems and how to use them, she has been the chairperson for AZOAUG, the Phoenix-area Oracle applications users group, for the past seven years, participating not only in organizing the events, but also as a lecturer.

Her career has taken her from a transaction processing clerk to an executive during an IPO, as well as co-owner of her husband's business, giving her a well-rounded and in-depth knowledge of business, from detailed transactions to their broader impact on the business itself. Lucky to find an organization where this breadth of knowledge can be used to assist other companies, Melanie now manages the E-Business Suite practice at MSS Technologies (www.MSSTech.com).

While participating in the high-tech world of business, Melanie keeps her feet firmly planted in the low-tech world of needlework, spending most of her non-working hours knitting and creating pieces of art with a needle, including needlepoint and Japanese embroidery. This, combined with a love for good food and cooking, helps to keep the pressures of our high-tech society at bay. Melanie lives in Phoenix, Arizona, with her husband, Bill, and two dogs, Josie and Yuki.

About the Technical Editor

Mr. Lucas Belter has extensive industry experience as an Oracle E-Business Suite Consultant, analyzing, designing, and implementing solutions for clients in a variety of industries, including high-tech manufacturing, health care, financial services, and distribution. He has experience with the full suite of EBS modules. Mr. Belter has worked as a team lead, trainer, and consultant on dozens of projects, including full lifecycle implementations, enhancement projects, and support initiatives. Mr. Belter has excellent knowledge of the Oracle Applications Implementation Methodology (AIM).

Contents

Acknowledgments ix
Introduction x

1   Procure-to-Pay Overview **1**
The Procure-to-Pay Family 2
    Purchasing 2
    iProcurement 2
    iSupplier Portal 3
    Services Procurement 3
    Sourcing 3
    Procurement Contracts 3
    Approval Management 3
    E-Business Tax 3
    iExpenses 3
    Payables 3
    Payments 4
    Subledger Accounting 4
A Word about Conversions 4
    Converting Suppliers 4
    Open Invoices 4
    Purchasing Conversions 5

2   Purchasing Setups **7**
Setups Completed with Other Modules 8
Locations for Delivery (Conditionally Required) 8
Organization Classification (Required) 10
    Inventory Parameters 12
    Costing Information 12
    Revision, Lot, Serial, and LPN 12
    Other Accounts 12
Defining Item Number Format in EBS (Optional) 13
Units of Measure (Conditionally Required) 13
    Setting Up Classes 14

Adding Additional Units of Measure to a Class 14
Unit of Measure Conversions 15
Creating Categories for Purchasing (Required) 16
Using Employees in Purchasing (Required) 19
Setting Up Approvers for Requisitions and Purchase Orders (Required) 20
Creating Buyers (Required) 22
Purchasing Options (Required) 24
Document Controls 24
Document Defaults 27
Document Numbering 30
Receiving Options 30
Accounting Options Available with Receiving Transactions 33
Cost Factors for Receipts 33
Financial Options (Required) 33
Line Types (Conditionally Required) 33
Requisition Templates (Optional) 34
Document Types (Conditionally Required) 35
Account Generator (Conditionally Required) 37

3   Processing Purchasing Documents **39**
Purchasing Documents 40
Requests for Quote 40
Requisitions 40
Purchase Orders and Agreements 40
Releases 40
Purchasing Documents, Step-by-Step 41
Requisitions 41
Using the Supplier Item Catalog to Create Requisition Lines 45
Requisition Distributions 47
Outside Processing 49
Defaulting Requisition Information 49
Approving Purchasing Documents 50
Approving a Requisition 51
Controlling Requisitions 52
Creating Purchase Orders from Requisitions 53
AutoCreate 54
Purchasing Documents 60
Setting Purchase Order Preferences 67
Approving Purchasing Orders 68
Controlling Purchasing Documents 68
Tracking Changes to Purchasing Documents 70
Releases 71
Buyers Work Center 71
Demand Workbench 72
Receiving 73
Receipts 74
Returns 76
Correcting Receiving and Return Transactions 76
Purchasing Month End and Accruals 77
Understanding EBS's Accrual Process 77

Loading Balances into the Accrual Tables 78
Additional Reconciliation Reports 78
Writing Off Accrual Transactions 79
Period End Accruals 79
Controlling Periods 80

4   **Suppliers** **81**
Technical Update 82
Creating Suppliers 82
Quick Update 83
Company Profile/Organization 86
Tax Details 88
Address Book 90
Contact Directory 93
Business Classification 93
Products and Services 94
Banking Details 95
Surveys 97
Terms and Control/Accounting 97
Tax and Reporting 99
Purchasing 100
Receiving 101
Payment Details 102
Invoice Management 104
Ongoing Supplier Maintenance 104
Identifying Duplicate Suppliers 105
Merging Suppliers 105

5   **Payables Setups** **107**
Required Setups 108
Operating Unit 108
Financial Options 108
Payables System Setups 112
Invoice Tolerances 113
Payables Options 114
Payment Terms 121
Special Calendars 123
Aging Periods 124
Bank Setups 125
Open First Payables Period 133
Profiles 133
Optional Setups 135
Hold and Release Reasons 135
Expense Report Templates 142
Distribution Sets 143
Folders 146

6   **Payables Processing** **149**
Invoices 150
Manual Invoices 150
Defaulting Information During Invoice Entry 151

Invoice Batch Window 152
Invoice Workbench 153
Invoice Information Tabs 160
Entering Quick Invoices 188
Expense Report Processing in Payables 190
Netting Outstanding Receivables and Payables 193
Recurring Invoices 198
Importing Invoices 202
1099 Processing 205
Payables Processing Flow from Beginning to End 208
Invoice Validation 210
Invoice Approval 210
Creating Accounting Entries 211
Inquiring on Payables Invoices 212
Closing and Reconciling Payables 214
Validate All Transactions 214
Reviewing the Invoice on Hold Report 215
Creating Accounting Entries 215
Transferring Data to the General Ledger 215
Ensuring All Transactions Are Accounted and Transferred Prior
      to Closing the Period 215
Controlling Payables Periods 216
Balancing Payables to the General Ledger 217

7   Payments Setups **219**
Setting Up Payments 220
Shared Setups 220
Disbursement-Specific Setups 233
System Profiles for Payments 244
Creating Templates for Streamlined Payment Processing 245

8   Payment Processing **249**
Introducing the Managers 250
Payment Batches vs. Single Payments 251
Generating Single Payments 251
Voiding, Stopping, and Reissuing Payments 256
Refunds 256
Using the Payment Manager 257
Creating Requests for Payment 257
Scheduling Settlement Batches 260
Bills Payable Settlements 262
Bills Payable Setups 262
Managing Payment Processing 262
Determining Cash Requirements 269
Bank Reconciliations 270
Updating Transactions 270
Bank Reconciliation Reports 271
Calculating Balances Owed to Suppliers 271

Glossary **275**

Index **281**

Acknowledgments

When acknowledging all the people involved in getting a book from concept to print, the list can be longer than the book itself! But there are always a few who stand out, both directly and indirectly. My parents, by always instilling in me that I could accomplish anything, have to top that list. My Mom, a lifelong teacher, is still a driving force behind my wanting to always learn more and find that ever-elusive answer to Why and then turning around and sharing the answer with anyone who wants to listen. My husband, in a much more subtle way, is always watching my back and looking out for me while I push forward in my endeavors.

Every technical author has two groups of people assisting to get the concept to market. The first is composed of the editors at their publisher, and Lisa McClain and her staff have been about as helpful and patient as any author can ask for. From late-night panic e-mails to re-explaining the formatting requirements yet again, these saints all deserve halos. Second are their technical editors. Lucas Belter spent evenings and weekends reviewing this information and ensuring it was complete and accurate and logical for the users.

The drive to write came at an early age, starting around eighth grade, and never left me. It was the encouragement of both past and current mentors who have kindled that flame and given it the sparks it needed to move forward and never die. Becky Tipton is such a person, showing me that writing and work do not have to be mutually exclusive. Mike Hawksworth, owner of MSS Technologies, is another, always there to remind me that yes, you can reach for the stars and even get there. No book is written alone, for it is the experiences of the author's life that are combined to make it happen. Thank you, everyone, for these experiences.

A special thanks also goes out to Pioter (Peter) Belter, who always found time to comment and give his opinion when a cloud was preventing me from seeing the path to clarity.

Introduction

Some of the greatest technological advancements in business have been made in the procure-to-pay processes, not only in automation, but also in connectivity between the supplier and the purchaser. As with all areas, when technology steps in and automates the processes, the steps required to perform the automation are swept away, where they linger, still the backbone for the process but lost to common knowledge. I have seen this repeated over and over throughout the years. As automation takes over, the steps, required to perform the task, are buried under a blanket of automation. In order to understand the automation, users *must* first understand the steps involved.

This lost knowledge became the premise for this book, identifying and outlining the manual tasks that automation is built on. This book, the *Oracle Procure-to-Pay Guide*, is designed to walk functional users and techies alike through the setup and processing steps to create an integrated and automated procure-to-pay system. Both new and old functionality is covered in detail, with field-by-field explanations and references back to the controlling setups. While functional users were my main focus when writing the book, support analysts and programmers will also greatly benefit from it. The setups are usually done by consultants, who then walk out the door with all the knowledge, and this book will assist in delivering some of that knowledge back to the company itself, and just may help you avoid creating a customization or two for a functionality that already exists, just begging to be found and used.

This book, while designed to read cover to cover, is also self-inclusive for each section, allowing the reader to go directly to a particular section and not be referenced back to other areas for more information. For Oracle or industry-specific terms, a glossary is included at the back for rapid access.

This book is broken down into three main sections: Purchasing, Payables, and Payments. The sections are tightly integrated, and the setups and processing steps refer back to these cross-over areas, showing how they intertwine to create transactions.

CHAPTER
1

Procure-to-Pay Overview

he Procure-to-Pay process is the heart of any organization—it's the flow that gets the goods required to do business. From the supplies that keep office staff productive to shop floor inventory that is delivered just in time for consumption in the manufacturing process, all organizations have a hard time functioning without this cycle.

Oracle E-Business Suite (EBS) has a comprehensive and integrated Procure-to-Pay cycle that can be set up to meet any company's needs. On the simple side, these needs may include manual purchase orders to procure items, receipts that are matched to invoices when they are delivered, and ultimately the creation of payments. Or they may entail a more complex cycle that is fully automated, where manufacturing demand generates purchase orders on which suppliers are determined by sourcing rules and sent out via XML, items are received into inventory according to supplier advanced shipping notifications, and invoices are created from the inspection process and paid with scheduled payment runs that remit the funds directly into the suppliers' bank accounts. While this automation is 100 percent within the functionality of the Oracle EBS Procure-to-Pay process, it is the steps performed by the system to make up these processes that need to be understood before they can be successfully automated.

Every company is different, and so are their needs for procurement. A high-tech consulting company is not going to have the same procurement needs as a high-tech manufacturing company. That is why EBS has a large array of capabilities, including both automated and manual processes.

This book is intended to cover what the Procure-to-Pay process can do, detailed setup descriptions, and instructions on how to process the steps manually; since without the manual understanding, the automated processes cannot be implemented or monitored.

The Procure-to-Pay Family

Multiple modules make up the Procure-to-Pay family in EBS. At the heart of it all are Purchasing and Payables, housing the core purchasing and invoice processing functions. Integrating tightly with these modules are iProcurement, iSupplier Portal, Services Procurement, Sourcing, Procurement Contracts, Approval Management, E-Business Tax, iExpenses, and Payments. Subledger Accounting is utilized to account for the transactions generated by all these systems. Some of these are actual modules, while others are features that can be turned on within the core areas of Purchasing and Payables.

Purchasing

The core Purchasing module controls the procurement functions within EBS, with the Buyers Work Center being the heart for controlling Request for Quotes (RFQ), Quotes, Requisitions, and Purchase Orders. With built-in and flexible approval structures, it offers the ability to tightly control this purchasing process. Purchasing also owns the receiving process.

iProcurement

iProcurement is a web-based module that allows users to create requisitions from shopping lists, stores, or punchouts to a supplier website; it incorporates an integrated approval process that can be viewed by the requestor and can receive items. Tightly integrated with Purchasing and Receiving functions, as well as Workflow and Approval Management, iProcurement provides an easy-to-use interface for ordering and receiving products.

iSupplier Portal

iSupplier Portal is designed for better collaboration with suppliers by granting them access to view information about their orders and payments in EBS, such as open orders and invoice statuses, to submit address or contact changes, to respond to RFQs, or to upload their catalogs into EBS for use by Purchasing.

Services Procurement

While purchasing services is closely related to the purchase of goods, dealing with the intangible components of services, such as the delivery of the invoiced hours, makes it harder to control. The Services Procurement processes that are integrated into Purchasing assist in this process, allowing for purchasing by hour or on a fixed-fee basis, integration into Oracle Project for tracking costs, and retainage amounts being withheld and invoiced at a later date. Flexible and detailed deliveries also assist in the accurate tracking of these services.

Sourcing

Sourcing becomes the core of any enterprise's procurement cycle, creating the rules and guidelines both suppliers and employees must follow to create and track RFQs and bids on projects, and ultimately to create a purchase order to proceed with the procurement of the sourced items.

Procurement Contracts

Every organization over a certain size eventually maintains purchasing contracts with suppliers for the procurement of goods, with specific terms and pricing. Procurement Contracts allows these agreements to be tracked and monitored for compliance throughout the Procure-to-Pay process.

Approval Management

Approval Management is an integrated module that allows rules and conditions to be defined for the approval of documents, such as purchase orders, requisitions, and invoices. While the standard features of the Purchasing and Payables modules allow for approval hierarchies based on positions or supervisors, along with approval limits, Approval Management allows complex rules surrounding the purchasing approval process to better enable an organization to control the purchasing cycle. An example would be requiring the director of information technology, in addition to the requestor's manager, to approve all computer-related purchases.

E-Business Tax

The E-Business Tax module calculates all aspects of transaction tax, from withholding to value-added. This module, tightly integrated with Purchasing, Payables, and Receivables, allows rules and rates to be defined for the taxation of products and services being purchased and consumed.

iExpenses

iExpenses is a web-based interface for users to enter expense reports for audit for compliance and payment. EBS includes approval processes and can enforce expense policies.

Payables

Sharing the Supplier Master data with Purchasing, Payables controls accounting and payment of invoices and can tightly integrate with Purchasing to achieve three- and four-way matching.

Payments

Payments, new in R12, is a module that controls all aspects of generating payments for suppliers (and to some extent, receiving payments from customers), beginning with payment selection rules, groupings, and validation and ultimately handling the process all the way through submission to the bank or printing the checks on a printer.

This book focuses mainly on Purchasing, Payables, and Payments, but to some extent, it must address the entire procure-to-pay process, due to the tightly integrated character of the EBS solution.

Subledger Accounting

Subledger Accounting is new in R12 as well, and it replaces all the various account generators that existed prior to it. This service will house the rules and create the accounting for receipts, month-end accruals, invoices, and payments.

A Word about Conversions

All new implementation projects need to address the aspect of data conversions. In EBS, it is best to address this in terms of open transactions as opposed to historical data, due to the integrated nature of the transactions. If an organization wants to record the past two years of historical purchasing data and is running Purchasing, Receiving, and Payables, this will require creating purchase orders that are matched correctly to receipts and invoices, which will have to record the exact payment history. These transactions will all need to reflect the same integration as the legacy system to be meaningful. This precise replication and integration is difficult to achieve and time-consuming to convert. There are basic data components that need to be addressed in any conversion: suppliers, items (if you are using them), unpaid invoices, and open and unreceived purchase orders.

Converting Suppliers

The minimum suppliers that will have to be created in EBS are those that are associated with any open invoice or purchase order that will be converted. Usually, an organization will look back over the past two to four years and convert all the suppliers it has done business with to ensure a good supply base is available for the users. Going back much farther than that may just be moving unnecessary baggage to the new home, and you should determine if there is a need prior to proceeding. Suppliers can always be added later on, but they cannot be deleted, only end-dated, once they are in EBS. This is also a good time to review supplier information for consistency (is it Mr. John Smith or Smith, John Mr.?) and valid address information. Ensure this is done early on in the project to avoid causing delays in the implementation. Assigning a separate team to this effort will also free up the core project team for other tasks.

Open Invoices

Though this sounds pretty straightforward, there actually two options when converting open invoices. Do I convert the invoices into EBS, or do I run out the invoices in the old system, booking the associated journal entries manually? The organization size is really the determining factor here, as well as the outstanding payables.

Purchasing Conversions

At the minimum, you will need to convert active purchase orders. If a computerized requisition process was utilized in the legacy system, then you should also convert requisitions that are in process (approved requisitions should have already become purchase orders prior to conversion, and it is the open purchase order that will be converted as opposed to the requisition).

All these transactions (suppliers, invoices, requisitions, and purchase orders) have open interfaces, or APIs (application programming interfaces), that can be used to import data. While this is an automated solution, companies with reasonable numbers of open transactions should not discount converting the data manually. This is an invaluable training tool for the new users, making them comfortable with the system prior to go live. Eight to ten hours is the cutoff point I use for manual conversion. This is where the training ends, boredom sets in, mistakes start to happen, and the cost in labor begins to outweigh the cost of developing an interface. The last option for converting data is the programs that exist today called keystroke mimickers, such as Data Loader, or spreadsheet integrators. These tools allow you to take data from Excel and load it into any form in EBS. Remember to look at using Folders or Form Personalizations, where fields can be moved and added, to potentially change the form format, making keystroke mimickers more easily used on more forms. At all costs, avoid loading data directly into the EBS tables at the database level. Besides making your system unsupported, the data will bypass all the validations written into forms and APIs and interfaces, potentially making garbage data the foundation for your new system.

With EBS, it is highly recommended that closed transactions never be converted in the submodules. The APIs Oracle has written were designed for open transactions and do not build all the links between transactional data, such as open invoices, and their resolution, the payment of the invoices. In order to load all transactions, you would have to load a Purchase Order and its corresponding receipts. Since the product relating to these receipts may no longer be in the company's warehouse, now the corresponding sales orders and shipments are needed. And this hypothetical company also uses lot control, so the proper lot numbers need to be recorded for each shipment. These shipments would create invoices in EBS automatically, with different numbers in the legacy system that would have to be matched to the proper payments.... You can see how quickly this snowballs into a complicated web of transactions, often leaving the systems with bad data or the company with a large programming bill that was probably not necessary. Keeping the legacy system up in inquiry mode through at least the next audit will satisfy most needs for legacy data, or alternatively, some companies create reports out of the legacy data to supply this data.

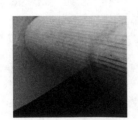

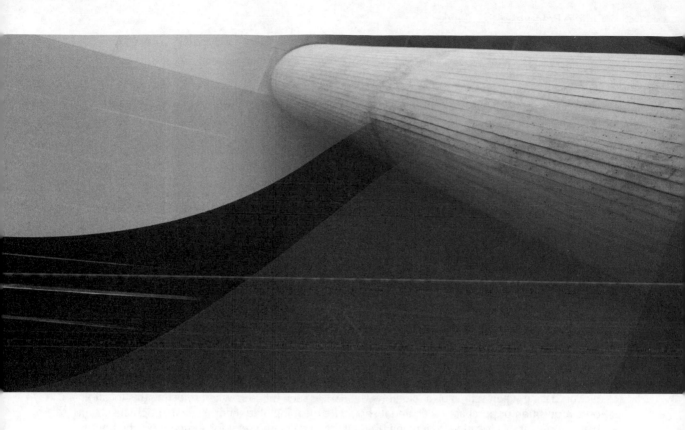

CHAPTER
2

Purchasing Setups

urchasing, Procurement, Supply Chain: call it what you will, but it is how your company gets all kinds of stuff. When this process is combined in an integrated enterprise resource planning (ERP) package such as Oracle E-Business Suite, things can get complicated pretty quickly. Understanding the setups involved that make the system tick can help uncomplicate things, providing the foundation needed to make EBS work for your company instead of the other way around. This chapter will be broken into two main sections: required setups to use the basics of the purchasing module, and optional setups to make the system do more of the work.

In its most simple terms, EBS allows a user to create a purchase order, approve it, print it, and match it to an invoice for payment. This section will outline the setups required to do just that.

Setups Completed with Other Modules

Several of the setups would have been completed with other module setups, such as System Administrator and General Ledger, and are outlined in Table 2-1 with descriptions of each step.

Locations for Delivery (Conditionally Required)

Locations are used for several purposes in EBS, including business locations that are associated with Legal Entities, physical locations that are associated with employees, and purchasing locations that represent where a product will be delivered. Figures 2-1 and 2-2 show the information used by Purchasing when setting up a location. The NAME is seen by users when selecting this location on a requisition or purchase order, and it should be meaningful to them. You can populate INACTIVE DATE to prevent this location from being used after that date, and set it for sometime in the future.

Setup Name	Area of EBS Responsible For	Description
Define Accounting Key Flexfields and load account numbers	General Ledger	General Ledger account numbers are required on several of the setup forms for purchasing as well as on the distributions added when creating a purchase order.
Setup Accounting Calendar	General Ledger	This associates dates with a specific accounting period.
Currencies	General Ledger	Any currency used on a purchase order must be enabled, and conversion types created and conversion rates entered.
Ledgers	General Ledger	All transactions are assigned to a specific Ledger for accounting.

TABLE 2-1 *Purchasing Setups Usually Completed with Other EBS Modules*

LEGAL ADDRESS is checked if this location was set up from the Legal Entity setups for Location; these addresses are reserved for Legal Entities and cannot be updated for any Purchasing information. Under the Address Details tab, the physical address of the location is added as well as the time zone that it resides in.

The Shipping Details page is the first place where purchasing specific information is entered. CONTACT is the direct contact for this location and can relate to either the site contact information or the buyer for that location. The SHIP-TO LOCATION determines the address where any product for this location is to be delivered to; it can be a different address than the actual location, if, for instance, you have a large building that has one address for the warehouse and a different one for the administrative buildings.

The next check boxes determine what this location can be used for. Locations that have SHIP-TO SITES can be used when creating purchase orders and requisitions for external entities, such as suppliers, whereas INTERNAL SITES are used for internal requisitions and purchase orders, representing purchases from another organization or location for your own company. RECEIVING SITES allow receiving transactions to be recorded against them, and BILL-TO SITES are used for tracking Payables invoices. The last choice is OFFICE SITE, which is used to track a physical office location and has some specific functionality with Europe localizations. The EXTRA INFORMATION button is used to enter Human Resources–specific information.

The Other Details tab associates an INVENTORY ORGANIZATION where any inventory items will be received into for this location, and EDI LOCATION identifies this location as the place where the Advanced Shipment Notifications will be received, both with and without invoices. The TAX CODES field is used in conjunction with E-Business Tax or third-party tax engines to calculate tax according to the location code as opposed to the item alone.

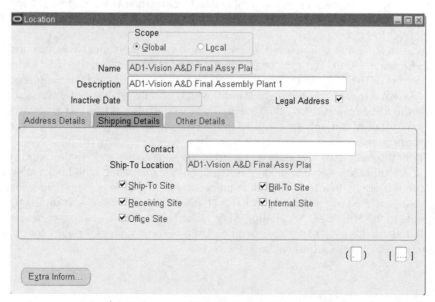

Purchasing Superuser | Setup | Organizations | Locations

FIGURE 2-1 *Purchasing-specific information on a location*

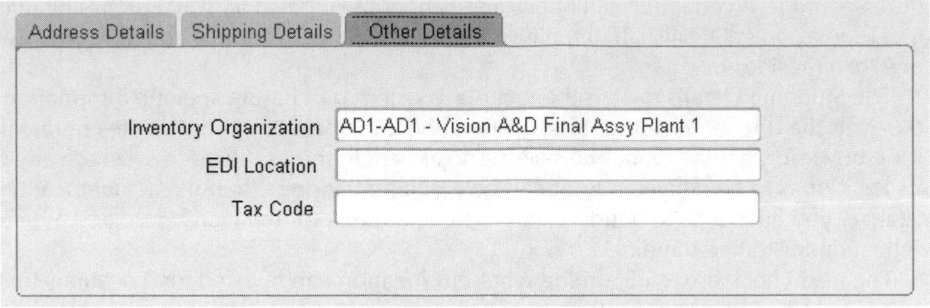

FIGURE 2-2 *Inventory- and Payables-specific information on a location*

Organization Classification (Required)

EBS comes with a large number of organizational classifications; the functionality being used determines which need to be set up. For Purchasing, the Organization setup required is called Operating Unit. The main purpose of an Operating Unit Organization is to associate a purchasing organization to the Ledger; this is a many-to-one relationship, where each Ledger can have multiple organizations associated to it, but each organization can be related to only one Ledger. Additional information for some of the advanced functionality in Purchasing can also be set up here, such as Bill To and Ship To Countries, Contract Terms, the Default Notify User for Contracts and Sales Assistance, as well as Quoting Defaults. Operating Units can be set up as part of the Ledger setups or added later as part of the Purchasing setups. To add them as part of the Purchasing setups, refer to Figure 2-3.

Create a NAME that will be used when selecting the Organization in setups and by the system for this Operating Unit. The TYPE classifies what type of Organization this is and is used for reporting purposes only. The DATES determine the period it is effective for, and the TO, or end, can be left blank. Assign a LOCATION to the organization, which usually relates to the physical address, and classify the location as INTERNAL or EXTERNAL. This classification is used when assigning employees to a location: they can only be assigned to Internal organizations. At this point the work must be saved prior to proceeding.

Under the ORGANIZATION CLASSIFICATIONS, add an OPERATING UNIT and ENABLE it, and again save the work. Click OTHER to receive additional information; the Operating Unit Information is required to associate this unit with a Ledger. Click in the NAME field to get the pop-up, and select a Primary Ledger—this is the Ledger that all purchasing transactions will create accounting transactions in, according to the Subledger Accounting (SLA) rules. The DEFAULT LEGAL CONTEXT has Ledgers listed as well and can be used to set up Operating Units without financial setups for non-financial transactions. Exiting this form will save the record.

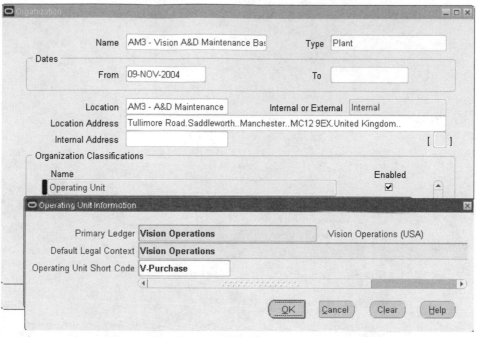

Purchasing Superuser | Setup| Organizations| Organizations

FIGURE 2-3 *Adding Operating Units as part of Purchasing setups*

EBS also requires an inventory organization to be set up when using purchasing. If Inventory is being implemented, this will be set up as part of the inventory setups. If not, you must set up a basic inventory organization at this time, as shown in Figure 2-4. Use the same screen as was used to set up an operating unit, but this time the ORGANIZATION CLASSIFICATION will be INVENTORY ORGANIZATION. As each organization can have more than one classification, both the Operating Unit and Inventory Organization setups can be assigned to the same organization.

Under the OTHER button, there are two required areas, even if inventory is not going to be used. Select ACCOUNTING INFORMATION and add the PRIMARY LEDGER, LEGAL ENTITY, and OPERATING UNIT that this inventory organization will be associated with.

Next, the inventory information will need to be added. As long as this inventory organization does not contain transactions against it, all the information on this form can be changed prior to use. This section is only going to cover the required fields on each tab, which are the minimal setups required for purchasing.

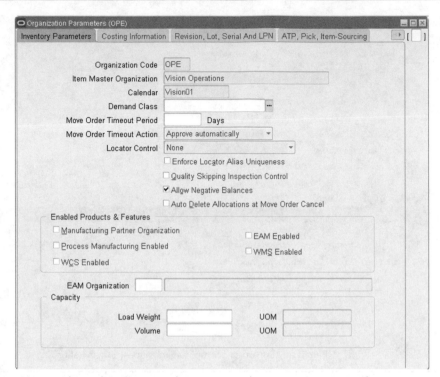

Purchasing Superuser | Setup| Organizations | Organizations | Inventory Organization | Inventory Management

FIGURE 2-4 *Creating an inventory organization*

Inventory Parameters

Enter an ORGANIZATION CODE, which is a distinct code up to three characters long for this organization that will appear on forms, and select the CALENDAR that will be used for transactions. This is not the same as the accounting calendar but is the Workday Calendar set up in manufacturing used to determine which days of the week are considered workdays (Inventory Superuser | Setup | Organizations | Calendars). Since this is a required field, a simple Monday–Friday calendar can be set up by giving the Workday Calendar a NAME, and saving it.

Costing Information

Enter a MATERIAL ACCOUNT that would be used if items were received into this inventory organization.

Revision, Lot, Serial, and LPN

Enter a STARTING SERIAL NUMBER, which is required even if serial numbers are not used, as well as a STARTING REVISION. Again, this is required even if this feature is not being used.

Other Accounts

Enter default account numbers for transaction processing, described in Table 2-2.

Field Name	Controls
Purchase Price Variance	Purchase Price Variance (PPV) is used to track any differences between the price on the purchase order and an actual price entered at time of receipt, which is either the actual cost from the supplier or the standard cost.
Invoice Price Variance	Invoice Price Variance (IPV) is used to track any differences between the purchase order and the actual invoice.
Inventory AP Accrual Account	This account is used for the perpetual accrual of items received and not yet invoiced. This account is usually used to accrue inventory, or asset, items.
Sales	This is the system default for sales accounts on customer orders. This account can be overridden with order management's Transaction Types or inventory item definition.
Cost of Goods Sold	This is the system default for cost of goods sold (COGS) transactions, created when items are shipped against an order. This account can be overridden with order management's Transaction Types or inventory item definition.
Deferred COGS Account	This account is used to match Cost of Goods Sold to Revenue by deferring the expense until the items are invoiced.

TABLE 2-2 *Inventory Organization Accounts and What They Are Used For*

Defining Item Number Format in EBS (Optional)

EBS allows Purchase Orders and Requisitions to be created by using Categories (Purchasing Superuser | Setups | Items | Categories) or Items (Purchasing Superuser | Items | Master Items). The advantage in using a Category or an Item is that reporting or analysis on types of purchases can be more easily done if there is a common classification, and either can be used to default account numbers onto requisitions or purchase orders. Items require more work to set up and use, as every new item will need to be created and all items maintained, but they are required if the orders are being received into EBS Inventory. If Inventory is utilized, items are set up as part of that module.

Units of Measure (Conditionally Required)

In EBS, product can be ordered with one unit of measure and then received and tracked in inventory with a different unit, referred to as the Base Unit of Measure. An example of this is ordering a Pallet, consisting of 12 cases, that is received one case at a time and issued out of inventory one item at a time. If Inventory is being used, Units of Measures (UOM) were set up as part of that module, but you should review these settings to ensure the needed units are set up for purchasing, and that the unit conversions between the inventory, or Primary Unit of Measure, and the Purchasing Unit of Measure, are accurate. UOM is also used when purchasing without an item number, and it is used with both item and category purchase orders to calculate the cost of the order, based on quantity ordered and unit of measure.

There are two main parts for UOM-Classes, which is a grouping of base Units, and Conversions between units assigned to the same class. For example, a Class of Package may be set up, with the conversion unit of Each. Then the individual Units of Measure of Each, Box, and Pallet are set up and assigned to that Class. A conversion can be set up to tell EBS that a Box has 12 Each, and a Pallet has 12 Boxes, and EBS will know a Pallet has a total of 144 Each.

Setting Up Classes

Classes get associated with each Unit of Measure that is set up, and this association creates a common basis for conversions between the purchasing and receiving (inventory) UOMs. When entering the Class form shown in Figure 2-5, you will be prompted to select an inventory organization. Attributes set up on an item, including Units of Measure and their associated classes, can be set at either the Master or the Item organization (Purchasing Superuser | Setup | Items | Attribute Controls). A Master organization is the controlling organization of the items themselves and common attributes, while the Item organization is where the actual item transactions take place (such as shipping and receiving), also called an inventory organization.

While most companies will have only one item master, it is possible to have more than one, creating distinct and unrelated item listings for each organization. When an attribute is set up to be controlled at the Master organization level, it is then shared across all item/inventory organizations using that master. When it is set at the Item organization level, then it is set at each individual inventory organization the item is assigned to. Ensure you select the proper organization when entering the class form. The NAME is what appears on the other forms, and the same BASE UNIT and UOM combination cannot be assigned to two different Classes.

Adding Additional Units of Measure to a Class

Once you have set up the Class, then you can assign additional Units to it. As seen in Figure 2-6, the unit of measure that is set up as a BASE UNIT will be the unit used for conversions between any other units of measure in a CLASS. In this example, SQUARE FOOT will be used to convert all units of measure assigned to the class AREA. When an item is set up, it is assigned a PRIMARY UNIT OF MEASURE, and then a UNIT OF ISSUE that is used to issue out the product. The unit of issue is limited to the units assigned to the same class as the Primary Unit of Measure. And Conversions are used to figure out the relationship between the two.

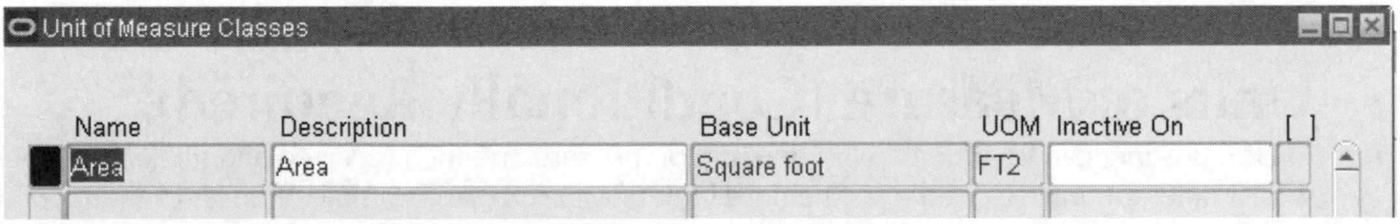

Name	Description	Base Unit	UOM	Inactive On	[ ]
Area	Area	Square foot	FT2		

Purchasing Superuser | Setup | Units of Measure | Classes

FIGURE 2-5 *Unit of Measure Classes*

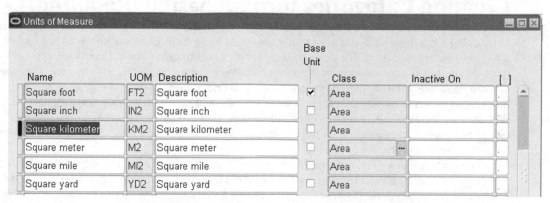

FIGURE 2-6 *Adding Additional Units of Measure to a Class*

Unit of Measure Conversions

You can set up three conversions for units of measure. Standard is the most generic and defines the conversions between any unit of measure and the assigned Base Unit for that class. This option is not available for the base units, as it is the conversions used to get *to* the base units in a class. IntraClass conversions are used to create conversions for a specific item that have a unit of measure assigned as their primary unit of measure, and the base unit of a class. This allows you to set up different conversion rates for different items with the same primary unit of measure. You can set up interclass conversions for base units and create a conversion rate between the base units of different classes. Figure 2-7 shows the Standard Conversion setup, where 1 square inch equals 0.006944 of a square foot.

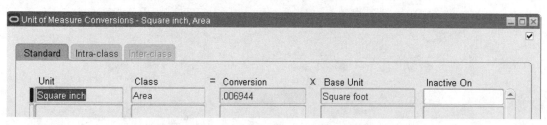

FIGURE 2-7 *Unit of Measure Conversions*

Creating Categories for Purchasing (Required)

As mentioned, you have two ways to create requisitions and purchase orders in EBS: with items, or by using a category with a description. Categories serve multiple purposes in EBS, a few of which are mentioned here. They can be assigned to items to group them for reporting or sourcing rules, or used to assign an account number and to derive the accounting information. Categories can also be assigned to approval groups, limiting the documents a person can approve. Also, buyers can be associated with a specific category, allowing them to AutoCreate purchase orders only for the category they are associated with. Categories are used in conjunction with several other features outside the scope of purchasing, such as tax classifications, iStore and iProcurement features, and inventory.

Categories are Key Flexfields, or fields required by EBS that allow flexibility in their formatting and qualifiers to be added for additional functionality. The default item category used by Purchasing Functional Area, called the PO Item Category, allows for multiple segments to be created (Purchasing Superuser | Setup | Flexfields | Key | Segments, select the Flexfield title of Item Categories). Ensure you unfreeze the Flexfield if any changes are needed or when setting up this Flexfield. Use caution in unfreezing a Flexfield when transactions are being created in the system that use this Flexfield because it may result in data corruption. As seen in Figure 2-8, a VALUE SET will need to be defined and added to the Flexfield, which will serve as a home for the actual values that can be used in

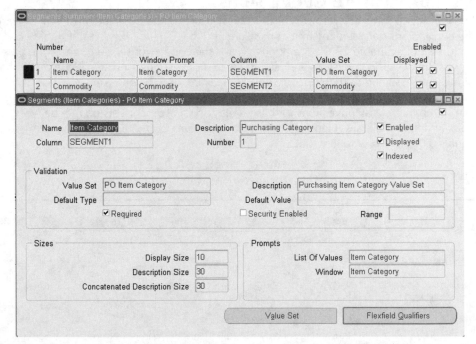

Purchasing Superuser | Setup | Flexfields | Key | Segments, select the Flexfield title of Item Categories

FIGURE 2-8 *Item PO Category Flexfield and Value Sets*

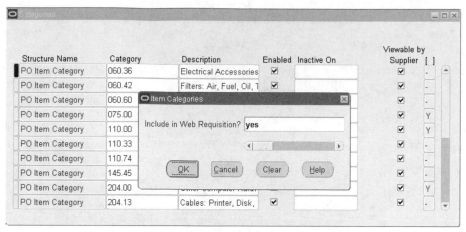

Purchasing Superuser | Setup | Items | Categories | Category Codes

FIGURE 2-9 *Purchasing category setup*

the system for this Key Flexfield (KFF). Once the KFF is saved and frozen, then values can be added for each segment of the category (Setup | Flexfields | Key | Values).

Once the values are set up, you can combine them for use as category codes and identify them as available for use on web requisitions that are created in iProcurement. In Figure 2-9, you can see the setup of a purchasing category. All item categories are seen on this screen, but this setup is geared toward PO Item Categories, identified by the STRUCTURE NAME. Select the CATEGORY values for each segment, and assign it a DESCRIPTION. This screen often has a bug, so if the list of values does not appear in the CATEGORY field, enter any character and press TAB and a pop-up box with the list will appear. ENABLED and INACTIVE ON determine if this category can be used (is enabled) and when (prior to the Inactive Date). Once a category is set up, it can be used on requisitions and purchase orders, as well as in the iSupplier portal and iProcurement. VIEWABLE BY SUPPLIER determines if iSupplier can use this category, and the Flexfield for INCLUDE IN WEB REQUISITION determines if iProcurement can see it.

After creating category codes, you can assign them to a category set to group them for searching and restricting information in iProcurement. Though there are many category sets in EBS, you will set up one default set for purchasing. Figure 2-10 shows category codes being assigned to a category set.

Ensure the category set you are adding the codes to is set up as the default category for Purchasing, as seen in Figure 2-11.

As mentioned earlier, categories can be used to default some or all of an account number on a requisition or a purchase order. Setting up Expense Account Rules assigns values to each segment in the Chart of Accounts, allowing these account values to then be used in the purchasing and requisition Account Generator to generate an account number. The Account Generator is a workflow that builds the account numbers on specific documents. Referring to Figure 2-12, click CREATE to add a new rule. The ACCOUNT RULE TYPE defaults to Item Category. From the list of values, the ACCOUNT

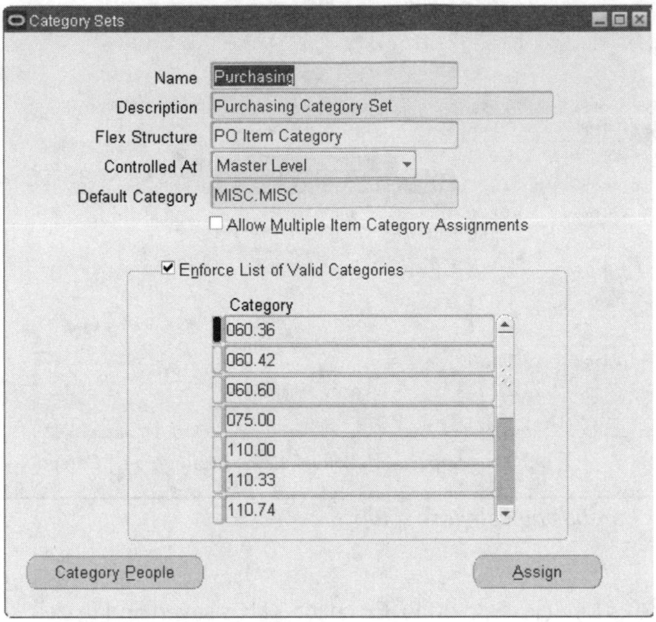

Purchasing Superuser | Setup | Items | Categories | Category Sets

FIGURE 2-10   *Adding category codes to category sets*

RULE VALUE can be populated with any valid category combination. Since categories are KFF in EBS, each organization's categories will look unique in not only the number of segments in the category, but also the values that populate it. Then select the SEGMENT NAME and VALUE to use as a default. Not all segments need to be populated, only the ones that will be used in the account generator.

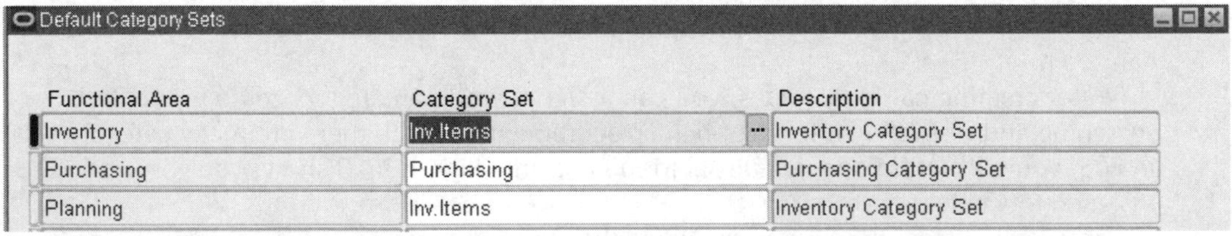

Purchasing Superuser | Setup | Items | Categories | Default Category Sets

FIGURE 2-11   *Default category sets for each functional area*

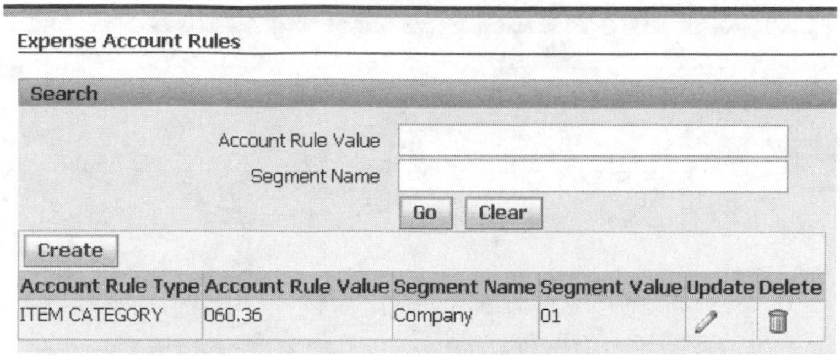
Expense Account Rules
Search
Account Rule Value
Segment Name
Go
Clear
Create
Account Rule Type
Account Rule Value
Segment Name
Segment Value
Update
Delete
ITEM CATEGORY
060.36
Company
01

Purchasing Superuser | Setup | Financials | Accounting | Expense Account Rules

FIGURE 2-12 *Adding default accounting information to a category*

Using Employees in Purchasing (Required)

Whether or not you are using Oracle Human Resources, employees must be set up in EBS for anyone who will be a buyer, requestor, or approver for purchase orders and requisitions. In EBS, buyers are defined as people creating purchase orders, whereas a requestor is the person asking for the goods. Approvers have the authority to approve either requisitions or purchase orders. Human Resources does not need to be implemented to use the Employee form to set up employee or position hierarchies for approvals in EBS.

When HR is partially installed, a modified employee form is available for use in a limited fashion (fewer required fields than when HR is implemented). On the employee record when Human Resources is a shared install (Purchasing Superuser | Setup| Personnel| Employees), you can set up the employee-supervisor relationships or employee positions used for approvals (see the next section, "Setting Up Approvers for Requisitions and Purchase Orders," for more), as well as the Ledger the employee is assigned to, plus a default expense account that can be used in the Purchasing and Requisition Account Generators, as seen in Figure 2-13.

One word of advice: if employees are being set up for purchasing or any type of approvals only and Human Resources is not installed, consider creating the Positions to agree to approval limits as opposed to actual job titles. This will make setup and maintenance much easier. For example, instead of setting up one position for marketing manager and another for accounting manager, both of whom can approve the same dollar amounts, set up a position called "1,000 limit" that can be assigned to both. Since there are usually fewer dollar amounts than there are positions, this is less work to maintain and makes research easier.

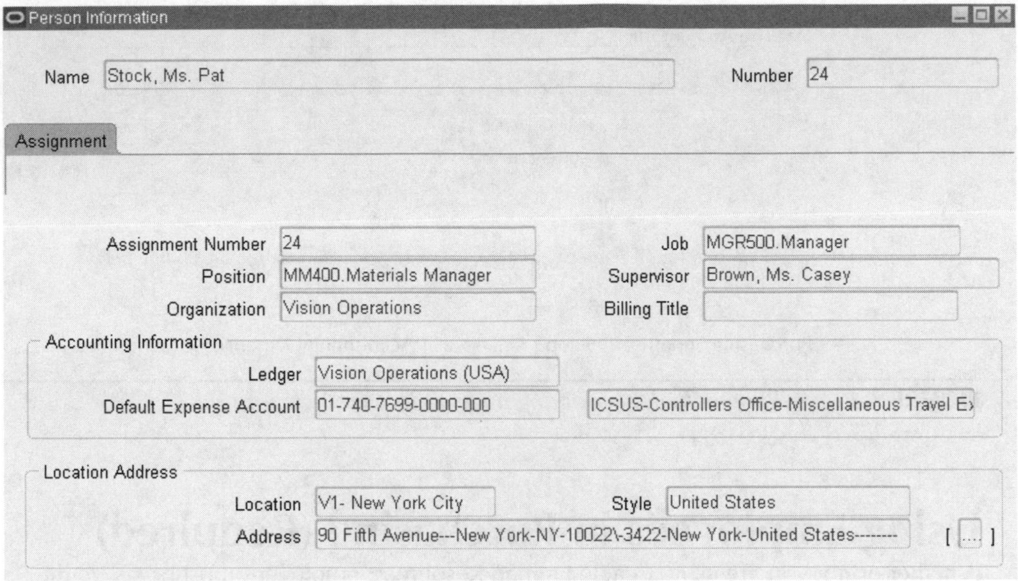

Purchasing Superuser | Setup | Personnel | Employees

FIGURE 2-13 *Employee Assignments when Human Resource is a shared install*

Setting Up Approvers for Requisitions and Purchase Orders (Required)

Both requisitions and purchase orders need to be approved before the documents are final and ready for the next step in the process. An approval process can range from something as simple as that any person creating a document can approve their own document, to a supervisor hierarchy approval process with limits based on an employee's position, or a complicated process where approvals are based on the item being purchased and the dollar amount of the document.

There are two options for creating these approval rules: the purchasing hierarchies, which can be used for both purchase orders and requisitions and have the limitation of a straight supervisor- or position-based hierarchical approval path, and Oracle Approval Management (AME), which is only available for requisition approvals. AME allows more complicated rules, such as all requisitions with the category of Computer Equipment must go to the CIO for approval. AME setups are beyond the scope of this book. Purchasing approvals will default to the supervisor hierarchy unless the Use Approval Hierarchy box is checked in the financial options (Purchasing Superuser | Setup | Organizations | Financial Options | Supplier-Purchasing tab). AME will be used when the Approval Transaction Type is populated on the document type selected on the requisition (Purchasing Superuser | Setup | Purchasing | Document Types).

To set up the purchasing approvals, groups are created to set up account numbers and dollar limits for one or more of the following criteria: document total, account ranges, item categories, item numbers, and ship- or deliver-to locations. The groups are then assigned to specific document types, such as requisition or purchase order, by the employee's position. Figure 2-14 shows a sample approval group. If you are using position hierarchies as opposed to approvals by supervisor, then at least document total and account ranges must be set up. Supervisor hierarchies only require one of the criteria to be set up.

Approval Groups are OPERATING UNIT specific, and the NAME and DESCRIPTION help to identify the group and what it does in EBS. The APPROVAL RULES themselves determine what each group can do. In the example for Director Production, this group has the authority to approve any document up to $100,000 only when the account number on the document is not for account 1570. The OBJECT determines what document element this rule pertains to, such as an account number or item. DOCUMENT TOTAL sets the approval limit for the entire document. ACCOUNT RANGE determines the account numbers that can be approved. Item Categories and Items assign specific ranges that can be either included or excluded for this group, and Location will restrict the approvals to a specific location. TYPE assigns the ranges that can be either included or excluded, with APPROVAL LIMITS being assigned only to the ranges that are included. LOW and HIGH VALUES are the ranges that will be included or excluded. Not shown on the screen is an INACTIVE DATE for each Object, allowing rules to be adjusted as needed. These rules can be set up fairly comprehensively for approval assignments.

Purchasing approvals, though hierarchical, have several options on how the approval is routed, based on the Forward Method assigned to the Document Type (Purchasing Superuser | Setup | Purchasing | Document Type). Direct will always proceed directly to the person with the ability to approve the document. This means that the document will be routed to the first person in the hierarchy who has the authority to approve all the elements of the document, possibly bypassing the direct supervisor of the requestor. Also available is Hierarchy, which will forward directly to each person in the hierarchy, requiring each to approve it before moving on.

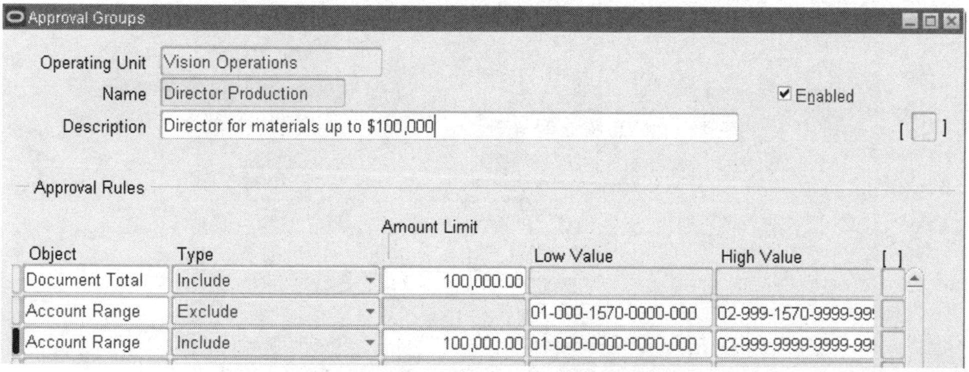

Purchasing Superuser | Setup | Approvals | Approval Groups

FIGURE 2-14   *Sample approval group*

Approval Groups, once they are set up, get assigned to Positions set up in Human Resources, as well as different types of documents. This association is seen in Figure 2-15. Positions are in turn assigned to employees, which will grant them the specific level of approvals. Select the POSITION from the list of values, and then select the DOCUMENT TYPE to assign the APPROVAL GROUPS to. Document types and their descriptions are listed in Table 2-3. Since not all document types require approval, only ones that do appear on this screen. For example, Request for Bid does not require approval and is not available in this screen.

To finish the Approval Assignments, add the APPROVAL GROUP to the DOCUMENT TYPE, and supply EFFECTIVE dates. It is not necessary to assign an approval group to every document type; not assigning one is the same as having no approval authority for that document.

Creating Buyers (Required)

In EBS, only employees setup as Buyers are allowed to create purchase orders, while any employee with the proper access can create requisitions and approve both documents. Buyers are the only users who can access the purchasing entry form in EBS. To make an employee a buyer, refer to Figure 2-16 and click ADD BUYER to add a new buyer. Select the employee name in the BUYER field, and optionally add CATEGORIES and SHIP-TO locations to restrict the purchase orders this buyer can create. Since an employee cannot be added more than one time, no employee can be assigned to multiple categories and locations. Enter effective dates to restrict when this buyer will have access to create purchase orders.

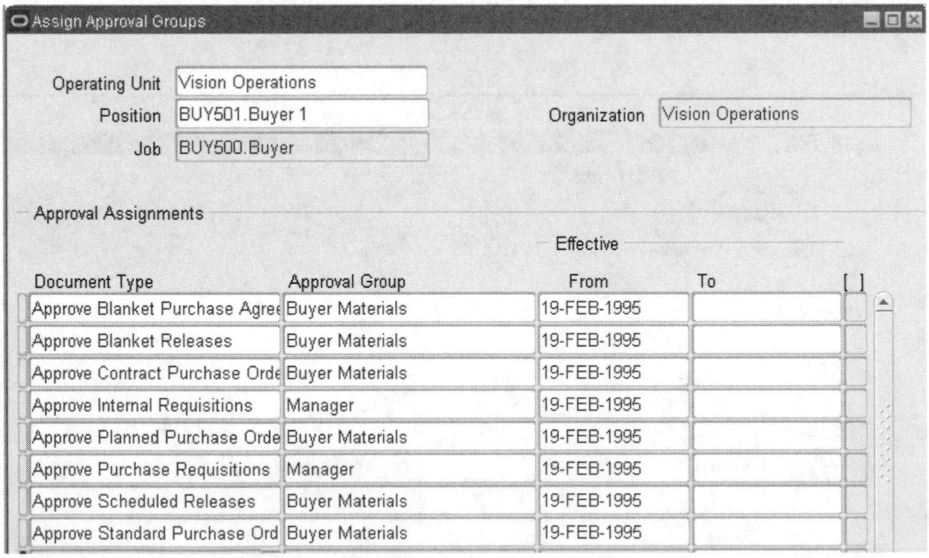

Purchasing Superuser | Setup | Approvals | Approval Assignments

FIGURE 2-15 *Assigning approval authorities to positions*

Document Type	Meaning
Blanket Purchase Agreements	Used for purchases that will be delivered according to an unknown schedule, or with negotiated prices. Releases are performed when a shipment is scheduled. Can be limited by Price, Quantity, and Effective Dates.
Blank Releases	Issued against Blanket Purchases for an actual scheduled order, and is constrained by Price, Quantity, and Effective Dates.
Contract Purchase Orders	Created when terms and conditions pertaining to goods or services are agreed upon in a contract. Standard purchase orders are issued against the contracts and are constrained to these terms and conditions.
Planned Purchase Orders	Used when a long-term agreement to buy goods or services from a source is made, and tentative delivery schedules are known.
Scheduled Releases	Used with Planned Purchase Orders to create the actual orders.
Standard Purchase Orders	Used for one-time purchases when the goods or services along with the estimated costs are known.
Internal Requisitions	Used to create requisitions for internally sourced items from locations and organizations set up in EBS.
Purchase Requisitions	Used to create requisitions for externally sourced items. Requisitions need to be turned into Purchase Orders or Releases prior to purchase.

TABLE 2-3 *Document Types That Allow Approvals*

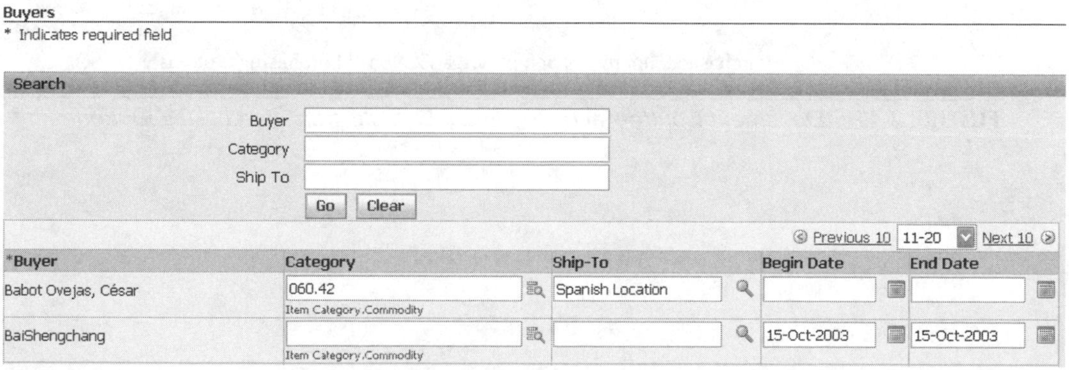

Buyers
* Indicates required field

Search

Buyer	
Category	
Ship To	

Go   Clear

Previous 10 11-20 Next 10

*Buyer	Category	Ship-To	Begin Date	End Date
Babot Ovejas, César	060.42 *Item Category /Commodity*	Spanish Location		
BaiShengchang	*Item Category /Commodity*		15-Oct-2003	15-Oct-2003

Purchasing Superuser | Setup | Personnel | Buyers

FIGURE 2-16 *Making employees authorized buyers*

Purchasing Options (Required)

Purchasing options are created to define defaults and controls for purchase orders and requisitions. Many of these options can be overridden on individual documents. Figure 2-17 shows the different areas of the purchasing options. These are set up for each individual Operating Unit, and you will be required to select the Operating Unit prior to starting the setups.

Document Controls

The Document Controls region of the Purchasing Options sets rules and limits on how documents are controlled for not only creation, but also closing. These are described in Table 2-4.

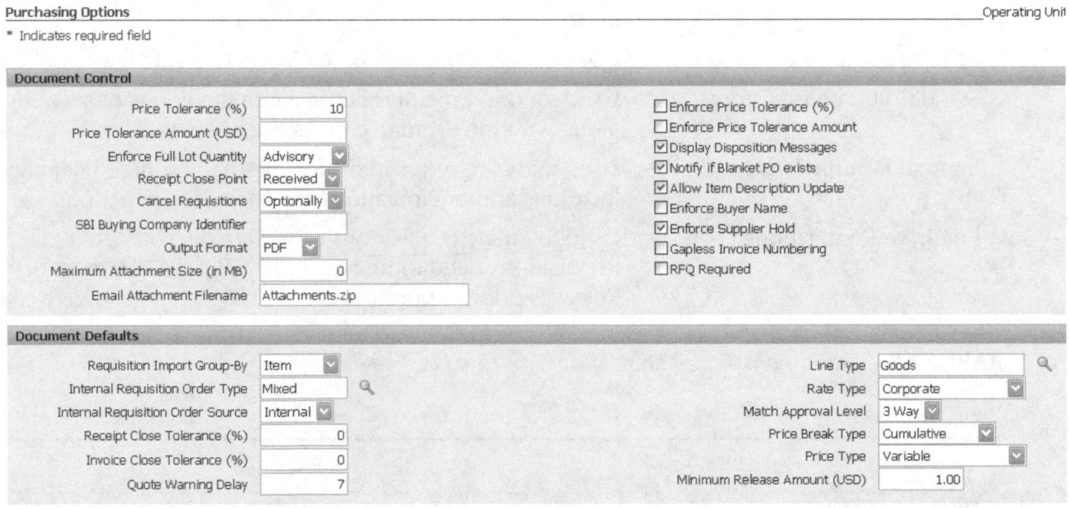

Purchasing Superuser | Setup | Organizations | Purchasing Options

FIGURE 2-17 *Document Controls and Document Defaults from Purchasing Options*

Field Name	Control
Price Tolerance (%)	Tolerances can be added for the amount that a purchase order can exceed a requisition it was created from. The % tolerance is the total percent any one line on a purchase order can exceed the price on the requisition line it was created from. This only refers to overages, not shortages.
Enforce Price Tolerance (%)	Prevents purchase orders from being approved when the price tolerance is exceeded. Not selecting this option will give the buyer a warning but allow the purchase order to be approved.
Price Tolerance Amount (in functional currency)	Assigns a hard dollar limit, up to which a purchase order line can exceed the associated requisition line. Can either be assigned alone or with the PRICE TOLERANCE FOR %, where the lower of the two tolerances will be enforced. (For example, if the % tolerance is 15%, which comes to $150, and the tolerance amount is set to $100, then the amount on the purchase order cannot exceed the requisition line by more than $100.)
Enforce Price Tolerance Amount	Prevents purchase orders from being approved when the price tolerance amount is exceeded. Not selecting this option will give the buyer a warning but allow the purchase order to be approved.
Enforce Full Lot Quantity	Used to determine how internal requisitions will create lines for items under lot control. None will allow any amount to be purchased, Automatic will default to the item rounding factor set up on the item, and Advisory will suggest that the line be rounded to the item rounding factor but allow the buyers to override the suggestion.
Receipt Close Point	Determines if a shipment is closed based on the Inspection (Accepted), Delivery, or Receipt of the item.

TABLE 2-4   *Document Control Options Available in Purchasing Options*

Field Name	Control
Cancel Requisitions	Determines how a requisition is handled when the associated purchase order is canceled. Always will cause both the purchase order and the requisition to be canceled, Never will leave the requisition open for later use or manual cancellation, and Optional will allow the buyer to determine if the requisition should be canceled or not.
SBI Buying Company Identifier	Used with the Self Billing (SBI) feature of EBS (Pay on Receipt), a unique identifier for Buying Company can be added to be part of the invoice number generated during self-billing. This will appear in the second segment of the self-billed invoice number.
Gapless Invoice Numbering	Determines if a gapless sequence will be generated for each Self Bill generated for a unique combination of SBI Buying Company Identifier, Selling Company Identifier (supplier), and Invoice Type.
Output Format	Determines the output format for purchase orders when they are printed, and can be set to PDF or Text. PDF will create a document that cannot be modified but can been seen from the Purchase Order windows, change history, iProcurement, and iSupplier portal. Text cannot be seen on these pages and can be modified in soft copy, so it is usually only used for printed documents.
Maximum Attachment Size (in MB)	When e-mailing purchase orders, any documents added as an attachment on the purchase order can be included in the e-mail. These attachments will be zipped when sent, and this field limits the file size that can be included.
Email Attachment Filename	Can be used to override the extension on the attachment, such as .zip, to prevent the attachments from being stopped by e-mail filters.
Display Disposition Messages	Determines if the instructions for disposal of an item are displayed on the requisition. These instructions would have been set up on the item themselves.
Notify if Blanket PO Exists	Notifies buyers when an active blanket purchase order exists for an item entered on a line of any document.
Allow Item Description Update	Determines the default for Allow Item Description Update when creating a new item. It is the item setting that will determine if a specific item on a purchasing document can have its description updated.

TABLE 2-4   *Document Control Options Available in Purchasing Options* (continued)

Field Name	Control
Enforce Buyer Name	Determines if buyers can create purchase orders with only their names or are allowed to change it to any qualified buyer's name.
Enforce Supplier Hold	Prevents purchase orders from being approved if the supplier is on hold, as defined on the Supply Base | Supplier | Invoice Management window.
RFQ Required	Prevents requisitions from being created into purchase orders if a Request for Quote is not received. This can be overridden on a requisition line.

TABLE 2-4   *Document Control Options Available in Purchasing Options* (continued)

Document Defaults

The Document Defaults region of the Purchasing Options defines how information can default onto a document when it is being created; these settings are described in Table 2-5.

Field Name	Control
Requisition Import Group-By	Controls how requisitions are grouped and combined when imported through the Requisition Open Interface, including requisitions created by Work In Process (WIP), Materials Requirements Planning (MRP), Order Management, and Inventory. All or Null will not group the requisitions, creating a unique requisition for each line. Fields available for grouping by include Buyer, Category, Item, Location, and Supplier.
Internal Requisition Order Type	Internal requisitions will be released and imported in Order Management under the order type identified here.
Internal Requisition Order Source	With only the selection of Internal, it is the source used to transfer internal requisition data from Purchasing to Order Management.

TABLE 2-5   *Defining Document Defaults*

Field Name	Control
Receipt Close Tolerance (%)	Controlling the closing point on documents in purchasing is a major decision that can increase or decrease a buyer's workload. If documents do not close automatically, then the buyer will need to manually monitor and close them. The Receipt Close Tolerance tells EBS when to close orders for receiving transactions. When the receipts made against an order reach within the tolerance percent of the quantity order, they will close for receiving, but will allow future receipts to be made against a closed order. This can be overridden when setting up individual items and purchase orders.
Invoice Close Tolerance (%)	Determines when EBS will close a purchase order that has been matched to an invoice. When the invoice matched to a purchase order line is within the tolerance percent of the line amount, the line will close for invoicing, but will still allow future invoices to be matched to the line. This can be overridden when setting up individual items and purchase orders.
Quote Warning Delay	Determines the number of days prior to the expiration date on a quote that a warning will be sent to the buyers.
Line Type	Determines the default line type for requisitions, purchase orders, quotes, and requests for quote. Line Types determine such things as the basis for calculating price and default category and pricing information.
Rate Type	Determines the default for where the exchange rate is derived from when entering a foreign currency document. Select from any rate type defined in the system, including User, which will require the person entering the document to provide a rate.
Match Approval Level	Determines how invoices are matched to purchase orders, and when the orders are closed: A 2-way match compares both the quantities and amounts of purchase orders to the invoices. A 3-way match adds a quantity invoiced comparison to the quantities received. A 4-way match includes the same criteria as a 3-way match but adds a quantity accepted comparison to the quantity received.

TABLE 2-5   *Defining Document Defaults* (continued)

Field Name	Control
Price Break Type	For blanket purchase orders, determines if price breaks are based on cumulative quantities for all shipments, or only an individual release (non-cumulative).
Price Type	Sets the default for the type of pricing used in the document. Additional Price Types can be added in the purchasing lookup codes (Purchasing Superuser | Setup | Purchasing | Lookup Codes).
Minimum Release Amount (Currency)	Determines the minimum amounts for releases on blanket, contract, and planned purchase orders.

TABLE 2-5 *Defining Document Defaults* (continued)

Receipt Accounting

Receipt Accounting controls how the system will handle accruals for both inventory and expense items. While accruing inventory items is mandatory, creating accrual transactions for expense items is optional. For either inventory or expense, accruals are recorded to reflect items that have been received but not yet invoiced in Payables (refer to Figure 2-18). ACCRUE EXPENSE ITEMS can be set either to accrue only uninvoiced items at Period End, or with every receipt. Most commonly used is PERIOD END, which will create a reversing accrual in the General Ledger, but AT RECEIPT can give a more accurate expense picture on a daily basis when using Daily Business Intelligence. ACCRUE INVENTORY ITEMS is always set to AT RECEIPT, where a clearing account is set up with each inventory receipt and relieved when it is matched to an invoice.

AUTOMATIC OFFSET METHOD determines how the account number for the Receiving Inspection account is created. When this option is set to NONE, the Receiving Inspection account from the destination organization is used. BALANCING will cause the balancing segment of the Receiving Inspection Account to be the same as the Balancing Segment of the Charge account that was transacted against at time of delivery, whereas ACCOUNT will overlay the Charge Account for all segments of the account string except for the natural account, which will come from the Receiving Inspection Account. Enter an account number for the EXPENSE AP ACCRUAL ACCOUNT, used to accrue expense receipts.

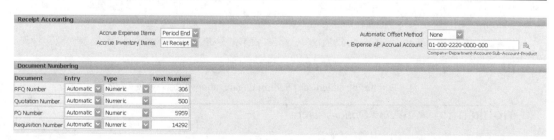

Purchasing Superuser | Setup | Organizations | Purchasing Options

FIGURE 2-18 *Receipt Accounting and Document Numbering from Purchasing Options*

Document Numbering

Document Numbering determines if document numbering is AUTOMATIC or MANUAL, based on the ENTRY field, and if the numbering is NUMERIC or ALPHANUMERIC. Only manual numbering can number documents Alphanumeric. The NEXT NUMBER field is the next number that will be used for automatic numbering. During data conversions, the document numbering can be set to manual, allowing the documents being converted to maintain their legacy numbers, and then switched back to AUTOMATIC. Ensure that the NEXT NUMBER is above any converted transactions to avoid problems with the creation of future documents.

Receiving Options (Required)

Receiving Options, seen in Figure 2-19, are used to default information on purchase orders for receipt of goods and services. Many of the options can be overridden when purchase orders are created, or when setting up specific suppliers or items. These defaults are specific to each inventory organization and are required to be set up for the organization defined as the Inventory Organization assigned in the Financial Options. (Purchasing Superuser | Setup | Organizations | Financial Options | Supplier-Purchasing) Typically, this will be the Item Master Organization.

Receiving Options

Table 2-6 describes the Receiving Options fields.

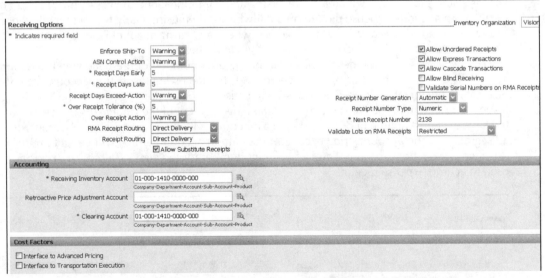

Purchasing Superuser | Setup | Organizations | Receiving Options

FIGURE 2-19 *Receiving Options setups*

Field Name	Control
Enforce Ship-To	Items are usually delivered according to the Ship-To location on the purchase order but at times can end up in another location. When None is selected, there is no warning when a user tries to receive the orders into a different location. Reject will not allow receipts to a location other than the Ship-To location on the purchase order, and Warning will notify the receiver that they are different, but allow the transaction to proceed.
ASN Control Action	ASNs, or Advanced Shipment Notices, are generated when product is shipped from a supplier, notifying EBS with specific receiving and arrival information that can be used to process the receipt. These can be received electronically in EBS. ASN Control Action determines if users are notified when processing a receipt where an ASN exists with a Warning, a Rejection that will not allow the receipt without using the ASN, or no notification at all.
Receipt Days Early	Number of days prior to the expected receipt date on the purchase order that receipts can be processed.
Receipt Days Late	Determines the number of days after the expected receipt date on the purchase order that receipts can be processed.
Receipt Days Exceed-Action	Determines action when the RECEIPT DAYS EARLY or LATE are exceeded: None allows the receipt, Warning notifies the user and still allows the transaction, and Reject will not allow the transaction to be processed if the days have been exceeded.
Over Receipt Tolerance (%)	Determines what amounts over the purchase order quantities that can be received against the order.
Over Receipt Action	When the quantity received is over the receipt tolerance, no action can be taken, which will allow the receipt without a warning, or a warning to appear to the users, or the receipt to be prevented altogether.
RMA Receipt Routing	Receipts for Return Materials Authorizations (RMA) have three options for how they are processed: Standard, which uses a receiving location prior to delivering an item to its final location, Direct Delivery, which performs these two steps in one transaction, and Inspection Required, which adds an inspection step into the receiving process.

TABLE 2-6 *Receiving Options Setups*

Field Name	Control
Receipt Routing	Purchase Order Receipts have three options for how they are processed: Standard, which uses a receipting location prior to delivering an item to its final location, Direct Delivery, which performs these two steps in one transaction, and Inspection Required, which adds an inspection step into the receiving process.
Allow Substitute Receipts	Select this option to allow a substitute receipt based on items set up as related (Items | Item Relationships).
Allow Unordered Receipts	When selected, allows receipts for items not on purchase orders, which can later be matched to a purchase order. This option can be overridden on both items and suppliers.
Allow Express Transactions	Determines if express receipts and deliveries are allowed, where EBS will select all lines on a specific order for the transaction, allowing the user to override them if needed.
Allow Cascade Transactions	Allows receipts and deliveries to be automatically distributed over multiple shipments and distributions based on the quantity received.
Allow Blind Receiving	EBS normally shows the quantities that are still due and were ordered at time of receiving. Blind receiving will hide this information, making users enter the quantities from the documentation received with the delivery.
Validate Serial Numbers on RMA Receipts	Restricts available serial numbers on an RMA to the numbers originally shipped with the order.
Receipt Number Generation	Determines if receipt numbers are manually entered or generated by the system. Receipt numbers must be unique within an inventory organization.
Receipt Number Type	Determines if receipts will be numeric or alphanumeric. EBS can only automatically generate numeric numbers, but alphanumeric can be selected with automatic numbering to allow interfaced receipts from other systems to be alphanumeric.
Next Receipt Number	When using automatic numbering, determines the next number that will be assigned by EBS.
Validate Lot on RMA Receipts	Restricts available lot numbers on RMA to the numbers originally shipped on the order.

TABLE 2-6   *Receiving Options Setups* (continued)

Accounting Options Available with Receiving Transactions

RECEIVING INVENTORY ACCOUNT is used when receipts are processed for all inventory purchase orders. This account is debited when the item is received and credited or cleared when the items are delivered into their inventory location. This clearing transaction can be set up to happen automatically when the RECEIPT ROUTING is set to Direct. RETROACTIVE PRICE ADJUSTMENT ACCOUNT is used when price adjustments are processed for items that have already been received. The final account set up here, CLEARING ACCOUNT, is used when an intercompany transaction is created for items received into one organization but purchased from another.

Cost Factors for Receipts

INTERFACE TO ADVANCED PRICING needs to be checked when the advanced pricing module is being used to calculate cost factors. INTERFACE TO TRANSPORTATION EXECUTION has to be checked if transportation costs are being calculated in Oracle Transportation Execution.

Financial Options (Required)

Financial Options are used predominantly by Payables but are required for Purchasing to function. Financial Options determine default account numbers, purchase order and requisition defaults, encumbrance options and employee defaults for expense reports. See Chapter 5, "Payables Setup," for a complete description of these setups.

Line Types (Conditionally Required)

Line types are used on both requisitions and purchase orders, and they determine how the amount is calculated on the line. Referring to Figure 2-20, the NAME on the line type is what the users will see when creating purchasing documents, so ensure it is meaningful to the users. DESCRIPTION adds information about the line type, but it is only available when using the List of Values to select the type, and not on the purchasing entry forms. Value Basis and Purchase Basis are the two key fields for line types and will determine how the order amount will be calculated, as described in Table 2-7.

Value Basis	Purchase Basis	Calculation
Amount	Services	Quantity entered becomes line amount. Price can not be updated and defaults to 1.
Fixed Price	Services Temp Labor	Only Amount can be entered. Quantity and Price are null.
Quantity	Goods	Quantity entered times Price entered equals line amount.
Rate	Temp Labor	Only Price can be entered; it becomes the line amount.

TABLE 2-7 *Basis for Line Types*

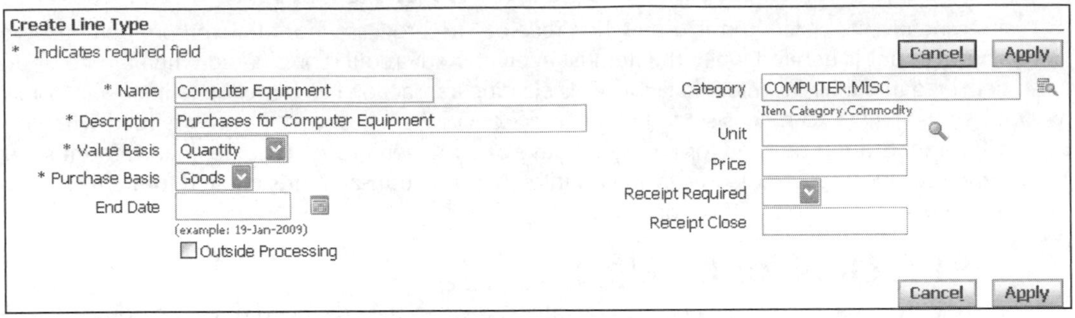

Create Line Type
* Indicates required field

* Name	Computer Equipment
* Description	Purchases for Computer Equipment
* Value Basis	Quantity
* Purchase Basis	Goods
End Date	(example: 19-Jan-2009)
	☐ Outside Processing

Category	COMPUTER.MISC
	Item Category.Commodity
Unit	
Price	
Receipt Required	
Receipt Close	

Cancel   Apply

Purchasing Superuser | Setup | Purchasing | Line Types

FIGURE 2-20   *Creating Line Types*

Adding an END DATE will determine when this line type can no longer be used. With the exception of UNIT when the VALUE BASIS is Amount, all other fields are options fields that can be used to default information on the line when this Line Type is selected.

Requisition Templates (Optional)

Requisition Templates can be defined and used with the Supplier Item Catalog. The Supplier Item Catalog is not only used to see where to purchase an item (Purchasing | Supplier Item Catalog), but also to enter lines based on a requisition using the Catalog feature. Most commonly, these templates are created to group like items, such as Computer Equipment or supplies kept in a supply closet at a specific location.

To create a Requisition Template, refer to Figure 2-21. After selecting the OPERATING UNIT this template will be used in, assign it a TEMPLATE name and a DESCRIPTION. The INACTIVE DATE is added to represent the date it can no longer be used; it can be left blank or set for a future date. Next, use the TYPE field to determine if the template will be used for Internal Requisitions or only Purchase Requisitions sourced outside of EBS. To assign a requisition a RESERVE PO NUMBER when it is created, select Yes, while Optional will allow the creator to decided. No prevents the user from reserving a purchase order number. When a PO number is reserved as part of the requisition process, the requisition cannot be combined with any other requisitions or split during the autocreate process, and the purchase order number will be lost if the requisition is eventually canceled. The option to reserve a PO number is only available when the requisitions are created in iProcurement.

Next, enter the specific items associated with this template. Select the line TYPE that will default in when this item is selected, and either an ITEM number or a CATEGORY name. Category is required and will default from the item, if one is entered, while the item is optional. The DESCRIPTION will default in from the item or category, and SOURCE TYPE determines if the item is purchased from a supplier or internally sourced from an internal location. A SUGGESTED QUANTITY can be added, which will default in when the template is used to create a line, and can then be updated by the user. This is especially beneficial when the item has price breaks associated with it. Depending on the line TYPE, enter either PRICE or AMOUNT to default on the order. Again, the requestor can update this information. Selecting NEGOTIATED SOURCE will identify this price as being created from a negotiation. Once this is saved, it will be available in the Supplier Item Catalog.

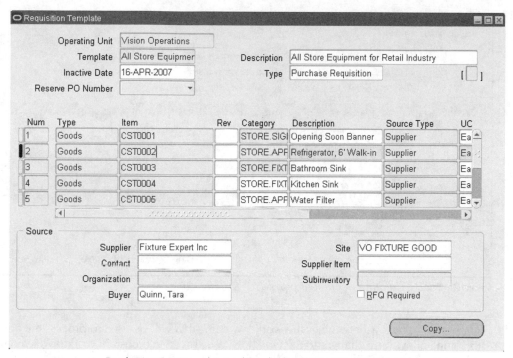

Purchasing Superuser | Setup | Purchasing | Requisition Templates

FIGURE 2-21   *Creating Requisition Templates*

Document Types (Conditionally Required)

Document Types, selected when entering a purchasing document, are used to set up approval options and controls for the document (see Figure 2-22). EBS comes seeded with document types that can be modified but not deleted. Select the update button for the document type to update it. The DOCUMENT LAYOUT fields refer to the XML layout that will be used to print this document, such as the Purchase Order format. These layouts are XML Templates that have been created and saved in the BI Publisher.

The Approval section defines some rules for approving this document. Selecting OWNER CAN APPROVE will start the approval process by looking at the approval limits of the person creating the document. If someone has the proper authority, that person will be able to approve his or her own request. When this is not checked, EBS will go to the next person in the approval chain to start the process. APPROVER CAN MODIFY determines if the person approving the document, when this is not the document owner, can make modifications to it, such as updating a distribution account number. CAN CHANGE FORWARD-TO and CAN CHANGE APPROVAL HIERARCHY both determine if the person submitting the document for approval can change the path the approval will follow. The Forward To person is the first person EBS selects to approve a document, based upon the hierarchy. The Hierarchy will follow either the person-supervisor hierarchy, the position hierarchy, or the custom designed hierarchy set up with Approval Management.

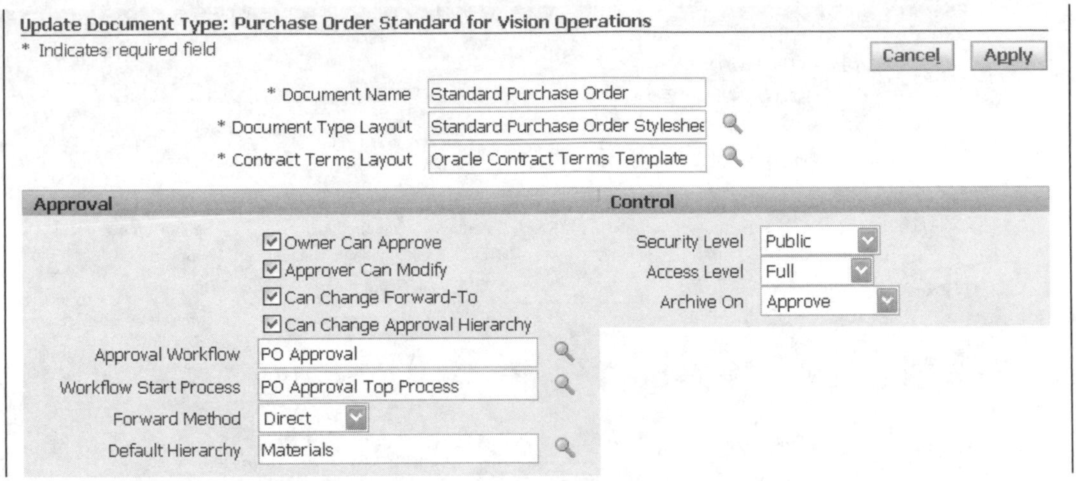

Update Document Type: Purchase Order Standard for Vision Operations

* Indicates required field

Cancel | Apply

* Document Name: Standard Purchase Order
* Document Type Layout: Standard Purchase Order Styleshee
* Contract Terms Layout: Oracle Contract Terms Template

Approval   **Control**

☑ Owner Can Approve   Security Level: Public
☑ Approver Can Modify   Access Level: Full
☑ Can Change Forward-To   Archive On: Approve
☑ Can Change Approval Hierarchy

Approval Workflow: PO Approval
Workflow Start Process: PO Approval Top Process
Forward Method: Direct
Default Hierarchy: Materials

Purchasing Superuser | Setup | Purchasing | Document Types

FIGURE 2-22 *Creating document types*

APPROVAL WORKFLOW determines the workflow name that will be used to process the approval. This setting allows any changes to the workflow to be saved in a custom workflow, leaving the seeded workflow intact for future reference or troubleshooting, and removing the risk of the customizations being overwritten during patching. WORKFLOW START PROCESS is the process in the workflow where the approvals will begin. FORWARD METHOD determines how the first person in the approval hierarchy is determined. When this is set to DIRECT, EBS will send the document to the first person in the chain with the authorization limits to approve the document. HIERARCHY, on the other hand, will require all persons in the chain to approve it until it reaches the person with the authority. For example, if someone on the warehouse staff enters a requisition that can only be approved by the VP of Operations, DIRECT will require only the VP of Operations to approve the document, whereas HIERARCHY will send it to the Warehouse Manager, to the Warehouse Director, and then to the VP of Operations. Each person in the chain must approve it to advance it to the next person.

The DEFAULT HIERARCHY can only be entered when the approval method is set to HIERARCHY in the Financial options (Human Resource tab, Use Approval Hierarchies). This will default the position hierarchy in the approval window, which can be updated when a document is submitted for approval if CAN CHANGE APPROVAL HIERARCHY is checked.

Several Control options exist here as well. SECURITY LEVEL determines who can access this specific document type. HIERARCHY will allow the owner (or creator) and any person above that person in the hierarchy to access a document, whereas PRIVATE will restrict access to only the owner. PUBLIC will allow all users to access all the documents, while the last option of PURCHASING limits access to the purchasing owner, who is also set up as a buyer. The ACCESS LEVEL determines what access is granted to people with the proper security level, selecting from FULL, which includes create, modify, and view; MODIFY, which does not allow document creation; and VIEW only. No matter what the ACCESS LEVEL is set to, the document owner will have access to create or modify his or her own documents—the access level only relates to documents created by other users.

Finally, ARCHIVE ON determines when changed, or updated, information for a document is archived. In order to see a document change history, this must be set to APPROVE, which archives the information once it is approved. Transmission archives the data when it is submitted for approval, and may not contain accurate information.

Account Generator (Conditionally Required)

A common misperception is that in R12, Account Generators were all replaced with Subledger Accounting (SLA), and this is not true. There is a distinct difference between what the two processes do. Account Generators are used to build account combinations, including the expense account and accrual accounts, which are added to such documents as Purchase Requisitions and Purchase Orders. SLA will generate the accounting entries for encumbrances as part of purchasing. And additional SLA transactions for what are typically considered purchasing transactions are actually owned by cost management and are found in the SLA setups there, including Receiving and Delivery accounting entries, Period End Accruals, and Price Adjustments on Purchase Orders. While SLA can utilize the accounts generated by the account generator, it does not have to.

The Account Generator for the expense account on requisitions and purchase orders is a seeded Oracle workflow that can be modified by companies to meet their specific needs. EBS calls the Account Generator based on the Workflow assigned in Payables Manager | Setup | Financial | Flexfields | Key | Accounts to the PO Account Generator ITEM TYPE. Without modifications, EBS will build the inventory account from the inventory setups, and expense accounts from either the expense account associated with an item or, when no item is used, the PO Expense Account associated with the requestor.

Once all the required setups are completed, Purchasing is ready to be used!

CHAPTER
3

Processing Purchasing Documents

he ultimate goal of a purchasing system is to ensure a company gets the "stuff" it needs to do business, delivered at the right time, and for the right cost. Understanding the documents and processes involved in accomplishing this is the first step in an efficient purchasing system.

Purchasing Documents

The main purchase documents used in the procurement cycle are requests for quote (RFQs), requisitions, and purchase orders. EBS also allows you to track any quotes received on an RFQ or requisition.

Requests for Quote

Requests for quote are created prior to actually purchasing any items, with the purpose of receiving price quotes from one or more suppliers. In EBS, these can be created directly from a requisition on which someone has already asked for goods, or created without any specific requests to prepare for future needs. Once the RFQ document is generated and sent out, responses, in the form of a quotation, can be tracked and reported on for analysis and supplier selection.

Requisitions

In the procurement world, the purchasing department is king and queen; everyone else in the organization is a pawn scurrying around asking for approval to buy goods or services. And there is a good reason for this: ensuring the best price is received on the products and services being purchased can save an organization a lot of money. Also, many industries and organizations have quality or specification standards that need to be adhered to, making it difficult for nonpurchasing employees to know all the rules.

For these reasons, requisitions are created in organizations to obtain approvals and then sent to the purchasing department, where the purchasing monarchy goes about procuring these goods. Requisitions can be set up to be approved by the departments responsible for the budgeted dollars prior to going to the purchasing department, keeping the approval and the budget controls with the same person. In EBS, requisitions can be created in both the core Purchasing application as well as iProcurement, a web-based interface that expands the requisition functionality.

Purchase Orders and Agreements

Purchase orders and purchase agreements can be created either based on requisitions or without them and serve as the legal agreement between the supplying and purchasing companies, setting pricing and terms of the sales. EBS has several types of Purchase Orders and Agreements, listed in Table 3-1.

Releases

Releases are documents created against planned, contract, and blanket purchase orders and have the specific shipment information each delivery. Multiple releases can be associated with each order.

Document Name	Usage
Blanket Purchase Agreement	Created when terms, such as payment terms and negotiated prices, and goods or services are known, but specific delivery dates are not. These can be either set up either for a specific organization or as global agreements for all organizations to access.
Contract Purchase Agreement	Created when the terms and conditions of a purchase are known but specific goods and services are not. When a line references a Contract Purchase Agreement, Oracle's Advanced Pricing features can be used for complex pricing schedules.
Planned Purchase Order	Created for long-term agreements where the items or services, terms, and at least a tentative delivery schedule are known.
Standard Purchase Order	One-time purchases for goods or services.

TABLE 3-1 *Types of Purchase Orders*

Purchasing Documents, Step-by-Step

Starting with requisitions, this section will walk through the steps and fields required when creating purchasing documents, including requisitions, purchase agreements, and releases.

Requisitions

Requisitions are created in the Purchasing subledger by entering information directly into the Requisition window, from requisitions entered into iProcurement, or from a variety of automated features, including Drop Shipments, Quotes, or by using Requisition Templates. Since EBS is an integrated system, automated requisitions can be created from Work in Process, Master Scheduling or MRP (Master Resource Planning) process, and Inventory demands.

No matter how the requisition is created, the document approval process is available for all requisitions, providing control over the purchasing process.

Manual Requisitions

There are two requisition windows: the first, where requisitions are entered, can display only incomplete or rejected requisitions. The second, a summary window, can display and control requisitions once they are routed for approval.

To enter a manual requisition, use the Requisitions window, shown in Figure 3-1. Since this is a Multi Org Access Controlled (MOAC) form, an OPERATING UNIT may need to be selected if you have access to more than one organization; if not, then the operating unit will default in and cannot be updated. The Purchasing Options (Purchasing Manager | Setup | Organization | Purchasing Options | Document Numbering region) will determine if a requisition number can be entered manually or if it is automatically assigned by the system. Either way, this field must be unique.

There are two types of requisitions: PURCHASE and INTERNAL. PURCHASE requisitions denote that a purchase is going to be made from a third-party supplier, while INTERNAL refers to a request to transfer materials from one inventory organization tracked within EBS to another inventory or expense location. Internal requisitions interface with Purchasing, Order Management, Shipping Execution, and Inventory modules in EBS. PREPARER will default to the person who is creating the requisition and cannot be changed; it may differ from the actual REQUESTER. Adding a DESCRIPTION will help ensure the buyer knows what the requisition is for. STATUS and TOTAL are maintained by EBS, showing the actual status of the requisition and the currency and total dollar amount associated with all the lines. Requisitions are broken into two parts, as are most transactions in EBS: a header and lines. The header tracks general information about the requisition that relates to all the lines, whereas lines have specific information about each item being purchased, including descriptions, delivery dates, quantities and price information, and supplier information.

The only requisition statuses that can be seen in this form are INCOMPLETE, REJECTED, and RETURNED. INCOMPLETE orders include any requisitions that have not yet been submitted for approval, while a REJECTED status denotes a requisition that has been submitted for approval and rejected by the approver. RETURNED orders have been returned to the requestor for additional information or because they are duplicates by the actual buyer. All these statuses can have changes made to them, be canceled, or be submitted for approval. All other requisition statuses can only be viewed in the Requisition Summary form, described in the next section.

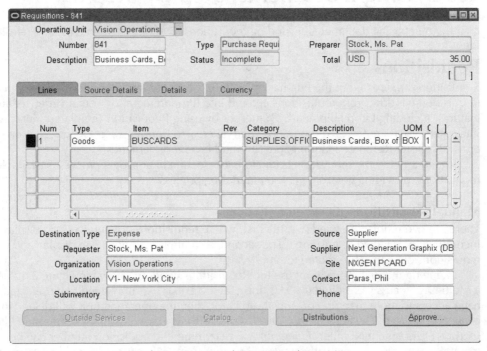

Purchasing Superuser | Requisitions | Requisitions

FIGURE 3-1 *Entering requisitions*

Entering Lines

When entering a line for a requisition, you have multiple options for adding information about the item being purchased. These options include using the item catalog, manually entering the information on the line, or automatically creating the requisition from demand created from another module in EBS. The same fields are utilized no matter how the requisition is created. Begin entering a manual requisition by adding a NUM to reflect the actual line number and a TYPE to denote the line type that is being created. This will default in from the Purchasing Options (Purchasing Manager | Setup | Organizations | Purchasing Options) setups and determine both the value and basis for the order, telling EBS how the amounts and quantities will be entered and calculated. ITEMS are not required to use purchasing in EBS unless the requisitions will be received into Inventory, but they can provide default information when creating an order, such as descriptions, supplier, unit of measure, default expense accounts that can be used by the account generator to build the requisition distributions, and purchase price. Items can also be used for expense requests for both inventory and non-inventory items being delivered to an expense location.

While setting up and maintaining items in your system does require additional time, there are benefits to doing so. The biggest advantages are the ability to source the purchases from specific approved suppliers, maintain purchase prices that will default onto orders, and assist in purchasing analysis by providing consistent information about the product being purchased. If items are not used, a CATEGORY must be manually entered for the requisition. CATEGORY will default in if an item is selected, and cannot be updated in this case.

Again, the DESCRIPTION will default in from the item, or it can be entered manually. If an item itself is set up to ALLOW DESCRIPTION UPDATE (Purchasing Manager | Items | Master Items or Organization Items), then EBS will allow the description field to be updated on both requisitions and purchase orders; otherwise, this field would not be updatable. When no item numbers are used, the buyer needs to type in a description for the purchase. UOM, or Unit of Measure, either defaults in from the item or can be added manually. This field is used not only to calculate the cost of the item on the requisitions and purchase order, but also to determine the actual cost when the items are received into inventory for average costing, and the purchase price variance for standard costing.

QUANTITY and PRICE are the two main fields used to calculate the costs associated with this order. If an item was used, and a LIST PRICE was entered on the item setup, this will default onto the requisition, but it can be updated by the preparer. Otherwise, it needs to be added manually. QUANTITY times PRICE will equal the total cost of the line, displayed in the AMOUNT field, and all the lines amount add up to become the TOTAL for the order. The NEED-BY date is the date the items are required, alerting not only the buyer but the supplier as well of the date the items are required.

SECONDARY UOM and SECONDARY QUANTITY, used with internal requisitions when Process Manufacturing (OPM) is enabled in both locations, are used for dual-controlled UOMs. SECONDARY UOM defaults in from the inventory item master, while the SECONDARY QUANTITY is calculated from the dual UOM indicator. If the OPM item is grade controlled, then the quality control GRADE can be entered. The CHARGE ACCOUNT, which is for display purposes only, defaults in to the charge account assigned on the Distribution. If more than one charge account is assigned, then the word MULTIPLE will display instead. RESERVED will be checked if budgetary funds are reserved for this line, usually associated with encumbrance accounting.

Source Details

Detailed information can be entered under the SOURCE DETAILS tab, such as a specific NOTE TO BUYER, providing information to the buyer about this particular purchase. A specific BUYER will default in if a DEFAULT BUYER was assigned to the item on the line, or a buyer's name can be added by the preparer. If this field is not populated, any buyer assigned to the category (Purchasing Manager | Setup | Personnel | Buyers) can work with the approved requisition to create the purchase order.

RFQ REQUIRED is usually used with an item number, denoting that the purchase of an item requires a request for quote, but it can also be checked by the preparer for non-item purchases. SUPPLIER ITEM either defaults in from the item or can be added by the preparer. This will default into the supplier item field when creating a purchase order from this requisition and will be printed on the purchasing document for the supplier to reference.

DOCUMENT TYPE, DOCUMENT, and LINE are all completed by EBS automatically when the requisition was created from either a blanket order, a contract, or a quotation; they link this requisition back to the source document. GLOBAL is checked when a blanket purchase agreement for the entire organization exists for the item being purchased, and the OWNING ORG will display as well, showing the organization who owns the agreement. This feature is usually seen when an organization is using a centralized purchasing model.

CONTRACT NUM references the associated contract agreement, along with the REV number. A contract agreement is basically an organization-wide agreement with a supplier for specific terms and conditions, but not prices or goods.

Adding Details

Additional details about the specific line item are added, such as if it is an urgent purchase or for a hazardous product, on the DETAILS tab. Checking URGENT will alert the buyer that this purchase is needed quickly, and a JUSTIFICATION for the purchase or reason for classifying it as urgent can be added. NOTE TO RECEIVER would include specific instructions for the person receiving the item, such as notifying a specific engineer when the item comes in.

TRANSACTION NATURE, a user-defined Lookup Code (Purchasing | Setup | Purchasing | Lookup Codes), can be added for information as to the nature of the purchase (such as Consumption or Resale). A REFERENCE NUMBER can provide a reference to a document in another system, such as a Work Order. A UN NUMBER (United Nations identification number for hazardous materials) can also be added. While EBS comes with UN numbers predefined, additional codes can be set up in Purchasing Superuser | Setup | Purchasing | UN Number. Here, the UN NUMBER, DESCRIPTION, and HAZARD CLASS can be added, or a previously set up UN NUMBER can be END DATED. After a UN NUMBER is added, the HAZARD class it is associated with will populate, or the HAZARD CLASS can be added without a UN NUMBER.

Currencies

Requisitions can be added in any currency set up in EBS by identifying the CURRENCY code and exchange RATE TYPE on the CURRENCY tab. EBS will calculate the Price and Amount for the functional currency based on the exchange rate. This tab also displays both the Base, or requisition, amount, and currency information, and the translated Functional currency amounts. The Functional currency relates to the primary currency that is set up for the Ledger.

Additional Line Information

You can add line information at the bottom of the requisition page, and it can be different for each line of the requisition. The DESTINATION TYPE has three options, and the item information entered determines the options. If an item is entered that is stocked in the purchasing organization, then the DESTINATION TYPE will default to INVENTORY, indicating that the item will be delivered into inventory directly upon receipt or after an inspection. If there is no item, or the item was set up in WORK IN PROCESS as being required by an outside processor, then SHOP FLOOR is available. The last destination type is EXPENSE, indicating that that line will be expensed immediately when received.

Adding a REQUESTER can help to drive the accounting in expense items by using the expense account associated with the employee, as well as by tracking the person who originally requested the purchase. (The expense account associated with an employee is set up on the employees record—Purchasing Manager | Setup | Personnel | Employee—under the ASSIGNMENTS tab.) ORGANIZATION refers to the inventory or receiving organization and will default to the organization associated with the requestor's default organization if a requestor was added. EBS requires at least one inventory organization to be set up to use Oracle Purchasing, even if Inventory is not being used.

LOCATION is the physical location to which the delivery should be made and can be set up, found in Setup | Organizations | Locations. If the DESTINATION TYPE was INVENTORY, a SUBINVENTORY can be added and will default in for the receipt, where it can be updated if required. If one is not provided, then the receiver will have to select one during the receiving process.

SOURCE determines whether the items being purchased will come from a third-party supplier or from an inventory organization within your own organization. When a requisition is sourced internally, it is called an Internal Requisition by EBS and allows the creation of an Internal Sales Order for the EBS organization it is sourced from, based on the ORGANIZATION entered. A SUBINVENTORY can also be identified. Both these fields appear by changing the SOURCE to Inventory.

For supplier-sourced inventory, the SUPPLIER, SITE, CONTACT, and PHONE can be added. While these fields all have the ability to select existing suppliers, sites, and contacts from the system, the requestor also has the option to enter names that do not exist as recommendations as to where to purchase a product. When the buyer converts this requisition into a purchase order will then have the option of creating the supplier or using a different one.

Using the Supplier Item Catalog to Create Requisition Lines

Requisition Templates uses the EBS Supplier Item Catalog to quickly find, review, and select items for purchase. Using this feature will decrease data entry for the requestor and allow the requestor to browse or shop from an existing catalog of items. This catalog is really an accumulation of purchasing information that exists in EBS. There are four tabs on the Supplier Item Catalog: Negotiated Sources, Prior Purchases, Sourcing Rules, and Requisition Templates, as seen in Figure 3-2. They are all a compilation of information from other data within EBS.

Negotiated Sources

The NEGOTIATED SOURCES region displays long-term agreements that may exist with a supplier, such as blanket purchase agreements, quotations, planned purchase orders, and global agreements.

Prior Purchases

EBS uses prior purchase orders and both scheduled and blanket releases to display historical purchase information.

Sourcing Rules

The SOURCING RULES tab displays any sourcing rules set up to automate requisition creation for items that are to be linked to purchase agreements or quotations from a supplier.

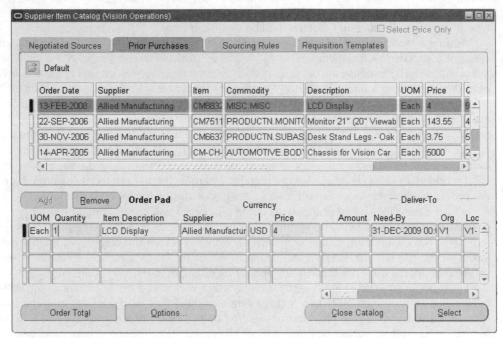

Purchasing Superuser | Requisitions | Requisitions | Catalog or Purchasing Superuser | Supplier Item Catalog

FIGURE 3-2 *Supplier Item Catalog*

Requisition Templates

The REQUISITION TEMPLATES tab displays the templates that are set up for faster purchasing. See Chapter 2 for more information on creating templates.

Using the Catalog

When you click the CATALOG button from a Requisition, your cursor must be on a requisition line as opposed to a header field. This will bring up the Find window, which can be used to narrow down the items that are displayed in the catalog. Some of the fields available to narrow down the selections are REQUISITION TEMPLATE, which will only display items associated with that template; ITEM, CATEGORY SETS, and DESCRIPTION; as well as supplier information, including SOURCED SUPPLIERS ONLY, which will limit the selection to items that are sourced from a specific supplier. Additional purchasing information, such as DUE DATE and LINE TYPE, can also be added when searching for prior purchases of an item. The catalog search screen is displayed in Figure 3-3.

After selecting Find, users will see the Catalog, previously shown in Figure 3-2, displaying information relating to the item they were looking to purchase. There are four tabs, listed previously in this section, and access to these tabs is controlled by the profile PO: Default Supplier Item Catalog Options (System Administrator | Profile | System). Here the option can be set to have access to all sources by leaving it blank or to display only a specific tab on the form. Once the item you wish to purchase is found, place the cursor on the line, and click ADD to add it to the Order Pad on the lower section of the form. This will default in all the information pertaining to the selected item

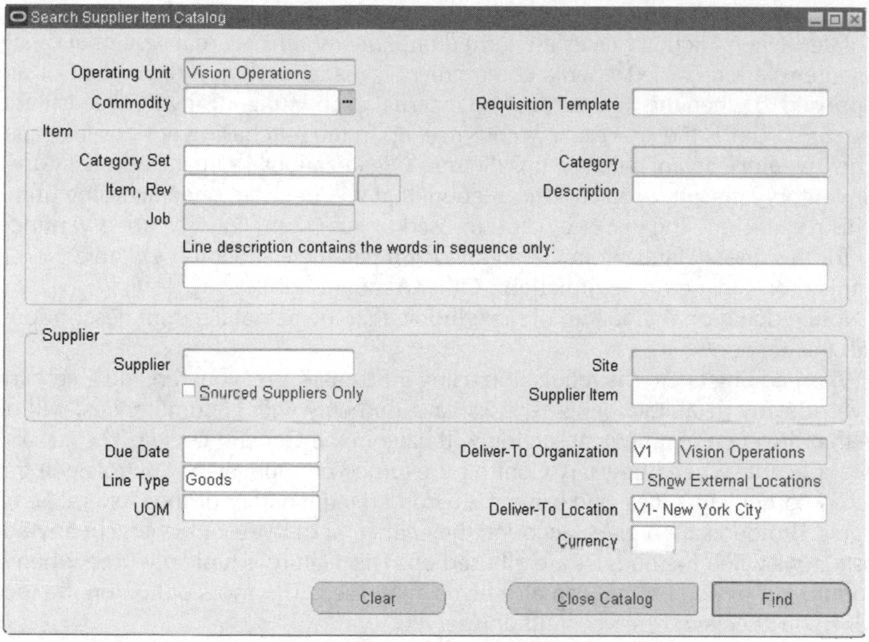

FIGURE 3-3 *Supplier Item Catalog Find window*

allowing the QUANTITY, PRICE, and delivery information, such as ORG, LOCATION, and DESTINATION, to be modified or added.

Use the OPTIONS button to default in some of this information when you are adding multiple lines with the catalog. There are two main options available: to default information from the item that is selected, or to default information from the previous line on the Order Pad. These defaults exist for the following fields: NEED-BY, DESTINATION TYPE, ORGANIZATION, LOCATION, REQUESTOR, SUBINVENTORY, and EXPENSE CHARGE ACCOUNT. Click ORDER TOTAL to display the total for all the lines added to the Order Pad so far. Click the SELECT button to finalize the catalog selection and add the lines to the requisition.

Requisition Distributions

At this point, specific distribution information will need to be added for each line. Distributions, added by clicking the DISTRIBUTIONS button, assign specific accounting or project information to each line.

Accounts

On the ACCOUNTS tab of the Distributions window (see Figure 3-4), the line NUM and QUANTITY will default in from the line on the requisition but can be modified to create multiple distributions for each line, splitting the accounting between more than one account. For expense requisitions, denoted by the DESTINATION TYPE on the preceding window, you will need to add the CHARGE ACCOUNT. Depending on how your system is set up, this may default in from an item or category if one was selected, the employee record, a project, or a combination of these places. These defaults are controlled by the account generator (See Chapter 2 for more details on the account generator).

Additional accounts that can be added on the distribution are the BUDGET, ACCRUAL, and VARIANCE ACCOUNTS. BUDGET ACCOUNT represents the accrual account set up for Encumbrances and is only populated when Encumbrances are turned on. *Encumbrances* are a type of accrual accounting where items are recorded when a commitment is made, such as a requisition or purchase order, as opposed to when the item is received (accrual accounting) or invoiced (cash accounting). The ACCRUAL ACCOUNT is the AP ACCRUAL ACCOUNT set up in the purchasing options for expense items, and on the inventory organization setups (Setup | Organizations | Organizations | Other Accounts tab) for inventory items; it represents the account that will be used when accruing uninvoiced receipts for this requisition. The VARIANCE ACCOUNT, used to record any Invoice Price Variances that would exist for this line, defaults from the organization parameters (Setup | Organization | Inventory Organization | Inventory Information | Other Accounts tab).

Notice down on the bottom of the window that the actual account descriptions are available for all the accounts.

When adding tax to the requisition using E-Business Tax, you can add a RECOVERY RATE override to override any default amounts. The GL DATE, used only with Encumbrances, will determine the date that the encumbrance transaction will have in the General Ledger. The RESERVED check box is only applicable when Budgetary Controls are turned on. Budgetary Controls will track requisitions, purchase orders, invoices, and expenses recorded in inventory or the General Ledger against the budgeted amounts for a given account; they either warn the user or prevent any additional transactions when the budgets are all used up. This feature is typically used when Encumbrance accounting is turned on, but can also be used by itself. The TOOLS option on the toolbar allows funds to be checked, reserved, and unreserved.

Project Information

When Oracle Project Costing is installed, requisitions, purchase orders, and invoices can all be charged to a specific project, causing them to interface to the Projects subledger and record the expenditure against the identified project. Project information includes PROJECT number, TASK, AWARD (if grants accounting is implemented), EXPENDITURE TYPE, ORG, and DATE. QUANTITY and line NUM are

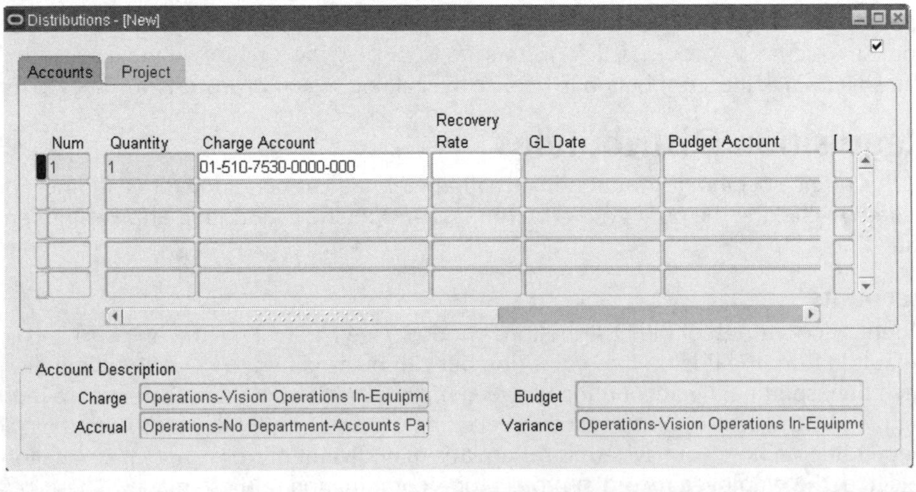

FIGURE 3-4 *Requisition distributions*

available, allowing the distributions to be split between multiple projects. CONTRACT LINE NUM, DELIVERABLE NUM, and UNIT NUM can all be added when Project Contracts is being used.

Outside Processing

When Work in Process is set up to utilize outside services to complete labor on a work order, you can add information relating to this process to the requisitions created to purchase these services. In order for a requisition to include outside processing, the DESTINATION TYPE must be set to SHOP FLOOR. This will enable the OUTSIDE SERVICES button, which opens a form that allows information specific to an item to be added. Enter either the Job or the assembly that will use this process, adding a line for the assembly if needed. Next select the OPERATION OR RESOURCE SEQUENCE this pertains to, and EBS will populate the rest of the information based on the selection.

Defaulting Requisition Information

If you are entering a large number of requisitions at one time, you can set up defaults, or preferences, and use them to decrease data entry. Preferences are not system defaults that are used every time, but session defaults that are set up each time you sign into Purchasing, and are saved only until you sign out of Purchasing (switching responsibilities will not lose your preferences, but signing out of the system will). To create a preference, click Tools | Preferences, and the Preferences window will open, as seen in Figure 3-5. Information entered on both the MAIN and PROJECT INFORMATION tabs will default in on all requisitions created until you sign out. This information can be overridden on any requisition. To make the preferences active, click APPLY.

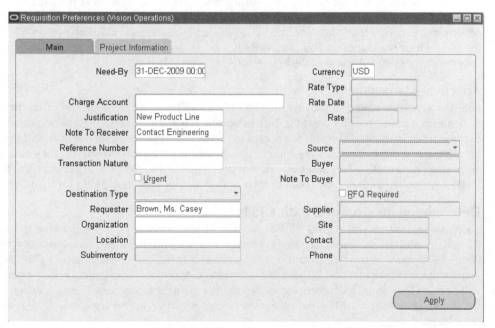

Purchasing Superuser| Requisitions | Requisitions | Tools | Preferences

FIGURE 3-5 *Requisition Preferences*

Approving Purchasing Documents

Purchasing Documents all require approval prior to being processed. The approval process will be a different in each organization, but EBS does require that approvals be set up. As mentioned in Chapter 2, Employees and Approvers, as part of the Approval Assignments and Approval Groups, must be set up prior to entering purchasing documents. EBS uses three main seeded paths for purchasing approvals: Employee Hierarchy, Position Hierarchy, or Oracle Approvals Management, which creates alternate hierarchies, rules, and conditions for the approvals to follow.

Employee Hierarchy

Using the Employee Hierarchy is pretty straightforward for approvals. EBS will look at the employee designated as the requestor for the requisition or purchase order, find his or her supervisor as set up on the EBS Person record (Setup | Personnel | Employees), and determine if that employee is authorized to approve the requisition given the document type, total amount, destination account number, item and category, and location. If the supervisor has the authority to approve, the requisition or purchase order is forwarded to him or her for approval. When the document type is set to OWNER CAN APPROVE (Purchasing Manager | Setup | Purchasing | Document Types), EBS will evaluate if the requestor or buyer has the authority to approve the document. If not, EBS will move on up the supervisor hierarchy to the next higher supervisor, checking the same criteria.

Position Hierarchy

Position Hierarchy has a slightly different way of finding the person who is in line to approve the documents, but it uses the exact same criteria as the Employee Hierarchy to determine if that person is authorized to approve the purchase. For Position Hierarchies, EBS will look not at a person's supervisor, but instead at that person's position, and find the next position in the hierarchy. For example, if an employee is set up as a Shop Floor Supervisor, and this position reports to the Shop Floor Manager, then EBS will send the requisition to the person who holds the Shop Floor Manager position. This does not necessarily have to be the requestor's assigned supervisor, or even someone in the requestor's supervisor hierarchy.

Approval Management

EBS has a module called Approvals Management (AME) that can be set up by using the employee or position hierarchy, or by creating its own unique hierarchy, as well by referring to as a group of defined rules to route documents for approval. These rules can be as simple as this: If the Category on the order equals Computer Equipment, send it to the CIO for approval. Or they can be as complicated as routing computer equipment purchases first to the person's supervisor, then to the IT Computer Specialist for configuration approval, and then to the CIO for final approval.

Determining the Approval Path EBS Is Using

There are two places you need to look to see how EBS is routing purchasing documents for approval. By default, EBS will use the Supervisor Hierarchy for approvals. If on the HUMAN RESOURCES tab of the Financial Options (Setup | Organizations | Financial Options), USE APPROVAL HIERARCHIES is checked, then Position Hierarchies will be used. To determine if Approval Management is being called, you will need to look at the Document Types (Setup | Purchasing | Document Types) for each individual document in question. AME is called for the document when the APPROVAL TRANSACTION TYPE is populated.

Approving a Requisition

No matter how your system is set up to route approvals, the approval process is the same. Once you have entered and saved all the required fields on a requisition, the APPROVAL button will be available. Figure 3-6 shows the approval window and options. The first section, ENCUMBRANCE, is only available for systems where Encumbrances are turned on. From here, you can RESERVE or UNRESERVE funds related to this requisition. These options are available if the Financial Options (Setup | Organizations | Financial Options) were set to RESERVE AT COMPLETION. Not all users have the authority to reserve funds, and if you do not, the funds will not be reserved until the person with the proper authority approves the requisition.

When reserving funds, you can update the options to USE GL OVERRIDE and USE DOCUMENT GL DATE TO UNRESERVE if the profile PO: Override Funds Reservation is set to YES. Setting PO: Used Document GL Date to Unreserve to YES will default the date to the date on the document when funds are unreserved. These can be set in System Administrator | Profile | System. When selected, this will allow funds to be reserved, even when absolute funds checking is turned on for the accounts on the requisition, up to be amount defined as the limit. EBS will default in the ACCOUNTING DATE and, when applicable, the UNRESERVE DATE.

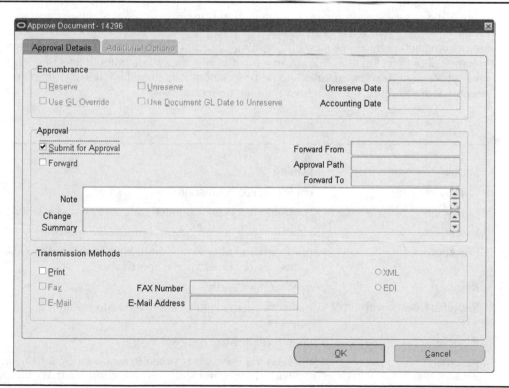

FIGURE 3-6 *Requisition approvals*

EBS will default a check in the SUBMIT FOR APPROVAL box, which will start the approval process. While the FORWARD feature can be selected at any time to populate the FORWARD FROM, APPROVAL PATH, and FORWARD TO fields, these fields can only be updated if the Document Type for Requisition Purchase has CAN CHANGE FORWARD-TO, CAN CHANGE FORWARD-FROM, and CAN CHANGE APPROVAL HIERARCHY checked. The profile PO: Allow Requisition Approval Forward Action must also be set to YES to use this feature. Otherwise, these are information-only fields.

A NOTE can be added for the approver and appears on the notification they receive. CHANGE SUMMARY will be populated by EBS only when the approval is for a change made to an already-approved requisition, and will highlight the changes for the approver. If business rules require it, the requisition can be printed, faxed, or e-mailed, and will default in both the FAX NUMBER and E-MAIL ADDRESS if a supplier and site were added to the requisition that has this information populated; otherwise, they can be added to this requisition. Selecting the OK button starts the approval process.

Controlling Requisitions

As mentioned at the beginning of this section, Requisitions can only be seen in the Requisition form with one of the following statuses: Incomplete, Rejected, or Returned. All Requisition Statuses are described in Table 3-2.

Managing requisitions really falls into three buckets. First, there are requisitions still in the requestor's court, which have the status of incomplete, rejected, or returned. Once the requestor submits the requisition for approval, it moves to the approvers bucket and the status becomes In Process, pending some type of an approval action. The last bucket is approved requisitions that are pending action by a buyer, usually creating a purchase order or rejecting it. In general, Incomplete or Rejected requisitions can remain as is in the system without affecting reports or other processes. The other statuses should be monitored on a regular basis and action taken as needed. Refer to Table 3-3 for actions required on requisitions.

Status	Meaning
Approved	Requisition has been approved.
In Process	Requisition has been submitted for approval and is still pending.
Incomplete	Requisition has not yet been submitted for approval.
Pre-Approved	Approver who has proper authority has forwarded requisition to another person for additional approvals.
Rejected	Approver rejected the requisition.
Requires Reapproval	Changes were made to an approved requisition, requiring it to be reapproved.
Reserved	Budgetary Funds are reserved for the requisition.
Returned	Approved requisition is returned to requestor by the buyer. Note that requisitions in this status are still considered in MRP, as they are approved. Canceling the requisition will remove it from MRP.

TABLE 3-2 *Requisition Statuses*

Status	Action Required
Returned	Returned requisitions need to be either rerouted for approval after changes are made or canceled.
Approved	Approved requisitions are ready to be added to a purchase order. Running the Buyers Requisition Action Required Report will show all approved requisitions that are waiting to be added to purchase orders. These requisitions appear on the AutoCreate window and will affect such processes as MRP and should be monitored closely.
In Process	In Process is a normal state for a requisition and is really only a problem if the requisition remains in process without approval for a long period of time (this time varies from organization to organization, but in general, 30 days or more is a good guideline). Often, an invalid workflow or invalid approver (such as a terminated approver) is the cause of the problem. Usually, they can be canceled. Sometimes, when the workflow was deleted in error or there is a problem with the approvals, they will need to be reset to Incomplete with a SQL script, PORESREQ.SQL. This script is available with Patch 5549427 and will only work if the system is not set up for encumbrances.
Pre-Approved	A requisition in this status should be treated the same as the In Process status.
Requires Reapproval	Requires that an approved requisition be resubmitted for approval due to a change on the document. These documents are managed the same as any In Process document.
Reserved	Requisitions that are in this status must be forwarded on for approval or unreserved. Available funds are reduced by the amount of the requisition when it is in this status.

TABLE 3-3 *Requisition Maintenance*

The Requisition Summary window can be used to control requisitions once they have been submitted for approval. After the requisition is queried, options will exist under the Tools menu by selecting Control. Most requisitions can be Canceled or Finally Closed from here. As with all areas of EBS, use caution when using Finally Closed on requisitions: no additional transactions can be made against a Finally Closed document, and it can not be reopened.

Creating Purchase Orders from Requisitions

A requisition, by definition, is only the act of asking for something to be obtained. A purchase order, on the other hand, is a legally binding offer between the buyer and seller to obtain those goods or services. Requisitions, in business, are internal documents used by multiple people in an organization to obtain permission and submit a request to purchase. These are then sent to the purchasing department, where they are sourced from different suppliers and grouped for purchasing.

EBS provides two features, AutoCreate and the Document Builder on the Buyers Workbench, to accomplish this task. The main difference between these two features involve the feel of how documents are transformed from a requisition into a purchase order: AutoCreate is a form in EBS, while Document Builder uses a web browser to accomplish the same task.

In addition to creating standard, planned, and blanket purchase orders, both forms can also create documents for requests for quote and auctions.

While all users with the proper security in the system can create requisitions, only employees set up as buyers can turn the requisitions into purchasing documents (Purchasing Superuser | Setup | Personnel | Buyers).

AutoCreate

Turning a document from a request to obtain to a legally binding document begins with finding and grouping the requests. This can be done in many different ways in the AutoCreate Find window, shown in Figure 3-7. A profile option affects the way AutoCreate works after the document is created. PO: Display the AutoCreated Document determines if the document is displayed once it is created. Setting this to Yes allows the buyers to review the purchase order and submit it for approval without having to query up the document. Documents can be reassigned easily in the Manage Buyer Workload form (Purchasing Superuser | Management | Manage Buyer Workload), where documents can be found and reassigned en masse.

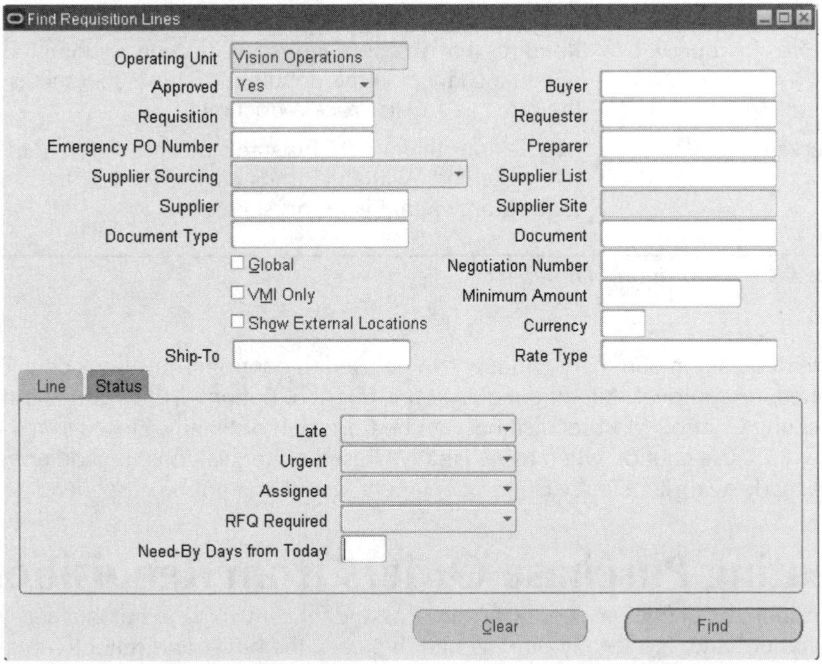

Purchasing Superuser | AutoCreate

FIGURE 3-7 *AutoCreate Find features*

When opening this form, four of the fields will default in: OPERATING UNIT, the SHIP-TO location associated with the OPERATING UNIT, APPROVED, and BUYER. Clicking CLEAR will remove the defaults except OPERATING UNIT and APPROVED, and these can be updated. While many of these fields are straightforward, such as Operating Unit, others require an explanation.

Requisitions can only be created for one OPERATING UNIT at a time, and this is the only required field on the form. While an unapproved requisition cannot be turned into purchase orders, it can be used to create a request for quote. Setting the APPROVED field to NO will show unapproved requisitions. In general, the Find window is used to group multiple requests into single documents, but this is not true all the time.

To find a single REQUISITION, the number can be selected from the list of values. EMERGENCY PO NUMBERS can also be selected. An emergency PO can be assigned when a requisition is created in iProcurement as opposed to the requisition form in purchasing, and when the purchase order number was reserved when the requisition was created. While this feature does help to satisfy the requirement some suppliers have in requiring a purchase order number when the order is placed, this does present potential EBS and company policy problems. If a user is supplying a purchase order number when the requisition is entered, and that user does not have the authority to approve that purchase, then actually contacting the supplier and supplying a purchase order number would be a policy violation. Also, once an emergency PO number is assigned to a requisition, this request cannot be added to any other requisitions, nor can other requisitions be added to it, when it is turned into a formal purchase order. If the requisition is rejected and never approved, that purchase order number will never have an associated document created for it.

The BUYER field is used to narrow down the requisitions assigned to a specific buyer when it was created. When this is populated, only requisitions assigned to this buyer will display. Access to updating this field is controlled by a profile option, PO: Allow Buyer Override in AutoCreate Find. When this profile is set to NO, then the buyer can only select requisitions with that buyer's name assigned as the buyer. REQUESTOR and PREPARER can also be added to narrow down the search. While these are often one and the same, it is possible to change the requestor on a requisition when this is a more centralized process or administrative staff is ordering for management.

If sourcing rules or approved supplier lists are set up, then selecting SUPPLIER SOURCING as SOURCED will limit the requisition lines available to items that are sourced to a specific supplier, while selecting UNSOURCED will show any line not associated with a purchasing sourcing document; leaving it blank will show both sourced and unsourced lines. While a SUPPLIER and a SUPPLIER SITE are not required when entering a requisition, they can be queried and grouped in AutoCreate by a supplier if one was assigned. EBS allows requisitions to have recommended suppliers that are not already set up in the system, but AutoCreate can only group on existing suppliers. They can also be grouped by the following DOCUMENT TYPES: Blanket Purchase Agreement, Contract Purchase Agreements, or Quotations, and the associated DOCUMENT number can be selected.

Supplier lists, which are created to group suppliers for the purchase of like items, such as Office Supplies or Computer Hardware, can be used to add the supplier to an RFQ. When they respond, the supplier responds with a quote, which can then be turned into a requisition, associating the supplier list to the requisition.

GLOBAL will select only requisition lines that were sourced form a global agreement. If your organization is using Oracle Sourcing, then the NEGOTIATION NUMBER can be added to limit the requisitions associated with a specific negotiation. You can select VMI, or Vendor Managed Inventory, to restrict the requisition lines to only those containing items that are under vendor management control. Locations can also be used to limit the search, by either selecting a specific SHIP-TO location or selecting to SHOW EXTERNAL LOCATIONS.

CATEGORY will default in from the buyer setup window (Setup | Personnel | Buyers) if one was populated for the buyer. The system profile PO: Allow Category Override in AutoCreate Find will determine if the buyer can update this field or not.

Finally, you can enter the MINIMUM AMOUNT on a requisition line, CURRENCY, and RATE TYPE. On the lower section of the form, you can add line-specific information to search by ITEM and REV, JOB, DESCRIPTION, and LINE TYPE. Under Status, you can add criteria to see only requisitions that are LATE, or past their NEED BY dates, marked as URGENT, ASSIGNED to a specific buyer, or have an RFQ REQUIRED. The last field is used to find all the requisitions that are needed within a certain number of days from today.

Once the requisitions have been queried up, you can AutoCreate them into specific types of documents, using a variety of methods and tools (see Figure 3-8). Once the requisitions have been approved, they are grouped by the buyer for purchasing or creating a request for quote. AutoCreate helps assist with these tasks.

ACTIONS that can be taken in the AutoCreate window include Create or Add To. Create will start a new document; Add To will add the selected requisition lines to an existing document. Next, it is the DOCUMENT TYPE that determines what document will be created. Documents include Standard PO, Planned PO, Blanket Release against an existing blanket purchase order, RFQ, Sourcing RFQ, or via an Auction. These last three options use EBS's ability to create requests for quote as well as hold auctions, and they are heavily tied into the module called iSupplier. iSupplier allows suppliers to be notified and respond to RFQs or an action online.

The last option is to determine how the requisition lines will be grouped for review and selection on the AutoCreate form. AutoCreate shows each requisition line, along with its associated header information, allowing the buyer to see all the requests for specific items, and to group them to maximize price breaks as well as reduce shipping costs. There are two options for how the lines are grouped on the form for selected. First is DEFAULT, which groups all the requisition lines by Item, Rev, Line Type, Unit of Measure, Supplier Item Number, and Transaction Reason. REQUISITION is the other, which will create documents based on the requisition number, not allowing lines from multiple requisitions to be combined onto one document.

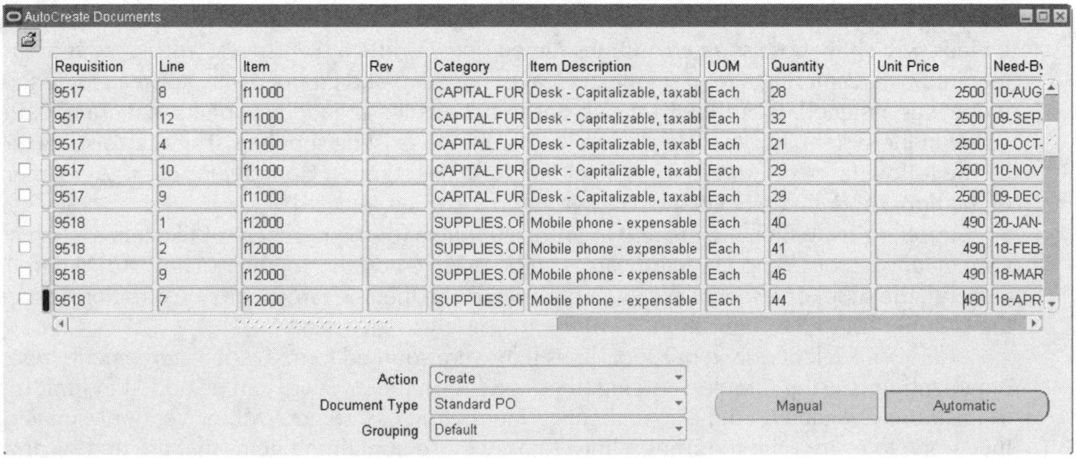

Requisition	Line	Item	Rev	Category	Item Description	UOM	Quantity	Unit Price	Need-By
9517	8	f11000		CAPITAL.FUR	Desk - Capitalizable, taxabl	Each	28	2500	10-AUG
9517	12	f11000		CAPITAL.FUR	Desk - Capitalizable, taxabl	Each	32	2500	09-SEP
9517	4	f11000		CAPITAL.FUR	Desk - Capitalizable, taxabl	Each	21	2500	10-OCT
9517	10	f11000		CAPITAL.FUR	Desk - Capitalizable, taxabl	Each	29	2500	10-NOV
9517	9	f11000		CAPITAL.FUR	Desk - Capitalizable, taxabl	Each	29	2500	09-DEC
9518	1	f12000		SUPPLIES.OF	Mobile phone - expensable	Each	40	490	20-JAN
9518	2	f12000		SUPPLIES.OF	Mobile phone - expensable	Each	41	490	18-FEB
9518	9	f12000		SUPPLIES.OF	Mobile phone - expensable	Each	46	490	18-MAR
9518	7	f12000		SUPPLIES.OF	Mobile phone - expensable	Each	44	490	18-APR

Action: Create
Document Type: Standard PO
Grouping: Default

Manual   Automatic

Purchasing Superuser | AutoCreate

FIGURE 3-8 *AutoCreate Documents*

There are two profile options that can be set to add additional criteria for the Grouping. First, PO: USE NEED-BY DATE FOR DEFAULT AUTOCREATE GROUPING will add the NEED-BY date to the previously described list of grouping criteria. The second, PO: USE SHIP-TO ORGANIZATION AND LOCATION FOR DEFAULT AUTOCREATE GROUPING, will allow the items to be viewed by ship-to organization and location as well. The other option for GROUPING is to group by REQUISITION, as opposed to line-specific criteria. This option does not allow documents to be grouped and created manually. The profile PO: DEFAULT REQUISITION GROUPING determines which of these two options (DEFAULT or REQUISITION) becomes the default on the form.

There are two paths that can be followed when creating documents: AUTOMATIC and MANUAL. To create a document automatically, select the requisition line(s) and click AUTOMATIC. This will open either the New Document form, if the ACTION was set to CREATE, or an Add To Document form, if it was set to ADD TO. To add a requisition line to an existing document, enter the document number you want to add it to from the list of values and select OK. This will open the document window (purchase orders will be used for the sake of consistency here, but you can also create a request for quote document), showing the lines the already existed on the purchase order as well as the newly selected lines.

Note that this feature is not limited to purchase orders that are created for the same supplier as the requisition; one of the features of AutoCreate is that the buyer has the option of reviewing the suggested supplier on the requisition and either accepting it or changing it. When more than one line is selected at a time, the grouping rules that were assigned previously will be used to group the requisitions onto a purchasing document.

If you selected CREATE instead of ADD TO, then you can add information prior to creating the actual purchase order (see Figure 3-9). If any of these fields were populated on the requisition, it will populate in this form, but it can be updated. If all the requisition lines were associated with a specific GLOBAL AGREEMENT (an organization-wide blanket agreement), then the agreement number will populate here. While the buyer can add a GLOBAL AGREEMENT number during the AutoCreate process, EBS will error out if multiple lines are selected that are associated to different Global Agreements. This field is available only for purchase orders, not for RFQs or blanket agreements.

A DOCUMENT NUMBER can be added only if Purchasing was set up to manually assign document numbers; otherwise, it will appear grayed out. When creating an RFQ only, the RFQ TYPE can be added. The SUPPLIER LIST NAME field will also be available for only RFQs. Supplier Lists are groups of suppliers set up in Supply Base | Supplier Lists, where the RFQ will go out to all suppliers listed in the Supplier List. RELEASE and RELEASE DATE will populate in when a release is being created with the requisition against a blanket purchase order, and will default to the next release number against the document and today's date.

SUPPLIER and SUPPLIER SITE will default from different information, depending on the document being created. When you are creating a release against a blanket purchase order, then the supplier and site will default in from the blanket and cannot be updated. If a standard purchase order is being created, then the supplier and site will populate in from the supplier on the requisition and, in the absence of one, will be blank. The buyer can add the supplier and site either at this time or after the document is created and prior to approving it.

The Currency for the purchasing document has some predefined defaults: The SOURCE can either be DEFAULT, FIRST REQUISITION LINE, or SPECIFY. DEFAULT looks first at the Supplier Site (Invoice Currency), and then the Supplier (Currency Preference on the Organization section) to see if there is one set. If not, then it will default to the functional currency setup for the organization. FIRST REQUISITION LINE will default the currency from the first line selected, and SPECIFY allows the buyer to select a requisition and requisition line to default the currency from, or to add a CURRENCY manually.

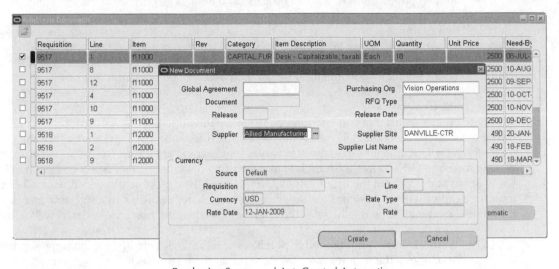

Purchasing Superuser | AutoCreate | Automatic

FIGURE 3-9 *Creating new documents automatically from AutoCreate*

Currency options are not available when adding a requisition line to an existing document, where the currency on the document will be used instead. When the CURRENCY selected for the purchase order does not match the currencies on the lines selected, you will have to provide a RATE TYPE and a RATE DATE prior to creating the document, which will be used to translate the currency on the lines to the new currency on the document. Selecting a RATE TYPE of USER will allow an actual Rate to be entered by the buyer. Remember, when any RATE TYPE other than User is selected, then you must set up the actual currency conversions for the requisition rates and the purchase order rate on the RATE DATE prior to creating the purchase order. Once all the data is entered, select CREATE to create the document, allowing additional information to be added prior to submitting it for approval.

When you have clicked the MANUAL button to AutoCreate documents, the same form is seen as described previously, but none of the information is defaulted in, requiring the buyer to add it in the AutoCreate window or on the actual document. This will also open up the Document Builder, where requisition lines can be selected and the lines built onto the document (see Figure 3-10). Once the Document Builder opens up, select a line by putting your cursor on it, and click ADD TO DOCUMENT button to add it to the document. It will now appear on the lower section of the form. Highlight it and click REMOVE to remove it from the document. The two buttons at the bottom are used to finish the process by either canceling the build or creating the document.

Not all requisitions will be created into documents by the buyers. Requisitions can be returned to the requestor for any number of reasons by selecting Tools | Return in the AutoCreate window. Some common business reasons would include a duplicate requisition or requisitions with missing or incorrect information. A reason can be added when this is done to inform the requestor of the problem. The requestor can then review the requisition in the Requisition window (Purchasing Superuser | Requisitions | Requisitions) and either adjust the information and resubmit it for approval, or cancel the requisition. This process will return all the lines in AutoCreate for the selected requisition.

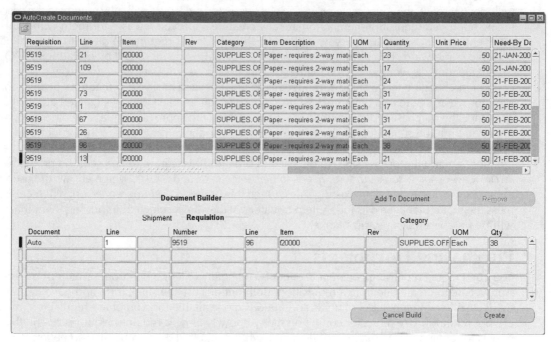

Requisition	Line	Item	Rev	Category	Item Description	UOM	Quantity	Unit Price	Need-By Da
9519	21	f20000		SUPPLIES.OF	Paper - requires 2-way mat	Each	23	50	21-JAN-200
9519	109	f20000		SUPPLIES.OF	Paper - requires 2-way mat	Each	17	50	21-JAN-200
9519	27	f20000		SUPPLIES.OF	Paper - requires 2-way mat	Each	24	50	21-FEB-200
9519	73	f20000		SUPPLIES.OF	Paper - requires 2-way mat	Each	31	50	21-FEB-200
9519	1	f20000		SUPPLIES.OF	Paper - requires 2-way mat	Each	17	50	21-FEB-200
9519	67	f20000		SUPPLIES.OF	Paper - requires 2-way mat	Each	31	50	21-FEB-200
9519	26	f20000		SUPPLIES.OF	Paper - requires 2-way mat	Each	24	50	21-FEB-200
9519	96	f20000		SUPPLIES.OF	Paper - requires 2-way mat	Each	38	50	21-FEB-200
9519	13	f20000		SUPPLIES.OF	Paper - requires 2-way mat	Each	21	50	21-FEB-200

Document Builder

Add To Document   Remove

Document	Line	Shipment	Requisition Number	Line	Item	Rev	Category	UOM	Qty
Auto	1		9519	96	f20000		SUPPLIES.OFF	Each	38

Cancel Build   Create

Purchasing Superuser | AutoCreate | Manual

FIGURE 3-10   *AutoCreate Document Builder*

The buyer can also modify a requisition by adding lines that will replace the existing line (select Tools | Modify). From here, the buyer can modify the information on any line by using the down arrow, which creates a new line that allows updates to be made to it. This will replace the existing line's information in the AutoCreate window when it is saved. This same feature can be used to split one requisition line into two lines by modifying the information on each line to reflect the new amounts or information. These changes will display on the requisition by zeroing out the amounts on the lines that were modified and adding the new lines that were created. A word of caution: EBS does not send this requisition back through the approval process, allowing the buyer to make the changes and proceed with the purchasing document creation.

The final action the buyer can take on a requisition in the Tools menu is to assign a requisition to another buyer. Select Tools | Reassign Buyer, and select the new buyer's name. This option reassigns only the line(s) that were selected, not the entire requisition.

Fully Automating AutoCreate

Auto-creation can be fully automated for releases against blanket agreements by using approved supplier lists (ASLs) and sourcing rules. After a blanket agreement is created and approved, run a process called Generate Sourcing Rules and ASLs form Blanket Agreements (View | Requests | Submit A New Request). This process will create both the sourcing rules and the approved supplier lists for the blanket, tying them together.

The one parameter on the request, Release Generation Method, determines how a requisition will move through the AutoCreate process. Selecting AUTOMATIC RELEASE will fully automate the process, taking approved requisitions and automatically creating approved releases for them without user intervention. AUTOMATIC RELEASE/REVIEW will create the release but require the buyer to review and approve it afterward. This submission for approval can also be automated by updating the PO Create Documents workflow by changing the ITEM ATTRIBUTE IS AUTOMATIC APPROVAL ALLOWED to YES. Use caution in changing this workflow, though, as setting this item attribute will automatically submit for approve any purchase order created from a requisition, not just the ones created automatically.

Once the purchase order is submitted, EBS uses the same approval rules as any other document, approving it if the submitter has the proper authority and forwarding it on to the proper person if he or she does not. RELEASE USING AUTOCREATE treats the requisition just like any other, making the creation a manual process using AutoCreate. In order for this feature to be used, the profile PO: ALLOW AUTO-GENERATE SOURCING RULES needs to be set to CREATE and UPDATE, which allows the users to create new rules and update existing rules. Once this process is set up, requestors will receive a message that a blanket exists for an item or category they have selected, informing them that it will be purchased against this blanket.

Purchasing Documents

You can create Purchasing documents either by manually entering one from scratch or by using AutoCreate to create one from a requisition. Both options use the same form and have the same fields. While a large number of fields and options are available for a purchase requisition, many are not required. Use the color coding on the window (yellow is required, white is optional, blue-gray is for defaulted information) to determine what is required. Remember that sometimes, adding data in one field can make another field required.

Purchase orders will be broken down into sections: Header, Lines, Shipments, and Distributions.

Purchase Order Headers

Header information on a purchase order is shared by the entire order (see Figure 3-11). If your responsibility has access to MOAC, then select the OPERATING UNIT this order is for; if not, it will default in. The PO number is either manually added or assigned by the system based on the Purchasing Options (Setup | Organizations | Purchasing Options). REV, which is maintained by the system, refers to the revision of the order, or the number of times changes have been made to key information after it was approved. CREATED will be populated by the system with the date and time the order was started.

TYPE represents the type of order that is being entered. Changing the TYPE will affect what fields are shown as well as required.

While the SUPPLIER, SITE, and CONTACT do not appear as required fields, they are required to submit an order for an approval, but not to save the order. Once a purchase document is approved, the system profile PO: Change Supplier Site will determine if the users can update the supplier site; the Supplier cannot be updated once saved. SHIP-TO will default in from either the buyer's personnel record, if it is populated, or the FINANCIAL OPTIONS on the Purchasing tab. None of these fields are required but can be left blank if the buyer is buying for multiple locations and added to the line information instead. BILL-TO is the location that the invoice should be sent to. Both of the fields will print on the purchase order. The BUYER will default in from the person who is signed into EBS. Note that a person must be set up as a buyer (Purchasing Superuser | Setup | Personnel | Buyers) in order to access this form. Users that are not buyers can access the view-only version of the form but cannot enter or update purchase orders.

Purchasing Superuser | Purchase Orders | Purchase Orders

FIGURE 3-11 *Purchase Order headers*

STATUS represents the status of the document. INCOMPLETE is the default status for all purchase orders until they are submitted for the first time for approval. This will change the status to IN PROCESS, where it will stay while it is routed for and approved. If you are set up to approve purchase orders, the document will evaluate your approval limits and either go directly to APPROVED or PRE-APPROVED, or be routed to the next person for approval. APPROVED represents purchase orders that are approved and can be received or matched to an invoice. PRE-APPROVED represents a document that has been approved by the proper person but forwarded to another person for an additional approval. REJECTED is the status of a purchase order was not approved by the approver. The final working status is REQUIRES REAPPROVAL, which means key information has been updated on the purchase order after it was previously approved, and it must be routed through the approval process again. This happens when the fields shown in Table 3-4 have changed.

Add a DESCRIPTION to each purchase order to identify the reason for the order or purchase. The CURRENCY will default in from either the supplier currency or the functional currency for the operating unit. If this purchase order was created from iProcurement using the Purchasing Card functionality, then the P-CARD field will populate with the procurement card number the order is for. The final field, TOTAL, represents the total of all the lines and charges entered on the purchase order.

Type of Field	Field Name
Header Fields	BUYER, SHIP-TO, BILL-TO
Supplier Information	CONTACT, CONFIRM, BRIEF NOTE TO SUPPLIER, ACCEPTANCE REQUIRED, ACCEPTANCE DUE DATE
Purchase Order Terms	PAYMENT TERMS, SHIP VIA, FOB, FREIGHT TERMS
Line information	UNIT PRICE, LINE NUMBER, ITEM, ITEM REVISION, ITEM DESCRIPTION, ITEM CATEGORY, QUANTITY, OR UNIT OF MEASURE. SOURCE QUOTATION HEADER OR LINE, HAZARD CLASS, CONTRACT NUMBER, SUPPLIER ITEM NUMBER, PRICE TYPE, UN NUMBER, BRIEF NOTE TO SUPPLIER, PROMISED DATE, NEED-BY DATE, and CAPITAL EXPENSE
Shipment and Distributions	Most updates in these areas will require reapproval, with the acceptance of accounting type information

TABLE 3-4 *Purchase Order Fields Where Changes Must Be Approved*

Line-Related Information on Purchase Orders

Lines are added to requisitions to include detailed information about the items that are being purchased. Each line will have a shipment and distribution, which will add the delivery and accounting information to it.

Lines Tab   The LINES tab will add item-specific information, as seen in Figure 3-12. NUM represents each line in the purchase order. While EBS allows you to select the first line number, it populates the rest of the lines in order after that, allowing you to override the line number that is assigned. EBS can also default this in on a purchase order that was created from a requisition in AutoCreate if the system profile PO: Use Requisition Line Numbers on AutoCreated Purchase Order was set to Yes.

TYPE is used to determine the type of product that is being purchased. TYPE (setup in Purchasing Superuser | Setup | Purchasing | Line Type) defaults information about how the amount on the line will be entered. There are four main line types for creating purchase orders: Amount, Fixed Price, Quantity, and Rate. Which is used depends on the VALUE BASIS entered on the Line Type. Amount orders, usually used when purchasing a service, allow only a quantity to be entered, which become the amount. This quantity then becomes the quantity to both receive and match to a purchase order. This option works well when a purchase order is issued for an estimate of services, where a portion of it can be received and billed.

Fixed Price, used to purchase either services or temporary labor, will allow the total amount or amount to be entered on the order. Quantity, most commonly used, allows a quantity, a unit of measure, and a unit price to be entered on the order. The last option, Rate, is used with Oracle's Services Procurement module. Services Procurement is designed to handle the complex purchasing requirements involved with services.

EBS allows the use of ITEM numbers on purchase orders. While this is not required, and not allowed for some types of purchases, such as services, it does allow better purchasing analysis and reduced entry for the person entering the order, as other fields will default in based on the item, such as Category, Description, and Unit of Measure. REV is only populated when an ITEM is entered and the item is under revision control. JOB is only allowed when Oracle Services Procurement is being used.

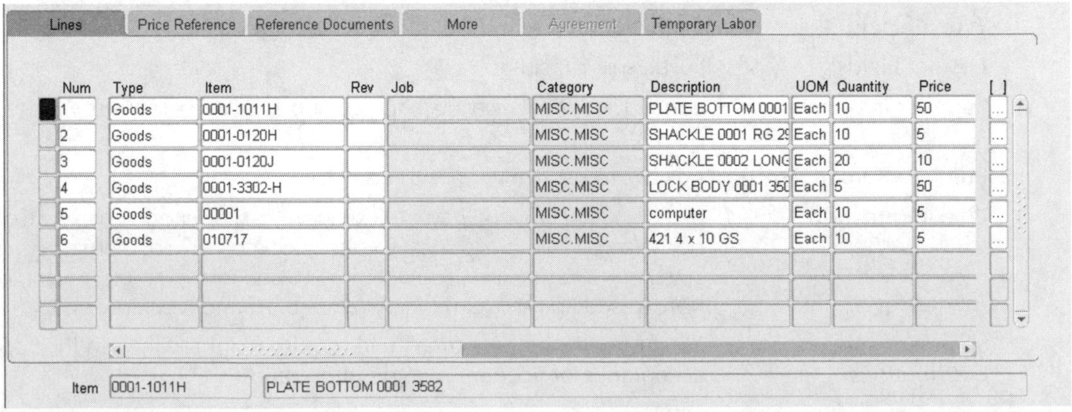

| Lines | Price Reference | Reference Documents | More | Agreement | Temporary Labor |

Num	Type	Item	Rev	Job	Category	Description	UOM	Quantity	Price	[ ]
1	Goods	0001-1011H			MISC.MISC	PLATE BOTTOM 0001	Each	10	50	...
2	Goods	0001-0120H			MISC.MISC	SHACKLE 0001 RG 29	Each	10	5	...
3	Goods	0001-0120J			MISC.MISC	SHACKLE 0002 LONG	Each	20	10	...
4	Goods	0001-3302-H			MISC.MISC	LOCK BODY 0001 350	Each	5	50	...
5	Goods	00001			MISC.MISC	computer	Each	10	5	...
6	Goods	010717			MISC.MISC	421 4 x 10 GS	Each	10	5	...

Item 0001-1011H   PLATE BOTTOM 0001 3582

FIGURE 3-12   *Adding lines to purchase orders*

While items are not required on purchase orders, CATEGORIES are. If an item was entered, this will default in and cannot be changed. If not, the buyer needs to add it. Categories are restricted to values that are predefined in Setup | Flexfields | Key | Values for the Item Category value set. DESCRIPTION, on the other hand, is a free-form field, allowing the buyer to add a description of the purchase. This will default in if an item was entered, but if the item was set up to ALLOW DESCRIPTION UPDATE (Items | Master Items or Organization Items | Purchasing tab), the buyer can modify or change the description. UOM, only required on certain types of purchase orders, is used not only to identify the units being purchased, but also to determine how an item can be received.

You can set up UOM conversion between the quantities purchased, received, and stored in inventory to calculate the correct quantities and costs. QUANTITY and PRICE are available, depending on the line type that was selected, and represent the number of units you wish to purchase as well as the unit price. Between the three fields QUANTITY, PRICE, and AMOUNT, at least one of them must be 1 or greater.

Both the PROMISED and NEED-BY dates represent the date that the supplier promised to deliver the goods and the date that your business requires them to be delivered. Both of these fields can be entered either on the line or as part of the shipment information. Since multiple shipments can be created for each line, it is possible to have multiple NEED-BY and PROMISED dates for each line. When the data is populated in one place, such as the line, then it will also display in the other, in this case, on the shipments. If multiple shipments are entered for a line with different dates, then the line will display "MULTIPLE" in these fields.

There are a few profiles that will affect the behavior of these dates. The first is PO: Check Open Periods, which determines if both the NEED BY and PROMISED dates have to be in an open period. When this is not set, then EBS does not require periods to be opened to create documents. PO: Default PO Promise Date from Need By Date will populate the promise date with the date entered in the NEED BY field. While neither of these fields show as required on the line or the shipment, one of the two must be entered in order to save the purchase order.

EBS allows a SUPPLIER ITEM to be added to a purchase order. At this time, though, there is no place to store these in the system. You can set up and store manufacturer part numbers, but not supplier item numbers if they are not the same. SUPPLIER CONFIG ID is used with iProcurement and is populated with a supplier configuration number when the requisition is created via a punchout to the supplier site. AMOUNT represents the total amount of the line. The CHARGE ACCOUNT, which cannot be entered on the line, will display the actual charge account entered on the distribution. If a line has multiple shipments, or the shipment has multiple distributions, then the CHARGE ACCOUNT will display Multiple (even if they all are the same account.)

RESERVED will be checked if budgetary control is enabled and the purchase order has reserved the funds. The final fields, SECONDARY UOM, SECONDARY QUANTITY, and GRADE, are used when Process Manufacturing is implemented. They are only available to process manufacturing users in purchasing organizations that are process manufacturing enabled.

Price Reference Tab   For each line, the LIST PRICE and MARKET PRICE will populate if an item was entered, and the list price is populated on the item itself; this can also be changed or entered by the buyer. Both of these fields are used on the Savings Analysis Reports EBS provides. These reports assist the buyers in analyzing the savings on each purchase order between the list, market, negotiated (when quotes are used), and actual costs.

You can add PRICE TYPE on each line for analysis as well. ALLOW PRICE OVERRIDE controls the releases on both blanket and planned purchase orders, determining if the amounts on the released documents can be over the PRICE LIMIT entered here. When this is not checked, the release will have the price from the main document and will not allow it to be updated; checking it will allow the price to be decreased or increased up to the PRICE LIMIT amount. This option is not available when the value basis for the line type is amount. NEGOTIATED is checked when the amount is less than the list price for this item, displaying that it was negotiated lower for the order. This field can be updated by the buyer as well.

Reference Documents Tab   For orders that are created from a contract or a source document, the information relating to that document is found here. When an order is created against a specific contract, the CONTRACT number, the OWNING ORG, and a check box to display if it is GLOBAL (across all organizations) are populated. For documents sourced from another document with sourcing rules or from a quote, the DOCUMENT TYPE, number and LINE, and SUPPLIER QUOTATION, as well as the CONTRACT NUM and REV are displayed. Of these fields, only CONTRACT, CONTRACT NUM, and REV can be entered by the buyer.

More Tab   Similar to the Details tab on a requisition, the MORE tab allows the buyer to add UN NUMBER information and HAZARD codes. A NOTE TO SUPPLIER can also be added, which can be displayed on the purchase order. This field is limited to 240 characters. The CAPITAL EXPENSE box can be checked to show that this line is a capital item, but this check box is for information only. A TRANSACTION NATURE can be added for the usage of the line, such as consumption or fixed assets. This is a purchasing lookup code, and more options can be added.

Agreement Tab   For blanket and contract orders only, you can add specific agreement information to control the order and releases. Adding a MINIMUM RELEASE amount will prevent releases from being created for less than a certain dollar amount. If there was an agreed-upon quantity for this order, you can add it in the QUANTITY AGREED field, as well as adding an AMOUNT AGREED. These two fields will not be automatically calculated when one or the other is entered, requiring the buyer to enter each field manually. They are used to print on the purchase order.

Once releases are made against the order, the QUANTITY and AMOUNT RELEASED fields will be populated by EBS, allowing the buyers to track how much is left on the agreement. Adding an EXPIRATION DATE will prevent releases against this order after that date. The CUMULATIVE PRICING check box is used in calculating price breaks on the order. The EBS default, used when this is not checked, evaluates each release for the price break points separately; checking this box considers both the current release and all the prior releases when calculating price breaks.

Temporary Labor Tab   The final tab, Temporary Labor, is only available when the purchase basis for the line is Temporary Labor. This allows the contractor information to be added, such as FIRST and LAST NAME, as well as a START DATE and an END DATE.

Adding Currencies and Using the Catalog

The CURRENCIES and CATALOG buttons at the bottom of the document window work the same for purchase orders as they do for requisitions. Currencies allows the currency for a specific line to be selected along with the conversion rates. This will default to either the supplier purchasing preference for currency, or the ledger functional currency. Catalog allows the buyer to use previous purchases, sourcing rules, and negotiated sources. The main difference between using the catalog on a purchase order as opposed to a requisition is that the REQUISITION TEMPLATE tab is not available.

Adding Terms

Terms are created for each purchase order in accordance with the supplier and system defaults, but they can be updated using the TERMS button at the bottom of the document window. The main terms associated with all orders include PAYMENT, which will default onto the invoice, FREIGHT, CARRIER, and FOB. PAY ON is used when Pay on Receipt (or Evaluated Receipt Settlement) is going to be used on this order. This is only available if the supplier site is set up as a Pay On Receipt site (this is not available if the site is set to Pay On Use). Populating this with RECEIPT will automatically create invoices for receipt transactions against this order. TRANSPORTATION ARRANGED determines if the Supplier or the Buying Organization will arrange the transportation. This field is used by EBS when Oracle Transportation is implemented.

When CONFIRMING ORDER is checked, it indicates that this is a confirmation to a verbal order. This will print on the actual purchase order "This is a confirming order. Do not duplicate." The FIRM check box is used internally by EBS to indicate that this shipment is an order that cannot be rescheduled by the master scheduling/MRP process. The ACCEPTANCE REQUIRED field indicates to the supplier if an acceptance of the purchase order and its terms and agreements is required, and BY what date. SUPPLY AGREEMENT, used with blanket agreements, indicates to EBS if any releases against this blank should be communicated to the supplier. This feature is used when Oracle Supplier Scheduling is implemented. RECEIVER and SUPPLIER NOTES can be added as well. These notes are associated with the purchasing document header, as opposed to the NOTE TO SUPPLIER field found on the MORE tab, which is line specific.

Agreement Controls are available for both blanket and contract agreements. EFFECTIVE dates are defined to assign the time period these agreements are in effect. Releases cannot be created if the dates do not fall within this date range. The AMOUNT LIMIT is the total amount that can be released against this agreement, while the MINIMUM AMOUNT is the smallest amount allowed on any release. This will default in from the AGREEMENTS tab if it was entered there. PRICE UPDATE TOLERANCE is used when price or sales catalog information is being imported from the supplier using the Purchasing Documents Open Interface. The tolerance will limit the amount the blanket purchase order can be increased for any new pricing.

Contract Terms can be added when Oracle Procurement Contracts is implemented.

The Encumbrance tab is available only if encumbrance accounting is turned on; it determines if this purchase order is encumbered or will create encumbrance accounting transactions, as well as assigning specific encumbrance and budgetary information. There is a profile option that will control the GL Date that appears here: PO: AutoCreate GL Date. The setting of this option will determine if the General Ledger date defaults to the date on the requisition or the date the purchase order is created using the AutoCreate window.

Adding Price Breaks

Price breaks can be added to blanket agreements only, and indicate any price advantages on the order. Multiple breaks can be added to each order by creating multiple lines on the price break form. Click the PRICE BREAK button at the bottom of the window to access the price breaks form. After assigning the line NUM, determine if this break is associated with a specific Organization and Ship-To. The ORG field is limited when an item is entered on the blanket agreement to the organizations that the item is assigned to. SHIP-TO locations are also limited according to the locations associated with the organization selected, or locations not assigned to any organization.

Enter a minimum QUANTITY to determine at what point an order will use the price break and EFFECTIVE FROM and TO dates. If these are not entered, the price break will be in effect for the entire duration of the order. BREAK PRICE is the discounted price that will take effect when orders for the QUANTITY are released. This will default to the actual amount on the line. DISCOUNT (%) will fill in, based on the difference between the line AMOUNT and the BREAK PRICE, or it can be added without entering a Break Price, which will calculate based on the Discount. Price Breaks are usually determined by the release quantities, but if CUMULATIVE PRICING was checked on the Agreement tab for the line, then it is based on the cumulative release quantities.

Shipment Details

Multiple shipments can be added to each line by clicking on the SHIPMENTS button, and add detailed information about where and when to ship a specific line on the order. The shipment NUM, ORG, SHIP-TO, QUANTITY, PROMISED DATE, and NEED-BY (if populated) will all default from the line and can be updated as needed. The NEED-BY date is required for inventory or master planned items. The ORIGINAL PROMISE date will be populated with the promised date that was entered first on the purchase order when the Promised Date is updated. UOM also defaults but cannot be updated except by updating the UOM on the line itself.

A NOTE FOR RECEIVER can be added or will populate from the requisition, just like the COUNTRY OF ORIGIN. The CHARGE ACCOUNT will display after the Distributions are added, and will reflect Multiple if more than one distribution is added for the shipment. AMOUNT reflects the line amount and can only be updated by changing the quantity, unit price, or amount on the line. RESERVED will display as checked when the funds on this line are reserved against the budget when budgetary controls are turned on. For Oracle Process Manufacturing items, SECONDARY UOM, QUANTITY, and GRADE will populate.

Using the More tab, tolerances can be updated for this specific order. These tolerances will either default from the supplier site, come from the supplier, or default in from the Purchasing Options, depending on which is populated (EBS looks first at the site, and then at the supplier, and finally at the Purchasing Options settings to find the defaults). RECEIPT CLOSE TOLERANCE (%) determines when this line will close for receiving, and the INVOICE CLOSE TOLERANCE (%) determines when this line will close for invoicing. There are three main close points for a purchase order: CLOSED FOR RECEIVING and CLOSED FOR INVOICING both relate to a specific line, while the purchase order itself has a closed status. The entire order will not close automatically if all the lines are not closed for both receiving and invoicing. A tolerance of 0% indicates that it will close when the total amount received or invoiced equals the amount on the order, whereas a close tolerance of 100% indicates that no receipts or invoices are required for this order, which will close the lines for receiving as soon as the order is approved. Reviewing these default close tolerances on a regular basis is a good idea to ensure orders are properly controlled and closed with minimal intervention by the purchasing agent.

The MATCH APPROVAL LEVEL determines if this order is set up for 2-Way (invoice to order only), 3-Way (invoice to both the receipt and the order), or 4-Way (invoice to delivery, receipt, and order); it is used to determine the close point for the order. A 4-Way match requires the receipt to be completed and delivered, and an invoice matched to the order prior to closing, while a 2-Way match only requires a receipt prior to closing the order. The INVOICE MATCH OPTION determines whether the invoice will be matched to the Receipt or the PO when using 3-Way matching.

When RECEIPT is selected, the invoice cannot be matched to this order until a receipt is actually made, but EBS will utilize the receipt date for exchange rate information when this is selected for foreign currency transactions. Selecting PO will allow the invoice to be entered prior to the receipt, and a system hold will be applied to the invoice until the receipt is performed. While matching to a receipt is not necessarily bad, ensure that the receipts are processed in a timely manner and prior to invoices being created to reduce problems when entering the invoices in the system. When this option is used, ensure there is a payables procedure in place for how to monitor those invoices that cannot be matched to the orders until the receipts are made.

Selecting ACCRUE AT RECEIPT indicates that the receipt for this line should create an accrual at the time of the receipt as opposed to at period end. Checking FIRM will indicate to MRP that this delivery cannot be changed. VMI will default as checked when the item selected for the line is part of a vendor-managed inventory, while the CONSIGNED box will check for items and suppliers where the product is on consignment.

The Status tab contains no fields that can be updated but stores important information about transactions against a given order. The STATUS field reflects the actual status of this shipment (such as Closed for Receiving), as well as the QUANTITY ORDER, RECEIVED, CANCELED, and BILLED (or Invoiced). It will also display the SECONDARY QUANTITY for ORDERED, RECEIVED, and CANCELED when the line is for an OPM item and organization.

Receiving Controls can be updated with the RECEIVING CONTROLS button for each shipment, but they do default from the supplier and system setups. You can set the DAYS EARLY and LATE the item can be received as well as the ACTION taken on these receipts, as well as determining any Over Receipt Tolerances and the ability to receive substitute items and how inventory items are delivered.

Distributions are required on all shipments to assign the accounting information. Again, multiple distributions can be added to each shipment. (As a recap, multiple distributions can be added to each shipment, multiple shipments to each line, and multiple lines to every order.) Distributions start by determining the TYPE of the distribution: Expense, Shop Floor, or Inventory. Any line can be set up as expense, but only lines with inventory items can have a Type of Inventory. If this order was created from a requisition, the REQUESTOR will default in from there; if not, it can be added by the buyer not just for information, but the expense account number associated with the requestor can be utilized in the account generator to determine the account number. The Requestor will default in the DELIVER-TO location, where it can be updated or manually added if there is no requestor.

The SUBINVENTORY is only available when the TYPE is set to INVENTORY; it determines which subinventory the item should be received into. QUANTITY will default in from the shipment and can be updated to create multiple distributions. A PO CHARGE ACCOUNT will default in if this line is associated with a project or an item, or it can default in from the requisition where it was created. It can also be added by the buyer. If the line is associated to a project, this can only be updated if the profile PA: ALLOW OVERRIDE OF PA DISTRIBUTIONS IN AP/PO is set to YES.

DESTINATION CHARGE ACCOUNT is only used for internally sourced orders; it indicates the account where the charge in the destination organization should go. Recovery Rate is populated when purchasing is set up to add tax to the purchase orders and the purchases are taxable. RESERVED and GL DATE, as always, are used for encumbranced and budget-controlled orders.

The More tab will display information about the requisition this order was created from, when there is one, as well as additional accrual and variance accounts. The accounts all default in from the setups and cannot be updated.

The Projects tab allows specific information about a project this purchase should be associated with in Oracle Projects. This will enable the cost associated with the project to be imported into Oracle Projects. Fields include PROJECT and TASK, AWARD for grants accounting users, and also EXPENDITURE-specific information. When project information is entered, the account generator will use this information to create the charge account for the distribution.

On the button of the distributions form, shipment-specific information is displayed for reference, as well as the descriptions of the accounts entered or defaulted in. At this point, the purchasing document is ready for approval.

Setting Purchase Order Preferences

Just as you can for requisitions, you can set Purchase Order Preferences to control specific information for this session (Tools | Preferences). These preferences are lost when you sign out of EBS. When creating large numbers of purchasing documents with similar data, such as Ship-To or Destination Type, or multiple orders for the same project, preferences can default the consistent information in for you, overriding the system defaults for these fields in this session only. These preferences will be lost when you sign out of EBS.

Approving Purchasing Orders

While an order can be saved at any point during the entry process, it can only be approved once all the required information is complete. While the APPROVE button will appear at any point after the order is saved, EBS checks prior to beginning approval to ensure all the required information is entered, and inform the buyer of any data that is missing. At a minimum, all orders must have a supplier, a line, and in all cases except blanket agreements, shipments and distributions for each line.

Once you have entered all the required data, click APPROVE button and the Approve Document window appears. This approval form works the same as the requisition approval form. All purchasing documents use notifications to inform the approver that the document requires approval. Notification can be viewed either in Notification Summary window (Purchasing Superuser | Notification Summary) or by setting up the Workflow Mailer in EBS to send out notifications to the approver's e-mail. One last note on approvals: If the person responsible for approving a document is out of the office and unable to reply, the document will remain In Process and not be forwarded on to the next approver.

Setting up a Vacation Rule will allow an approver to delegate his or her response to a notification, or to transfer ownership of the notification to another person. When delegating a notification response, this will make any responses appear as if the original owner responded to the notification, not the person it was delegated to, and this may become an issue during audits or with internal policies. Transferring ownership will transfer the notification to the person covering the approvals, requiring that person to have the proper authorities to approve the document. If he or she does not, it will move up the ladder from this point, not from the original owner. More details on Approvals can be found earlier in this chapter in "Approving Purchasing Documents."

Transmission Methods are more heavily used on purchase orders than on requisitions; they determine how the orders will be transmitted to the supplier for fulfillment. There are three ways EBS supports sending the document to the supplier: printing a hard copy to main or fax manually, faxing it directly from the system, and e-mailing it directly or electronically via XML or EDI. The first three methods will default in from the supplier site (Supply Base | Supplier | Address Book | Manage Sites| Communications | Notification Methods). The preferred method can be set here to Email, Fax, Print, or None, and both a fax number and an e-mail address can be entered.

The system profile PO: Secondary Email Address can be set up to add an e-mail address to which a duplicate of all e-mailed documents are sent. This is often set to the buyer. When a purchase order is e-mailed, EBS uses the Workflow Notification Mailer to send an e-mail with the purchase document attached to the supplier. The Notification Mailer requires extra database configurations prior to being used. Faxing, on the other hand, requires that RightFax FCL (Fax Command Language)–compatible software be installed prior to using this feature. EDI and XML both require additional setups and interfaces to be created in purchasing. EDI uses the Oracle e-Commerce Gateway to transmit and receive documents, while XML uses the XML Gateway. When a supplier is set up as a Trading Partner in the e-Commerce Gateway for EDI and in the XML Gateway for purchase documents, the appropriate boxes will be checked. With the exception of EDI and XML, the buyer has the option to change how the purchase order is sent.

Besides printing a document when it is approved, you can print one at any time by running a request for Printed Change Orders, Printed Purchase Orders, Printed RFQs, and Printed Requisitions. These reports come in both Landscape and Portrait orientations.

Controlling Purchasing Documents

In a perfect world, all purchasing documents will always be needed, and they will close automatically when the items are received and paid for. Reality requires a little bit more care and feeding. Purchasing documents have two general conditions that need to be monitored:

orders that are created and will never be delivered or invoiced, and orders that will not be used 100 percent and need to be closed manually.

Canceling Purchase Documents

Any purchasing document can be canceled at any time. This includes a document that has receipts associated with it. While there are valid business reasons for canceling an order that is received, be aware that the receiving transactions will not be available for update or return to the supplier once the document is canceled. More often than not, it will be unreceived documents that are canceled. This will remove the documents from the purchasing reports, keeping them more usable in length. To cancel either an order or a specific line on the order, go to the Purchase Order or Summary window (Purchasing Superuser | Purchase Orders | Purchase Orders or Purchase Order Summary).

Once the order is queried, put your cursor on the purchase order header to cancel the entire order, or on a specific line to cancel only one line. Select Tools | Cancel and the cancellation box will appear, allowing a reason to be added, as well as determining if the associated requisition will be canceled as well as the order. You can also select if the cancellation will be sent to the supplier. Once an order or line is canceled, it cannot be reactivated in the future.

Price Changes on Blanket Agreements

An additional feature EBS provides is the ability to apply pricing changes to the releases associated with the blanket agreement. The profile option PO: ALLOW RETROACTIVE PRICING OF POS controls how this feature works. When this is set to ALL RELEASES, every release against the blanket agreements will be updated, including releases that have already been received or invoiced. OPEN RELEASES ONLY will update on releases that are still open and not received. No matter which of these options is selected, only releases that have a status of APPROVED or CLOSED and are not encumbranced will be considered. The final option is NEVER, which disables this feature.

Once the profile is set, there are two options for updating the existing releases. Making a pricing update to a blanket agreement creates a new Rev of the agreement, requiring it to be reapproved. On the Approval window, select the ADDITIONAL OPTIONS tab and check APPLY PRICE UPDATE TO EXISTING POS AND RELEASES. This will cause all the releases to be updated where they meet the criteria (status = approved or closed) and based on the setting assigned the profile option PO: ALLOW RETROACTIVE PRICING OF POS. In order for the retroactive pricing to take effect, run the concurrent program called Retroactive Price Update of Purchasing Documents Program to update the releases.

Also available is the option to COMMUNICATE PRICE UPDATES to the supplier, which will e-mail all the purchase orders and releases that are impacted with the new pricing. When this box is not checked, only this blanket agreement is communicated to the supplier. This communication follows the Transmission Method selected. The second option is to run the concurrent request called RETROACTIVE PRICE UPDATE OF PURCHASING DOCUMENTS PROGRAM. Since this can be run for all documents for the same supplier at one time, it is a good option when multiple blanket agreements were updated.

Closing Orders

As mentioned, orders will self-close when the invoice and receiving tolerances are met. The requirement to close an order is that the lines all be closed for invoicing and receiving. One common misunderstanding about EBS is that a closed order cannot have any additional receipts or invoices matched to it, which is incorrect. To receive a closed order, ensure the INCLUDE CLOSED POS check box is selected when finding expected receipts. Invoices can be matched to any purchase order except those that are canceled.

Orders can only be manually closed from the Purchase Order Summary form (Purchasing Superuser | Purchase Orders | Purchase Order Summary). Find the order you want to control, and select Control from the Tools menu. This will open the Control Document form. From here, the purchase order can be updated with the actions listed in Table 3-5.

Tracking Changes to Purchasing Documents

When a change is made in a purchasing document to key information that requires reapproval and creates a new revision of the order, EBS tracks these changes. They can be seen in the PO Change History form, shown in Figure 3-13. After finding the history by selecting the Organization and either the purchase order number or supplier, among the other find fields, choose whether you want to compare the latest version of the order to the previous saved document, to compare it to the original order, or to see all the purchase order changes. This will display all the changes made on the document, including the header, line, shipment, or distribution level.

Action	Description
Cancel PO	Cancels the entire PO, allowing no further actions on the order or any associated receipts.
Close	Closes the purchase order so that it will no longer appear on reports.
Close for Invoicing	Closes the order of invoicing only.
Close for Receiving	Closes the order for receiving only.
Finally Close	I can never say this enough: Final is Final. Once an order is Finally Closed, no additional transactions can happen to the order or any of its associated transactions. This can *not* be undone via any standard functionality in the applications, and it will lock up any pending or future transactions that are attempted against the order (such as matching it to an invoice or adjusting an invoice that is matched to it).
Freeze	Prevents any future modifications to the order but allows receipts and invoices against it. This is removed by unfreezing the order.
Place on Hold	Placing an order on hold will not only unapprove it, but will also prevent printing, receiving, invoicing, and reapproval until the hold is removed by selecting RELEASE HOLD. At this time, the order will require reapproval.
Open for Invoicing	This is only available when the order or line is closed for invoicing; it allows it to be reopened.
Open for Receiving	This is only available when the order or line is closed for receiving; it allows it to be reopened. As mentioned earlier, closed lines can still be received, so this is more about reporting than the actual receipt.

TABLE 3-5 *Actions Available to Control Purchase Documents*

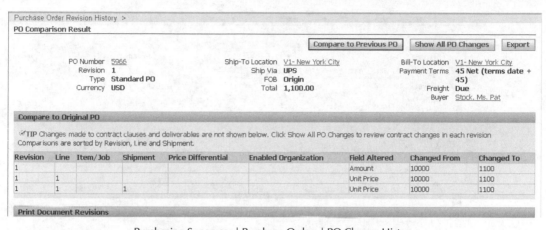

FIGURE 3-13   *History of purchase document changes*

Releases

Releases are created against both blanket and planned purchase orders, and they become the shipments and distributions against these orders. The releases add shipment information that allows receipts and invoices to be processed against them (see Figure 3-14). In order to create a release, enter the PO number from the list of values. If you entered the release form from the Purchase Order Summary form, then the PO number will populate for you. The RELEASE number will populate with the next available number in the system, but this number can be updated. The release header information will all default in from the source document and, with the exception of BUYER, cannot be updated.

The rest of this window works like a purchase order shipment, allowing shipping and distribution information to be added, along with receiving controls and agreements. The one field that is different is the SHIPMENT field. This is used only when the release is against a planned order, known as a planned release, and it references the shipment on the order this release relates to. Once the information on the release is updated, the release needs to be approved, just like any other purchasing document.

Buyers Work Center

The Buyers Work Center is an interactive web-based interface that allows buyers to find requisitions and use the Document Builder to create orders, manage and update orders, manage the negotiation process, maintain suppliers, and manage procurement contract deliverables (only available when Procurement Contracts is installed). Many of these features are available in other forms already covered, as noted in Table 3-6.

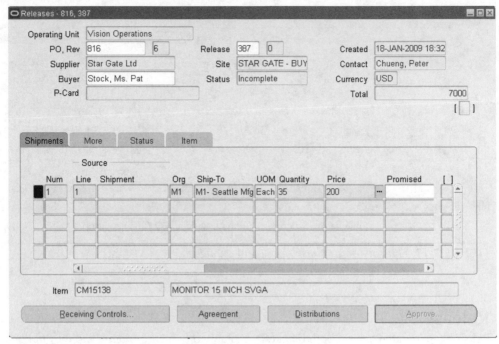

Purchase Superuser | Purchase Orders | Releases or Purchase Order Summary | Query A Blanket or Planned Order | Release button

FIGURE 3-14   *Releasing shipments against blanket and planned orders*

Demand Workbench

The Demand Workbench for requisitions has a few features worth covering, as seen in Figure 3-15. It can query data based on a previously saved View or by entering specific search criteria. There

Buyer Work Center Feature	Form
Requisitions	Demand Workbench	AutoCreate
Requisitions	Summary	Requisitions	Requisition Summary
Orders	Purchase Orders	Purchase Orders
Agreements	Purchase Orders	Purchase Orders with the type of blanket or contract agreements
Deliverables	There is no comparable form for this information
Negotiations	Much of the information can be found in RFQs and Quotations, while the work center provides a summarized recap
Suppliers	Supply Base	Suppliers

TABLE 3-6   *Buyer Work Center Compared to Other Forms*

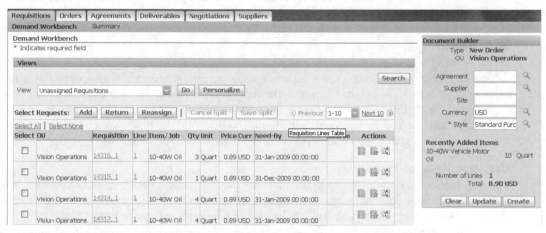

Purchasing Superuser | Buyer Work Center | Requisitions

FIGURE 3-15 *Demand Workbench in the Buyer Work Center*

is no ability to perform what is commonly called a "blind query" in this form that will return all the data (in other words, you cannot query all approved requisitions waiting to be created into documents). The view (which is really just a search where the criteria are saved and the fields displayed can be selected) or search must contact one of 20 fields, such as BUYER or REQUISITION NUMBER.

Once the requisitions are found, the same actions that can be taken in AutoCreate can be taken here. Check the requisition(s) you want to take action on, and ADD it to an existing document or create a new document, RETURN it to a requestor, or REASSIGN it to another buyer by using the buttons next to SELECT REQUESTS. The icons under ACTIONS allow a requisition line to have a new item purchased, from either the Catalog or the buyers personal favorites, or for the lines to be split into more than one line.

Once requisition lines are added to the Document Builder on the right side of the form, select CREATE and the purchase order form will open up for the document to be created and submitted for approval.

Receiving

Receiving is typically thought of as an inventory function where items are received and credited into inventory. In reality, it is a purchasing process against the purchase order, where the destination determines whether the purchases are received into inventory and thus increase the value, or only received against the order, creating a record for accruals and eventual payment. Users can be notified of expected receipts, reminding them of outstanding receipts and providing a quick link to receive a particular purchase order by running the workflow notification for the item type PO Confirm Receipt. This reminder can be sent to their e-mail if the Workflow Notification Mailer is turned on in EBS, or as a notification within EBS.

Users can also be notified in iProcurement if it is implemented, with a reminder appearing on their home pages when they sign in. These notifications are generated according to the Need-By date on the purchase order, reminding the requestor on a set schedule after the Need-By date is reached. Besides using the workflow PO Confirm Receipt notifications or iProcurement to receive transactions, receipts can also be performed from the purchasing menus.

EBS provides three main features for receiving: the receipt itself, returns for damaged or unneeded items, and the ability to perform corrections on receipts.

Receipts

When creating a receipt, EBS provides a large number of fields that can be used to find the expected receipt, the most obvious being the PURCHASE ORDER or REQUISITION number. Additional fields, such as ITEM or CATEGORY, and DATE RANGES for when the receipt is expected, are also available. Once the expected receipt is found, the actual receipt is performed in two steps: first by creating a header for the receipt, and then by providing individual line information. The report called Expected Receipts Report also allows purchasing and accounting to track outstanding receipts.

Creating Receipt Headers

Receipt Headers, shown in Figure 3-16, allow the user to create a new receipt or add to an existing receipt, as well as add generic information that will pertain to an entire receipt. EBS defaults the receipt to NEW RECEIPT, but this setting can be changed by clicking ADD TO RECEIPT and entering a RECEIPT number when prompted. This will not change the existing receipt but add additional lines to the transaction. The RECEIPT DATE will default in to the current date and time but can be updated to any date in an open purchase and for items received into inventory and inventory period. This traditionally represents the date the item is received in the organization, as opposed to the SHIPPED DATE, which is recorded in the next field.

Additional fields are available to add information for SHIPMENT, PACKING SLIP, WAYBILL/AIRBILL, and BILL OF LADING numbers. A FREIGHT CARRIER can only be entered for freight carriers that are set up in the system (Purchasing Superuser | Setup | Purchasing | Freight Carriers). CONTAINERS, representing the number of containers in the delivery, and COMMENTS can also be added. The SUPPLIER will default in based on the selection made on the Find window, and RECEIVED BY will default to the employee associated with the user signed into EBS but can be updated. Updating the receiver will not change the user associated with the transaction, tracked in the CREATED BY field in the database and displayed from the menu item, Help | Record History. With the exception of RECEIVED BY and RECEIPT DATE, none of this information is actually required to perform a receipt.

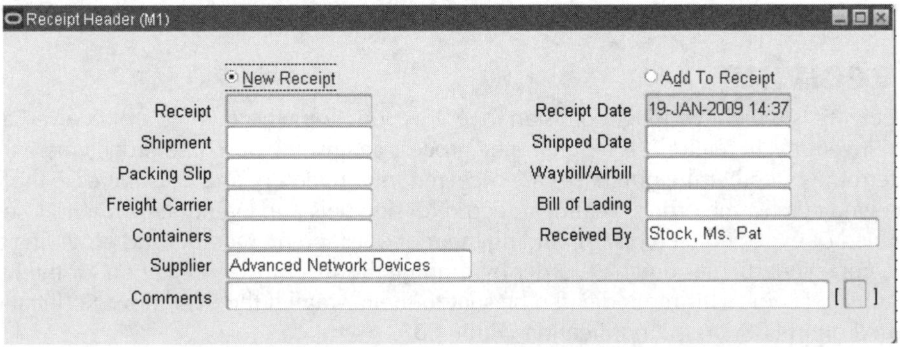

Purchasing Superuser | Receiving | Receipts

FIGURE 3-16 *Creating a Receipt Header*

Adding Receipt Lines

Lines are used to record the actual receipt for each line on an order. Much of the information will default in for the receiver, allowing him or her to make updates as required (see Figure 3-17). The QUANTITY will default in to the remaining amount due on the order, while actual amount on the order can be found on the Order Information tab. When ALLOW BLIND RECEIVING is checked on the receiving options for the organizations (Purchase Superuser | Setup | Organization | Receiving Options), then both of these fields will reflect zero, forcing the receiver to use the shipping paperwork to enter the quantities.

To receive a specific line, use the check box on the left of the window, and enter the QUANTITY received. Information about the receipt will default in from the purchase order, including delivery information such as DESTINATION TYPE and SUBINVENTORY. This information can be accepted as is or updated to the proper receiving data. The Details tab will have additional information that can be added for each line, including PACKING SLIP, SUPPLIER LOT to track items to a specific lot from the supplier, REASON CODE for the transaction, and COMMENTS.

The final check box, RECEIPT EXCEPTION, does a few things with this receipt when it is selected. First, the purchase order the receipt is associated with cannot be closed for receiving, and second, this receipt will appear on the Receipt Exception Report, allowing these receipts to be tracked. This feature allows items to be processed into the system, reflecting their status as received from the supplier, but also to be monitored to ensure that any exceptions, such as quantity, item, or damaged goods, are monitored and corrected.

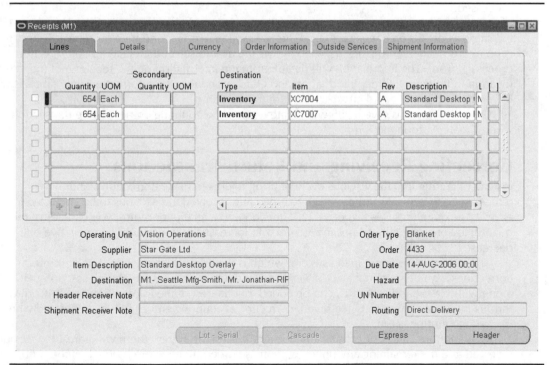

FIGURE 3-17 *Receiving lines*

Finally, any invoices matched to a receipt marked with an exception or purchase order line it was recorded against will go on hold, alerting accounting to a potential problem with the receipt. The payables person can remove this hold to process the invoice. All the other tabs on the Receipts form are informational about the line being received, available to help the receiver ensure he or she is processing the correct order.

When Blind Receiving is not turned on, users can create Express Receipts by selecting the EXPRESS button. This will prompt the receivers if they want to receive the product into its final destination, or into the receiving location, and it will select all lines for the remaining quantity on the order to receive. Saving receipts will process them in EBS.

Returns

Returns are processed almost exactly the same way as receipts are, using the Returns window instead (Purchasing Superuser | Receiving| Returns). Instead of finding expected receipts, the system will find all previously processed receipts that meet the search criteria. The QUANTITY to return will need to be entered, as well as where the product is being RETURNED TO. This is the field I tend to see the most mistakes made in. On Inventory items, the user needs to select SUPPLIER to remove the quantities from inventory, whereas selecting RECEIVING will move the items back to the receiving location, but the quantities will still remains in inventory for this location. An RMA (Return Material Authorization) NUMBER from the supplier can be entered for tracking purposes, and when the supplier is set up for Pay on Receipt (or ERS, Evaluated Receipt Settlement), checking CREATE DEBIT MEMO will automatically create the debit memo when the return is processed.

Unlike with receipts, additional information can be added on the other tabs. The DETAILS tab is the same as details on a receipt, except the TRANSACTION DATE is found here for returns, since there is no return header. The RETURN FROM tab allows the user to select the place the return is being processed from. The information will default from the information on the receipt, not the latest location in inventory. Order Information and Outside Services are information-only tabs. As with Receipts, saving the record creates the return transaction.

Once the return is saved, EBS will create reversing accounting entries for the transaction when Create Accounting is run.

Correcting Receiving and Return Transactions

Instead of getting into the viscious cycle of using returns to make corrections, and then rereceiving the items, EBS allows both returned and received transactions to be corrected for an error in the quantities (see Figure 3-18). After you find a receipt or return, you can adjust the quantity by entering either a positive QUANTITY to increase the transaction or a negative one to decrease it.

The current transaction in the system, which is the original transaction plus or minus any corrections, can be seen in the PARENT QUANTITY field. On the DETAILS tab, the TRANSACTION DATE, along with REASON and COMMENTS, can be added, but the rest of the information on the Corrections form is informational only. Once saved, correcting accounting entries will be generated when Create Accounting is run.

While Returns and Corrections function similarly in the system (both will adjust the amount received and the remaining amount on a purchase order), Returns are used when the product is physically returned to the supplier, while Corrections are usually performed to correct human errors.

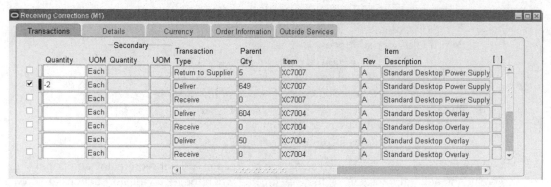

Purchasing Superuser | Receiving | Corrections

FIGURE 3-18 *Correcting receiving and returned transactions*

Purchasing Month End and Accruals

As with all subledgers in EBS, purchasing has month-end steps that need to be performed and transactions that need to be reconciled to the General Ledger journal entries. While the close steps can be performed in any department, the reconciliation steps are traditionally owned by the accounting department.

Understanding EBS's Accrual Process

Purchasing has two types of accruals available for transactions that have been received but not yet invoiced to record the organization's liability. Perpetual accruals are traditionally used with inventory items, where a liability is set up for transactions when they are received, and is relieved when the invoice is matched to the receipt or purchase order. These accruals are created as part of the receiving transaction and relieved with the invoice transaction. Alternatively, Reversing accruals, traditionally used for Expense items, can be created each month end as a journal entry that is reversed on the first of the subsequent month. EBS does allow expense accruals to also be created as perpetual accruals, but this option is rarely used and requires more reconciliations. Listed next are the associated accounting entries for both types of accruals.

Perpetual Accruals
    Receipt (Standard Costing)
        Dr Inventory @ Standard
            Cr Received Not Invoice Liability @ PO Price
        Dr/Cr Purchase Price Variance for difference between PO and Standard Price
    Receipt (Average Costing)
        Dr Inventory @ Actual Cost
            Cr Received Not Invoice Liability @ PO Price
        Dr/Cr Purchase Price Variance for difference between PO and Actual Cost
    Invoice
        Dr Received Not Invoiced Liability @ PO Prices
            Cr Payables Liability @ Invoice Amount
        Dr/Cr Invoice Price Variance for differences between PO and Invoice

Expense or Reversing Accruals
    Receipt
        No Transaction
    Period End Accrual Process
        Dr Expense for Received items on Purchase Orders
            Cr AP Accrual
            This entry is reversed on the first day of the next period
    Invoice
        Dr Expense for Invoiced Amount
            Cr Payables Liability

Perpetual accruals, also known as Accrue on Receipt, do not require any additional steps to create the accrual transactions; they are created when the receiving transactions are created throughout the month. The AP Accrual account balance will typically be made up of Uninvoiced Receipts and Overinvoiced Receipts, as well as any inevitable mistakes. Differences found in the accounts may be due to a pricing or a quantity discrepancy.

Perpetual Accruals are used when the accrual method is set to At Receipt for either Inventory or Expense Items in the Purchasing Options (Purchasing Superuser | Setup | Organization | Purchasing Option). The accrual account for the perpetual accrual is on the organization parameters for Inventory | Other Accounts (Purchasing Superuser | Setup | Organizations | Organizations for the inventory organization).

Loading Balances into the Accrual Tables

The Accrual Reconciliation Load Run program will select, analyze, and report on transactions associated with the Accrual Accounts defined on the Select Accrual Accounts form (Purchasing Superuser | Accrual Write Offs | Select Accrual Accounts). After the accounts are added to this window, the Accrual Reconciliation Load Run program can be run to load all receipts and invoices into the accrual table, as well as any written-off transactions. This program, typically run once a month after the processing for the month is complete, should not be run for each subsequent month without completing the reconciliation for the prior month, as it will cumulatively load additional transactions and can *not* be taken back to a prior point in time.

The date parameters are used to limit the time period the updates are made for, but since the table is not truncated, or deleted and reloaded, each month, any transaction without an update in the defined time period will *not* be updated and will have the same balance as the last load. The FROM date provided on the report is only to inform EBS how far back to consider for loading data; it usually is one or two days prior to the current month (when reconciling for June, then the FROM date would be May 30, 2008). This date should *always* predate the prior month end and the day it was closed. The data in the accrual tables will not be updated prior to the date entered in the FROM date. This reduces the amount of data considered to load the information, thus making the report run faster. The TO date should always be the last day of the month you are reconciling.

Additional Reconciliation Reports

The Summary Accrual Reconciliation Report summarizes balances of the accrual accounts. This report will always reflect the last data loaded in with the Accrual Reconciliation Load Run program. The AP and PO Accrual Reconciliation Report is a detailed report of all AP and PO matched transactions (receipts, write-offs, and invoices), including ones that matched and are no longer part of the balance. This report is always inclusive of the latest information in the system and *cannot* be backdated. The Miscellaneous Accrual Reconciliation Report has all Inventory and Payables transactions that were not associated with a purchase order that hits the accrual accounts. These are potentially issues during the accrual reconciliation process.

Writing Off Accrual Transactions

While EBS will take care of 99 percent of the perpetual accruals, there will be times when the balance needs to be written off. In R12, this process has been enhanced to now include a journal entry for all written-off transactions. The main reason transactions need to be written off is that the receipt quantity is different than the quantity matched to an invoice. The write-off form (Purchasing Superuse | Accounting | Accrual Write Offs | AP and PO) will display all transactions that make up the accrual balance—the same transactions that appear on the AP and PO Accrual Reconciliation Report. Using the Find window will narrow down the transactions you need to write off.

You can query up all the transactions and export them easily to Excel for analysis (File | Export. Ensure that your Internet Options on Internet Explorer are set to prompt downloads. Tools | Internet Options | Security Settings | Downloads | Automatic Prompting for file downloads should be enabled). Selecting the AUTO-SELECT RESULTS FOR WRITE-OFF box will check all the transactions found to be written off. Make sure you do not check this box and save after you navigate away from the Write Off window, without reviewing the selected transactions.

Transactions may need to be written off for many reasons. There could be a duplicate invoice, or two invoices relating to different purchase orders that were matched incorrectly. Problems such as this are probably better fixed in Payables than in the Write Off window. If the invoice is a duplicate, it needs to be removed. If the invoice should have been matched to another PO, then that PO is probably also appearing as an unmatched receipt. While writing off both the unmatched receipt and the invoice that was matched incorrectly will remove them from the report, the purchase order that was not matched will also need to be manually closed in Purchasing to prevent another invoice from being matched to it in error. Other problems, such as a correction to the receiving transaction that is also returned to the supplier, may also be an out-of-balance condition in the inventory that needs to be resolved. If a physical inventory or cycle count has happened since the transactions but prior to finding the problem, chances are it is already fixed in Inventory. This scenario would make a good candidate for write-offs.

As you can see, problems that exist in the accrual accounts can often be an indication of a larger problem, so monitoring this account and researching the differences on a timely basis is critical not just from an accrual balancing perspective, but also from a system perspective. To write off a transaction, select the check box next to the transaction(s) and save. This will open up the Write Off Transactions window, allowing a DATE, REASON, and COMMENT to be added. Also, the total of all the lines checked is seen in the WRITE OFF BALANCE box. These written-off transactions will create journal entries against the Accrual account and the Invoice Price Variance account associated with the purchase order. This entry may actually be an offset for an invoice price variance that was recorded earlier.

Period End Accruals

When accruals are recorded at the end of a period, usually for expense receipts that have been received and not yet invoiced, the Receipt Accrual–Period End request is run to prepare the transactions for the Create Accounting Process to pick up and create the journal entries. If needed, this process can be run multiple times during the month, as it is cumulative for each period and does not reaccrue the same receipt for the same period more than one time. This process looks at expense receipts that are not yet matched to invoices, and accrues the amount received by debiting the purchase order distribution account and crediting the AP Expense Accrual account, set up in the Purchasing Options (Setup | Options | Purchasing Options). A reversing entry for the accrual is created when the next month is opened in Purchasing. This accrual should always agree with the Uninvoice Receipts Report for the same time period.

Controlling Periods

Purchasing periods, as in other modules, are opened and closed each month. Periods should be closed after all the receipts are entered for the period, and are accounted and sent to the General Ledger with the Create Accounting process. Opening and closing periods are done in the Control Purchasing Periods form (Purchasing Superuser | Setup | Financials | Accounting | Control Purchasing Periods). From here, periods can be opened, closed, or permanently closed.

   To open a period in Purchasing to allow transactions, the corresponding General Ledger and Payables periods must be either opened or set to future-entry. Once the period is closed, then no additional receipts are allowed in the period. Purchasing does allow a period to be reopened if required. Permanently closing a period, though, does not allow the period to be reopened to correct receipts or other potential problems. In general, controlling access to the period windows is a better way of controlling the periods than permanently closing a period, allowing flexibility for potential problems. Purchasing also has access to open and close payables periods (Purchasing Superuser | Setup| Financials| Accounting | Open and Close Periods), and this screen should not be confused with the Control Purchasing Periods screen.

CHAPTER
4

Suppliers

12 made a significant change in the supplier model, adding it to the Trading Community Architecture (TCA), where Customers already existed. This results not only in new windows for tracking supplier information, but also in a new set of underlying tables to store all the supplier information and added functionality. Since customers and suppliers now share the same TCA structures, parties created for one can be utilized by the other, allowing payables and receivables for the same party to be recognized with EBS's new E-Business Tax module.

If you are upgrading to R12 from an earlier version of EBS and have customizations such as reports or interfaces that refer to supplier information, ensure you review these customizations to see what updates are needed to the coding. Please note that many of the features added to the supplier record require additional setups for use. Refer to Chapter 2 on Purchasing setups and Chapter 5 for Payables setups for additional implementation steps.

Technical Update

There are two major changes in the table structures for suppliers that will affect custom reports, imported data, and troubleshooting.

First, suppliers created from employee records (both in the shared Human Resource [HR] model and fully installed environments) no longer have the employee data duplicated in the new supplier tables; instead, R12 maintains the data in the HR tables for security purposes. This is for suppliers that are set up with the Supplier Type of Employee, where the employee record is linked to the supplier.

Second, in the Payables schema, there are three new tables for suppliers: AP_SUPPLIERS, AP_SUPPLIER_SITES_ALL, and AP_SUPPLIER_CONTACTS. Their main purpose is to store supplier-specific information. The core supplier information exists in the HZ schema in the following tables: HZ_PARTIES, HZ_PARTY_USG_ASSIGNMENTS, and HZ_ORGANIZATIONS_PROFILES. The AP tables and HZ tables are linked using the POS_SUPPLIER_MAPPINGS table. The final table, IBY_EXTERNAL_PAYEES_ALL, tracks specific payment information for each supplier. The old tables for suppliers still exist as views, which reference the new tables listed here, but caution should be used in relying on these views. When customers were moved to the TCA format, the views for the old customer tables were left in place, and over time it was found that they were not accurate, causing incorrect reporting.

Additional information on these tables can be found on MetaLink in the Electronic Technical Reference Manuals (e-TRM).

Creating Suppliers

Supplier setups, used by Payables, Purchasing, Assets, Property Manager, and iSupplier Portal, determine how the suppliers and their addresses can be used, as well as storing specific processing information. The supplier setup is broken down into multiple windows, which group the setup information by what data or processes it controls. The Suppliers window, shown in Figure 4-1, can be accessed from Payables under Supplier | Entry, and in Purchasing from Supply Base | Suppliers. Navigation from either responsibility takes you to the same window. Once you enter the form, either search for an existing supplier or click CREATE SUPPLIER to enter a new supplier that does not yet exist.

When you create a supplier, some base information is added. This includes adding the supplier name in the ORGANIZATION NAME field and identifying the supplier as a TYPE of Standard Supplier or a Supplier Used to Process Expense Reports to Internal Employees, which requires

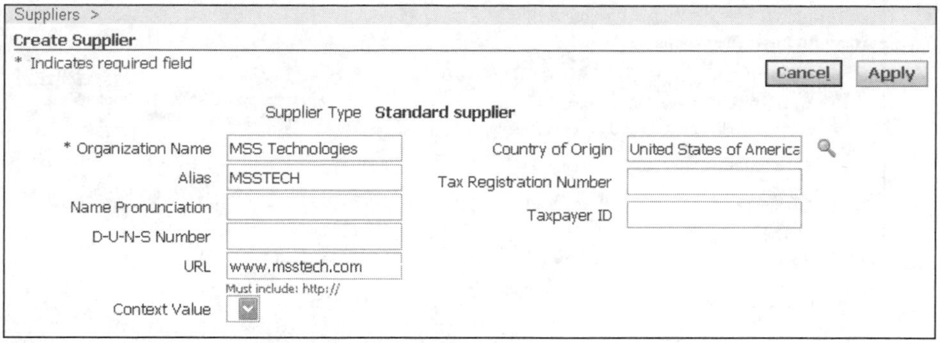

Payables Manager | Suppliers | Entry | Create Supplier

FIGURE 4-1 *Creating a new supplier*

that the supplier be linked to an employee set up in Oracle Human Resources. Once the base information has been entered for a new supplier, you are taken to the Quick Update, where you can add or modify information, just as for any existing supplier.

Quick Update

The Quick Update window, seen in Figure 4-2, enables you to update basic supplier information, such as names for active suppliers, and to assign sites with some of the key purchasing and payables information. SUPPLIER NAME is the legal name of the entity being paid and will be populated from the ORGANIZATION NAME entered on the prior window. This field is a unique field for data entry, but nonunique suppliers can be imported via an interface or upgraded from a previous version. Since not allowing duplicate supplier names to be created in EBS is a key system control to prevent duplicate payments, taking the time to create a naming convention for suppliers is critical. Naming conventions should cover such aspects as case, abbreviations, and format.

SUPPLIER NUMBER, a unique number, was assigned when the supplier was created, either by the system, or manually, depending on the Payables System setups (Payables Manager | Setup | Options | Payables System Setups). An ALTERNATE SUPPLIER NAME can be added to phonetically spell out the pronunciation of the supplier. REGISTRY ID is the Party Number assigned as part of the TCA module; this number is manually assigned (and appears on the create supplier form) when the system profile HZ: Generate Party Number is set to NO (System Administrator | Profile | System). When this option is set to YES, the party number is automatically generated by the system, and the field is not visible when creating a supplier. An INACTIVE DATE can be added to reflect the day this supplier is no longer available for transactions. An ALIAS can be added if the supplier is known by more than one name or uses a common abbreviation.

On the right side of the page, supplier holds can be added to this supplier. PURCHASE ORDER HOLDS will place a hold on all new orders entered in the system. Once this is selected, a field to add a reason for the hold will become available, and this field is not linked to a list of values but can be any reason a user enters. All future purchase orders will advise the creator that this supplier is on purchasing hold, and not allow the document to be approved. PAYMENT HOLDS are added for All Invoice, Unmatched Invoices, or Unvalidated Invoices, preventing these invoices from being paid until the hold is released on the invoice, by either removing a specific invoice hold manually or by removing the hold on the supplier and revalidating the invoices.

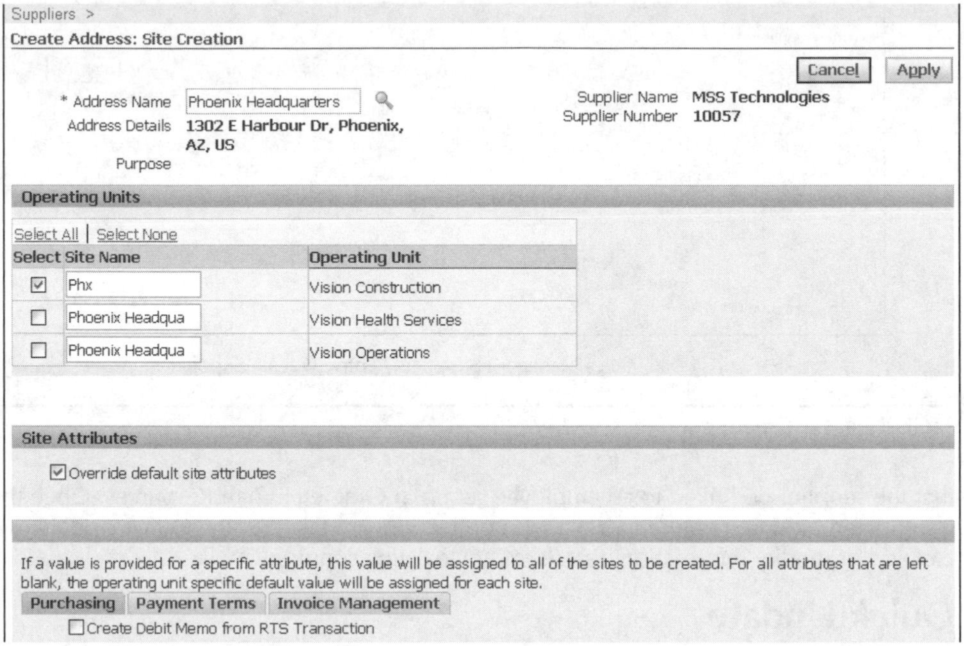

FIGURE 4-2 *Quick Update, creating a new site*

From here, you can modify Key Purchasing and Key Payment setups for supplier sites already assigned to an operating unit, or you can create a new site from an existing address by clicking CREATE. Note in Figure 4-2 that the address must already exist for this supplier. EBS has Addresses and Sites broken out into two separate features in R12, allowing one address to be associated with multiple operating units. The advantage to this feature is that updates to the addresses affect all operating units, reducing the duplicate updates that were required in previous versions. Defaults from the Key Purchasing and Key Payables setups will be applied to this address unless OVERRIDE DETAIL SITE ATTRIBUTES is selected, allowing the attributes to be updated for this address.

Key Purchasing Setups

Key Purchasing setups, shown in Figure 4-3, will default operating unit–specific information when creating requisitions or purchase orders for this supplier site. The SHIP-TO LOCATION is the default shipping location and can be left blank if it is used for multiple locations, requiring the user to select the proper location. The BILL-TO LOCATION, when populated, will default in on the documents as well. Both of these fields default in on the supplier setups from the Purchasing tab of the Financial Options if they are populated. SHIP VIA is the default shipment method for this supplier.

The PAY ON field should be populated with PAY ON RECEIPT to use the evaluated receipt settlement (ERS) feature of EBS, or left null to invoice traditionally. ERS is used to self-invoice for products purchased with a purchase order and then received in EBS, where the invoice in Payables is then automatically created based on the purchase order price and the quantities received. The options to PAY ON USE or USE ON RECEIPT are not yet valid in the purchasing application for ERS transactions. ALTERNATE PAY SITE is used as the bill-to site when ERS is used, and can be any active pay site for the supplier. INVOICE SUMMARY LEVEL, again, used with ERS, determines if the self-invoices are grouped and created based on the Receipt, Pay Site, or Packing Slip. CREATE DEBIT MEMO FROM RTS TRANSACTION, when checked, will generate a debit memo in Payables for return to supplier (RTS) transactions that were matched to a receipt. The distributions on this will be prorated across all the distributions associated with the original receipt.

Check GAPLESS INVOICE NUMBERING, also used by ERS, to assign sequential invoice numbers or debit memo numbers to all sites for this supplier who have the same SELLING COMPANY IDENTIFIER. The identifier creates a unique invoice sequence for all the pay sites within a specific supplier, ensuring there are no gaps in the invoices generated for the supplier across all sites. This number must be unique across suppliers but can be repeated within the same supplier for different sites. Purchasing Terms can have defaults set, for such things as FOB, FREIGHT TERMS, TRANSPORTATION ARRANGED, and COUNTRY OF ORIGIN.

Key Payment Setups

Payment setups, shown in Figure 4-4, control both invoices and payments against the invoices. An INVOICE AMOUNT LIMIT can be added for each SITE and OPERATING UNIT, placing any invoice entered over the limit on hold to allow review prior to payment. The INVOICE TOLERANCE enforces the quantities ordered, quantities received, and price tolerances when matching invoices to a purchase order that is goods based and has a quantity ordered. A SERVICES TOLERANCE can be added for purchase orders that were set up as services, where the price is based on the amount of the order as opposed to the quantity ordered (see Chapter 2). If this is not completed, then the tolerances will default from the Matching tab on the Payables options.

The INVOICE MATCH OPTION will determine how this supplier site will match to purchase order lines or receipt lines. When RECEIPT is selected, it cannot be matched until the receipt is actually made, which may delay entering the invoice into the system. The other option, PURCHASE ORDER, can be matched at any point after the purchase order has been approved, and will apply any holds as needed, such as a Receiving Hold when the receipt is not completed. Invoices can be

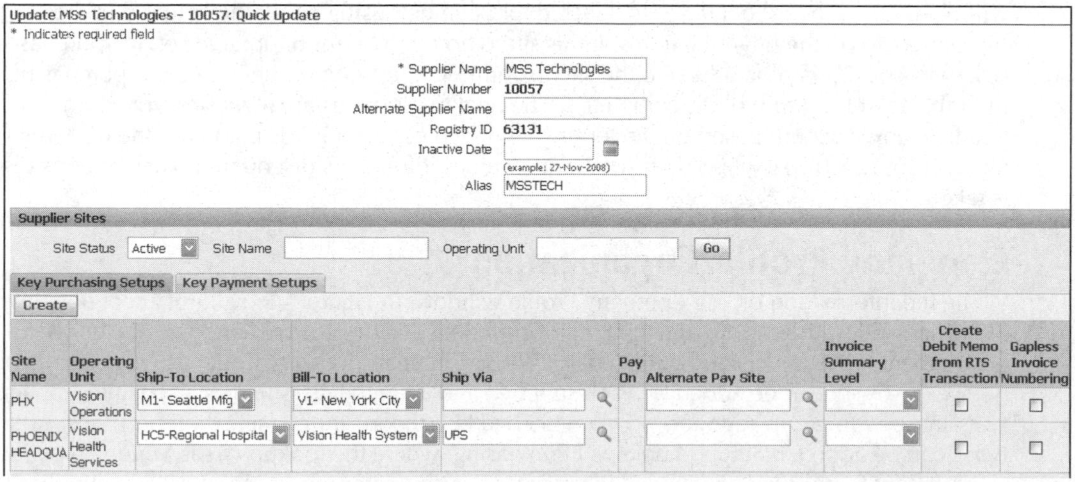

FIGURE 4-3 *Quick Update, Site Key Purchasing setups*

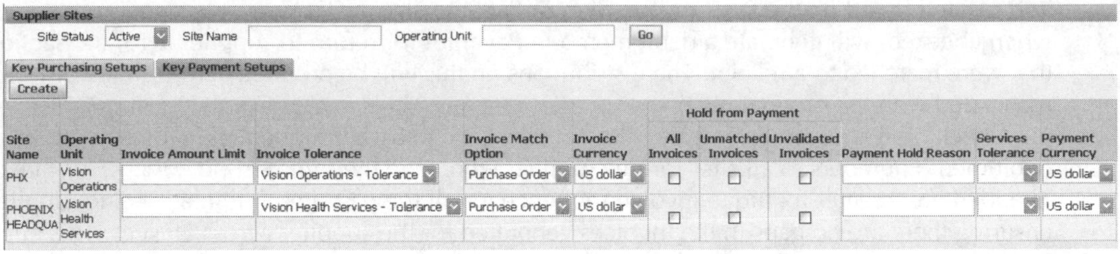

Supplier Sites													
Site Status Active ▾ Site Name [ ] Operating Unit [ ] [Go]													

Key Purchasing Setups   **Key Payment Setups**

[Create]

							Hold from Payment					
Site Name	Operating Unit	Invoice Amount Limit	Invoice Tolerance	Invoice Match Option	Invoice Currency	All Invoices	Unmatched Invoices	Unvalidated Invoices	Payment Hold Reason	Services Tolerance	Payment Currency	
PHX	Vision Operations	[ ]	Vision Operations - Tolerance ▾	Purchase Order ▾	US dollar ▾	☐	☐	☐	[ ] ▾		US dollar ▾	
PHOENIX HEADQUA	Vision Health Services	[ ]	Vision Health Services - Tolerance ▾	Purchase Order ▾	US dollar ▾	☐	☐	☐	[ ] ▾		US dollar ▾	

FIGURE 4-4   *Quick Update, Site Key Payment setups*

HELD FROM PAYMENT for a specific pay site as well as for the entire supplier, for all invoices, unmatched invoices, and unvalidated invoices. If one of these is checked, then you can enter a PAYMENT HOLD REASON—again, this is a free-form field and not linked to a list of values. The PAYMENT CURRENCY will default to the INVOICE CURRENCY but can be updated to allow invoices to be recorded in one currency and paid in a different one. The PAYMENT PRIORITY and PAY GROUP are assigned to supplier sites to group invoices into different payment processing requests for payment.

When creating an electronic payment, setting the DEDUCT BANK CHARGE FROM PAYMENT option will determine if the bank charges associated with that payment are paid by you (NO), by the supplier at a negotiated rate, or by the supplier at the standard bank rate, as defined in the Setup | Payment | Bank Charge Calculation window.

You can add default TERMS for each site, as well as the TERMS DATE BASIS. There are four dates in EBS that can be used to default the terms: Goods Received, Invoice, Invoice Received, or System. With the exception of System, the date used as the basis for the payment terms must be populated in order for the terms date to populate. While INVOICE DATE is a required field when entering an invoice, both the GOODS RECEIVED and INVOICE RECEIVED DATES are not.

The default for TERMS DATE BASIS will come from the Payables System Setup default (Payables Manager | Setup | Options | Payables System Setup) and can be updated if needed. PAY DATE BASIS will determine when the invoice is selected for payment, using either the actual due date or the discount date on the payment terms. If this site is going to be used for large service purchases, a RETAINAGE RATE (%) can be added to the site to withhold a portion of the invoice or purchasing line until the agreed-upon work is completed. The final two options are ALWAYS TAKE DISCOUNT, which will take any discount based on the terms of the invoice, even if it is paid after the discount date, and EXCLUDE FREIGHT FROM DISCOUNT, which determines if freight is discounted when a terms discount is taken.

Company Profile/Organization

While the information on the Company Profile window, in Figure 4-5, will not affect how invoices are processed, it does allow the tracking of supplier-specific information that may be useful in government reporting or for internal analysis. A SIC (Standard Industry Code) as well as a NATIONAL INSURANCE NUMBER can be added for each supplier, and it can be classified as a specific supplier TYPE. TYPES are used to group suppliers on many seeded EBS reports for classification purposes. Additional types can be added in Setup | Lookups | Purchasing, where the lookup TYPE is Vendor Type.

A Parent Supplier can be added to any supplier (the parent must also exist as a supplier in EBS), to create a hierarchy in EBS, but this relationship is not used for any processing functionality. If the supplier provides a CUSTOMER NUMBER that relates to your organization in its system, it can be

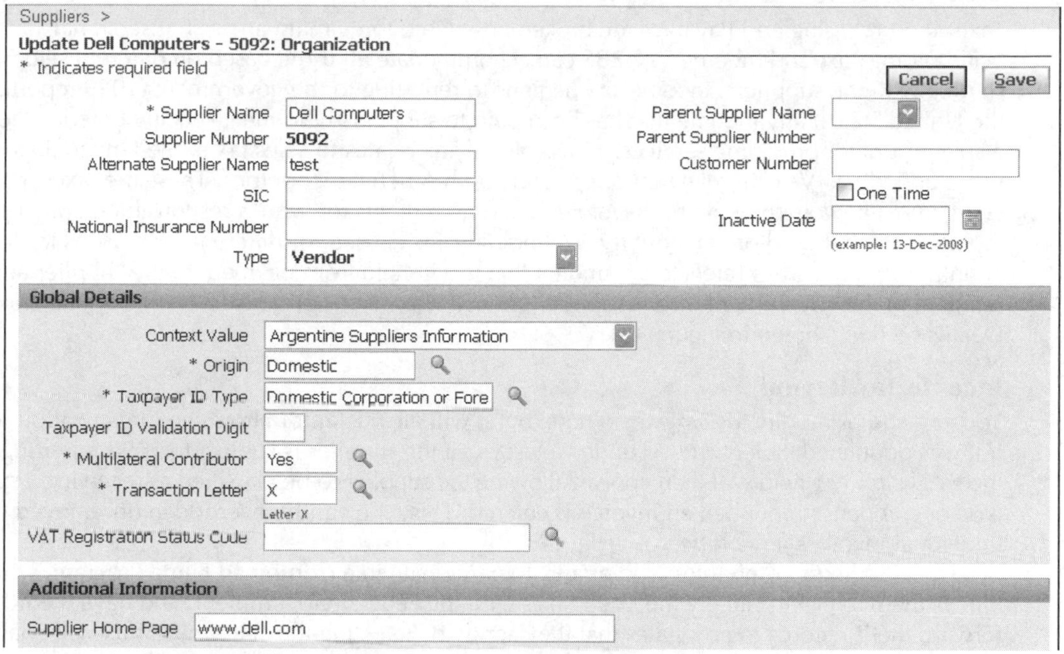

FIGURE 4-5 *Organization information about a company profile*

referenced on this window and used on purchasing documents. Selecting ONE TIME supplier will show this was a supplier that is only going to be used one time; this field is informational only and does not prevent repeat transactions with the supplier.

Global Details can be added if you have any localizations installed where additional supplier information is allowed. Select the specific country from the CONTEXT VALUE list of values to show that country's specific fields.

The URL for the supplier's web site can be added under SUPPLIER HOME PAGE, under Additional Information.

In the Organization section, information such as D.U.N.S. (Data Universal Numbering System, assigned to track businesses in Dun and Bradstreet), YEAR ESTABLISHED and INCORPORATED, MISSION STATEMENTS, and CEO name and title can be added. To track the size of the organizations you do business with, the Total Employees section has fields for both the ORGANIZATION and CORPORATE TOTAL employees.

Tax and Financial Information tracks the specific financial information about an organization, such as ANNUAL or POTENTIAL REVENUE, as well as a CURRENCY PREFERENCE. The TAXPAYER ID number is required for all suppliers who by law must receive a 1099 at the end of the year (for the United States). This is usually a Social Security number for an individual or a Tax Identification Number for a small business. Since this field is required to tag an invoice as 1099-able, entering 000000000 as a placeholder while the proper paperwork is received will cause EBS to mark all invoices as 1099s, while showing a blank taxpayer ID on the reports to indicate that the number is still missing. TAX REGISTRATION NUM is where the VAT registration number is stored for suppliers subject to value-added tax.

Tax Details

Taxes in Purchasing and Payables are broken down into three main areas: Transactional Tax, Withholding Tax, and Income Tax. EBS can accommodate all three based on different setups, starting with the suppliers. Income Tax pertains to reporting to the government (1099 reporting in the United States) any income that has been paid to suppliers who meet specific criteria, such as a sole proprietor providing services. Transactional Tax relates to sales tax in the United States, and value-added tax (VAT) in many European and South American countries. These are taxes that are charged by the government and have different requirements for who is responsible in paying and reporting them, based on the country. Withholding Tax is used for different tax reasons in many countries, but it always refers to an amount that is withheld from payment to the supplier and remitted to the government on the supplier's behalf. Tax setups are create in the Supplier Tax Details section, shown in Figure 4-6.

Income Tax Region

You can add or modify the TAXPAYER ID here, but it will also default in from the Organization region if it was populated. Select FEDERAL under REPORTABLE if the supplier is subject to 1099 reporting, and the INCOME TAX TYPE field will then appear, allowing the supplier to be classified as receiving a specific type of compensation when an invoice is entered. This type can be overridden or removed from individual invoices if need be.

The IRS allows companies who qualify to participate in a Combined Filing Program, which allows them to electronically file 1099 taxes with the Federal Government, and have the IRS forward the B records to any states that they apply to. Selecting the STATE check box will enable this reporting feature. Before using this feature, you must apply to the IRS and be approved.

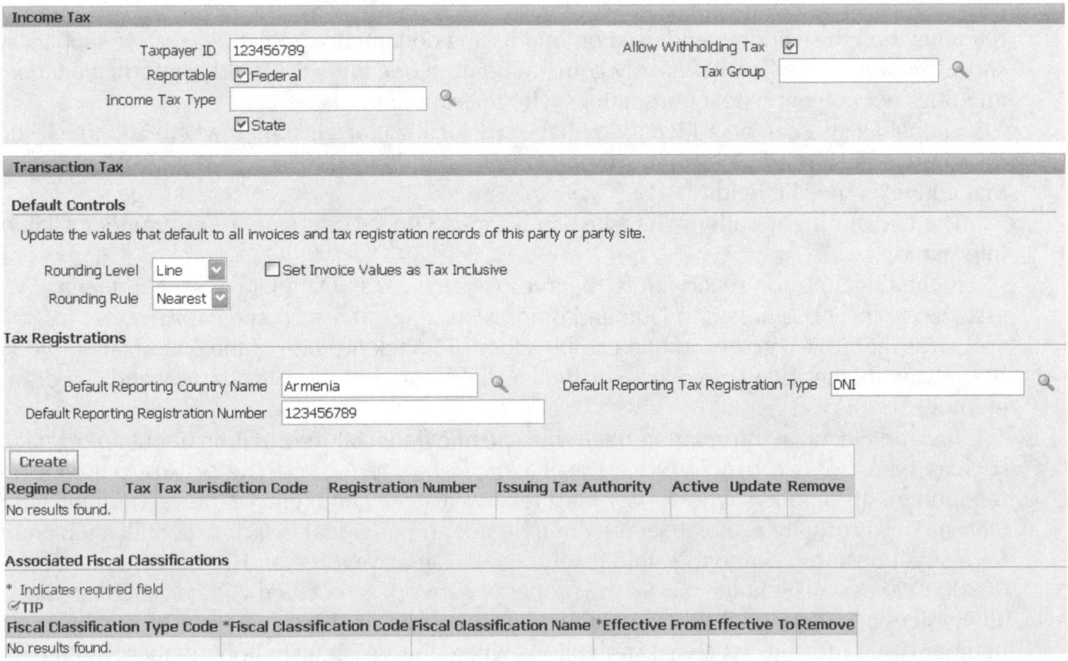

Income Tax

Taxpayer ID	123456789	Allow Withholding Tax	☑
Reportable	☑ Federal	Tax Group	🔍
Income Tax Type	🔍		
	☑ State		

Transaction Tax

Default Controls

Update the values that default to all invoices and tax registration records of this party or party site.

Rounding Level Line ▾   ☐ Set Invoice Values as Tax Inclusive
Rounding Rule Nearest ▾

Tax Registrations

Default Reporting Country Name Armenia 🔍   Default Reporting Tax Registration Type DNI 🔍
Default Reporting Registration Number 123456789

[Create]

Regime Code	Tax	Tax Jurisdiction Code	Registration Number	Issuing Tax Authority	Active	Update	Remove
No results found.							

Associated Fiscal Classifications

* Indicates required field
✓ TIP

Fiscal Classification Type Code	*Fiscal Classification Code	Fiscal Classification Name	*Effective From	Effective To	Remove
No results found.					

FIGURE 4-6 *Supplier Tax Details*

ALLOW WITHHOLDING TAX allows EBS to withhold a specific percentage from payment to the supplier and submit it to the government. This feature is usually used in countries where a percent of every transaction is required to be paid to the government and in the United States when an organization is withholding Sales Tax that was not charged by the supplier, and is remitting it on the supplier's behalf. It is also used to withhold taxes from a supplier who has not submitted proper W9 information. Once this option is checked, the TAX GROUP field becomes available, and the withholding group can be added. This group identifies the percent of tax withheld and the reason for withholding.

Transaction Tax

Under the Transaction Tax section, default controls can be set for the rounding of taxes. The ROUNDING LEVEL can be set to either LINE or HEADING, and the RULE options are NEAREST, or UP or DOWN, and determines rounding on tax calculations. Selecting SET INVOICE VALUES AS TAX INCLUSIVE is the tax percent based on the total tax paid as a percent of the total cost of the item, including taxes and freight, as opposed to the tax paid as a percent of the base cost of an item. For example, the Tax Inclusive rate for a $100 item with a $30 tax is about 23 percent, or the tax / the total cost (30/130), whereas the Tax Exclusive rate is 30 percent, the amount the item cost without taxes times the rate (100 * 30%). As you can see from the example, this will have an impact on the tax rates that are entered into the system.

Tax Registrations are entered to determine the country where the tax is reported, as well as a DEFAULT REPORTING REGISTRATION NUMBER and a DEFAULT REPORTING TAX REGISTRATION TYPE, such as value-added tax (VAT) or distributed net income (DNI).

Tax Regimes, or sets of tax rules for any given country or supplier, are added by clicking the CREATE button above the Regime Code region of the Tax form. Regimes, which are created and maintained in Oracle's E-Business Tax module, can also be assigned to a supplier in the Tax Manager responsibility (Parties | Party Tax Profile), where the PARTY TYPE is THIRD PARTY, as shown in Figure 4-7. Select a TAX REGIME CODE to identify the type of tax being charged or withheld. TAX is then added—only the taxes that are assigned to the TAX REGIME CODE previously selected will be available from the list. Taxes determine such things as the type of tax (such as Deferred or Exempt), the geographic regions, and the actual reporting code for the tax. Adding a TAX JURISDICTION CODE identifies a specific geographical area where the tax is effective, usually relating to a specific country or region of that country.

Sometimes companies do business (DBA) under one name but are registered with the government under a different name for tax reporting. The COMPANY REPORTING NAME stores the name by which the company is registered with the government and that will appear on tax reports. The TAX REGISTRATION TYPE field is used to identify the actual type of tax being recorded, and the government-issued number the supplier is assigned for tax reporting from the government is recorded under TAX REGISTRATION NUMBER. The TAX REGISTRATION STATUS, such as REGISTERED or AGENT, can also be assigned.

Once tax-related information is added to the supplier, it becomes the default for setting up tax information on each individual site. Each site's tax information is created under the Supplier Site section of this form. Site setups, which are country specific, will ultimately be the driver to tax transactions created for the supplier.

Select the address of the legal entity responsible for reporting the tax from the LEGAL REGISTRATION ADDRESS (this is your company's address, not the supplier's address), and add the ISSUING TAX AUTHORITY. Under the Invoice Controls region, you can set ROUNDING RULES again, as well as identify if the invoices are entered as TAX INCLUSIVE and if this is a SELF ASSESSMENT.

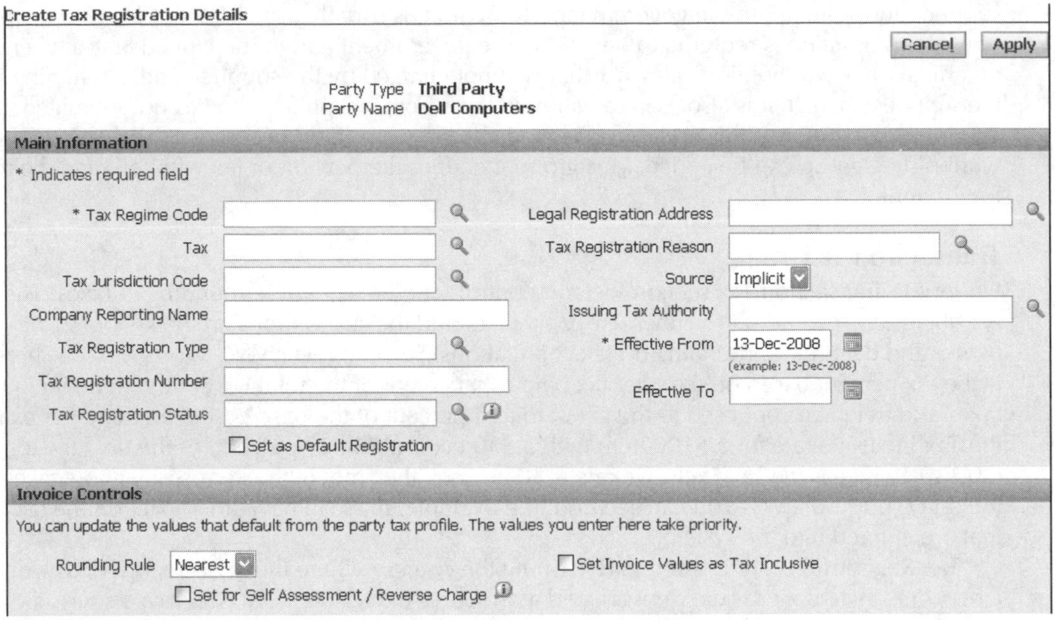

FIGURE 4-7 *Creating Tax Regimes*

Back on the main Tax Details window, Fiscal Classifications can also be added to the supplier, which are used when different transactions are taxed at a different rate or with a different tax code. Each Site also is marked as having withholding tax and a tax group, and can be assigned a Regime and Fiscal Classification. Tax capturing and reporting, in and of itself, is a complicated process, and so are the setups. This is only the portion of the Oracle E-Business Tax setups required to use tax. There are additional setups required in the Tax Manager responsibility.

Address Book

In R12, Addresses and Sites are separate for suppliers. Addresses, seen in Figure 4-8, are where a physical or mailing location resides, while Sites store payables- and purchasing-specific information about the supplier. More importantly, addresses, like suppliers always were, are shared across all legal entities and operating units, while the sites associated with them are operating unit specific.

Creating Addresses

The typical address information is entered by clicking the CREATE button for any physical or mailing location a supplier might have. While only the ADDRESS LINE 1 and COUNTRY are marked as required, State, County, City, and Postal Code may be required if they are set up to be validated in the Trading Community Architecture module (Trading Community Manager | Trading Community | Administration | Geography Hierarchy | Manage Validations). ADDRESS NAME will become the actual name in the system, and will default in as the site name as well, where it can be overridden. Table 4-1 shows additional fields that can be added to an address when you click the UPDATE button.

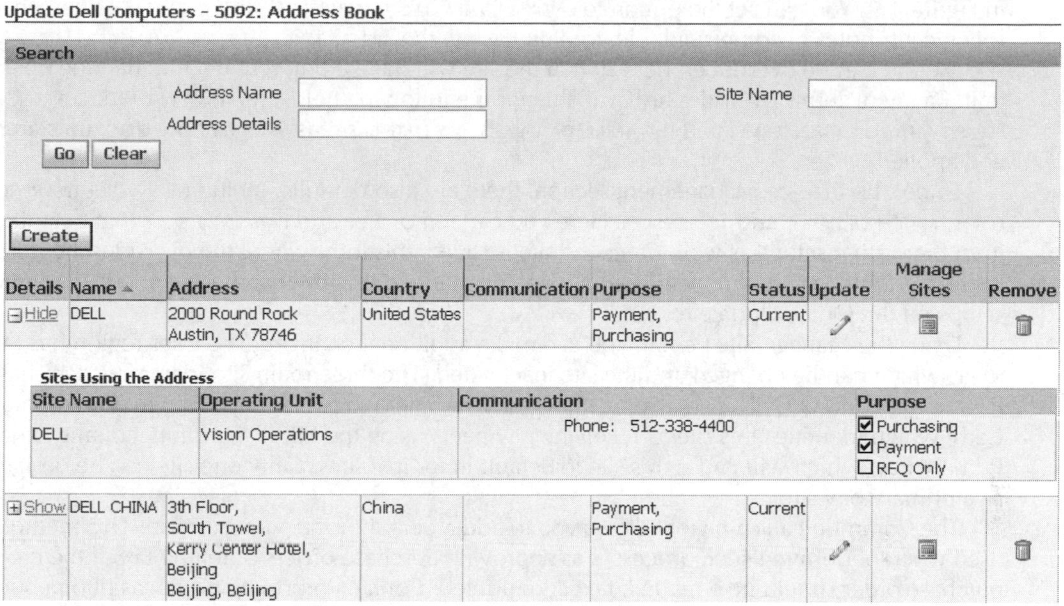

Update Dell Computers – 5092: Address Book

Search

Address Name   Site Name

Address Details

[Go] [Clear]

[Create]

Details	Name ▲	Address	Country	Communication	Purpose	Status	Update	Manage Sites	Remove
⊟ Hide	DELL	2000 Round Rock Austin, TX 78746	United States		Payment, Purchasing	Current	🖉	🖾	🗑

    Sites Using the Address

Site Name	Operating Unit	Communication	Purpose
DELL	Vision Operations	Phone: 512-338-4400	☑ Purchasing ☑ Payment ☐ RFQ Only

Details	Name ▲	Address	Country	Communication	Purpose	Status	Update	Manage Sites	Remove
⊞ Show	DELL CHINA	3th Floor, South Towel, Kerry Center Hotel, Beijing Beijing, Beijing	China		Payment, Purchasing	Current	🖉	🖾	🗑

FIGURE 4-8   *Supplier addresses*

Field Name	Usage
Addressee	Alternative address name, usually when the address location belongs to another entity (for example, the payments are being sent to a third-party collection agency; the agency would be the addressee).
Geography Code Override	Allows override to tax jurisdiction when integrating Vertex for tax calculations.
Language	Determines what language (if multiple languages are installed in EBS) all notifications, including purchasing documents, are sent to the supplier in.
Update to all new sites created for this address	Makes this address the default for communication details and purpose.
Email Address	E-mail used for this address for notifications and documents sent to the supplier electronically.
Address Purpose	Identifies this address as being used for Purchasing documents, Payments, or only for Request for Quotes (RFQ).

TABLE 4-1   *Additional Address Fields*

Once you've applied the address, you must assign it to one or more operating units, as seen in Figure 4-9. You can set the option to OVERRIDE DEFAULT SITE ATTRIBUTES here as well. When checked, specific attributes become available; for Purchasing, the ABILITY TO CREATE DEBIT MEMO FROM RTS TRANSACTION can be overridden here so that the site will have a different default than the operating unit. Payment Terms overrides are available for the following fields: PAYMENT METHOD, CURRENCY, PRIORITY, PAY GROUPS, TERMS, and the TERMS DATE BASIS, PAY DATE BASIS, as well as how discounts are taken and applied.

Under the Invoice Management section, there are also defaults, including INVOICE CURRENCY, LIMITS, MATCH OPTIONS, and TOLERANCES. Here you can remove or add PAYMENT HOLDS that defaulted from the system setups as well. Once the site is saved, this form where the overrides are made is not available, and any updates will need to be made in the Key Purchasing and Key Payment setups on the Quick Update region.

Using the Manage Site pencil, you can make additional changes. The Uses region has the SITE NAME, which can be changed and the site inactivated. The three main site identifiers, Purchasing, Payment, and RFQ Only, can also be changed here, and two more are available: Procurement Card, which identifies this site as receiving payments using the EBS P-Card functionality, and Primary Pay, which will cause this site to default in for invoices. Only one site can be designated as a primary pay site.

The Communication region allows you to add a default NOTIFICATION METHOD. This method is used when performing such processes as approving purchase orders or telling EBS if the created purchase order should be e-mailed, faxed, or printed. Contact information such as phone numbers and the e-mail address used for communication is also stored here.

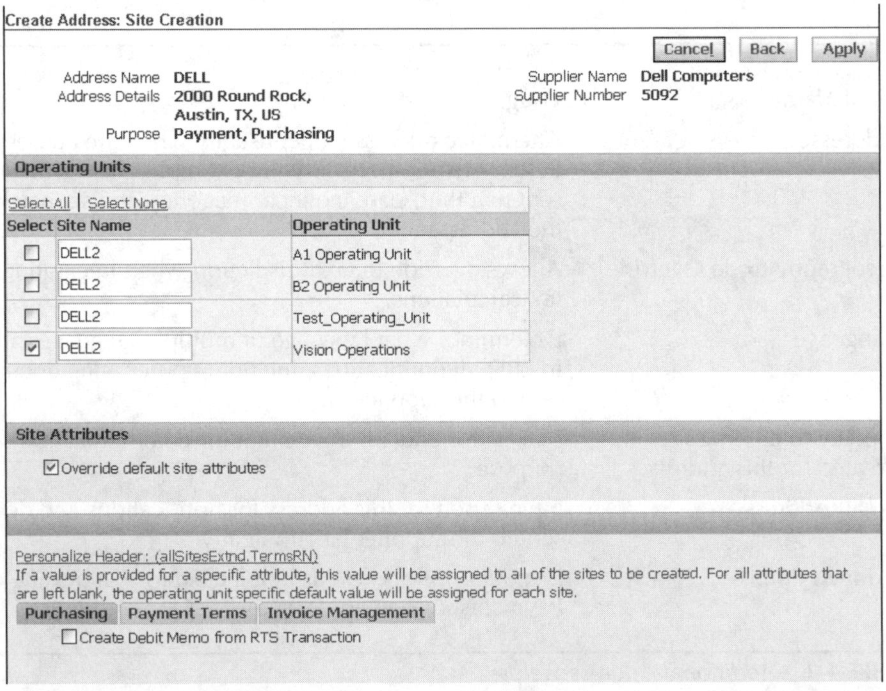

FIGURE 4-9 *Adding operating units and overrides to supplier sites*

The Identification region allows your CUSTOMER NUMBER with the supplier to be stored and used on documents, as well as the EDI LOCATION used for Electronic Data Interchange payments and transactions. (The EDI location code is a unique code assigned by the Uniform Commercial Code [UCC] to any given location of a legal entity.) An ALTERNATE SITE NAME can be added for organizations that have the need to store names in more than one character set, such as Kanji.

The ALTERNATIVE NAME field is not available for sorting unless the Payables option Sort By Alternate Fields is turned on. Adding a SHIPPING NETWORK LOCATION from the list of locations will make an address (Purchasing Manager | Setup | Organization | Location) that is not related to this supplier available on the SHIP-TO LOCATION field when entering a purchase order. This allows products to be shipped to an address other than one belonging to the supplier. This is often used when creating a purchase order for items that have multiple outside processes being completed by different vendors.

Contact Directory

Contacts can be added for each supplier in the Contact Directory, shown in Figure 4-10, storing such information as title, phone numbers, and specific addresses for the contact. For an address to be added to a contact, it must first be created in the Address Book. When using iSupplier, contacts can be granted access to iSupplier by selecting CREATE USER ACCOUNT FOR THIS CONTACT.

Business Classification

Many organizations, either for internal tracking purposes or for government regulations, need to track suppliers under different classifications. EBS tracks the classifications shown in Table 4-2.

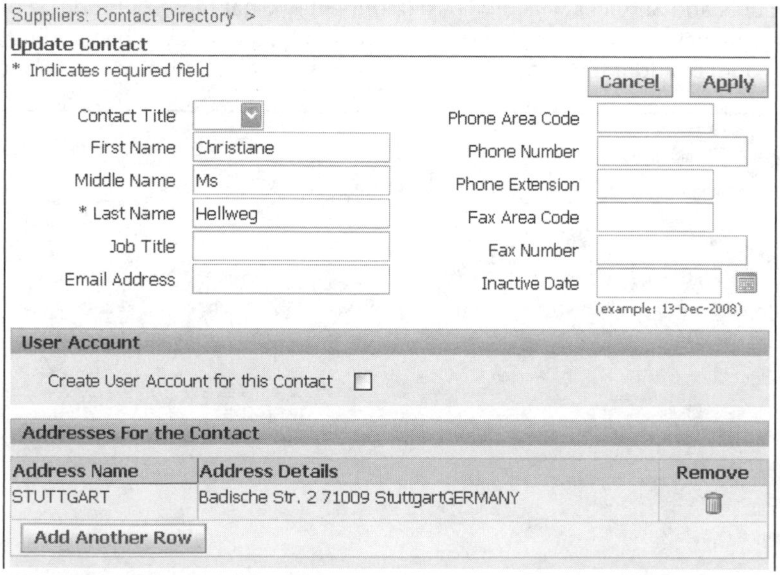

FIGURE 4-10   *Supplier contacts*

Classification	Description
Hub Zone	Identifies a business that has been classified by the Small Business Administration as a small business in a distressed area, or Historically Underutilized Business Zone, giving it more access to Federal contracting opportunities.
Minority Owned	Classifies a business as being owed by a person who is classified as a minority, such as American Indian.
Service-Disabled Veteran Owned	Classifies a business as being owed by a veteran who was disabled during military service.
Small Business	Business are classified as small when they are under certain limits in revenues or number of employees, as classified by the Small Business Act. These size requirements vary by industry.
Veteran Owned	Classifies a business as being owed by a military veteran.
Women Owned	Identifies this supplier as being owned as a woman.

TABLE 4-2 *Business Classifications*

Each classification is selected by checking the APPLICABLE box, and providing CERTIFICATION NUMBERS and the CERTIFYING AGENCY, as shown in Figure 4-11. A STATUS of APPROVED or PENDING can be assigned, and all statuses come in from iSupplier as pending until reviewed and accepted by a buyer.

Products and Services

The Products and Services window is used to identify what types of products or services the supplier provides to your organization, as shown in Figure 4-12. When adding a product or service, you can add it either as a broad category, such as Computer Accessories, or as one

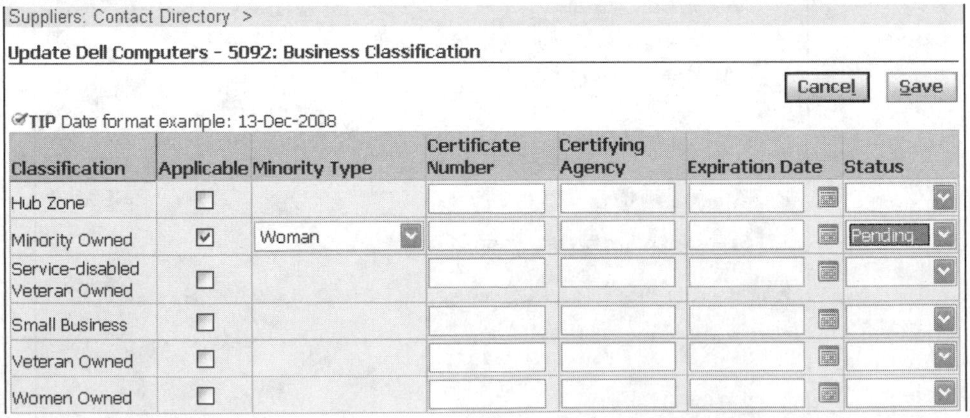

FIGURE 4-11 *Supplier classifications*

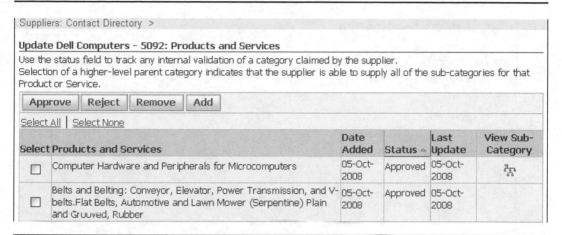

FIGURE 4-12   *Adding products and services to a supplier*

of the child categories, such as Monitors or Diskettes. Once a product is added, it needs to be approved or rejected by a buyer.

The listing of products and services is actually the PO Item Category descriptions, where the Parent is an independent value, and the Child is a dependent second segment. This listing can be completed by an person internal to your organization, or you can request suppliers to complete this themselves using iSupplier. This information can then be used when generating RFQs by finding all the supplier names who provide the product or service you are looking for.

Banking Details

Bank accounts need to be added to supplier records, as shown in Figure 4-13, to use with electronic funds transfer (EFT) or wire payments. In R12, banks are shared within a legal entity and no longer striped by operating unit, but are grouped by country instead. Bank-specific information, such as bank and branch number, account number, and check digits, are regulated by many countries, and the country groupings allow the formats of this information to be validated. The countries currently validated are Austria, Belgium, Denmark, Finland, France, Netherlands, Norway, Portugal, Spain, Brazil, Colombia, Germany, Greece, Iceland, Ireland, Italy, Luxembourg, Poland, Sweden, Switzerland, the United Kingdom, and the United States. In addition to becoming global access operating units, bank accounts are now owned by the Cash Management module (CE tables).

When adding a bank account to a supplier, it can be set up for the supplier's bank itself, or for a factor's bank account. A *factor* is an entity or company that purchases the outstanding receivables from your company at a discounted rate, in exchange for immediate working capital. When this happens, the payment for the receivables may be sent directly to the factor's bank account.

The data entered to create a factor or supplier bank account are the same, with one exception: when entering a factor bank account, a PAYMENT FACTOR NAME is selected from the list of values to show the actual supplier the payment is being made to. The rest of the fields are explained in Table 4-3. When creating a new account for a supplier, for either an existing or new bank, ensure you save the changes (click the SAVE button on the bottom right of the form) after clicking APPLY. The data is not committed to the database until it is saved.

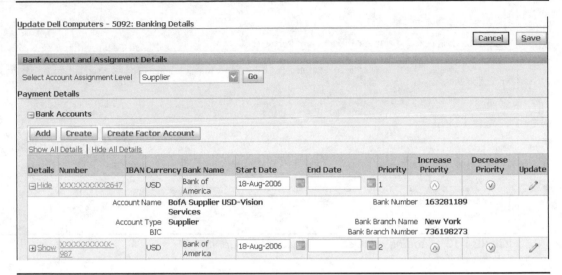

FIGURE 4-13 *Adding supplier banking details*

Under the section Account Owners, additional suppliers can be added who will have access to this account. These need to be added from a supplier who already has access to the account.

Field Name	Required?	Explanation
Country	Yes	Country where the bank resides, used to validate specific bank information based on the country requirements.
Allow International Payments	No	Check this field if payments are going to be made to any supplier in a country outside of the country the account is assigned to.
Bank – Select Existing Bank – Bank Name	Yes	Select the BANK NAME from the list of values. Only banks assigned to the Country, Legal Entity, and Payables can be seen in the list.
Branch – Select Existing Branch – Branch Name	Yes	Select the BRANCH NAME from the list of values. Only branches assigned to the bank and country can be selected.
Bank Account – Account Number	Yes	Add the ACCOUNT NUMBER for this bank. EBS provides different levels of security to ensure that bank account numbers, once entered in the system, are hidden from users who should not have access to them.
Check Digits	No	Provides authentication to a bank that the account number is being used by an authorized user. This is not commonly used in the United States. The number is provided by the banking institution.

TABLE 4-3 *Banking Details for Suppliers*

Field Name	Required?	Explanation
IBAN	No	International Bank Account Number, a unique account number used in the EuroZone nations for banking across country borders.
Account Name	Yes	Unique name for the bank account.
Currency	No	Currency in which transactions are normally processed for this bank account.

TABLE 4-3 *Banking Details for Suppliers* (continued)

Surveys

Surveys are normally used when iSupplier has been implemented. iSupplier is a self-service module that allows suppliers to access your ERP system and view open purchase orders, shipments, sales orders, receivables, and payment statuses. Surveys allow questionnaires to be sent to suppliers using the iSupplier portal and Oracle's Survey tool, where responses are gathered and analyzed.

Terms and Control/Accounting

The Accounting window allows sites to be added to the supplier, as well as accounting-related defaults, as seen already created in Figure 4-14. Click CREATE to add a new site. In order to select the ADDRESS NAME from the list, ensure that only addresses where the PURPOSE is either Payables or Purchasing or both is selected. Addresses that were not set up as Payables or Purchasing cannot be added in the accounting region. Once an address is selected, click SELECT next to the SITE NAME. The SITE NAME, which will default to the ADDRESS NAME, can now be updated. Note that an address can be added more than one time to a supplier by making the site name unique, if this is required for your business purposes.

Under the Site Attributions section, check OVERRIDE DEFAULT SITE ATTRIBUTES to make additional fields available for update, overriding the defaults. For Purchasing, the ABILITY TO CREATE DEBIT MEMO FROM RTS TRANSACTION is available. Payment Terms overrides are available for the following fields: PAYMENT METHOD, CURRENCY AND PRIORITY, PAY GROUPS, TERMS, and the TERMS DATE BASIS, PAY DATE BASIS, as well as how discounts are taken and applied.

Invoice Management also has Payables defaults, including INVOICE CURRENCY, LIMITS, MATCH OPTIONS, AND TOLERANCES. Payment Holds that defaulted from the system setups can be removed, or added, here as well. Once the site is saved, this form where the overrides are made is not available, and any updates will need to be made in the Key Purchasing and Key Payment setups on the Quick Update region.

Once a site has been added, then specific accounting information can be updated from the system defaults if needed, as shown in Figure 4-15. Under the Liability tab, you can update the LIABILITY ACCOUNT that invoices will offset against for this supplier, allowing liabilities to be tracked in separate accounts for different suppliers or sites. You can also change a PREPAYMENT ACCOUNT from the system default for each site under the Prepayment tab. BILLS PAYABLE, the new term for Future Dated Payments in EBS, allows you to chose the account that will be used for all Bills Payables at a future date, and you can add a DISTRIBUTION SET to default distribution line accounting for invoices (see Chapter 5 for more information on distribution sets). The Legal Entity, Operating Unit, and Site Names can be seen on these tabs as well, but this information cannot be updated. The Legal Entity ID that appears on the Liability tab is the system identification for that legal entity and is not normally used by users.

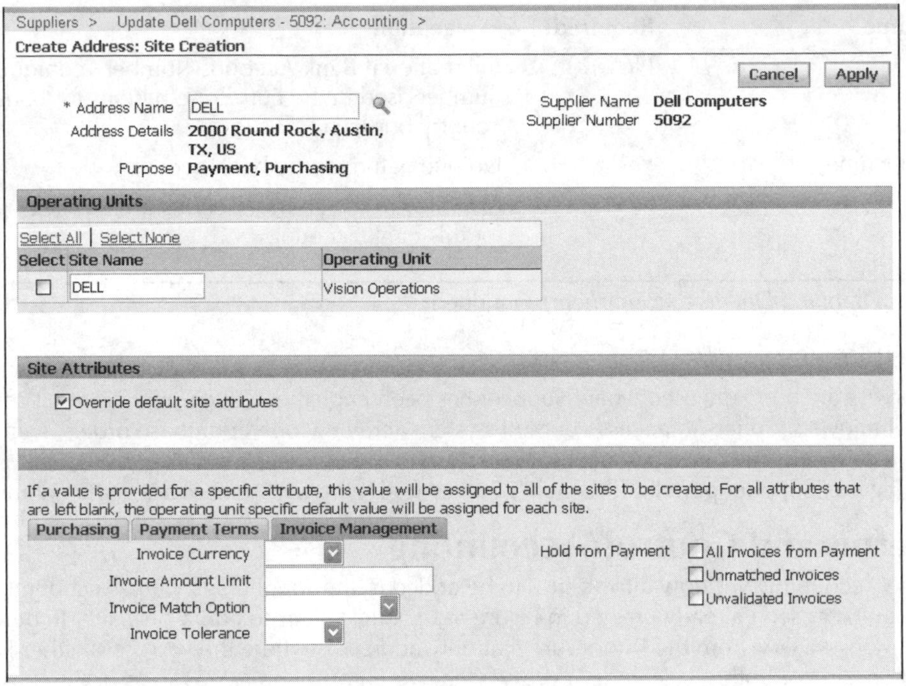

FIGURE 4-14 *Adding new sites and specific information*

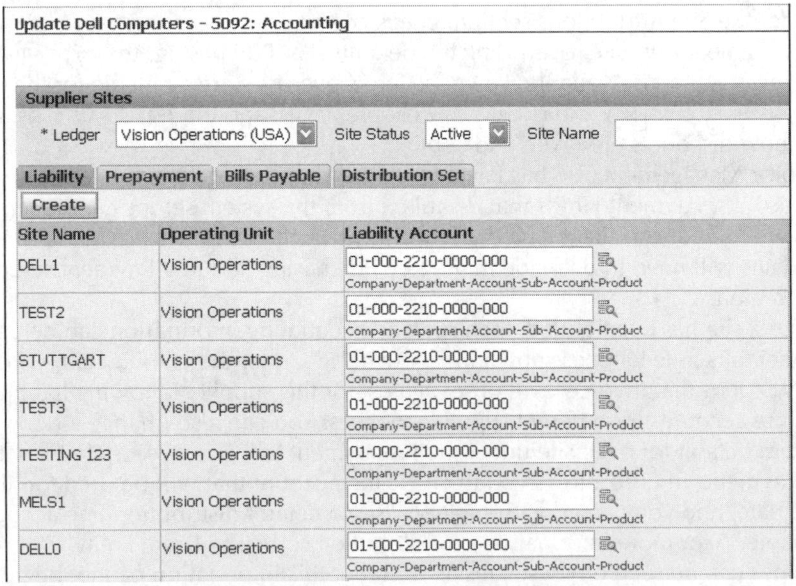

FIGURE 4-15 *Adding accounting information to sites*

Tax and Reporting

EBS has introduced a new module called E-Business Tax in R12, which is the Oracle sales and use tax engine. The Tax and Reporting region of suppliers is utilized with E-Business Tax to ensure tax is assessed and reported properly for any given supplier.

Sometimes, an entity does business under more than one name, and the supplier name entered in your system may not be the name that is registered with the IRS for income tax reporting. As seen in Figure 4-16, use the REPORTING NAME field to enter the supplier's tax reporting name, and this name will appear on all 1099 reports. NAME CONTROL is used when reporting 1099s electronically to the IRS, and will appear on the supplier's B record. VERIFICATION DATE can be entered to track the last time a W9 was received from this supplier. ORGANIZATION TYPE appears on the electronic filing reports for the IRS, but not the printed copies.

For Transaction Tax calculations, several options are available to be set on the supplier and on individual sites. Selecting ALLOW TAX APPLICABILITY will allow automatic tax calculations for this supplier. Since not all suppliers or sites have the same requirements for this field, it can be set at the system, supplier, and site levels. SET FOR SELF ASSESSMENT/REVERSE CHARGE allows self-assessed taxes, commonly known as Consumer Use Tax in the United States, to be created. ALLOW OFFSET TAXES, commonly used with VAT taxes, will offset all VAT taxes while maintain a record of them for reporting. TAX CLASSIFICATIONS are used by E-Business Tax for tax calculation purposes.

You can add TAX REPORTING CODES for both internal and country-specific tax reporting.

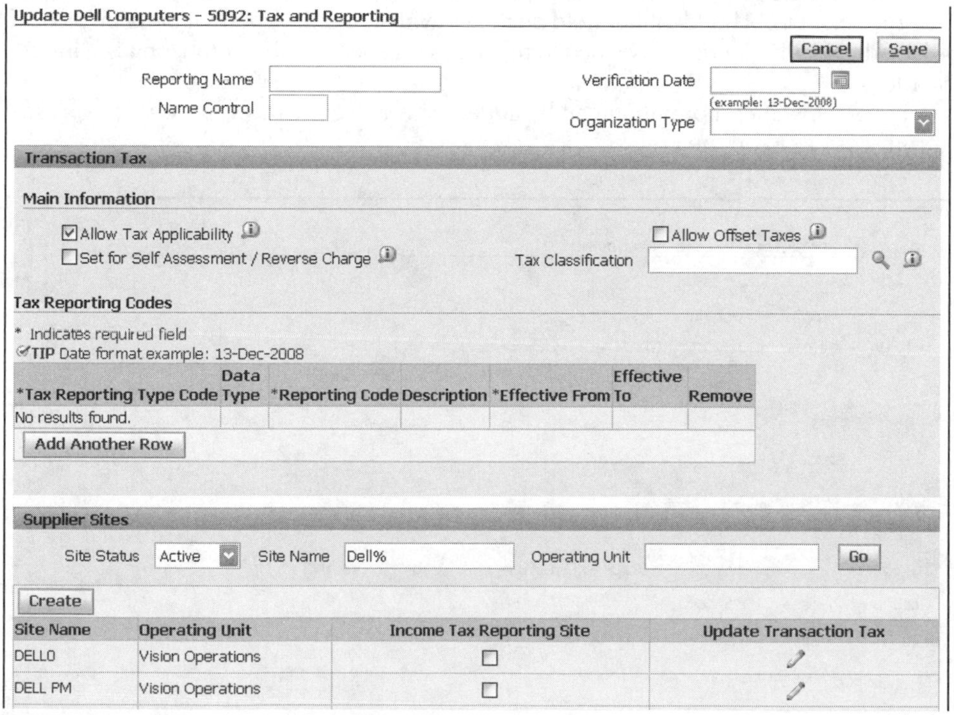

FIGURE 4-16 *Supplier Tax and Reporting setups*

Purchasing

The Purchasing region, shown in Figure 4-17, allows purchase orders to be put on hold as well as default purchasing information by supplier site. To hold all future purchase orders, select PURCHASE ORDER HOLD, ALL NEW ORDERS and assign a PURCHASE ORDER HOLD REASON. The hold reason does not have a list of values to select from but allows any reason to be typed in. Checking CREATE DEBIT MEMO FROM RTS TRANSACTION will automatically create a debit memo for the supplier if that supplier was set up as self-billing and a Return to Supplier is performed.

Sites can be added on this screen by clicking CREATE and selecting an address from the list of values. Once it has been added, SHIP-TO and BILL-TO LOCATIONS can be modified fore each site. These will become the default ship-to and bill-to locations for purchasing documents entered using the site. SHIP VIA can also be added for each site, defaulting in the shipping method.

When an address connected to the site is a payables address, self-billing information can be added. If the address was not set up as a payables site, then self-billing cannot be turned on. Remember that address names can be changed when added as site names. To see the Site Names created from a specific address, go to the Address Book region of suppliers, and click SHOW under Details. All the Site Names set up for that address will appear, as well as the site Purpose.

The fields that can be added on the Self Billing tab of the Purchasing region include PAY ON, which will determine if the invoice is generated when a product is used, received, or received and used. An ALTERNATE PAY SITE can be added here for an address, instead of using the same site for both purchasing and payables. When a self-bill is generated, the INVOICE LEVEL SUMMARY determines how the transactions are grouped onto invoices. The option to CREATE DEBIT MEMO FROM RTS TRANSACTIONS is available here as well, and GAPLESS INVOICE NUMBERING can be set to assign sequential invoice numbers or debit memo numbers to all sites in this supplier who have the same SELLING COMPANY IDENTIFIER. The Identifier field becomes available only when Gapless Invoice Numbering is selected, and it is a number assigned to multiple sites to ensure the numbering is gapless for self bill invoices.

Freight-specific information can be added for FOB, FREIGHT TERMS, TRANSPORTATION ARRANGED, and COUNTRY OF ORIGIN on the Freight tab.

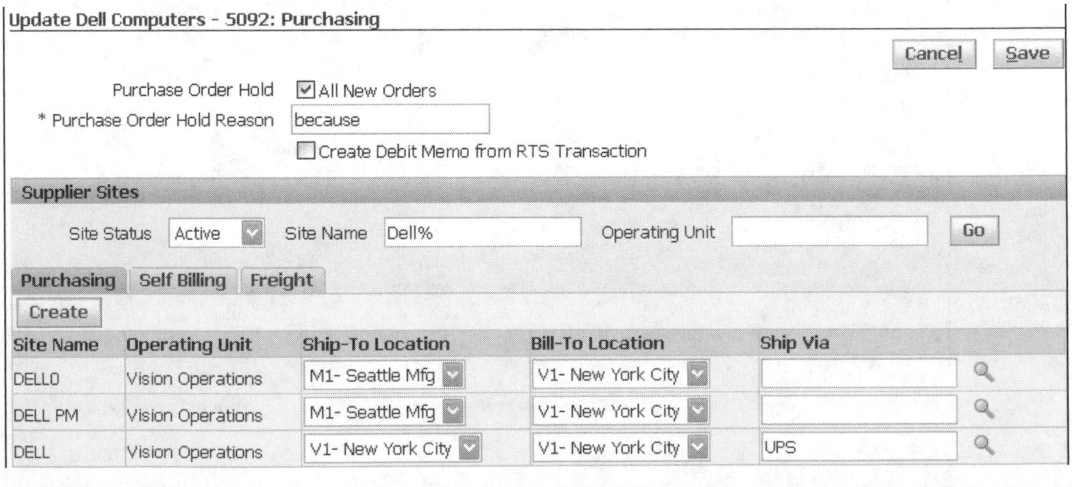

FIGURE 4-17   *Purchasing-related supplier setups*

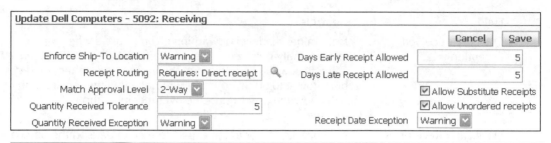

FIGURE 4-18 *Receiving options*

Receiving

Receiving defaults will populate based on the Receiving options set up in Purchasing (see Figure 4-18). While these can be overridden on each specific purchase order, any defaults that are unique for a specific supplier can be modified here, eliminating the need to manually change them. The defaults are explained in Table 4-4.

Field	Controls
Enforce Ship-To Location	Items are usually delivered based on the Ship-To location on the purchase order, but at times they can end up being received in another location. When NONE is selected, there is no warning when this happens. REJECT will not allow receipts to a location other than the Ship-To location on the order, and WARNING will notify the receiver that they are different but allow them to proceed.
Receipt Routing	Receipts have three options for how they are processed: STANDARD, which uses a receiving location prior to delivering an item to its final location, DIRECT DELIVERY, which performs the receiving and delivery steps in one transaction, and INSPECTION REQUIRED, which adds an inspection step into the receiving process.
Match Approval Level	Determines how transactions are matched to purchase orders, and the matching is used to determine when the orders are closed: 2-WAY MATCH compares both the quantities and amounts of purchase orders and invoices. 3-WAY MATCH adds a quantity invoiced comparison to the quantity received. 4-WAY MATCH includes the same criteria as 3-way match, and adds quantity accepted compared to quantity received.
Quantity Received Tolerance	Determines how much over the purchase order quantity can be received.

TABLE 4-4 *Supplier Receiving Defaults*

Field	Controls
Quantity Received Exception	Determines the level of warning given to users when the total quantity received is greater than the Quantity Received Tolerance. WARNING will inform the person performing the receipt but allow it to be saved. REJECT will not allow the receipt, and NONE will allow the user to save the over-receipt without notification that the item is over the tolerance.
Days Early Receipt Allowed	Number days prior to the expected receipt date on the purchase order receipts can be transacted.
Days Late Receipt Allowed	Number of days after the expected receipt date on the purchase order receipts can be transacted.
Allow substitute Receipts	Select this option to allow substitute receipts based on items set up as related (Items | Item Relationships). While a substitute receipt will close the purchase order for receiving and can be matched to an invoice, it does not replace the original item number transactions, and care should be used with planning and reservations when this feature is turned on (both will use the old item number that was not received).
Allow unordered Receipts	Allows receipts for items not on purchase orders, which can later be matched to a purchase order. This option can be overridden at both the item and supplier levels.
Receipt Date Exception	Determines action when the Receipt Days Early or Late are exceeded: NONE allows the receipt, WARNING notifies the user but allows the transaction, and REJECT will not allow the days to be exceeded.

TABLE 4-4   *Supplier Receiving Defaults* (continued)

Payment Details

The Payment Details region, seen in Figure 4-19, is used to set default payment information for each supplier, and the same fields can be set at the site levels as well, making each site have different defaults.

Each supplier can have multiple PAYMENT METHODS, with one being set as the default method. Payment methods refer to the medium in which a payment will be remitted to a supplier, such as Check, Wire, Electronic Funds Transfer (EFT), or Credit Card. A supplier in EBS cannot remit funds using a specific method until the corresponding method has been assigned to the supplier or site. Invoices will adapt the DEFAULT method when they are entered, but can be changed to any method assigned to the supplier or site.

Payment Delivery Attributes can be added for electronic processing of payments. The DELIVERY CHANNEL is a unique code handed out by either a company's central bank or government; it will directly identify how the payments will be delivered or processed in that specific country. These codes unique for each country. In the United States, the most common delivery channels used are

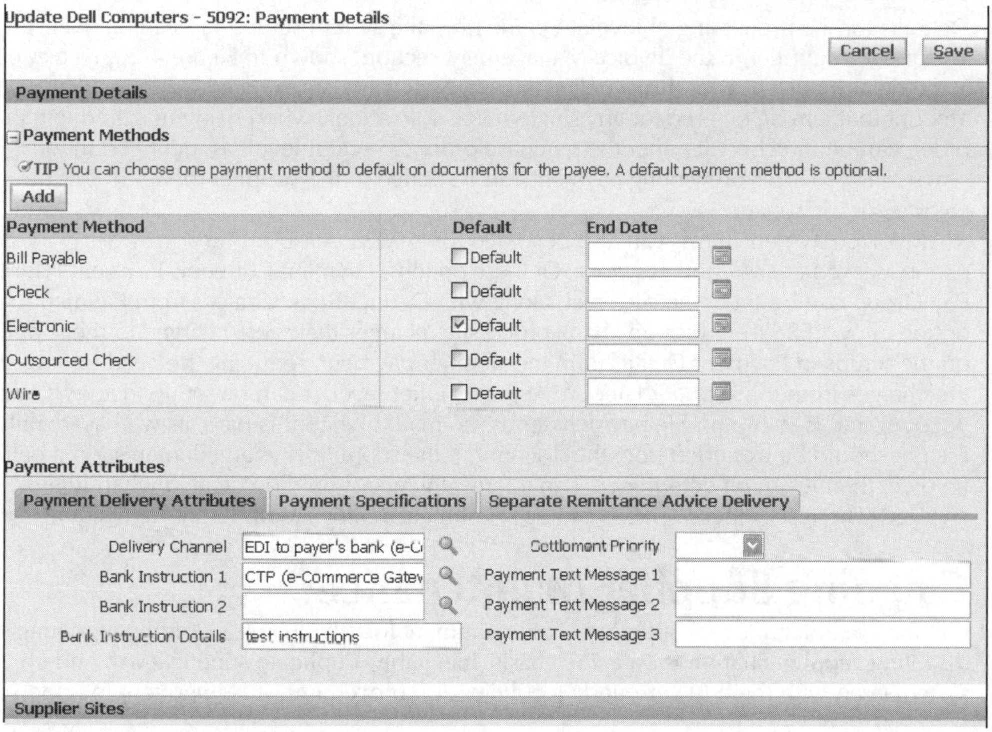

FIGURE 4-19   *Supplier payment options*

for EDI (Electronic Data Interchange) transactions. Working with the DELIVERY CHANNEL code, two sets of BANK INSTRUCTIONS can be added to further tell the banking institution how to handle the funds when they are received. Under BANK INSTRUCTION DETAILS, additional instructions can be typed in. SETTLEMENT PRIORITY informs the bank of the priority of the transaction. PAYMENT TEXT can be added and passed on to the payees from the payment system.

Payment Specifications provides EBS with instructions on how to process invoices for payment. PAY EACH DOCUMENT ALONE will produce one payment per invoice, as opposed to grouping them for payment on one document. BANK CHARGE BEARER can be added to determine who will bear the cost of the bank charges added to process the payment. When submitting a payment to the central bank for processing, note that some governments require that the reason for payment be included with the transaction; this reason is stored in the PAYMENT REASON field. PAYMENT REASON COMMENTS can be included as well. Payment Formats, which are linked to Payment Methods in Oracle Payments, can be added as a default for the payee, ensuring all payments are processed using this format.

When a payment is made, EBS can include a separate remittance advice. This advice can be delivered either by Mail, E-Mail, or Fax, and an e-mail address or fax number can be set up on the Separate Remittance Advice Delivery tab.

Invoice Management

Defaults for the processing of invoices come from the system setups and can be overridden and set for each supplier in the Invoice Management section, shown in Figure 4-20. INVOICE CURRENCY is the default currency for this supplier. INVOICE AMOUNT LIMITS can be added to restrict the dollar amount that can be entered for any single invoice. Invoices, when being matched to a purchase order, can be matched at either the purchase order or receipt level, as identified in the INVOICE MATCH OPTION. Holds preventing payment can be added to the supplier for ALL INVOICES, UNMATCHED INVOICES, or UNVALIDATED INVOICES.

Invoice Payment Terms can also be added for PAYMENT CURRENCY, PAYMENT PRIORITY, TERMS, TERMS DATE BASIS, PAY DATE BASIS, and PAY GROUP. Of these options, Payment Currency, Payment Priority, and Pay Group can be set at the site level, along with Deduct Bank Charges from Payment. This option allows EBS to reduce any bank processing charges that were charged to the supplier based on the setups in Payment Details from the supplier payment, reducing the need to have to collect the charges from the supplier later on. At the supplier level, it can be set up to ALWAYS TAKE THE DISCOUNT that is set up on the payment terms, no matter when it is paid, as well as identifying if Freight should be excluded from the discount. If the supplier is charged interest on a delinquent invoice, then it can be determined if an Interest Invoice should be created when interest is charged. The rest of these options can be set at the supplier site under the Terms tab.

Ongoing Supplier Maintenance

Ongoing maintenance for suppliers is a requirement for any business. Adding, updating, and disabling suppliers happens on a daily basis. Inevitably, duplicate suppliers will end up in the system even with the best surrounding policies and procedures. It is important to understand that

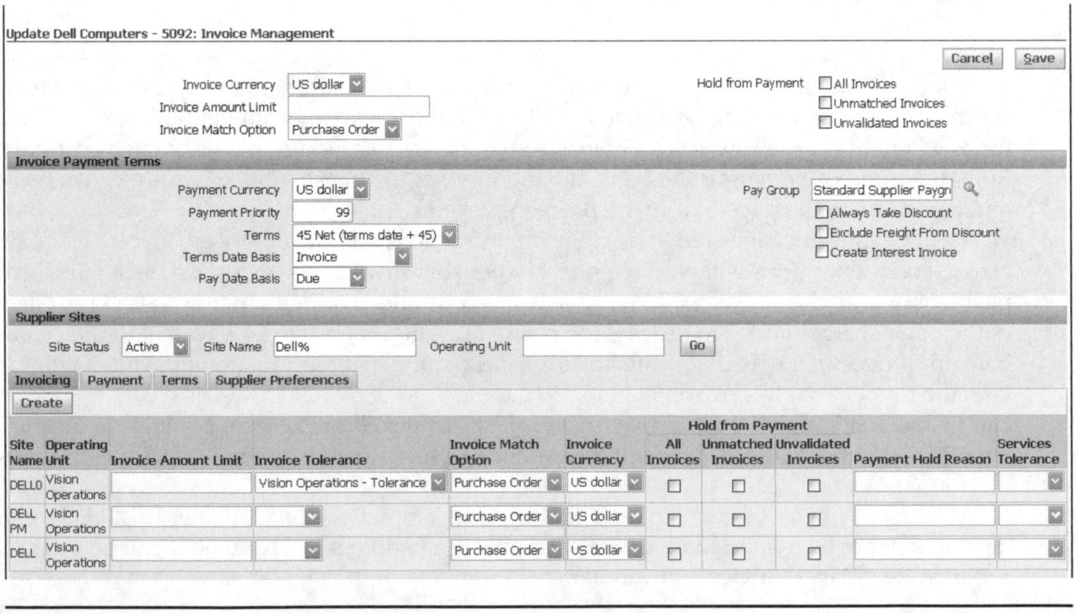

FIGURE 4-20 *Supplier invoice defaults*

no suppliers can be deleted from EBS. They can be inactivated and eventually purged, but they cannot be outright deleted. Updates to supplier information can be done by querying up the supplier and adding, end dating, or modifying information that already exists. If Sarbanes-Oxley (SOX) audits require that changes to suppliers (or any other data in EBS) be monitored, there are two options: using the database auditing feature in System Administrator or implementing Oracle's Governance, Risk, and Compliance (GRC) module. Both track changes at the database level, for which the GRC module will also provide reporting for the changes.

Identifying Duplicate Suppliers

Duplicate suppliers will happen from time to time, even though EBS does not allow suppliers to be entered with the same name. Duplicates refer to two or more suppliers that have variations of the same name, such as Dell and Dell Inc, or the same tax identification number.

The Supplier Audit Report, shown in Figure 4-21, is the best way to identify duplicate supplier names in the system. The report will match names up to a certain number of characters, which are entered by the person running the report. Running this report on a regular basis can not only help keep the supplier master as accurate as possible, it can also reduce the possibility of duplicate payments or fraud. EBS allows the same invoice number to be entered for different suppliers, but not the same supplier, so when there are multiple supplier numbers set up for the same company, duplicates are less readily found.

Merging Suppliers

Once duplicate suppliers are identified, or if a company is involved with a merger or name change, the ability to merge two suppliers is available. Supplier data can be merged for both invoices and purchase orders, and you can move transactions into an existing supplier site or create a new one, depending on the site information where the data is coming from. Use the Supplier Merge window shown in Figure 4-22 to merge supplier information.

When INVOICES are merged, you have the option to move ALL, PAID, or NONE. Moving ALL invoices changes the supplier on both paid and unpaid invoices in the system but will leave the Paid-To name on the payment screen the actual name that the check was cut to. EBS cannot move over invoices where the number already exists in the new supplier. If all transactions should be moved, the invoice number will have to be changed in one of the suppliers prior to running the merge process. The invoice number can be updated when the invoices are not paid or fully accounted, but invoices in these statuses cannot be updated.

```
Vision Operations (USA)                                                  Report Date: 14-DEC-2008 16:21
                                       Supplier Audit Report             Page:                       1
                                   Suppliers Matching in first 10 letters
Supplier
Number          Supplier Name               Site              Address                  City        State Zip
--------------- --------------------------- ----------------- ------------------------ ------------ ----- -----
5074            Automotive Supplier #1      DETROIT           5555 Big Beaver Road     Troy        Michi 48084
5075            Automotive Supplier #2      CLEVELAND         3 Summit Park Drive       Independence Ohio  44131
20008           Automotive Supplier #3      CAMBRIDGE         3500 Auto 3 Way          Cambridge
20009           Automotive Supplier #4      MEXICO CITY       2455 Auto 4 Parkway      Mexico City
20088           Building Maintenance, Inc.  EAM-ERS           1000 Abernathy Road      Atlanta     GA    30305
2012            Building Management Inc.     HQ - NYC          345 Industrial Way        New York    NY    10234
20174           Commissioner Of Customs Authority
20175           Commissioner Of Excise
```

FIGURE 4-21 *Supplier Audit Report for identifying duplicate suppliers*

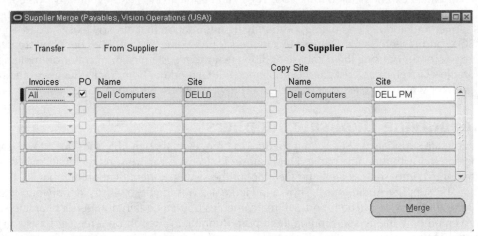

Payables Manager | Suppliers | Supplier Merge

FIGURE 4-22 *Merging suppliers*

Adding an additional distribution line for zero dollars will change the status to partially accounted, allowing the invoice number to be updated. Once the duplicate invoice is merged, it can be voided or canceled if need be. Invoices that exist in the Payables Open Interface will *not* be considered for the merge, and they will error out if the old supplier and site are end-dated, so ensure that all transactions are imported prior to merging data.

When PO is selected, then all purchase orders will be transferred over to the new supplier number. EBS also moves any purchasing-related information to the new supplier, including receipts, quotes, supplier schedules, sourcing rules, approved supplier lists, and MRP (Manufacturing Resource Planning) related records. This ensures that the purchasing, as well as payables, systems are well set to use the new supplier and supplier sites. With both invoices and purchase orders are moved over, the old supplier site and (if there are no longer any active sites) the supplier will be disabled as part of the merge process.

From the list of values, select the NAME and SITE for the FROM SUPPLIER. If you want to merge all sites for a supplier, each site must be merged separately. Check COPY SITE to create the existing site in the new supplier, or the data can be merged in an existing SITE on the TO SUPPLIER. When merging to an existing site, note that to merge invoices, the existing site must be marked as a Pay site, and to merge purchase orders, it must be a Purchasing site. It is possible to merge one site for a supplier into a different site for the same supplier.

Click MERGE and a report will print out detailing the merged transactions. This report gives detailed information of all merged suppliers, sites, and transactions, as well as printing any invoices that did not merge due to duplicate invoice numbers. Use caution when merging suppliers and sites—this feature cannot be undone once EBS has processed the merge.

CHAPTER
5

Payables Setups

ayables is an integrated subledger that can be used to control the accounting transactions and remittances due to third-party suppliers and subsidiaries. These transactions are tightly controlled by Subledger Accounting to create financial transactions, and setups which control accuracy while maximizing cash outflows. Payments has been broken out in R12 to a separate module with its own controls, and will be covered in the Chapter 7. Setups in Payables are broken down into three different types: required, conditionally required (referring to setups that come seeded but can be modified or changed), and optional.

Required Setups

Certain setups are necessary for processing all transactions in Payables. These include Operating Units, Financial and Payables Options, System Setups, Tolerances, Calendars and Aging Periods, and Bank-related information, such as for opening the first period for processing transactions.

Operating Unit

Prior to beginning the setups in Payables, an Operating Unit must be defined. This step may have been completed already if other subledgers are being used. The main purpose of an Operating Unit is to associate the payables transactions to the Ledger and segregate data, and Operating Units are often aligned with an organization's structure. These Operating Units can be used by multiple subledgers at the same time.

To set up an Operating Unit, you use the Organization form (Payables Manager | Setup | Organizations). Create a NAME that will be used in setups and by the system for this Operating Unit. The TYPE is a reporting field that allows the Organization to be classified for reporting purposes; it is not required unless you plan on entering employees into EBS, in which case the TYPE should be set to BUSINESS GROUP. The DATES determine what period the Operating Unit is effective for, and the TO can be left blank for organizations that are still active. Assign a LOCATION to the organization, usually relating to the physical address, and classify the location as INTERNAL or EXTERNAL. This classification is used when assigning employees to a location; they can only be assigned to Internal organizations.

At this point your work must be saved to proceed. Under the ORGANIZATION CLASSIFICATION, select OPERATING UNIT and ENABLE it, and again save the work. Click OTHER to access additional information screens; only Operating Unit information is required, which will associate this unit with a Ledger. Click in the NAME field to get the pop-up, and select a Primary Ledger; this is the Ledger that all purchasing transactions will create accounting transactions in according to the Subledger Accounting (SLA) rules. Exiting this window will save the record.

Financial Options

Financial Options are used predominantly by Payables but are required for some Purchasing functionality. Financial Options, shown in Figure 5-1, determine default account numbers, purchase order and requisition defaults, encumbrance options, and employee defaults for expense reports. Financial Options will need to be set up for each Operating Unit Payables will be processed for. How MOAC (Multi-Org Access Control) is set up will determine whether the Operating Unit will default in or will need to be selected when entering the screen.

Accounting Tab

On the Accounting tab, default account numbers are assigned for transactions. LIABILITY, PREPAYMENT, DISCOUNT TAKEN, PO RATE VARIANCE GAIN, and PO RATE VARIANCE LOSS are all required, even if you are

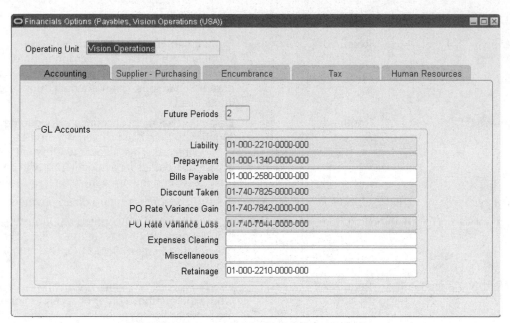

Payables Manager | Setup | Options | Financial Options

FIGURE 5-1 *Financial Options*

using Purchasing as a stand-alone purchasing system without integrating it with Payables or General Ledger. These accounts will become the defaults for suppliers when they are set up, and they can be changed there to create supplier-specific accounting. With the introduction of Subledger Accounting, these accounts may be used as part of the final accounting solution, but SLA may override them on the actual transactions for the accounting sent to the General Ledger. Table 5-1 gives a short description of what each of the required and optional fields is used for.

Supplier-Purchasing Tab

The information completed on the Supplier-Purchasing tab will create defaults for several key supplier setups. Checking RFQ ONLY SITE will cause all new suppliers to be valid only for request for quotes, not purchase orders or invoices. This allows users to follow a supplier process and ensures the supplier information, both EBS data and company-required data, is complete prior to use.

SHIP-TO LOCATION is the default shipping location for all new suppliers. This field is not mandatory, and it may not be appropriate to have a default if you have more than one location used by a majority of the suppliers. BILL-TO LOCATION is the default billing address that will appear on purchase orders when creating suppliers. INVENTORY ORGANIZATION is a required field even if you are not using inventories; it will determine which items can be purchased from this organization—only items that are set up in this inventory organization can be purchased. Since this is a required field, you can set up a shell inventory organization under Payables Manager | Setup | Organization and assign the ORGANIZATION CLASSIFICATION as an Inventory Organization. Under the OTHER button, you will need to add Accounting Information to link this inventory organization with the Ledger, Legal Entity, and Operating Unit.

Field	Required or Optional	Usage
Liability	Required	Default liability account assigned to new suppliers, which can be overridden on each supplier record. This account can be used as part of SLA setups, or another account used altogether.
Prepayment	Required	Default prepayment account assigned to new suppliers, which can be overridden on each supplier record. This account would only create accounting entries if payment terms with discounts were used, and the discount was taken.
Bills Payable	Optional	Default account for future dated payments.
Discount Taken	Required	Account used for discounted amounts when the Discount Method is set to System Account (Payables Manager | Setup | Options | Payables Options).
PO Rate Variance Gain	Required	Used to record rate gains for inventory items where the purchase order or receipt rates are not the same as the invoice. The matching method (purchase order or receipt) determines which foreign currency rate is compared to the invoice.
PO Rate Variance Loss	Required	Records rate losses for inventory items where the purchase order or receipt rates are not the same as the invoice. The matching method (purchase order or receipt) determines which foreign currency rate is compared to the invoice.
Expenses Clearing	Optional	Used as a clearing account for credit card transactions where the company pays the credit card directly but matches the payments up to expense reports entered in iExpenses.
Miscellaneous	Optional	Used for any Miscellaneous charges received in XML, either via the XML Gateway or iSupplier. If this is not filled in, Miscellaneous charges will be prorated against all the other lines on the XML invoice.
Retainage	Optional	Account used to record retainages, or contractually withheld payments. Usually withheld from progress payments on long-term or high-dollar contracts.

TABLE 5-1   *Required and Optional Fields on the Accounting Tab of Financial Options*

SHIP VIA can be populated if you have a preferred freight carrier that should default on purchase orders. FOB, or Free On Board Terms, are a group of terms that dictate specifics about a sale such as who owns the product during shipping. The FOB entered here will default on all purchase orders. FREIGHT TERMS determine who is responsible for paying the freight charges, and will default on purchase orders when it is populated.

Encumbrance Tab

Under the Encumbrance tab, Payables can be set up to use both Requisition and PO Encumbrances, as well as determine whether funds can be reserved by the requisition preparer (RESERVE AT COMPLETION is checked) or if only approvers can reserve funds. Encumbrance accounting records accounting entries for both requisitions and purchase orders, as opposed to waiting for the receipt or invoice against an order, where the accounting is typically performed and the liability recognized. Encumbrance Accounting is often used in U.S. federal government accounting or in organizations where budgets strictly control costs.

Tax Tab

The Tax tab on the financial options is used exclusively with value-added tax (VAT). A MEMBER STATE can be added and is used by Payables to determine if the state is a member of the European Union. The VAT REGISTRATION NUMBER is the VAT number for your organization and prints on some of the value-added tax reports.

Human Resource Tab

The Human Resource tab is used to default data when setting up employees in EBS. Employees can be added to EBS to create a hierarchy for Purchasing document approvals, invoice approvals, and journal entry approvals. When HR is not fully implemented in EBS, in what is called a Shared Install, there is a modified People window that allows accounting-related information, such as employee name, address, supervisor, and default distribution account, to be added and used by Purchasing and other subledgers.

A BUSINESS GROUP is assigned here, so that the employees will all be registered in that group. When Organizations are created, at least one organization needs to be classified as a Business Group. When Human Resources is not fully implemented, the Operating Unit can be set up as the Default Business Group. The EXPENSE REPORT ADDRESS for employees can be set to OFFICE or HOME and will determine which address on the Personnel record will print on expense reports.

USE APPROVAL HIERARCHIES should be checked when an employee's position hierarchy is going to be used for approving purchasing documents; left unchecked, it will cause EBS to use the supervisor hierarchies as opposed to positions. POSITION HIERARCHIES relates to the positions, or jobs, an employee is assigned to, which may be different than the actual supervisor associated with an employee. An example of this is that John Doe, a Line Supervisor, may directly relate to Jane Dee, the Plant Supervisor, while the position of Line Supervisor may report to the Plant Manager instead. Using supervisor or position hierarchies is not the only option when creating approvals in EBS. A module called Application Management (AME) can also be utilized, where separate rules and hierarchies are defined and assigned for approvals.

Employee Numbers can be assigned either automatically or manually, as determined with the METHOD, and the NEXT AUTOMATIC NUMBER will be populated when automatic numbering is selected. This next number can be reset at any time, but ensure that it is reset to a number greater than the last number assigned to prevent problems when adding employees.

Payables System Setups

Payables System setups control some key setup defaults and controls for Suppliers, Invoices, and Payments, as seen in Figure 5-2.

Supplier Numbers

The numbering of suppliers is controlled here, determining if a new supplier number is assigned automatically or manually in the ENTRY field. While this field can be switched back and forth between the two options, ensure that the automatically assigned numbers do not overlap with any supplier numbers that were manually created in the system or imported. One safe way to ensure this is to have manually assigned numbers be alphanumeric.

Switching back and forth is a useful option as you do data conversion for new divisions or acquisitions, allowing numbers from legacy systems to be maintained. The TYPE determines if the supplier number field allows alphanumeric or numeric data only. Only numeric numbers can be assigned automatically, but the type can still be set to alphanumeric to allow manual entry of this type. NEXT AUTOMATIC NUMBER determines the next number the system will use, and can be updated as needed. Ensure that when updating the next number, it is always set one larger than the last used number in the database to prevent errors when entering suppliers.

Invoice Controls

The INVOICE MATCH OPTION determines whether invoices are matched to the receipt itself or to the purchase order, which indirectly links it to the receipt. Even when PURCHASE ORDER is selected, an invoice cannot be paid if a 3-way match is selected and the receipt is not yet made, but it does allow entering the invoice in the system with an automatic hold, preventing payment until the receipt is made and the hold is released by the system.

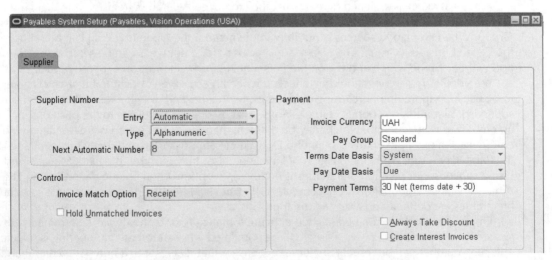

Payables Manager | Setup | Options | Payables System Setup

FIGURE 5-2 *Payables System setups*

When this field is set to RECEIPT, the invoice cannot be matched until the receipt is actually transacted in EBS, delaying the invoice entry and causing the transaction to be manually monitored until the receipt is made and allows matching to it. Selecting HOLD UNMATCHED INVOICES will cause any invoice entered into Payables to be held if it was not matched to a purchase order; this option is useful if all invoices are matched to purchase orders.

Payment Defaults

The Payment section allows a default INVOICE CURRENCY to be entered, which can be overridden when entering an invoice if one is received for a different currency. This option can also be set at the supplier level, but it defaults on each new supplier from here. If this is not set in the Payables System setups, then the currency will default from the Ledger setups. PAYGROUPS, used to group invoices into a single payment request, can be added as a default for all invoices.

When entering an invoice into Payables, you can use any of several dates to default the payment terms, as set in the TERMS DATE BASIS. SYSTEM will use the current date in EBS to determine the terms. GOODS RECEIVED will default the date the items were received against the purchase order; this should only be selected if all invoices are matched to receipts, or the GOODS RECEIVED date will have to be manually added for all unmatched invoices. INVOICE will use the Invoice Date as the basis for the payment terms, and the INVOICE RECEIVED date will use the date recorded as the invoice received date on the invoice entry screen. Of these options, both INVOICE RECEIVED and GOODS RECEIVED are not required fields and will leave the Terms Date null if they are not entered when entering the invoice. The Terms Date, along with the terms assigned to the invoice, is used by EBS to determine when an invoice should be paid and how it is aged in the invoice aging reports.

PAY DATE BASIS determines if invoices are selected for payment based on the Due date or the Discount date, as defined with the payment terms. PAYMENT TERMS will default the terms on all suppliers entered into EBS, which in turn defaults onto the invoices entered against that supplier. This default can be overridden at both the supplier and the invoice levels. Selecting ALWAYS TAKE DISCOUNT will cause EBS to take the discount associated with a payment term no matter when the invoice is paid. EBS has the ability to accrue interest on overdue invoices, and create a separate interest invoice when the invoice is paid. Selecting CREATE INTEREST INVOICES will cause this to happen.

Invoice Tolerances

Invoice Tolerances are utilized when Payables is integrated with Oracle Purchasing. In R12, the Invoice Tolerances are assigned to the Payables Options on the Matching tab (Setup | Options | Payables Options, see the next section). These become the defaults for new suppliers when they are set up, and any changes at the supplier level will override the system defaults. To create tolerances, refer to Figure 5-3, and assign a NAME and a DESCRIPTION for the tolerance being set up. There are two TYPES of tolerances set up here: GOODS and SERVICES. When GOODS is selected, these tolerances will pertain to purchase orders where the quantity is the basis of the order, whereas SERVICES represents orders that are based on an amount.

In order for each individual tolerance to be considered or set up, the check box to the right of the field needs to be checked. The HOLD NAME will default in based on the tolerance and cannot be updated. The ORDERED tolerance controls the quantity above the shipment entered on a purchase order that can be matched to an invoice without going on hold. The Amount is used for Services tolerances instead of quantity. The MAXIMUM QUANTITY ORDERED is a quantity-ordered limit that would apply to any purchase order matched to an invoice, no matter what the actual transaction was set up for. Use this option only if a majority of the purchase orders have the same quantity. These options are used when performing 2-way matches (invoice to purchase order).

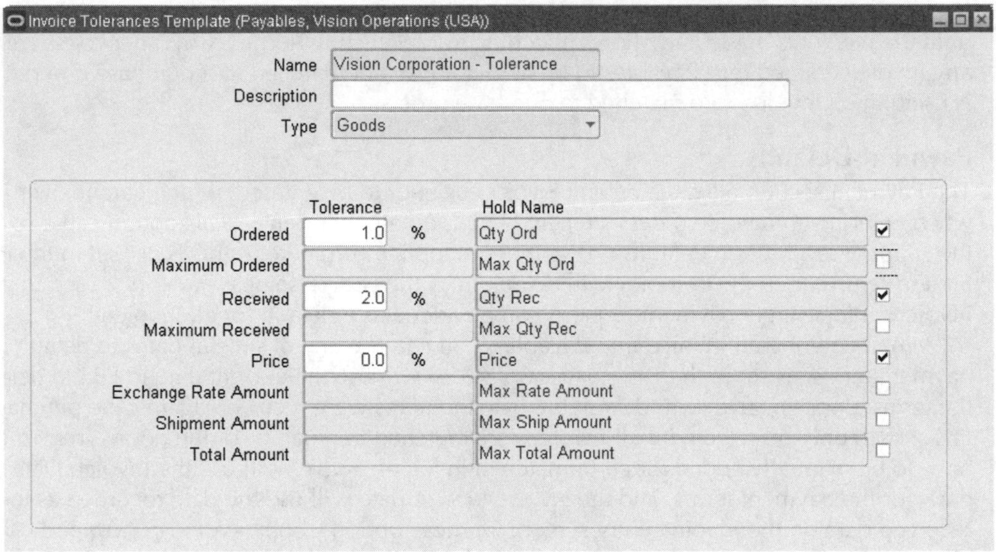

Payables Manager | Setup | Invoice | Tolerances

FIGURE 5-3 *Setting up Tolerances*

RECEIVED tolerances are used when matching an invoice to a receipt, and represent the percentage over the actual receipt that can be matched without going on hold. Quantity is used for goods, and the dollar amount for services. Setting the MAXIMUM RECEIVED quantity tolerance would hold any match where the amount matched was greater than this amount. These tolerances are used when 3-way matching is utilized (invoice to purchase order and receipt). This does not require that the matching be set to default to the receipt; matching to a purchase order still has a link to the receipt associated with that order.

The PRICE tolerance is used when comparing the purchasing order shipment line amount to an invoice and will hold any invoice where this amount tolerance is reached, based on the quantity for goods and a dollar amount for services. EXCHANGE RATE AMOUNT is used when entering foreign currency transactions; it compares two invoice and purchase order exchange rates. The SHIPMENT AMOUNTS tolerance is for matching an invoice to a shipment recorded against a purchase order when transacting in a foreign currency. The TOTAL AMOUNT, again used with foreign currencies, takes both the Exchange Rate and Shipment Amount variances, and determines if the total is greater than the tolerance allowed here.

Payables Options

You use Payables Options to control and create defaults in a large part of Payables. At the top of this window, the first thing you select is the operating unit, determining which operating unit these defaults relate to. All the setups will pertain to this operating unit only, as seen in Figure 5-4.

Accounting Options

Payment Accounting options determine when specific transactions related to payments are accounted. Payments can be accounted for either when the payment is issued—for instance, when

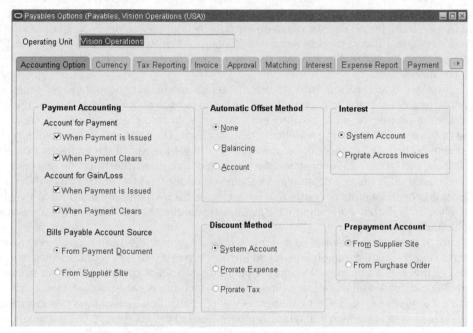

Payables Manager | Setup | Options | Payables Options

FIGURE 5-4 *Payables Options*

the check run is confirmed—or when a payment is cleared using Oracle Cash Management. If both are selected, then Subledger Accounting creates a transaction when the check is cut and a second transaction when the payment is cleared, using a clearing account. Once the accounting for payment is selected, it cannot be changed, with one exception: if you are accounting for a payment when it is issued, you can add to account for it when it clears; no other changes are allowed.

Transactional Gains and Losses can be accounted either when the payment is issued, when it clears, or both. In an accrual-based system, the Gain/Loss calculated when the payment is issued is based on the rate assigned to the invoice, and the rate assigned to the payment, using either the payment date or, for bills payable (future-dated payments), the maturity date. WHEN PAYMENT CLEARS will calculate the difference between the invoice rate and the rate on the date the payment clears the bank. If both are selected, then it will record these differences in increments, first recording the difference between the invoice date and the payment date, and then the difference from the payment date to the clearing date.

A payment must be accounted prior to the system creating the gain/loss transaction, so when you are creating a gain/loss entry, the Account for Payment must also be selected at the same level. You can account for the payment at both levels, and the gain and loss at only one of the two levels. (In other words, if you create accounting for the gain/loss when the payment is issued, it must be accounted for when the payment is issued as well.) Once saved, the only change allowed here is to add accounting when the payment clears.

Bills Payable, or future-dated payments, determines if the account numbers used are from either the payment document or the supplier site. The PAYMENT DOCUMENT will use the account number set up in the Future Dated Payment field on the bank account (Payables Manager | Setup | Payment | Bank Accounts | Bank | Update Accounts | Options when Payables is checked). Selecting FROM SUPPLIER SITE will use the Bills Payable account in the Bills Payable tab of the Accounting Region on the supplier setups.

AUTOMATIC OFFSET METHODS, used to determine how the liability account is generated for each transaction, defaults to the account that is assigned to each supplier. EBS also has the ability to modify the supplier account by using the BALANCING segment entered on an invoice. along with the rest of the segments from the supplier liability account. The final option is to use only the ACCOUNT segment of the liability account on the supplier, and get the rest of the segments from the invoice distributions. Table 5-2 demonstrates the difference in these methods. While this option can be changed after it is set, use caution and ensure you understand the impact this will have on the General Ledger. Liability accounts that were created for invoices entered prior to the change may be offset in the liability account that is generated after the change, causing the accounts to be out of balance.

DISCOUNT METHODS are used to determine how a payment discount is applied across the accounting on the distribution lines on an invoice. When SYSTEM ACCOUNT is selected, the account number that was set up in the Financial Options for DISCOUNT TAKEN is used. PRORATE EXPENSE will take the discount against all the expense lines evenly; if EXCLUDE TAX FROM DISCOUNT CALCULATION is checked on the Payments tab of this form, then taxes will not have the discount taken against them. The final option is PRORATE TAX, which will take an amount equal to the tax percent (for instance, if your taxes are 18 percent, then 18 percent of the discount is used) to credit the tax lines, with the remaining discount hitting the DISCOUNT TAKEN account set up on the financial options.

INTEREST settings are used when interest is charged against an invoice and an interest invoice will be created. The SYSTEM ACCOUNT will use the expense account entered on the Interest tab on this form. PRORATE ACROSS INVOICES will use the distribution string from the expense line, substituting the natural account from the account on the Interest tab, and will prorate the interest across all the account combinations.

PREPAYMENT ACCOUNT is used when a prepayment is created for a supplier; it can either hit the prepayment account assigned on a supplier site or, when FROM PURCHASE ORDER is selected, the prepayment will use the default distribution account on the purchase order.

Currency

The Currency tab has the defaults for transactions that are entered in foreign currencies, which includes any currency that is different from the main currency assigned to the Ledger. Selecting USE MULTIPLE CURRENCIES allows invoices and payments to be transacted in foreign currencies. This will also require payment formats to be set up for the currencies you want to make payments in, as well as the bank account to be enabled for multiple currencies. If this option needs to be

Supplier Liability Account	Invoice Distribution	Offset Method	Liability Account
01-000-210000-0000	02-210-520000-0000	None	01-000-210000-0000
01-000-210000-0000	02-210-520000-0000	Balancing	02-000-210000-0000
01-000-210000-0000	02-210-520000-0000	Account	02-210-210000-0000

TABLE 5-2 *Automatic Offset Methods Example*

disabled, the bank account (Setup | Payment | Bank Accounts) and payment methods (Payments Setup Administrator | Payment Method Defaulting Rules) must be disabled first. Selecting REQUIRE EXCHANGE RATE ENTRY will require an exchange rate to be entered on a transaction prior to saving it; when this option is not checked, transactions can be entered without an exchange rate, allowing it to be added or defaulted in prior to accounting using AutoRate.

CALCULATE USER EXCHANGE RATE allows the users to enter a transaction in a foreign currency and the Ledger currency, and EBS will calculate the exchange rate for the transaction. EXCHANGE RATE TYPE determines which exchange rate will default in for transactions when it is entered, or when AutoRate is used. If this option is set to USER, EBS requires the user to enter the rate when the transaction is entered, as it will not default in. The General Ledger accounts that relate to foreign currency transactions are set up here, including realized gains and losses, and any rounding differences for transactions. The gain and loss accounts are used to calculate the difference between the invoice rate and the payment rate, recording the gain or loss on the transaction.

When working with gains and losses between invoice exchange rates and payment exchange rates, you can run a report called Payments Gain and Loss Report to see all the payments during a time period that had a gain or loss resulting in a different exchange rate. This report also displays the account numbers these transactions were recorded to.

Tax Reporting

When filing 1099s using an electronic medium to submit the 1099s to the government, selecting COMBINED FILING PROGRAM will also file the K-records for all regions that participate in the federal combined filing program. Ensure you are approved with the federal government to participate in the combined filing program prior to selecting this option. When the COMBINED FILING PROGRAM option is selected, selecting USE PAY SITE TAX REGION will default the tax region for each transaction from the supplier tax region. Alternatively, if USE PAY SITE TAX REGION is not selected, an INCOME TAX REGION can be added as a default for all transactions. Either of these defaults can be overridden when entering an invoice into the system where 1099 is applicable.

Invoice

The Invoice tab will control many defaults for invoice transactions; options are outlined in Table 5-3.

Option	Control
Confirm Date as Invoice Number	Whenever an invoice number is not entered when tabbing past the field, then EBS will default in the Invoice Date for the number. Enabling this check box will prompt users to confirm that they want to use the invoice date for the invoice number.
Allow Online Validation	Check this option if you want users to be able to validate invoices from the action button on the invoice or invoice batch screen. If this is not enabled, the users must submit the Invoice Validation concurrent request to validate an invoice or batch.
Allow Document Category Override	Determines if Document Categories, used to determine the numbering sequence used for a transaction, can be changed by the user.
Allow Adjustment to Paid Invoices	Once an invoice is paid, the invoice distributions are locked, preventing any changes. Enabling this option will allow changes to the distribution account numbers on the invoice as well as the purchase order lines or receipts the invoice is matched to, but not the total amount of the invoice. This option will not enable changes to the purchase order or receipts themselves.

TABLE 5-3   *Payables Options Invoice Settings*

Option	Control
Recalculate Scheduled Payment	The due date for an invoice is based on the field selected in the Payables System Option when the invoice is entered. Selecting this option will recalculate the due date when the invoice is validated, based on the latest information on the invoice, to create the most optimal, or latest, due date. When this is selected, EBS will not override any manual changes or splits that have been made to the payment schedule for the invoice.
Receipt Acceptance Days	When Recalculate Scheduled Payments is selected, one of the options for basing the terms date is Goods Received. Goods Received can add a few days to the date of the receipt as specified in the Receipt Acceptance Date, to allow for processing time.
Allow Remit-To Account Override	When suppliers are created, default bank accounts are added and used for funds remittance, and will be used when the invoice is paid. Checking this option will allow the users to override the bank account that defaults in from the supplier to any other bank account associated with the supplier.
GL Date Basis	Just as the due date can be calculated from different dates on the invoice, so can the General Ledger date, which is used to determine the period the invoice affects in the GL. Selections include Invoice Date, System Date, and Goods Received Date. Since the goods may not be received when the invoice is entered, it can default to the Invoice Date or the System Date when the received date is null.
Freight Account	When an account number is entered here, the distribution account will automatically populate on an invoice line when the line type is Freight.
Tax Tolerance-Tax	Allows tolerances to be set up for Sales, Offset, and User-Defined tax calculations. Invoices with tax lines that do not fall within this tolerances will be placed on hold. This tolerance is based on a percentage.
Tax Tolerance-Tax Amount Range	Creates a dollar range for taxes entered versus taxes calculated by the system where invoices will go on hold.
Prepayment Payment Terms	The terms entered here will default in for all prepayments, overriding the terms on the supplier.
Prepayment Settlement Days	The settlement date of a prepayment is the earliest date when EBS allows invoices to be matched to the prepayment. The settlement date is calculated by taking the payment date and adding the number of days entered here. When this field is not populated, then EBS uses the days from the supplier site terms date. (If the terms are set to net 30, then the prepayment settlement date is 30 days after the prepayment is paid.)
Prepayment Tax Difference Account	When populated, the tax difference account is used for any differences in the taxes paid on the prepayment and the taxes on the invoice applied to the prepayment.

TABLE 5-3   *Payables Options Invoice Settings* (continued)

Approval

Invoices, when entered in EBS, can be set up to require an approval prior to payment. This is a very good control if invoices are not being matched to purchase orders; it utilizes workflow notifications to get an approval prior to payment. This approval process is enabled when USE INVOICE APPROVAL WORKFLOW is checked. When invoices require approval, they must be either approved or rejected once the approval process is started. Approvals can utilize either a strict supervisor or a position hierarchy, or else they can have flexibility on who approves them by implementing Approval Management (AME). Selecting ALLOW FORCE APPROVAL will enable a designated person (this function can and should be restricted with the menu function Force Approve Invoices) to force the approval of an invoice for either payment or cancellation. There are two options on when the approval is required: either after validation or after the accounting has been performed.

When approvals are being used for invoices, the sequence of events for approval, accounting, and validation can be assigned in the APPROVAL PROCESSING SEQUENCE section. Select REQUIRE VALIDATION BEFORE APPROVAL if the invoice needs to be validated prior to being routed for approval, and REQUIRE ACCOUNTING BEFORE APPROVAL to ensure the system applies any subledger accounting rules to an invoice prior to routing it for approval. If neither of these are selected and approvals are being used, the invoice will be routed for approval once it is saved and meets two main criteria: the invoice header amount must equal the invoice distribution lines, and the check box READY FOR APPROVAL must be checked on the invoice window. This box is checked by default, but a user can uncheck it to prevent an invoice from being routed for approval while research is being done on the invoice.

Matching

The Matching tab determines how invoices are matched to purchase orders. ALLOW FINAL MATCHING will cause the match to the purchase order for this invoice to be the last action allowed to the purchase order, and it updates the PO status to Finally Closed. By definition, final matching of an invoice to the purchase order creates a status where no more invoices can be matched, and no changes can be made to the purchase order. Before selecting this option, understand that final is *final*; once the invoice is validated, no updates are allowed for incorrect matches or incorrect distribution lines on the purchase order or incorrect receipts.

Selecting ALLOW DISTRIBUTION LEVEL MATCHING will allow an invoice to be matched to one or more individual distributions that are associated with each shipment. When this is not selected, then invoices can only be matched to the shipment level. When an invoice is matched to a purchase order, the distribution account from the purchase order will default in as the distribution line for the invoice. ALLOW MATCHING ACCOUNT OVERRIDE gives the payables person the ability to override this default with a different account.

Descriptive Flexfields (DFFs) are fields that can be set up as required by your organization to track additional information about a transaction. DFFs that are set up on purchase orders can be transferred to the corresponding DFF on an invoice if TRANSFER PO DESCRIPTIVE FLEXFIELD INFORMATION is selected. In order for this option to work, the DFF structures on both the purchase order and the invoice will need to be exactly the same.

GOODS and SERVICES TOLERANCES are used to default the tolerances used when matching invoices to purchase orders. These tolerances are the system defaults both for creating new supplier sites and for transactions if there are no tolerances assigned to a supplier site. Select the tolerance set up during the purchasing setups that is appropriate for your organization (Payables Manager | Setup | Invoice | Tolerance).

Interest

When an invoice is past due for payment, EBS can be set up to automatically calculate interest and create interest invoices at time of settlement. ALLOW INTEREST INVOICES needs to be checked when using this functionality. A MINIMUM INTEREST AMOUNT can be set for generating an interest invoice, and the EXPENSE and LIABILITY accounts for the interest invoice transaction will need to be supplied.

Expense Report

Oracle EBS has two solutions for entering expense reports. The first comes embedded in Payables and allows the expense reports to be entered directly into a window in Payables. This option is usually used by the AP department when they enter expense reports for the rest of the organization. The second is a separate module called iExpenses, a web interface that allows users to enter expense reports, using predefined rules, download expense transactions for credit card companies, route them for approval, and send them to Payables for auditing and processing.

Both options use a template to build the expense report account numbers and provide a list of predefined expense categories. Select the DEFAULT TEMPLATE for the system, which will default in for all users but can be overridden based on the users' rights and the iExpense setups. APPLY ADVANCES will take any outstanding advances associated with the employee in Payables and reduce it from any expense report entered for that employee. If this option is not selected, Payables users can still manually apply prepayments to expense reports.

Whether EBS is using the full install of Human Resources or a partial install, employees can be linked to supplier records and maintained for payments. Selecting AUTOMATICALLY CREATE EMPLOYEE AS SUPPLIER will cause any employee with an expense report to be created as a supplier record, with the supplier type of Employee, and will also make any updates in names or addresses from Human Resources to Payables to update the supplier records. Default PAYMENT TERMS, PAY GROUPS, and PAYMENT PRIORITIES can be set for employee suppliers. The last option that can be set is if any expense reports created for suppliers should be held when they are not matched to a purchase order.

Payment

The Payment tab determines specific defaults for payments, such as whether tax should be excluded from a discount calculation. The ability to predate a single payment, or to allow the payments to be voided and reissued is also controlled here. When a single payment is created, EBS has the ability to enter a different mailing address than the one on the supplier record; check ALLOW ADDRESS CHANGE to enable this feature. Most organizations incur bank charges when funds are wired or electronically sent to the receiver's bank. Payables allows the bank charges to be passed on to the suppliers by reducing the amount from the payment when ENABLE BANK CHARGE DEDUCTION FROM PAYMENT is selected. Once turned on, the deduction can be set to a standard rate for the supplier or a negotiated rate.

Withholding Tax

Withholding tax, or the reduction of a tax obligation from the supplier settlement, can be set up in EBS to comply with different government regulations. Commonly used in other countries, this is usually used in the United States when there is a problem with the 1099 information reported to the government, and a company is required to withhold the flat rate of 28 percent (as of 2008) for all payments. USE WITHHOLDING TAX needs to be checked to use this feature. Selecting ALLOW MANUAL WITHHOLDING allows the user processing payables transactions to manually add a withholding transaction to a payment, and the TAX GROUP needs to be added to default the withholding taxes that should be calculated. Withholding Taxes can be set up to NEVER withhold, requiring all transactions to be manually withheld, or to be withheld when the invoice is validated, or when it is paid.

INCLUDE INCOME TAX TYPE ON WITHHOLDING DISTRIBUTIONS is used with 1099 withholding and will update the tax code for federal income tax withholding (Misc4) on the invoice lines. When calculating withholding, it is usually done only on the invoice and freight lines, but by selecting INCLUDE TAX AMOUNT, any tax lines will be included in the withholding calculation. When INCLUDE

DISCOUNT AMOUNT is selected, the withholding will apply to the full amount of the invoice as opposed to the discounted amount paid. The CREATE WITHHOLDING INVOICE option determines if an invoice is created for the amounts withheld, usually to the tax authority supplier, and can be created at time of validation or payment.

Reports

The Reports tab is used to determine if specific reports can be sorted by the Alternate Names field for Supplier, Supplier Site, or Bank Account. These are the only reports that use this feature:

- Accounting Entries Audit Report
- Cash Requirements Report
- Invoice Aging Report
- Invoice on Hold Report
- Invoice Register
- Preliminary/Final and Rejected Purged Listing
- Supplier Mailing Label
- Suppliers Paid Invoice History
- Supplier Report
- Unaccounted Transactions Report

Payment Terms

Payment Terms are required when entering an invoice; they determine the due date for the invoice. The due date is used by EBS when selecting invoices for settlement (along with other options), as well as determining the bucket the invoice will fall into on the Invoice Aging report. Referring to Figure 5-5, enter a NAME for the term. This is the name the users will see when reviewing or entering transactions and should be meaningful enough for them to know what this term is doing. Add a DESCRIPTION with additional information. The EFFECTIVE DATES will determine when this term can be used. Only a FROM date is required; the TO date should be left blank while the term is still being used, or it can be set to a future date if your company plans on not offering this term at a specific date in the future.

The CUT-OFF DAY is used for terms where the payment is due on the specific day of a month; it determines if the invoice should be due this month or the next. When an invoice is dated prior to the cut-off day, the due date will be the current month. When an invoice is dated after the cut-off day, then the invoice will have a due date of next month. This field is only used with DAY OF MONTH terms.

RANK is used with the RECALCULATE SCHEDULED PAYMENT option that was set on the Payables Options window (Payables Manager | Setup | Options | Payables Options). This feature allows EBS to recalculate a payment schedule, or the due date, each time an invoice is validated, based on the most recent information in EBS. Ranking comes into play when there is a different payment term on the purchase order than on the invoice that is matched to it. EBS will look at the two terms and use the most favorable terms for the company, pushing the payment out as far as possible. Rank is not the order in which the terms are used but notifies EBS that this term can be recalculated for the payment schedule.

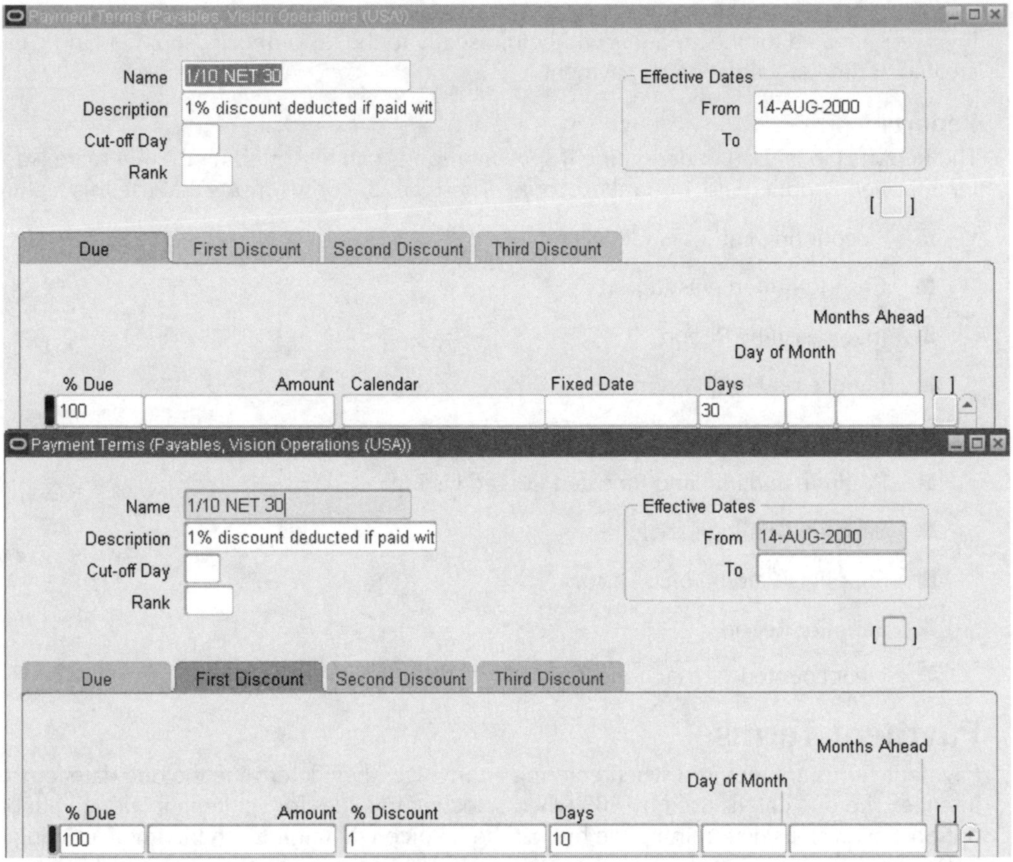

Payables Manager | Setup | Invoice | Payment Terms

FIGURE 5-5 *Payment Terms*

Payment Terms can range from something as simple as Net 30, or due in 30 days, to a complicated tiered schedule that requires a calendar and provides discounts. Ensuring the terms are set up correctly in EBS can help ensure cash flow is maximized (for instance, they can ensure that you do not pay invoices before they are really due, and any available discounts are taken). The % DUE setting is the amount of the invoice this line of the Term pertains to; it must total 100 percent for all lines. An AMOUNT can be added instead of a percent of the invoice, but ensure that the amounts entered equal the invoices this payment term is used on. AMOUNT and % DUE cannot be combined on one line or one payment term.

Once the amount of the invoice that a line is responsible for is defined, then the payment schedule needs to be identified. This schedule can be based on a Calendar, Fixed Date, Number of Days, or Day of the Month, all combined with a set number of Months Ahead. Table 5-4 shows how each of these different schedules is used to create the due date of an invoice. There are a few dates on an invoice that need to be understood when looking at these meanings. Terms Date is the date that EBS uses to calculate the payment terms, or actual due date, and is determined based on the Terms Date Basis assigned in the Payables System setup (Payable Manager | Setup |

Schedule	Meaning
Calendar	Special Calendars (see the next section for details on how to set up a special calendar) can be set up and used with Payment Terms to determine the date an invoice is due based on the terms date. For example, if the terms date of an invoice is between Jan 1 and Jan 15, then the due date for the invoice is Jan 31.
Fixed Date	This is used when the payment terms are due on a specific date—day, month, and year. Ensure this is used with caution, as it is a fixed date and cannot be dynamically changed.
Days	Days refers to the number of days after the terms date that the invoice will be due. If this is set to 30, then the invoice will be due 30 days after the terms date.
Day of Month	Day of Month is a specific day of the month that a payment is due. To default the due date to the last day of any given month, set this field to 31 and EBS automatically adjusts it to the last day of the month. This is the only schedule that can be used with the MONTHS AHEAD field, or alone.
Months Ahead	Used when a specific DAY OF MONTH is entered, it will determine which month the Day of Month will pertain to. If the Day of Month is set to 31 and Months Ahead is set to 0, then all invoices entered up to and including the last day of the current month will be due on the last day of that month (entered May 30, due May 31). If the Months Ahead is set to 1, then invoices entered in May will be due on June 30.

TABLE 5-4 *Schedules for Determining Payment Due Date*

Options | Payables System Setup). Due date, which is found on the Scheduled Payments tab of an invoice, shows the actual due date of an invoice and is based on the Terms Date and Payment Terms. It is the Due Date that is used when running an Invoice Aging or a settlement batch.

Up to three discounts can be added for each line of a term. The % DUE and AMOUNT will default in from the previous form, and updating it in either location will update both the term and the discount. Add a % DISCOUNT to identify the percent of the invoice that will be taken as a discount, and determine if that discount is available a set number of DAYS after the terms date or a specific DAY OF MONTH, either for the current month or a set number of MONTHS AHEAD. EBS has the ability to take a discount identified on a payment term even if the invoice was not paid within the discount period. This is set on the Payables System Options, with the ALWAYS TAKE DISCOUNT option.

Special Calendars

Special calendars (Payables Manager | Setup | Calendar | Special Calendar) are used for specific reasons in Payables, including Recurring Invoices, Withholding Tax, Payment Terms, and Key Indicators. Recurring Invoices use the calendar to determine the frequency that an invoice can be generated for. Withholding Tax uses the calendars to limit the amount of tax that can be withheld in any given time period. Payment Terms uses the calendar to determine the due dates for invoices with terms dates in a set time period, and Key Indicators refers to the time periods that the Key Indicators report will gather data for.

Give the calendar a NAME and DESCRIPTION, and determine the PERIODS PER YEAR that the calendar will have. This can be set to any number of periods, as long as they are all set up in the calendar. Select the TYPE OF CALENDAR that is being set up, based on the four usages described in the preceding paragraph. The next part of the calendar is set up exactly the same as an accounting calendar, assigning a PERIOD NAME, and the YEAR it pertains to. The SYSTEM NAME will default in as a combination of these two fields and can be overridden if need be. DUE DATE is only used for Payment Terms, and is the actual due date for any invoices where the terms date falls between the FROM and TO dates. REPORT RUN is only used with Key Indicators; it allows the Key Indicators report to be run using this calendar.

Aging Periods

The other type of calendar used in Payables determines the Aging Periods, or buckets, that appear on the Invoice Aging Report. When running this report, the Aging Period can be selected, allowing for multiple aging buckets to be set up to accommodate different organizational needs.

Add both a NAME and a DESCRIPTION for the aging periods, and ensure ACTIVE is checked, as seen in Figure 5-6. The COLUMN ORDER is the order that the columns will appear on the report, with 1 being to the farthest left. The FROM days value is the number of days from the invoice due date today is. Since the Invoice Aging report cannot be back-dated, it is always as of the current date. The TO days value represents the upper end of this bucket. Negative days are not yet due, and positive days are already past due. Remember when entering the day that *all* past due invoices and future-dated invoices are selected if you want this to be a balanced aging, showing all outstanding invoices. Starting the FROM value at -30 will never pick up any invoices that have a due date of more than 30 days from today, and only going out to 120 days will never pick up an invoices that are more than 4 months past due. COLUMN HEADINGS will appear on the report when it is printed.

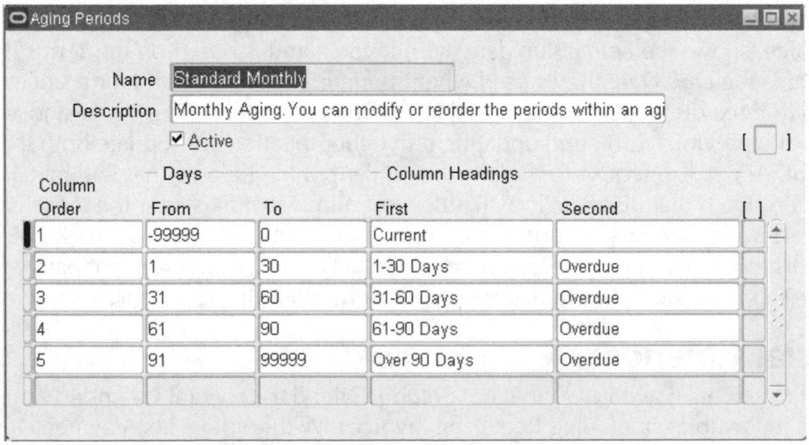

Payables Manager | Setup | Calendar | Aging Period

FIGURE 5-6 *Invoice aging calendar for periods*

Bank Setups

Banking information is entered for two reasons in Payables: to identify the bank account the funds are being disbursed from (internally owned) or to identify the bank account funds are being sent to (externally owned). In R12, banks are now owned by a combination of Cash Management and Trading Community Architecture, and they can be shared across operating units assigned to the same legal entity and country. Banks are grouped by country, giving EBS the ability to validate country-specific address formats as well as bank account formats. Also, while banks are shared across the system, bank accounts that are defined for suppliers are now separated from the bank accounts belonging to the organization. Bank Accounts for the suppliers are added to either a new bank or an existing bank in the bank details region of the supplier (Supplier | Entry | Banking Details).

Banks consist of the actual bank, branches, specific account(s), and payment documents associated with the account. From a technical standpoint, the tables underlying these components have also changed. Banks and their associated accounts were part of the AP schema in previous versions, but they have now been moved into Cash Management (CE). The new tables are described in Table 5-5.

Banks

Banks are set up and shared for both internally and externally owned banks. Internally owned banks are banks and their accounts owned by your organization, while externally owned banks are owned by the supplier themselves. Figure 5-7 shows the main bank setups. When creating a new bank, you have the option to either CREATE NEW BANK or SELECT AN EXISTING PARTY AND ADD BANK DETAILS. The main difference between the two is that the existing party (parties are suppliers) option links the bank directly to the supplier and names it the supplier name, while non-party accounts are not linked to suppliers and are named the actual name of the banking institution.

Select the COUNTRY the bank resides in and assign a BANK NAME. Then go back and select if this is creating a new bank or using an existing party to add additional bank details to. You can add an ALTERNATE BANK NAME if this banking institution or supplier bank has a second legal or commonly used name. The SHORT BANK NAME is seen on some of the forms in EBS. The BANK NUMBER can be added as an identifying number for this institution. Note that this is not the bank account number, as this bank can be used for multiple accounts. Add a DESCRIPTION for why this bank is used, remembering that banks can have multiple internal and external accounts associated with them. Two tax fields are available for tax identification numbers: TAXPAYER ID, which is used in the United States for the tax identifier issued by the government, and TAX REGISTRATION NUMBER, which is used in other countries for tax identification.

Table Name	Usage
CE_BANK_ACCOUNTS	Contains bank information at the legal entity level.
CE_BANK_ACCT_USES_ALL	Operating Unit bank account information is stored here.
CE_PAYMENT_DOCUMENTS	Payment document data available to banks.

TABLE 5-5 *New Bank Tables*

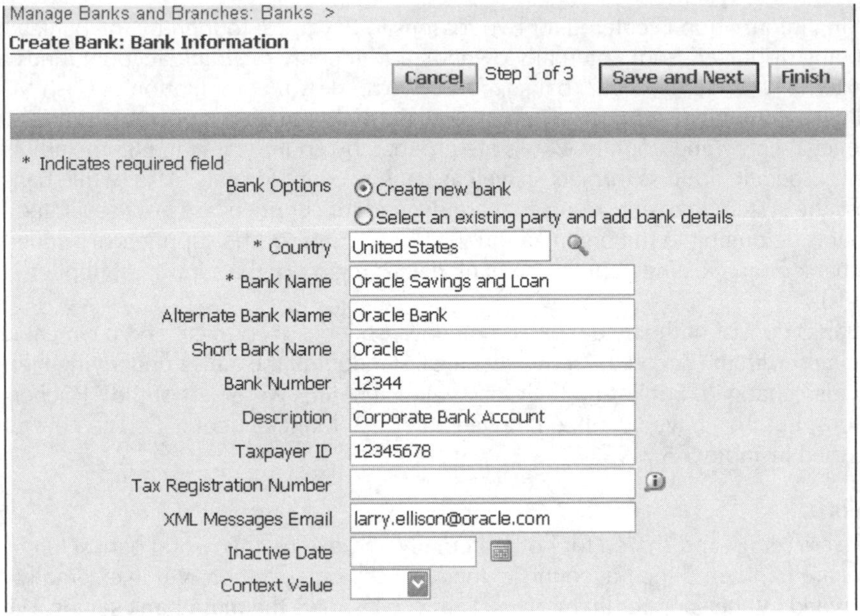

Payables Manager | Setup | Payment | Banks and Bank Branches | Banks tab

FIGURE 5-7 *Setting up banks*

Cash Management now has the ability to process XML bank statements via Oracle's XML Gateway. When this feature is used, an XML MESSAGES EMAIL address can be added to notify a person at the bank that validation failed for the transmitted file. The INACTIVE DATE is a date when this bank is no longer usable, and CONTEXT VALUES can be added for descriptive Flexfields that are enabled for the bank.

Once the Bank Information region is completed, Addresses and Contacts can be added to the bank. You can accomplished this by clicking SAVE AND PROCEED, or by returning later and adding them to the saved bank. The Address format is dictated by the country that was selected on the bank itself, allowing for address validation. In the United States, City, State, County, and Postal Code fields are suggested, but the address can be saved after receiving a warning if these are not completed. Only ADDRESS LINE 1 is actually required. An ADDRESSEE can be added to print with the address, such as Attention: Accounts Payable. The address can be inactivated with the STATUS field. A GEOGRAPHY CODE OVERRIDE can be added when this bank needs to integrate with Vertex and a third-party tax solution.

When adding a Contact, specific persons and contact information, such as e-mail addresses, phone numbers, and postal addresses, can also be saved. In addition to first, middle, and last names, the previous last name is tracked as well as an ALIAS. There is a field for PRONUNCIATION to store the phonetic spelling. The contacts JOB TITLE and DEPARTMENT can be added; they are particularly useful when multiple contacts exist. The only required fields are a START DATE and a REGISTRY ID. The REGISTRY ID is shown when the profile HZ: Generate Party Number is set to NO (System Administrator |

Profile | System), requiring the user to enter a unique identifying number for this contact. When this profile is set to YES, the ID is generated automatically by the system, and not seen on this screen.

Bank Branches

Once the Bank is saved, you can add a Branch, as seen in Figure 5-8. The COUNTRY and BANK NAME will default from the Bank when you click the CREATE BRANCH button next to the bank name in the Bank window. Again, Branches can be created new or added to an existing party. Then add either a BRANCH or PARTY NAME, along with an ALTERNATE NAME. The ROUTING TRANSIT NUMBER for the branch can be added here for this branch, as well as a BIC (Bank Identification Code) for the branch. The BANK CODE identifies the branch as using a CHIPS Code, a CHIPS Participation ID, or a Federal Routing Number that was listed in the Routing Transit Number field.

The BRANCH TYPE, used to identify the clearing house used for the payments, can be set to ABA for Federal Reserve System Routing, CHIPS for Clearing House Interbank Payments System, or SWIFT (Society for Worldwide Interbank Financial Telecommunication) for routing payments across country borders. If this branch is going to be used for EDI transactions, then the EDI LOCATION can be added. The company number provided by the banking institution can be added in the EFT NUMBER field for more accurate matching of Electronic Funds Transfer. The Regional Financial Centers (RFCs) are processing centers for banking institutions and are identified as AFC for Austin, BFC for Birmingham, CFC for Chicago, KFC for Kansas City, PFC for Philadelphia, and SFC for San Francisco. Once the branch is saved, contacts and addresses can be added to it.

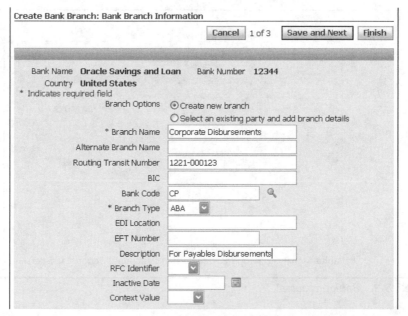

Payables Manager | Setup | Payment | Banks and Bank Branches | Bank Branches tab

FIGURE 5-8 *Bank branches*

Bank Accounts

Bank Accounts can only be created after the Bank and Bank Branch have been set up. After clicking CREATE in the Bank Account window, select the COUNTRY, BANK, and BANK BRANCH this account is to be associated with. At this point, specific account information can be added. Account information is broken down into five subcategories: Owner and Use, Information, Controls, Access, and Contact.

Account Owner and Use To create the account owner and usage, refer to Figure 5-9. First, select the OWNER of the account, which is the Legal Entity who has the legal rights over it. Then select the account uses, selecting from PAYABLES, PAYROLL, RECEIVABLES, and/or TREASURY (more than one use can be selected). The account uses will determine what subledgers can use the account, and what transactions can be created from it. Payables allows payments to be created, but it does involve additional setups, as outlined in Chapter 7. Payroll integrates with Oracle Payroll and is used for paying employees. Receivables transactions include funds received for open receivables and miscellaneous other reasons. Treasury, or Cash Management, encompasses bank charges, interest, and adjustments for deposits or disbursements, which are usually created with an interface with the bank.

Bank Account Information Next, specific account information can be added, as described in Table 5-6.

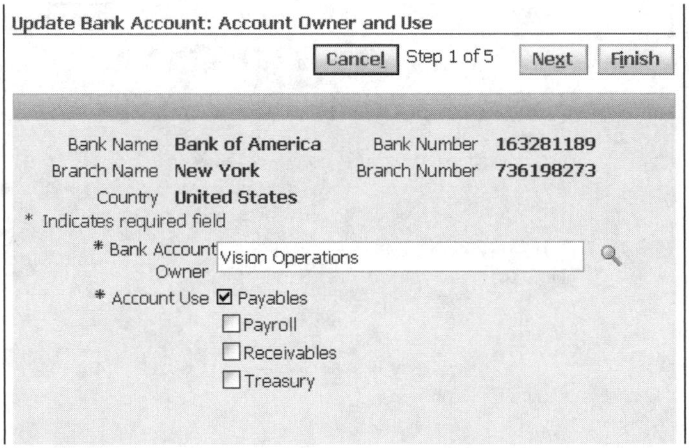

Payables Manager | Setup | Payment | Bank Account | Account Owner And Use

FIGURE 5-9 *Bank accounts*

Account Information	Required?	Description
Account Name	Yes	Name or usage of the bank account. Visible when assigning accounts to payment templates.
Alternate Account Name	No	Alternate name or spelling of a bank account. Can be used to select an account on a payment template.
Short Account Name	No	Name that appears on some windows; is limited to 30 characters.
Account Number	Yes	Actual bank account number.
Check Digit	No	Provides authentication to a bank that the account number is being used by an authorized user. This is not commonly used in the United States. The number is provided by the banking institution.
Currency	Yes	Select the main currency for the bank account. If the currency selected is not the same as the Ledger currency, ensure conversion rates are maintained.
Multiple Currencies Allowed	No	When selected, allows foreign currency disbursements to be cut out of this account (foreign being anything other than the Ledger currency)
IBAN	No	International Bank Account Number: a unique account number used in the EuroZone nation for banking across country borders.
Account Type	No	Select the type of account at the bank, such as Checking or Savings.
Account Suffix	No	Number assigned as an identifying segment of the account, used to determine the type of account. This length varies by country.
EFT Number	No	Unique number assigned to electronic funds transfers (EFTs), similar to a check number.
Secondary Account Reference	No	Additional referencing information for the bank account for internal use only.
Account Holder	No	Name of the person within the organization who is responsible for this account.
Alternate Account Holder	No	Alternate name of the person within the organization who is responsible for this account.
Description	No	Description of the account usage.
Start Date	No	First date the account allows transactions.
End Date	No	Last date the account will be used and allows transactions.

TABLE 5-6 *Bank Account Information Fields*

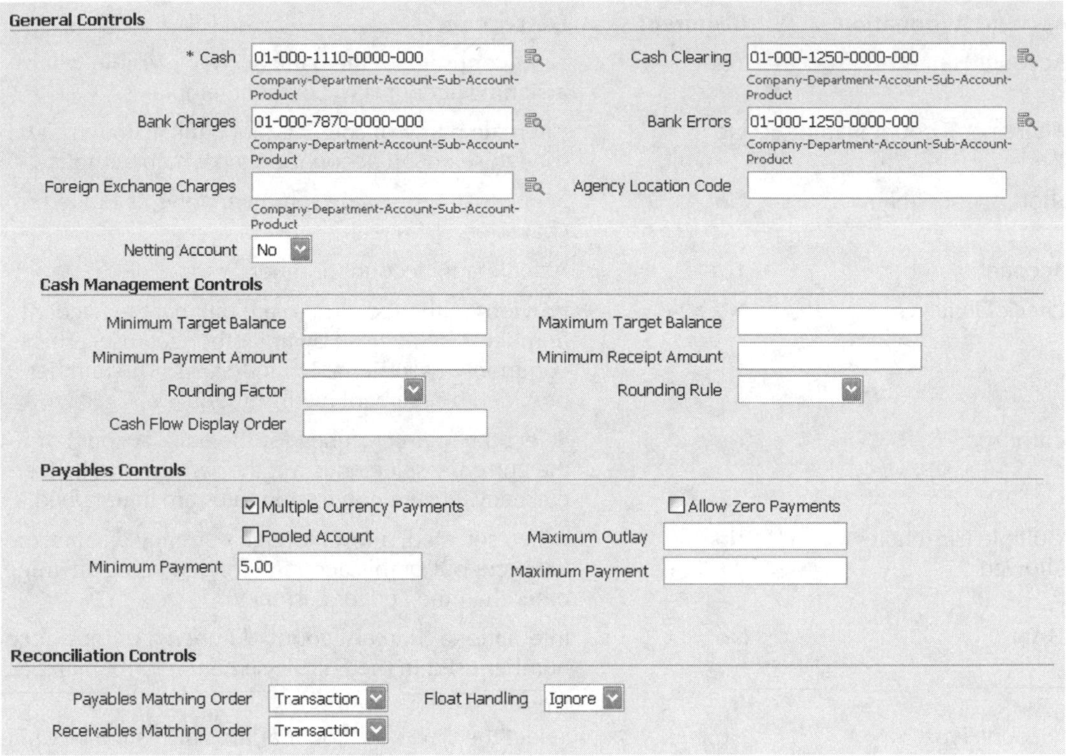

General Controls

* Cash	01-000-1110-0000-000	Cash Clearing	01-000-1250-0000-000
	Company-Department-Account-Sub-Account-Product		Company-Department-Account-Sub-Account-Product
Bank Charges	01-000-7870-0000-000	Bank Errors	01-000-1250-0000-000
	Company-Department-Account-Sub-Account-Product		Company-Department-Account-Sub-Account-Product
Foreign Exchange Charges		Agency Location Code	
	Company-Department-Account-Sub-Account-Product		
Netting Account	No		

Cash Management Controls

Minimum Target Balance		Maximum Target Balance	
Minimum Payment Amount		Minimum Receipt Amount	
Rounding Factor		Rounding Rule	
Cash Flow Display Order			

Payables Controls

☑ Multiple Currency Payments   ☐ Allow Zero Payments
☐ Pooled Account   Maximum Outlay
Minimum Payment 5.00   Maximum Payment

Reconciliation Controls

Payables Matching Order Transaction   Float Handling Ignore
Receivables Matching Order Transaction

Payables Manager | Setup | Payment | Bank Account | Update Account | Account Controls

FIGURE 5-10 *Bank account controls*

Bank Account Controls   Bank Account controls are added next to assign General and Reconciling controls for each module. Refer to Figure 5-10 for this next section.

The first section, General Controls, is where the General Ledger account numbers are assigned to the account. The CASH account is the actual asset account that will track the account balance. CASH CLEARING will get used, depending on the options select in the Payment Account section of the Payables Options (Setup | Options | Payables Options | Accounting Options tab). When Payments are set up to account when the payment clears, as opposed to Issued, then the Clearing Account is used. The BANK CHARGES account will be used to record any bank charges entered into Cash Management, a module used to reconcile bank accounts. The BANK ERRORS, used again by cash management, is where differences within the defined tolerances are recorded for checks created in Payables and reconciled to a bank statement in cash management. The FOREIGN EXCHANGE CHARGES account records differences in foreign transactions reconciled in cash management. An AGENCY LOCATION CODE can be added for United States federal government agencies. If this account is going to be used to net Receivables and Payables transactions, select YES for NETTING ACCOUNT.

In the next section, you can add Cash Management Controls, which are used in cash projections, including MINIMUM and MAXIMUM TARGET BALANCES, and ROUNDING FACTORS, determining if the data is displayed in thousands, millions, and so on, and ROUNDING RULES of NEAREST, UP, or DOWN. You can set a MINIMUM PAYMENT amount, preventing checks from being cut for under a certain dollar amount, as well as a MINIMUM RECEIPT AMOUNT for automatic receipts in accounts receivable. CASH FLOW DISPLAY ORDER can be populated to dictate the order a bank account is shown for a specific currency. For example, setting this field to 1 will ensure that this bank account will display first for all USD selections.

Add Payables Controls to determine if the account can be used for MULTIPLE CURRENCY PAYMENTS or not. This option is only available if MULTIPLE CURRENCIES ALLOWED was selected under the General Controls. Sometimes it is necessary to make zero dollar payments to clear invoices and credit memos from the Payables aging, which are permitted on this account when ALLOW ZERO PAYMENTS is checked.

Select POOLED ACCOUNT when the Automatic Offset Method in the Payables Options (Setup | Options | Payables Options | Accounting Options tab) is set to Balancing. This will allow a single cash accounting entry to be made from each liability account, as opposed to one entry per transaction based on the Cash Account set up on the bank account.

Set the MAXIMUM OUTLAY to cause a warning to the users when the total outlay for a payment batch is greater than this amount, although it will still allow the payments to be processed. The MINIMUM PAYMENT and MAXIMUM PAYMENT are used when creating payment batches to determine the transactions that are selected for payment. Both of these fields in the Payables Controls will override the minimums and maximums set in the Cash Management section of bank accounts.

For Receivables, select MULTIPLE CURRENCY RECEIPTS to allow receipts to be recorded in a currency other than the primary Ledger currency. This can only be selected if MULTIPLE CURRENCIES ALLOWED was selected under the General Controls.

Reconciliation Controls are set for reconciling transactions in Cash Management to bank accounts. PAYABLES MATCHING ORDER, or the order that the transactions are processed to match the bank statements, can be set to either TRANSACTION or BATCH, depending on the level of details received from the bank. This matching order can also be set for receivables transactions. FLOAT HANDLING determines how effective dates later than the current dates will be handled when the lines are reconciled. IGNORE will reconcile future dated lines, while Error handling depends on whether automatic reconciliations are being used or not. If they are, then these transactions will error out during the automated reconciliation. When using manual reconciliations, then the transactions will give the user a warning, allowing that user to reconcile the line by ignoring the error, or not to reconcile the statement line.

Foreign Currency Banks, seen in Figure 5-11, should be assigned a default EXCHANGE RATE TYPE as well as a DATE. The date used to determine the exchange rate has several options: BANK STATEMENT DATE or GL DATE, STATEMENT LINE DATE, or based on dates on the transaction, such as the TRANSACTION CREATION DATE, GL DATE, or EXCHANGE RATE DATE.

Open Interface Controls are used by the AutoReconciliation program and determine how transactions are mated during the process. Selecting USE RECONCILIATION OPEN INTERFACES will enable this feature, while the OPEN INTERFACE MATCHING CRITERIA setting determines how transactions will be matched during autoreconciliation. The choices are DATE AND AMOUNT or TRANSACTION NUMBER. FLOAT STATUS identifies the status of transactions that are available for clearing, while the CLEAR STATUS is the status assigned to the transaction after it is cleared.

Under Manual Reconciliation Tolerances, TOLERANCE AMOUNTS and TOLERANCE PERCENTAGES can be set for matching check amounts from Payables to the bank statements, with any transactions falling within the tolerances creating a journal in the Bank Errors or Charges account. TOLERANCE DIFFERENCES determines which of these two accounts are used. FOREIGN TOLERANCE DIFFERENCES determines how differences are handles when the currency conversions are out of balance with the bank: Booked into the Charges/Errors account, as a Gain/Loss, or no action at all. These same tolerances are available for Receipts, Cashflows, and Open Interface.

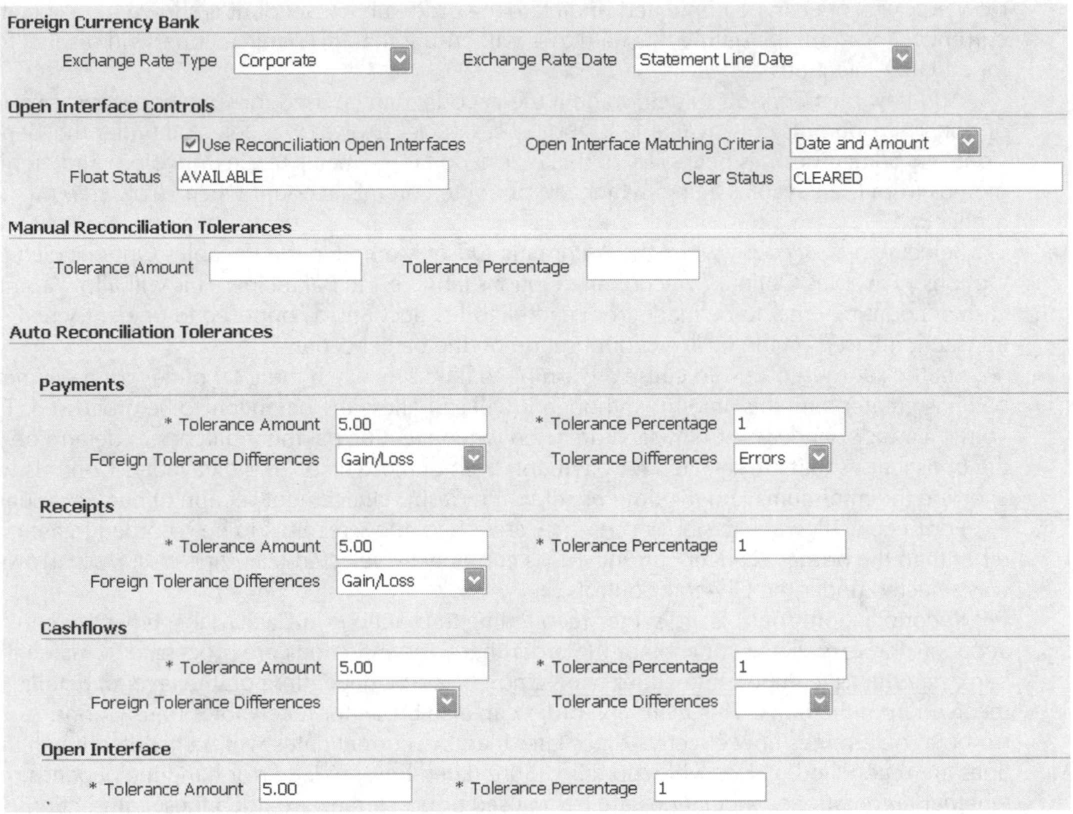

FIGURE 5-11 *Additional bank account controls*

Next is to add the Organization Access to a bank account, shown in Figure 5-12. Select ADD ORGANIZATION ACCESS, and check if the ACCOUNT USE will include PAYABLES, PAYROLL, RECEIVABLES, or TREASURY. Each bank account can be used for multiple purposes. Then select the ORGANIZATION you want to grant access to. When this account is not going to be used in this Organization any more, add an END DATE. This can be repeated multiple times to grant access to multiple organizations.

Next, you can add specific payables options to override accounts set up in the preceding step, for CASH, CASH CLEARING, BANK CHARGES, and BANK ERRORS. All of these will default from the General Controls and can be overridden for each Organization, giving account control not to the bank account, but to the organization. You can set up additional accounts for Realized Gain and Loss, as well as Future Dated Payments, also called Bills Payables in other locations in R12. You can

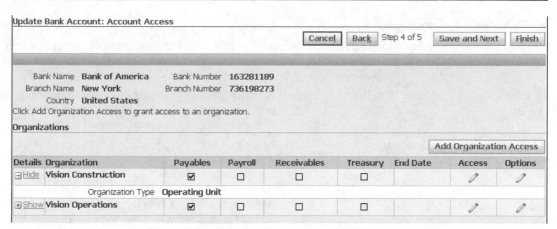

Payables Manager | Setup | Payment | Bank Account | Account Access

FIGURE 5-12   *Bank account access*

assign a default payment document category to the organization, as well as assign specific payment document categories to a specific payment method, ensuring the correct categories are used.

You can also add contacts for this specific bank account.

Once the account is saved, it can be queried back up, and two options are available: UPDATE ACCOUNT and MANAGE PAYMENT DOCUMENTS. The UPDATE ACCOUNT button will allow any of the information just saved to be modified. MANAGE PAYMENT DOCUMENTS allows a review of any skipped documents that were recorded during the payment process, as well as marking these checks or documents as Void at this time. This is usually used with preprinted forms.

Open First Payables Period

Before processing can begin in Payables, the first period needs to be opened. Payables periods are controlled independently of other subledger periods, such as General Ledger, though they do use the same calendar. This means that the Payables calendar is set up at the same time the General Ledger calendar is, but they are opened and closed independently. The Payables periods are controlled in Payable Manager | Accounting | Control Payables Period.

Profiles

The final required step in setting up Payables is setting the profile options. Both required and optional profiles are listed in Table 5-7.

Profile Name	Required?	Controls
MO: Operating Unit	Required, no default	Set this profile to identify a specific operating unit for a responsibility. In R12, this should not be set at the site level, or it will not allow using MOAC.
MO: Security Profile	Conditionally, no default	Set this profile to grant access to a responsibility to multiple operating units. Either the Security Profile or the Operating Unit profile must be set.
AP: Notification Receipt E-mail	Optional	Adding a user's e-mail address to this profile will cause a notification to be sent to that user every time the Concurrent Request Notification is completed. This process can be added to a request set so that a specific person or e-mail address is notified when the request set completes successfully.
AP: Use Invoice Batch Controls	Optional, defaults to No	Determines if invoices are entered in Batches for balancing purposes, or as individual invoices. This must be set to YES to create batches from the Payables Open Interface Import. EBS does not allow invoices to be entered in both batch and non-batch modes at the same time.
AP: Show Finally Closed POs	Optional, defaults to No	Determines if Finally Closed purchase orders are seen when matching from an invoice. Even when set to YES, invoices cannot be matched to POs that are finally closed, and the information is for reference only.
AP: Invoice Approval Workflow User	Optional	Person who has access to perform system approvals or rejections during the Payables approval process
Default Country	Optional	When set, this profile will default the country in when entering supplier addresses. The default can be overridden during data entry.
Folders: Allow Customization	Optional, defaults to Yes	Can be set at the user level to prevent updates to folders assigned to a user.
Sequential Numbering	Optional, defaults to Not Used	Determines if sequential numbering on transactions is ALWAYS USED, PARTIALLY USED on some transactions, or NOT USED.

TABLE 5-7   *Payables Profiles*

Optional Setups

There are additional setups that are only required when specific functionality will be used or when adding additional selections, such as Hold Reasons

Hold and Release Reasons

EBS comes with the ability to place holds on invoices to prevent payment, both manually and automatically by the system. System holds are placed and released during the invoice validation process, while manual holds can be added at any time to prevent payment. Some system holds can only be released by the system, while others can be released by the system or manually; manual holds can only be released manually. Using manual holds in EBS allows for better tracking of outstanding invoices, while preventing payment with the hold processes. For example, if an invoice needs to go to the CFO prior to approval, and invoice approvals is not being used in EBS, then it can be entered in the system and placed on hold, ensuring that it is accounted for, and that it appears on the hold report for monitoring and follow-up. Setting up hold names and releases ensures that the reasons for the holds are known for greater tracking and follow-up.

System Holds

System holds are placed either when a supplier or system setup triggers one, such as when 3-way match is turned on and the purchase order is not received or when the distribution lines do not equal the total of an invoice. The system holds are both placed and released when the problem is resolved during the invoice validation process. While some system holds have to be resolved and released via validation, some can also be released manually. Table 5-8 lists the seeded system and manual holds and releases. While most system holds allow for accounting, there are a few that do not and the problem must be resolved before Subledger Accounting can be completed on that invoice and the transaction sent to the General Ledger.

Adding New Manual Holds and Releases

You can add more manual holds and releases in EBS, as shown in Figure 5-13. The NAME is what the users will see when selecting either a hold or a release, and should be meaningful to them, while the DESCRIPTION appears on the hold report. The HOLD TYPE determines if it is a hold or a release. Also, the type determines where the hold is applied or released. Manual holds can be applied to either an Invoice or a Line, and manual releases in the Quick Release window, to Invoice, Line, or Matching or Variance issues. ACCOUNT ALLOWED determines if the Subledger Accounting process can take place on an invoice. When this is not selected, then the hold must be resolved prior to the transaction being accounted.

Hold Name	Description	System or Manual?	Hold Type	Allow Accounting?	Manual Release?	Correction when Manual Release not allowed
Invalid PO	Invoice has invalid or missing PO number	Manual Hold	Invoice Hold Reason	Yes	Yes	
Invoice Cancel	Invoice cannot be canceled	Manual Hold	Invoice Hold Reason	Yes	Yes	
Payment Approval	Awaiting payment approval	Manual Hold	Invoice Hold Reason		Yes	
Secondary Approval	Awaiting secondary approval	Manual Hold	Invoice Hold Reason		Yes	
Holds Quick Released	Holds released	Manual Release	Hold Quick Release Reason	Yes	Yes	
Invoice Quick Released	Invoice released	Manual Release	Inv Quick Release Reason		Yes	
Natural Account Tax OK	Tax code updated to match natural account	Manual Release	Invoice Release Reason		Yes	
Reduced Amount	Invoice amount lowered	Manual Release	Invoice Release Reason		Yes	
Supplier Updated	Supplier or site updated	Manual Release	Invoice Release Reason		Yes	
Validated	Hold released	Manual Release	Invoice Release Reason		Yes	
Match Override	Matching hold approved	Manual Release	Matching Release Reason		Yes	
Matched	Passed matching condition	Manual Release	Matching Release Reason		Yes	
Variance Corrected	Invoice variance corrected	Manual Release	Variance Release Reason		Yes	
Variance Override	Variance hold released	Manual Release	Variance Release Reason		Yes	
Awt Acct Invalid	Automatic withholding tax account is invalid	System Hold	Acct Hold Reason			Correct the automatic withholding tax
Dist Acct Invalid	Distribution account is invalid	System Hold	Acct Hold Reason			Either change the distribution account, or enable the account causing the problem

TABLE 5-8   *Seeded System and Manual Holds and Releases*

Hold Name	Description	System or Manual?	Hold Type	Allow Accounting?	Manual Release?	Correction when Manual Release not allowed
ERV Acct Invalid	Cannot create exchange rate variance account when using Automatic Offsets	System Hold	Acct Hold Reason			Enter a valid exchange rate account
Funds Check	Funds checking could not be performed because no budget exists for the account and accounting period, or the invoice account is not the same as the purchase order account, or the detail account is no longer assigned to a parent	System Hold	Funds Hold Reason			Use a different account, or enter a budget for the account selected
Insufficient Funds	Insufficient funds exist for this invoice distribution	System Hold	Funds Hold Reason		Yes	
No Rate	Invoice is not in functional currency and has no exchange rate	System Hold	Insufficient Information			Enter a valid exchange rate
Amount	Invoice amount exceeded limit specified on the supplier site	System Hold	Invoice Hold Reason	Yes	Yes	
Exchange Protocol Hold	Awaiting exchange protocol approval	System Hold	Invoice Hold Reason		Yes	
Exp. Report – No Bill	Waiting for a bill to back up an expense report	System Hold	Invoice Hold Reason		Yes	
Natural Account Tax	Invoice tax code does not match the natural account tax code set up in the Tax Options. This is used when the E-Tax option to Enforce Tax from Account is set.	System Hold	Invoice Hold Reason		Yes	
Supplier	Hold all unvalidated invoices for supplier, and is assigned when the supplier site is set up to Hold Unvalidated Invoices	System Hold	Invoice Hold Reason	Yes	Yes	
Withholding Tax	Can't perform automatic withholding tax	System Hold	Invoice Hold Reason		Yes	
Can not Execute Allocation	Allocation generates an invalid account	System Hold	Line Hold Reason			Correct Allocation account or enable account

TABLE 5-8 *Seeded System and Manual Holds and Releases* (continued)

Hold Name	Description	System or Manual?	Hold Type	Allow Accounting?	Manual Release?	Correction when Manual Release not allowed
Can not Generate Distributions	Line does not contain enough data to produce distributions, applied when automatic distributions are generated	System Hold	Line Hold Reason			Correct reason for distributions not generated, usually an invalid account number
Can not Overlay Account	Overlay generates an invalid account	System Hold	Line Hold Reason			Correct account number being generated
Inactive Distribution Set	Line references an inactive Distribution Set	System Hold	Line Hold Reason			Reactivate the distribution, or remove the reference
Invalid Default account	Line references an invalid default account	System Hold	Line Hold Reason			Correct default account or enable default account
Line Variance	Total of invoice lines does not equal invoice amount	System Hold	Line Hold Reason			Correct Line or Invoice amounts to agree
Skeleton Distribution Set	Line references a skeleton Distribution Set	System Hold	Line Hold Reason			Enter amounts on the Distribution Set
Amt Ord	Amount billed exceeds amount ordered, above the tolerances	System Hold	Matching Hold Reason	Yes	Yes	
Amt Rec	Amount billed exceeds amount received, above the tolerances	System Hold	Matching Hold Reason	Yes	Yes	
Can't Close PO	Cannot close PO before shipment is fully delivered when Online Receipt Accruals are enabled	System Hold	Matching Hold Reason	Yes	Yes	
Can't Try PO Close	Cannot try PO close because invoice has unreleased holds	System Hold	Matching Hold Reason	Yes		Correct the holds on the invoice to close the PO
Currency Difference	Invoice currency different from PO currency	System Hold	Matching Hold Reason	Yes	Yes	
Final Matching	PO has already been finally matched to another invoice	System Hold	Matching Hold Reason	Yes		Match the invoice to a PO that is not finally closed
Matching Required	Invoice is not matched to any PO, and is applied when Hold Unmatched Invoices is enabled in the supplier site	System Hold	Matching Hold Reason	Yes	Yes	
Max Amt Ord	Amount billed exceeds amount ordered by Maximum Amount Ordered tolerance amount	System Hold	Matching Hold Reason	Yes	Yes	

TABLE 5-8 *Seeded System and Manual Holds and Releases* (continued)

Hold Name	Description	System or Manual?	Hold Type	Allow Accounting?	Manual Release?	Correction when Manual Release not allowed
Max Amt Rec	Amount billed exceeds amount received by Maximum Amount Received tolerance amount	System Hold	Matching Hold Reason	Yes	Yes	
Max Qty Ord	Quantity billed exceeds quantity ordered by Quantity Ordered tolerance amount	System Hold	Matching Hold Reason	Yes	Yes	
Max Qty Rec	Quantity billed exceeds quantity received by Quantity Received tolerance amount	System Hold	Matching Hold Reason	Yes	Yes	
Max Rate Amount	Exchange rate variance exceeds limit set in tolerances	System Hold	Matching Hold Reason	Yes	Yes	
Max Ship Amount	Variance between invoice and shipment amount exceeds Amount tolerance limit	System Hold	Matching Hold Reason	Yes	Yes	
Max Total Amount	Sum of invoice and exchange rate variances exceeds limit	System Hold	Matching Hold Reason	Yes	Yes	
Milestone	Invoiced quantity/amount is not equal to Milestone pay item	System Hold	Matching Hold Reason			Update the milestone or the invoiced amounts matched to the milestone
PO Not Approved	PO has not been approved	System Hold	Matching Hold Reason	Yes	Yes	
Price	Invoice price exceeds purchase order price by more than the tolerance. This is based on a weighted average of all the distribution lines and price corrections	System Hold	Matching Hold Reason	Yes	Yes	
Qty Ord	Quantity billed exceeds quantity ordered by more than the tolerance	System Hold	Matching Hold Reason	Yes	Yes	
Qty Rec	Quantity billed exceeds quantity received by Quantity Received tolerance amount	System Hold	Matching Hold Reason	Yes	Yes	
Quality	Quantity billed exceeds quantity accepted	System Hold	Matching Hold Reason	Yes	Yes	
Rec Exception	Receiving Exception on receipt	System Hold	Matching Hold Reason	Yes	Yes	

TABLE 5-8 *Seeded System and Manual Holds and Releases* (continued)

Hold Name	Description	System or Manual?	Hold Type	Allow Accounting?	Manual Release?	Correction when Manual Release not allowed
Tax Difference	Invoice tax code different from PO tax code, or they are the same but the Taxable Flag on the purchase order shipment is set to No	System Hold	Matching Hold Reason	Yes	Yes	Correct Line or Invoice amounts to agree
Dist Variance	Total of invoice distributions does not equal invoice amount	System Hold	Variance Hold Reason			
Prepaid Amount	The prepaid amount including tax exceeds the invoice amount	System Hold	Variance Hold Reason	Yes		Unapply the prepayment and reapply a lower amount
Tax Amount Range	Invoice tax amount does not fall within range, including the tolerance	System Hold	Variance Hold Reason	Yes	Yes	
Tax Variance	Invoice tax amount is not equal to the calculated tax amount, including the tolerance	System Hold	Variance Hold Reason	Yes	Yes	
Awt Acct Valid	Automatic Withholding Tax Account is now valid	System Release	Acct Release Reason			n/a
Dist Acct Valid	Distribution account is now valid	System Release	Acct Release Reason			n/a
ERV Acct Valid	Exchange rate variance account is now valid	System Release	Acct Release Reason			n/a
Funds Now Available	Sufficient funds now exist	System Release	Funds Release Reason			n/a
Passed Funds Check	Funds checking was performed	System Release	Funds Release Reason			n/a
Exp. Report-Received bill	Released Holding Expense Report – Received bill and reviewed it	System Release	Invoice Release Reason			n/a
Tax Withheld	Performed automatic withholding tax	System Release	Invoice Release Reason			n/a
Workflow Process	Release of hold by supervisor/manager	System Release	Invoice Release Reason			n/a
Rate Exists	Invoice exchange rate is now available	System Release	Sufficient Information			n/a

TABLE 5-8 *Seeded System and Manual Holds and Releases* (continued)

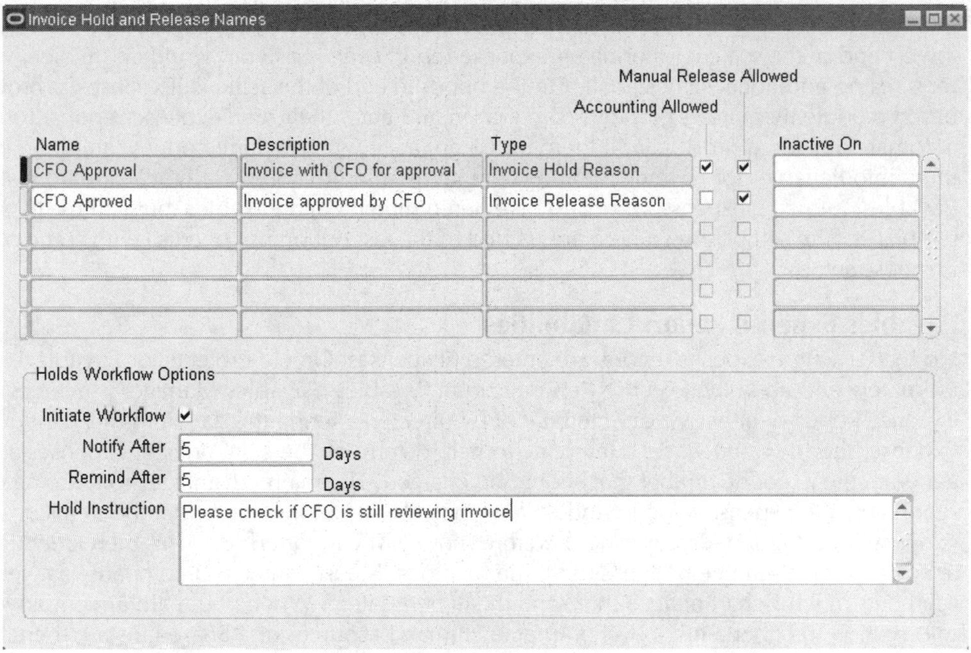

Payables Manager | Setup | Invoice | Hold and Release Name

FIGURE 5-13 *Creating holds and release reasons*

One of the criteria for month end is that all transactions must be accounted, or else the transaction will have to be swept, or moved, into the next period. Leaving transactions on a hold where accounting is not allowed will cause this to happen. MANUAL RELEASE ALLOWED determines if a user can release the hold, or if the reason for the hold needs to be resolved within the system. An example of this would be, do you want users to be able to release invoices put on hold because the 3-way match tolerances are not met by a receipt, or do you want to release the hold only by fixing the problem (as by receiving the transaction or removing the match to the purchase order)? Adding an INACTIVE ON date will prevent a hold or release from being applied after that date.

Holds Workflow Options is a nice feature that sends out notifications when the Holds Resolution workflow is set up; using this feature, a hold can be applied that can be manually released, using Oracle's Application Manager (AME) to determine who is going to be notified. This will send out a notification to the person identified, informing him or her of the hold. To set up EBS to send out hold notifications, first add the INITIATE WORKFLOW option to any hold that is set up with MANUAL RELEASE ALLOWED. Add the number of days for the first notification to go out in NOTIFY AFTER, and a second notification in REMIND AFTER. A message for the notification can added in the HOLD INSTRUCTIONS. Once this is completed, then AME needs to be set up for the transaction type APHLD. AME is a module that integrates with many subledgers, such as Payables and Human Resources, to set up approval hierarchies and conditions. The Holds Workflow will use AME to determine who should receive the notification about a hold.

Expense Report Templates

EBS has several options for processing expense reports, with varying degrees of features. At the lowest end of the scale is entering an expense report exactly as you would an invoice, which requires no additional setups at all. On the opposite end of the scale is iExpenses, a browser-based module that allows employees to sign in and enter their own expense reports, route them automatically for approval, audit them for compliance with corporate policy, and then integrate them into Payables for payment. Somewhere in the middle of these fall the standard features of Payables, allowing expense reports to be entered directly into Payables, but still using predefined templates. The setups shown here are related to the last option but overlap with some of the iExpense setups.

Payables Expense Report Capabilities

No matter where expense reports are entered (iExpenses, Oracle Projects, or Payables), they all ultimately end up in the Expense Report form in Payables (Payables Manager | Invoices | Entry | Expense Reports), either via an interface or by directly entering the data into this window. The Expense Report window uses a template to help determine the categories of expenses and to generate the account number that should be charged. The main advantages to entering expense reports via the Expense Report window as opposed to as an invoice is that the items on an expense report are predefined and therefore more easily reported on. Also, the General Ledger account number can be built based off the employee's cost center and company (as well as other segments in your chart of accounts), and the expense item. When you maintain employee address information in either a full install of Oracle Human Resources or a Shared Install, then the address and name information will be automatically updated when expense reports are created from the employee record.

Expense Report Template Setups for Payables

Expense reports are defined and entered by OPERATING UNIT, as assigned on the template shown in Figure 5-14. The TEMPLATE NAME is seen by the users when they enter expense reports in Payables. Adding an INACTIVE ON will make this template no longer available for use after this date. Selecting ENABLE FOR INTERNET EXPENSES will allow this template to be used in iExpenses as well as Payables Expense Reports. Selecting the ASSIGN CARD EXPENSE TYPE works with the integration if employee credit cards and iExpenses, creating a cross-reference between the credit card expenses and the template expense items.

   Enter a meaningful name for the EXPENSE ITEM; this is what appears on the Expense Report window when entering expenses. EXPENSE CATEGORY, used with iExpenses only, allows additional fields for information to be added, such as Airline when Airfare is selected. If taxes are required to be calculated on expense reports, add a TAX CODE to default in for all transactions entered against this expense item. The GL ACCOUNT determines how the account number is built for the expense report; it uses the client extension called AP_WEB_ACCTG_PKG.Build Account.

   Out of the box, the account number on an expense report uses the GL Account assigned to an expense item, combined with the Default Expense Account assigned on the employee record under Assignments region, on the Purchase Order Information tab. The way the default engine works is that any segment assigned on the Expense Report Template will override the employee account number. If the employee is assigned Company 01 Department 500 Account 7710 (01.500.7710), and the template has defaults for Company of 02 and Account of 7520 (02.(null).7520), then the account number assigned to the expense report will be 02.500.7520. With the exception of an END DATE, all the other fields on the templates pertain to iExpenses.

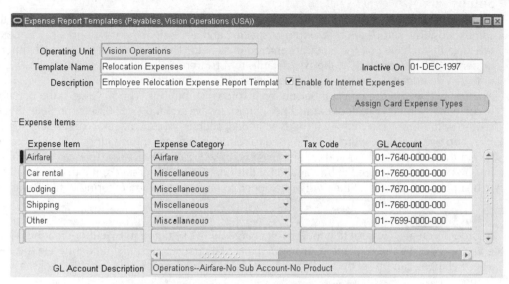

FIGURE 5-14 *Expense Report Template setup*

Once the template is saved, it can be either manually selected when entering an expense report or assigned on the Expense Report tab in Payables Options (Payables Manager | Setup | Options | Payables Options) as a default, which can be overridden in Payables when entering an expense report.

Distribution Sets

When entering invoices in Payables, you will find many times that a supplier or a specific type of invoice will have the same distributions assigned to it. Whether these distributions are just for the account numbers or for account numbers and a percentage of the bill, a Distribution Set can be used to reduce the amount of key punching, as well as potential typos, when entering the account numbers. Distribution Sets can be assigned as a default to a supplier site (Supplier | Accounting | Distribution Set) or added when entering an invoice or batch.

Skeleton Distribution Sets

Skeleton Sets assign only the account number, and not any amounts, when an invoice is entered. These work well when the invoice is provided with the breakout needed in relation to activity, such as a phone bill that comes with the expenses split by cost center, but the amount changes on a monthly basis, depending on actual usage. The accounts this invoice will be created for are static, but the amounts will change on a regular basis.

Fully Distributed Sets

A Fully Distributed Set will not only assign the account numbers, but using a percentage, it will assign an amount to each line item based on a percentage. This works well for invoices where a set percentage is allocated to a specific account or department and is not based on actual usage.

Setups

Both distribution set types are set up in the same window, shown in Figure 5-15, and use the same fields. The setups are OPERATING UNIT specific and get assigned a NAME and a DESCRIPTION. The TYPE defaults in based on the amounts entered in % field. The percentage must equal either 100 or zero. When it equals 100, the TYPE defaults to FULL. Zero will default to SKELETON. An INACTIVE ON date can be added when this distribution set should no longer be used.

NUM will create the line number on the invoice distributions. The % value is the percent of the invoice that should default onto this line; it must always equal 0 or 100 percent. Selecting PROJECT RELATED will allow PROJECT INFORMATION to be added, such as PROJECT, TASK, AWARD NUMBER, EXPENDITURE TYPE, and ORGANIZATION, which will be used to send the expense information to Oracle Projects. Select the default ACCOUNT and line DESCRIPTION, as will as the INCOME TAX TYPE tax reporting information that will need to be tracked for this line. Once this is saved, it can either be assigned to a supplier to default all the time or be added to an invoice when entering it into Payables.

Bank Charges

In order to create a transaction for a bank charge during settlement (by either creating a journal entry or reducing the settlement amount), the actual charges must first be defined in the system. These charges can be set up across the board for all banks, or for only specific banks, as seen in Figure 5-16.

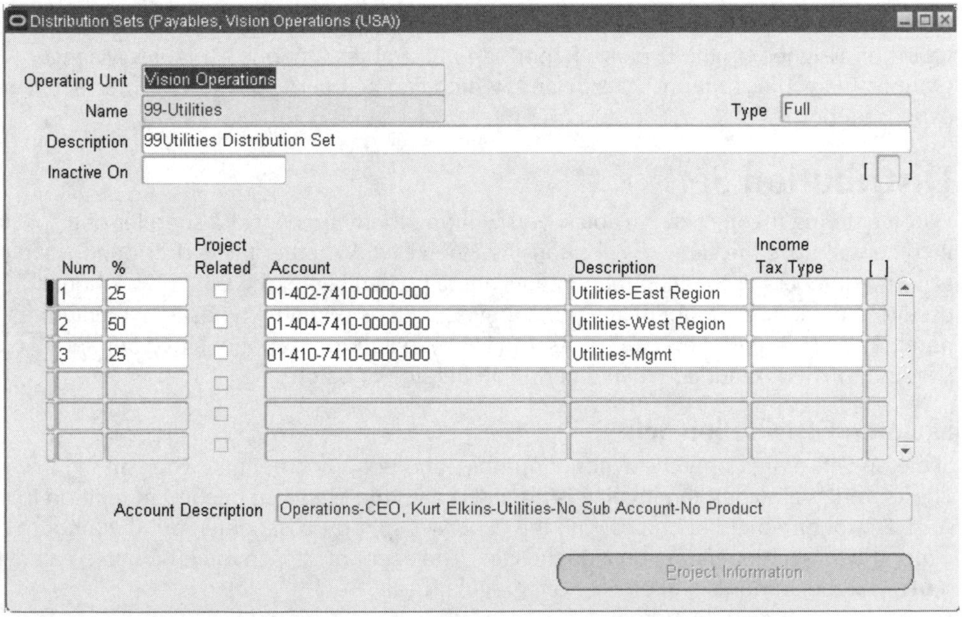

Payables Manager | Setup | Invoices | Distribution Sets

FIGURE 5-15 *Setting up Distribution Sets*

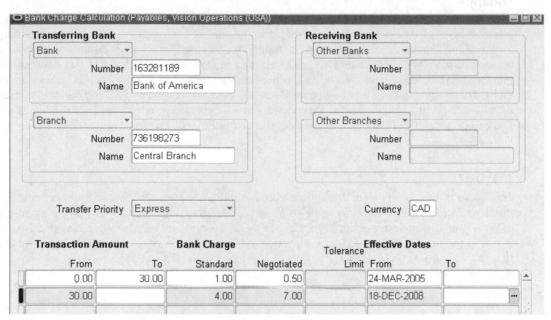

Payables Manager | Setup | Payment | Bank Charge Calculation

FIGURE 5-16 *Bank Charge setups*

First, enter the banking information for the Transferring Bank. Select either a specific BANK or ALL BANKS. When a specific bank is desired, add the NAME or NUMBER for the bank from the list of values. The same options are available for the BRANCH, selecting either a specific branch or ALL BRANCHES, but you also have a third option, ALL OTHER. Selecting this will generate bank charges when the Transferring Bank sends funds to any bank outside of itself.

This information is repeated for the Receiving Bank. The Transferring Bank is the bank owned by your company's legal entity, who is responsible for making a payment, while the Receiving Bank is the financial institution the funds are being sent to and is owned by the supplier you are paying. Since bank charges are only associated with electronic funds settlements and not check settlements, the receiving bank will have to be set up in EBS.

Next, determine if the TRANSFER PRIORITY will be for EXPRESS payments, NORMAL payments, or ANY payment. When the settlement is created, it will be identified as EXPRESS or NORMAL, which determines if charges will be incurred. Also, identify the CURRENCY for the settlement that relates to this charge. If you want the charges to relate to multiple currencies, then multiple bank charges will need to be set up.

For the Transaction Amount, only a FROM amount is required. You can add a TO amount to tier the charges based on the dollar amount of the transaction, but at least one TO field must be left open for all other amounts. You must enter amounts in these fields in dollars and cents (10.00), or an error will be encountered. You then enter both STANDARD and NEGOTIATED rates, and the setups for the supplier or invoice will determine which amount is used. Use a TOLERANCE LIMIT when bank charges are set up for receivables transactions, to indicate the tolerance allowed for any incoming bank charges. Add EFFECTIVE DATES for the charges, indicating the time period they are effective for.

Lookups

Throughout the system EBS uses the concepts of Lookups, which determines what data can be selected from a list of values when entering data. Besides being module-specific (there are lookups for Payables, Purchase, Employee, and Subledger Accounting that affect Payables transactions and windows), there are also different access levels for a lookup. An access level of USER denotes a field that can be updated or new lines added, while EXTENSIBLE lookups can only have new lines added to them. The existing data cannot be updated. SYSTEM is data that is used by EBS and cannot be changed or added to. When updating a list that appears in a list of values, note that it is usually either a Lookup or a Key Flexfield (such as Item or Account numbers). The lookup window is seen in Figure 5-17.

Folders

The folder option is prevalent throughout EBS, but it heavily impacts the data entry process for invoices. Folders allow the order of fields as well as the actual fields that are seen on a window to be changed. While this feature is not available on every window, it is denoted with a small file folder in the upper-left portion of the form when it is. Invoice Entry is an example of one of the places this feature can be used. There is a Folder menu as well as a Folder toolbar. Table 5-9 describes each option.

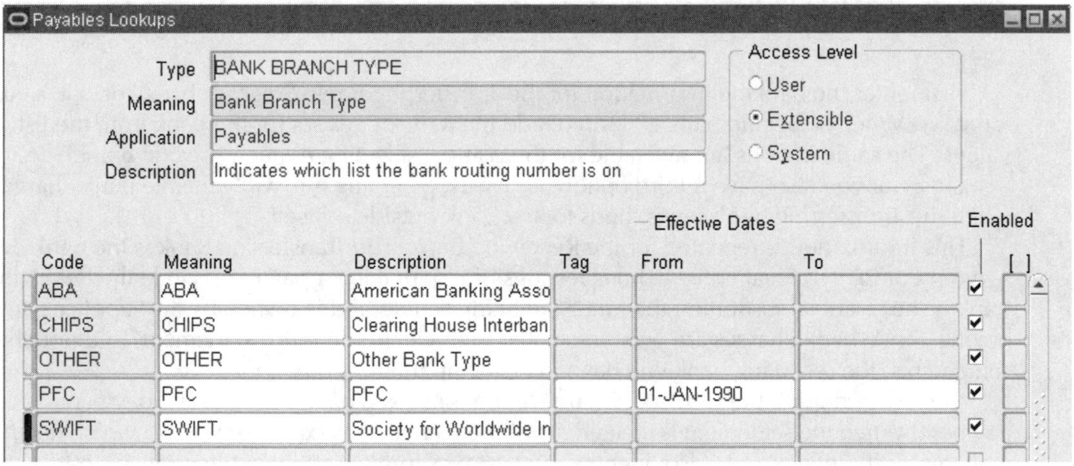

Payables Manager | Setup | Lookups

FIGURE 5-17 *Payables lookups*

Folder Option	Description	How to Use
New	Saves a new folder	Make the desired folder changes and save the folder as a New folder prior to closing the window.
Open	Opens an existing folder	Used to open any personal or shared folder.
Save	Saves changes to a folder	Save is used to save changes to any personal folder.
Save As	Saves a shared folder	When a folder is shared, any changes must be made under a personal folder, using Save As and changing the name.
Delete	Deletes any folder created by you	Folders can only be deleted by the creator or a system administrator.
Show Field	Shows additional fields	Many fields on windows that allow folders have hidden fields with data, which can be selected and shown.
Hide Field	Hides a visible field	Most fields can be hidden to reduce the data seen on the screen, but some required fields cannot be hidden.
Move Left, Right, Up, Down	Moves a field one position over	Fields can be moved by using this menu option or by putting the mouse over the field name to get a plus sign with arrows on the ends, then using the right mouse button to drag it to the desired position.
Widen Field	Increases field width	Fields can be increased or decreased to better view the data.
Shrink Field	Decreases field width	Fields can be increased or decreased to better view the data.
Change Prompt	Changes the name of a field in this folder only	Field Names can be changed within the folder only using this option, making them more in line with a company's lingo or policies. Right-clicking the prompt will also engage this feature.
Autosize All	Autoadjusts the field widths to the data in the fields	Uses a sampling of data in the underlying table, based on a record sampling of 10, 50, or 100.
Sort Data	Sorts data in form based on the first three data entry fields	This option will always sort on the first three fields only.

TABLE 5-9   *Folders Menu Options*

Folder Option	Description	How to Use
View Query	Displays query	Folders have the ability to save a query in a form, which can then be seen with this menu option.
Reset Query	Erases any queries in the folder	Resets the folder so that there is no query on it.
Folder Tools	Brings up the Folder toolbar	The folder toolbar can perform many (but not all) of the functions listed in the Folder menu.

TABLE 5-9   *Folders Menu Options* (continued)

Folders can only be saved by the person who created them. Any changes made to a public folder by a user who does not own it will have to be saved as his or her own folder, preventing one user from making changes to another person's folder. The main caution needed, when creating a folder, is that a query associated with a folder is only saved when it is really required. If a folder has a query, and is the default view for users, they will only be able to see data within the query, not all the data in the system, so ensure this is what is needed prior to saving.

When saving a folder, besides assigning a FOLDER name, there are a few other options available. AUTOQUERY can be set to ALWAYS, NEVER, or ASK EACH TIME. NEVER or ASK EACH TIME are safe options to ensure that data is not inadvertently restricted. Selecting OPEN AS DEFAULT causes the folder to always be a user's default, and unchecking this box and saving the folder will bring back the original view the next time the window is opened. Selecting PUBLIC will allow other users to select this folder for use as well.

Folders are not only powerful for reducing data entry; they ensure that data important to your organization is visible to the users. Before beginning to use folders, you can set a profile option to restrict what users can do with folders, called Folders: Allow Customization. If this is not set to NO (the default of NULL does give them access to customize folders), then all users will be able to create and modify folders. When this restriction is turned on, then users can only open existing public folders. Finally, users with access to the System Administrator responsibility, have the ability to modify, assign, or remove all folders.

CHAPTER
6

Payables Processing

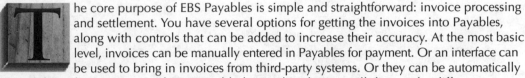he core purpose of EBS Payables is simple and straightforward: invoice processing and settlement. You have several options for getting the invoices into Payables, along with controls that can be added to increase their accuracy. At the most basic level, invoices can be manually entered in Payables for payment. Or an interface can be used to bring in invoices from third-party systems. Or they can be automatically created through activities in other EBS subledgers. This chapter will discuss the different processing options, as well as how to monitor and control the accuracy of the invoices and month-end processing.

Invoices

No matter how an invoice is entered into EBS, there are certain controls that take place prior to payment. Invoice Validation is the first of these controls, confirming that the invoice and line information is accurate in terms of the system setups and controls, and validations will also apply or release system holds according to the latest information pertaining to the invoice. Validation also creates system tax and miscellaneous transactions where applicable. Invoice Approvals can be used to route invoices for payment approval. Create Accounting is the last step in controlling the invoices, generating both the Payables liability and other offsetting distribution accounts to prepare the journal entries and send them over to the General Ledger.

Invoices in EBS have three main components: a header, lines, and distributions. The header relates to invoice-specific information generic to all lines, such as the invoice number, while lines identify the specific details relating to the goods or services received, tax, freight, and any miscellaneous charges. To create these details, multiple lines can be associated with each invoice header. Distributions contain detailed accounting information about each line, and again, multiple distributions can be created for a line.

Manual Invoices

Invoices can be created directly in Payables with a few different windows. While the entry points are different, the ultimate home for all these invoices is the Invoice Entry screen. The advantage of having different entry points is to reduce data entry time and increase accuracy by defaulting as much data as possible on an invoice. This section will discuss the following input windows for invoices:

- Creating batches for invoices
- Invoices
- Quick invoice entry
- Recurring invoices
- Expense report processing

Invoice Batches

The Batch window is used to group invoices and use a running total and counts for balancing, as well as defaulting batch specific information and the ability to perform Invoice Validation and Create Accounting for the entire batch. The default information added to a batch will be used on all the invoices in that batch, overriding supplier and system defaults. Invoices cannot be entered both with a batch and without one using the same setups; either one or the other has to be used, based on the profile AP: Use Invoice Batch Controls (System Administrator | Profile | System).

Invoices

This same window is used both when entering a single invoice or individual invoices within a batch, and allows the control of prepayments, entry of debit memos, applying credit memos to invoices, and creation of tax distributions, as well as performing actions on the invoice, such as validation or payment. The Invoice window is the ultimate home for all invoices entered into Payables.

Quick Invoice

The Quick Invoice window provides a streamlined entry screen for invoices, usually used for less complex transactions. Some of the advanced features, such as prepayments and matching credit memos, are not available in this window. When data is entered here, a process is run to move the transactions to the Invoices window via the Payables Open Interface, where additional validations take place.

Recurring Invoices

Not all payables transactions come with an invoice, but still require monthly payment. Rent is a good example of this. Recurring Invoices can be set up and generated each month as a consistent reminder to make these payments.

Expense Reports

While employee expense reimbursements can be entered as a regular invoice, using the Expense Report window provides a predefined list of expenditures, which helps to reduce data entry and increase accuracy, by generating account numbers based on the type of expense and account number associated with the employee record in EBS. The iExpense module, a web-based interface for entering expense reports, is also available, where expense reports can be routed for approval and audited by Payables for policy compliance.

Defaulting Information During Invoice Entry

After reading about setting up Payables in Chapter 5, and as you go through this next section on invoice processing, you will see that much of the controlling data on invoices defaults in from various sources. A hierarchy exists for these defaults, and understanding this hierarchy will help you to tune Payables setups to create accurate defaults and controls.

Controls begin with the system setups. While a majority of these default setups are found in the Payables Options (Setup | Options | Payables Options) and Financial Options (Setup | Options | Financial Options), there are additional places where default information is stored. The default setups will control the information that is populated when creating Suppliers, and can be overridden and updated on the address sites, where controlling information also resides. The site information is used as defaults for both purchase orders and invoices, with the purchase order information taking precedence when an invoice is matched to it.

Finally, when entering transactions using a Batch, additional defaults can be added that will override any system, supplier, or site defaults for this specific batch.

During invoice entry, the system works backward to determine the defaults for each invoice. First it looks to see if the invoice is matched to a purchase order and will take the controlling information from there. When the invoice is not matched to a purchase order, it checks if the invoice was entered in a batch which included any defaulting batch information. If not, it turns to the supplier site, and then the supplier setups themselves, to see what data should be used. The last place it looks is the system setups.

Let's take payment terms as an example. After the terms are set up in Setup | Invoice | Payment Terms, they can be added as a default in the Payables System Setups (Setup | Options | Payables System Setups). From here, this assigned payment term becomes the default terms when creating suppliers, which in turn default down to the supplier site. Invoice batches allow default terms to be identified for all invoices in the batch. When entering an invoice, note that the system looks first to see if it is matched to a purchase order that has terms associated with it, and if not, to see if it is in an invoice batch. If the terms are set on the batch, then these terms are adopted for the invoice. If it still does not find any default terms, the system checks the supplier sites, then the supplier, and finally the Payables System Setups. Following this hierarchy, the terms will default in from the first place term information is found.

The final overriding feature is for the accounting information on an invoice, which is added to invoices by the Subledger Accounting (SLA) process, creating liability and distribution accounts based on the SLA setups.

Invoice Batch Window

Batching invoices into groups for data entry assists not only with controlling the default data on invoices, but also with balancing. While batches cannot ensure the distribution account was correctly entered on an invoice, they can ensure that an invoice for $125 is not entered and paid for $1,250 by mistake. EBS accomplishes this by creating a control total that can be used for balancing. Also, if a large number of employees are entering invoices, it makes it easier to not only find, but also control, their individual invoices.

As seen in Figure 6-1, a BATCH NAME is assigned to each batch and must be unique. Developing a naming and batching convention early on in an implementation is beneficial in keeping the names consistent. Invoices can be batched into any grouping that makes sense for your organization, such as one based on type or entering person, and date. For a person- and date-based batching policy, a common naming convention is initials and date (MAC123108). The DATE defaults from the system date in EBS. CONTROL COUNT represents the number of invoices that you intend to enter, while the CONTROL AMOUNT is the total dollar amount. These numbers can be entered or changed at any point during the batching process; they are used by EBS to compare to the ACTUAL INVOICE COUNT and ACTUAL INVOICE TOTAL entered into the batch.

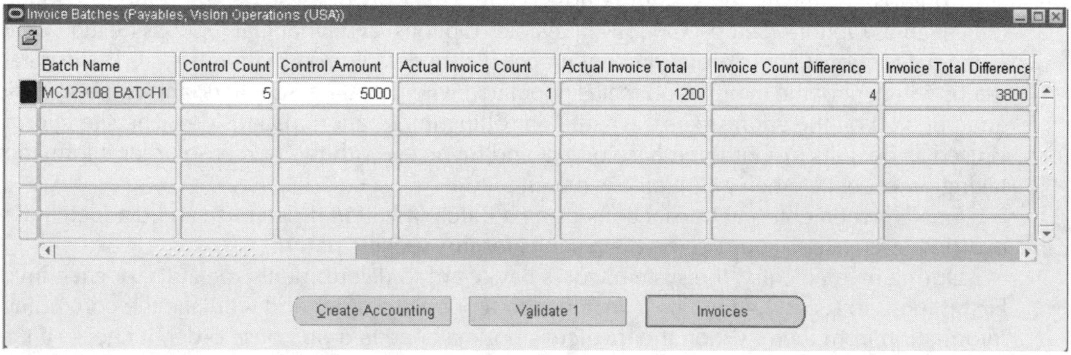

Batch Name	Control Count	Control Amount	Actual Invoice Count	Actual Invoice Total	Invoice Count Difference	Invoice Total Difference
MC123108 BATCH1	5	5000	1	1200	4	3800

Create Accounting   Validate 1   Invoices

Payables Manager| Invoices | Entry | Invoice Batches

FIGURE 6-1 *Entering invoice batches*

When using a daily batching policy, you can enter invoices throughout the day, and postpone entering the control totals onto the batch for balancing until the end of the day. EBS calculates both an INVOICE COUNT DIFFERENCE and an INVOICE TOTAL DIFFERENCE based on the entered control totals and the actual transactions. While this balancing is useful, it is important to understand that unbalanced batches, as well as batches without totals, can be saved in EBS with only a warning.

At this point, you can add default information to override system and supplier defaults on all the invoices entered in the batch. INVOICE CURR can be added when the invoices are in a different currency than the Ledger; this currency will populate into the PAYMENT CURR, which can be changed if needed. PAYMENT TERMS entered here will override any supplier-specific terms. Invoices can be entered as different types and will default from the INVOICE TYPE field. This and all the defaults can be overridden on each individual invoice as they are entered. PAY GROUP and PAYMENT PRIORITY, used when selecting invoices for payment, can be assigned at the batch level, as can the GL DATE. The last fields are HOLD NAME, to apply holds to an entire batch during data entry along with the HOLD REASON, and OPERATING UNIT if multiple units are accessible to this responsibility. Once an operating unit is selected, the LIABILITY ACCOUNT can be added to a batch to override the supplier defaults. You can also add a DOCUMENT CATEGORY, used with sequential numbering for invoices.

Because of these defaults, your organization's batching policy should be considered carefully; you should group like invoices and reduce data entry as well as potential errors. Batch default information must be populated prior to entering invoices, and adding information after the entry of invoices will *not* update any existing invoices in the batch, only becoming the defaults for any new transactions entered. Also, EBS will inform you if you exit a batch that is out of balance, but it will not prevent this batch from being saved or processed in any way. There are two reports, Batch Control Report by Batch Name and Batch Control Report by Entered By, that can be run and reviewed to ensure all batches are in balance.

Once all the invoices are entered for a batch, the entire batch can be validated from the Batch window if ALLOW ONLINE VALIDATION was selected in the Payables Options (Setup | Options | Payables Options). Selecting CREATE ACCOUNTING will create a draft accounting for all the invoices in the batch.

Invoice Workbench

Whether the batching feature is used or not, the same window is used for invoice entry. Invoice Inquiry (Invoices | Inquiry | Invoices), allowing invoices to be viewed but not updated, has the same fields as the Invoice Workbench window. When using batches, you can still query individual invoices and make updates to them in the Invoice Workbench. Notice in Figure 6-2 that the Invoice Workbench is a Folder window, denoted by the folder icon in the upper-left portion of the screen, allowing the fields to be rearranged, shown, or hidden for faster data entry using the Folder menu.

The Invoice Workbench has required, optional, and informational fields. These fields are color-coded, as are all windows in EBS. When using the standard EBS color palette, blue-gray represents informational data that cannot be updated, white is optional data, and yellow is required data. On web forms, most required fields are denoted with an asterisk (*) next to the field name, but this is not as accurate as the color coding on the forms. Data that is informational and cannot be updated does not appear in a box on the web-based windows. Sometimes fields will change between required, informational, and optional, based on other data previously entered.

Data relating to invoices can be broken down into groupings: Invoice, Processing, Projects, Settlement, and Tax. Invoice data relates to the invoice itself, while Processing fields pertain to the accounting processing and coding of an invoice. Projects-related fields are used when the EBS Projects Costing subledger is implemented and invoices are tracked as expenditures against

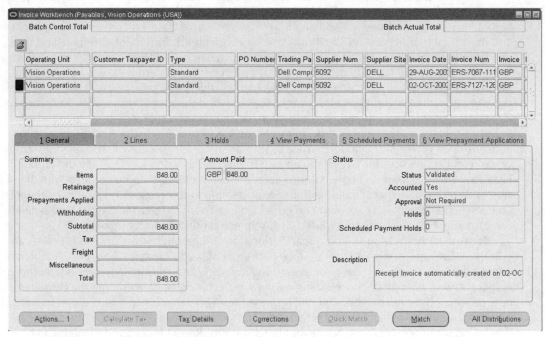

Payables Manager | Invoices | Entry | Invoices or Payables Manager | Invoices | Entry | Invoice Batches,
Invoice button

FIGURE 6-2 *Invoice entry*

a specific project. Settlement includes information that directly affects the payment of the invoice, while Tax fields track specific information about all the taxes related to an invoice (Withholding, VAT, Sales and Use, and so on). For easier grouping, the fields in the Invoice Workbench will be grouped in these categories, with fields hidden with the folder identified with a (H). The fields are listed in alphabetical order for easier reference.

Invoice-Related Fields

Invoice-related fields track information directly related to the invoice itself, either defaulting from the supplier records and system defaults or input manually. APPROVAL DESCRIPTION (H), APPROVAL STATUS (H), and APPROVED AMOUNT (H) are reference fields that can be populated by the user, and are not related to the invoice approval process. While not used by EBS for transacting the invoice, these fields can be helpful when invoices are approved manually or force approved in the system.

BATCH NAME (H) is assigned when using the invoice batching feature, but it will always be blank for invoices entered without a batch. The field is populated by EBS and cannot be updated by the user at the invoice level.

Once an invoice is entered into the system, it can be deleted at any point prior to the invoice validation process. When it is deleted, there will be no record of the invoice ever being entered into the system. After the invoice is validated, it can be canceled, which zeroes out the line and closes the invoice, removing it from the aging and ensuring it cannot be selected during payment processing. The difference between deleting an invoice and canceling it is that deleting removes it from the database, while canceling reverses all the accounting but maintains a record of the invoice entry in Payables. Once an invoice has been canceled, information about the cancellation can be found in the CANCELED AMOUNT (H), CANCELED BY (H), and CANCELED DATE (H) fields. EBS automatically populates these fields during the cancellation process.

Received dates can be used when determining the due date of an invoice, depending on how the system is set up (Setup | Options | Payables System Setup). The DATE GOODS RECEIVED (H) field is populated from the receiving transaction against a purchase order. This field can also be used to determine the GL date (determined by the Setup | Options | Payables Options | Invoice tab). The DATE INVOICE RECEIVED (H) is entered by the person entering the invoice and can be used to determine the date the terms are based on. If the system is set up to use the DATE INVOICE RECEIVED, a folder should be created to show this field during data entry. DESCRIPTION should be added for all invoices and will default on the lines in the line description field when populated. Entering informative descriptions into EBS on all records helps to identify the data being entered and can reduce the amount of research and referencing to hard-copy backups.

When an invoice has a payment term that includes a discount, EBS can calculate the amount that is eligible for discount; it populates that amount in the DISCOUNTABLE AMOUNT (H) field. This field can either be populated by the person entering the invoice or else default in when the invoice is validated (the total invoice amount will default in). If an invoice includes tax lines, either manually entered or calculated by EBS, you have the option of setting up EBS to include or exclude tax from the discounted amount (Setup | Options | Payables Options | Payment tab | Exclude Tax From Discount option). When this is selected, EBS will reduce the discountable amount by the amount of tax during invoice validation.

DOCUMENT NEEDS REAPPROVAL (H), when checked, will reprocess an invoice through the invoice approval workflow by resetting the approval status to Needs Reapproval. The READY FOR APPROVAL (H) check box must be checked when using the invoice approval workflow process to approve invoices; it signifies that the invoice is eligible for the workflow to evaluate if it is ready to process. By default, this box is always checked, but it can be unchecked if need be.

The last field used when approving invoices is the REQUESTOR (H) field. The person's name populated in this field will be the starting point for EBS to evaluate who the invoice should be sent to for approval. You do not have to enter the final approver in this field, but the person who actually requested the goods or services, and EBS will route the invoice for approval based on this person's name and how the Approval Manager is set up. Even when not using the standard invoice approval process, you can still populate this field if you want to track who requested a specific invoice for payment. All invoices will display a WF APPROVAL STATUS (H) whether invoice approval is turned on or not. When approvals are not turned on, it will display Not Required, or the actual status of the approval process when approvals are being used.

EBS does allow for sequential numbering for invoices, where the system will assign a sequential number based on the DOCUMENT CATEGORY NAME. This sequential number does not replace invoice numbers but is in addition to invoice numbers. The sequence itself that is assigned to the invoice will display in the DOCUMENT SEQUENCE NAME field, which defaults in based on the document category. When the sequence number is assigned, it will appear in the VOUCHER NUMBER (H) field.

Multiple types of invoices can be entered into EBS for payment; they are defined by the TYPE field, described in Table 6-1.

Type	Usage
Adjustment and PO Price Adjustment	System-generated invoices for changes to purchase order prices when Retroactive Pricing is turned on using the profile option PO: Allow Retroactive Pricing of PO.
Credit Memo	Credits, or reductions to the amount owed a supplier, where a credit invoice is received from the supplier itself.
Debit Memo	Adjustments to amounts owed the supplier when a credit memo or other adjusting document is not received.
Expense Report	Expense reports for employees entered using the Expense Report window or iExpenses.
Mixed	Used to enter invoices both matched and not matched to purchase orders; it can be either a negative or positive amount.
Prepayment	An invoice entered to create a prepayment to a supplier for services or goods not yet received, where the actual invoice will be received from the supplier at a later date. When applied to an invoice, a prepayment will reduce the amount due.
Retainage Release	An invoice created for a withheld amount, or retainage, against a periodic payment. This is usually associated with service purchases.
Standard	General invoices, either matched or not matched to a purchase order.
Transportation Invoice	Freight invoices interfaced from the Oracle Transportation Management module.
Withholding Tax	An invoice created for tax withholding that is due to a government agency.

TABLE 6-1   *Invoice Types*

When matching an invoice to a Purchase Order, you can enter a PO NUMBER. This will default the Supplier (TRADING PARTNER), SUPPLIER NUM, and SUPPLIER SITE from the purchase order itself. These cannot be changed when they are populated from the purchase order. MATCH ACTION will determine, based on the purchase order, if an invoice is matched to the purchase order itself or the receipt. When deciding to match to purchase orders or receipts, consider the fact that an invoice cannot be matched to a receipt that has not been made in EBS yet, creating the need to manually track when the receipt is performed. If you match to a purchase order, 3-way matching still takes place, but allows the invoice to be entered and matched prior to the actual receipt transaction, automatically placing the invoice on hold and releasing it once the receipt is performed. When a credit memo is matched to an invoice (by using the CORRECTIONS button), that will also be reflected in this field. If the invoice is not matched to the purchase order, then either the TRADING PARTNER or SUPPLIER NUM will need to be entered manually. Entering one of these fields will populate the other. SUPPLIER SITE defaults in if there is only one Pay Site active on the supplier, or if one of the Pay Sites was marked as Primary Pay (Suppliers | Entry | Address Book | Manage Sites). If the supplier selected is set up as an employee and linked to the employee record in the Oracle Human Resource screen, then the EMPLOYEE NUMBER (H) will populate in for reference.

INVOICE DATE can either be manually entered or will populate when tabbing over the screen with the current system date if the period is opened, or the last day of the prior month or the first day of the next month. INVOICE NUM is the actual invoice number referenced on the invoice and must be unique for all invoices entered for a specific Supplier Site. You should establish and follow naming conventions for case, spaces, and the like to ensure the integrity of this field and to prevent duplicate invoices from being entered and paid. If no invoice number is entered, the system will default the INVOICE DATE in this field. When CONFIRM DATE AS INVOICE NUMBER is checked on the Payables Options (Setup | Options | Payables Options | Invoice tab), EBS will prompt the user to confirm that this is correct.

The INVOICE CURR will default from the supplier INVOICE CURRENCY or the invoice batch, but it can be overridden. Entering a currency other than the Ledger currency will require a conversion rate to either default from the setups or entered by the user. INVOICE AMOUNT is the actual amount of the liability in the invoice currency for this invoice, including any tax or freight amounts, and should not be reduced for any potential discounts based on the payment terms. EBS will calculate these automatically and book the discount when the payment is made.

Invoices can be entered in either the main currency of the Ledger assigned to Payables, also called the functional currency, or in a foreign currency, and is determined by the INVOICE CURR field. When a foreign currency invoice is entered, the RATE TYPE, EXCHANGE DATE, and EXCHANGE RATE need to be populated. RATE TYPE will default in from the Currency tab of the Payables Options (Setup | Options | Payables Options) and determines where the EXCHANGE RATE is derived from, either a rate defined in the system or a rate entered by the user. The EXCHANGE DATE determines which rate will default in if it is not user entered, or else it reflects the actual date of the exchange rate the user entered. EBS will automatically calculate, based on this exchange information, the FUNCTIONAL CURR AMOUNT (H) for the invoice and display the FUNCTIONAL CURRENCY (H) itself for reference.

RELEASE AMOUNT NET OF TAX will display the amount of an invoice that is released and not retained. Portions of invoices can be retained for large project where the amounts are withheld from payment pending the completion of a specific task or duty.

Processing-Related Fields

Each invoice will have a GL DATE, which will relate directly to the period that this invoice will be accounted for in the General Ledger. This field will populate automatically according to the GL DATE BASIS that is selected in the Payables Options (Setup | Options | Payables Options | Invoice tab). If the basis, such as invoice date, would create a GL date that is in a closed period, this field will not populate automatically but will require the user to enter it.

DISTRIBUTION SET, used to populate account distributions for an invoice, will default in from any supplier site that has a distribution set associated with it, or you can manually add it at this time. Any DESCRIPTION added to the invoice header will not only be available to print on check stubs or remittance advised, but will also default to the line descriptions, where it can be overridden.

LEGAL ENTITY (H) reflects the entity responsible for paying the obligation and is the name that will appear on 1099s. LIABILITY ACCOUNT (H) and LIABILITY DESCRIPTION (H), which default in from the supplier setups, are used when creating accounting to generate the offsetting transaction.

OPERATING UNIT is a required field for all transactions but can only be updated or entered if a user has access to multiple operating units (determined with the profile MO: Security Profile). This cannot be updated if the user only has access to one operating unit, and will default in if that user has access to multiple units but the profile MO: Default Operating Unit is set up.

Projects-Related Fields

When the Oracle Projects subledger is used, invoices can be linked directly to a specific PROJECT, TASK, EXPENDITURE TYPE, and EXPENDITURE ORGANIZATION, as well as added to an EXPENDITURE ITEM DATE. Such invoices can be interfaced with Projects, creating an expenditure against the related project. Any changes to the project information, once the transaction is in projects, can then be interfaced back to Payables, creating the reversing as well as new distribution lines to keep the two subledgers in synch.

AWARD NUMBER (H), only populated when Grants Accounting is being used with Projects, reflects the award that will be credited for this invoice.

Settlement-Related Fields

When funds are remitted to suppliers electronically, you must decide whether you are responsible for any related bank charges or the supplier is. EBS functionality allows you to reduce the amount of the settlement if the supplier is responsible. BANK CHARGE BEARER (H) is populated when the USE BANK CHARGES option is enabled (Setup | Options | Payables Options | Payment tab) and will deduct the bank charges from the payment if this is populated with Supplier/Negotiated or Supplier/Standard. On each invoice, BANK CHARGE BEARER can be set to PAYEE, PAYOR, PAYEE EXPRESS CHARGES, or SHARED. Remember, discounts associated with payment terms cannot be used when Bank Charges is enabled.

DELIVERY CHANNEL (H) will be populated according to the channel entered on the Supplier setup, in the Payments Detail region, and determines how the payment will be delivered to the supplier when processed electronically. The REMIT TO BANK ACCOUNT NAME will default in from the primary bank set up on the supplier site. If the supplier site does not have a bank account, then it will default in from the supplier. This is set up in the Banking Details region of the supplier. A bank account must be associated with either the supplier or the supplier site to make an electronic payment.

When the NET OF RETAINAGE (H) box is checked, the invoice amount on the header should be the net of any amounts retained. This box is checked by default in EBS.

Invoices are usually paid in the same currency as the invoice themselves, which will default into the PAYMENT CURR field, but the user can update the payment currency to create a payment in a currency that is different than the invoice. When a currency other than the Ledger currency is entered, the PAYMENT RATE DATE is used to determine which system rates are used for the translation of the transaction. PAYMENT RATE TYPE, when it is other than the user, will populate the PAYMENT RATE from the currency tables, based on the rate associated with the date entered in the PAYMENT RATE DATE. When this is set to USER, or the rate is not entered for the PAYMENT RATE DATE, the user can enter the PAYMENT RATE into the system. The amount due on an invoice in the payment currency is displayed in the PAYMENT AMOUNT (H) field.

The TERMS DATE will populate according to the TERMS DATE BASIS that is assigned at the supplier site. These options are GOODS RECEIVED, INVOICE, INVOICE RECEIVED, and SYSTEM date. If this is set to the INVOICE RECEIVED date, since this is a hidden field, it should be shown by creating a folder so that users have access to enter it (see Chapter 5 for more information on folders). TERMS will also default in from the invoice batch or supplier site but can be overridden by the user. PAYMENT METHOD determines the way the funds will be settled with the supplier, such as credit card, electronic, or check; they default in from the supplier site. The payment method on an invoice must agree to the payment method when completing a settlement batch in order for the invoice to be selected. PAY GROUP, again, used to select invoices for a settlement batch, will also default in from first the batch and then the supplier site but can be overridden. Selecting the PAY ALONE (H) flag will cause one settlement document to be generated for each invoice, as opposed to paying multiple invoices with one document. This can be set manually on an invoice or default in from the supplier record, in the Payment Details region, under Payment Specification.

PREPAID AMOUNT will reflect the total of the prepayments that have been applied to this invoice, and is maintained by the system when prepayments are applied or unapplied. When a prepayment is applied, the prepayment invoice number will appear in the RELATED INVOICE field. There are two types of prepayments that can be entered into EBS: Temporary or Permanent. The permanent PREPAYMENT TYPE is used when payments are deposits; it cannot be applied to invoices later received. Temporary prepayments are paid in advance of an invoice and are applied to the invoice or expense report when it is received. SETTLEMENT DATE determines when the temporary prepayments can be applied to an invoice; it defaults to the invoice date. SETTLEMENT PRIORITY can be added and used for grouping payments when they are created, or it will default in from the supplier record.

QUICK CREDIT and CREDITED INVOICE are used with the transaction types of Credit Memo and Debit Memo and populated when an entire invoice has been credited. To use this feature, enter a credit or debit memo for a negative amount equal to the amount of the invoice you want to credit. Check QUICK CREDIT, and select the invoice number from the list of values in the CREDITED INVOICE field that you want to credit. This will automatically create distribution lines based on the invoice distributions when the transaction is saved, eliminating the need to manually enter the accounting information.

MATCH ACTION determines if the invoice will be matched to a purchase order, a receipt, or an invoice. When matching a credit or debit memo to an invoice, this links the two transactions for informational purposes but does not close the invoice or memos, both of which will continue to appear on the aging until they are selected for payment (more on this in Chapter 8, under zero dollar payments.)

The UNIQUE REMITTANCE IDENTIFIER will capture any IBLC (Institut Belgo-Luxembourgeoise du Change, used with Belgium electronic remittances) that is associated with the Payment Reason Code on the supplier site.

Tax-Related Fields

EBS introduced a new tax engine called E-Business Tax, in R12, which is used to calculate sales and use taxes on invoices. It determines taxes from several fields, including BUSINESS CATEGORY, FISCAL CLASSIFICATION, INVOICE SUBTYPE, and TAXATION COUNTRY. BUSINESS CATEGORY refers to the type of transaction that is being performed, such as processing an expense report or creating a purchase transaction. FISCAL CLASSIFICATION is simply a grouping of determining taxation factors that can be assigned to multiple business categories. The FISCAL CLASSIFICATION often line up with the tax laws of a country, so the United States might have a FISCAL CLASSIFICATION for Liquor and another for Gasoline. These could then be assigned to multiple BUSINESS CATEGORY, such as Purchase and Sales transactions.

Be aware that the TRANSACTION BUSINESS CATEGORY does not default in automatically on an invoice but needs to be manually added. The SELF-ASSESSED TAX AMOUNT reflects the amount the supplier does not include as tax on an invoice and that you are adding on yourself. When tax is assessed based on a purchase order, then the SUPPLIER TAX INVOICE DATE will populate from there, reflecting the date that the supplier charged the tax on. When the tax was not recorded on the purchase order, then the INTERNAL RECORDING DATE reflects the tax reporting date. The SUPPLIER TAX INVOICE EXCHANGE RATE shows the exchange rate for any tax assessed in a foreign currency.

If more than one legal entity is assigned to the Ledger associated with the operating unit, then the user will have the option of selecting a legal entity and registration number in the CUSTOMER TAXPAYER ID field. This is only needed when taxes (withholding, 1099 tax reporting, VAT) are being applied to the transaction. The TAX AMOUNT, though it still appears on the form, is no longer used in R12. The TAX CONTROL AMOUNT can be entered as the control amount for the calculated tax entries associated with the invoice lines. When the E-Business Tax calculations add up to more or less than the control amount, then EBS will prorate the control amount over the lines.

When using automatic withholding, EBS will display any WITHHELD AMOUNT for an invoice in this field. The WITHHOLDING TAX GROUP (H) will default in if a withholding tax is assigned to the supplier, or it can be manually added. In addition to adding the withholding tax group to the invoice header, it can also be added to the individual lines.

Invoice Information Tabs

The Invoice window is broken into upper (header) and lower (line and additional information) regions. The header region, described in the preceding section, contains all the data entry fields relating to the entire invoice, while the lower region is located just under the tabs has status and processing information about an invoice as well as line-specific information. The data that is displayed in the lower region pertains to the invoice that your cursor is on (denoted by the dark tab to the left of Operating Unit). Because this is a multiregion screen, the details for only one invoice can be displayed at a time in the lower section. Scrolling down or up on the invoices will display the details for additional invoices.

General Tab

The General tab shows general status information about the invoice. In the Summary section, a summary of the invoice components appear, footing down to the TOTAL amount of the invoice. AMOUNT PAID is the currency and invoice amount that has been paid so far. The Status section is one of the most important sections when troubleshooting processing problems on an invoice. STATUS shows the status of the invoice, which directly affects what transactions can take place on the invoice. The different statuses are described in Table 6-2. While this field cannot be manually updated, running the Invoice Validation process will update the status for the current system conditions.

Status	Explanation
Available	Denotes a temporary prepayment that has been validated and still has an amount available for application.
Canceled	An invoice has been canceled and no longer appears on the aging or is available for payment. Canceling an invoice reverses any accounting entries for the invoice.
Fully Applied	Denotes a temporary prepayment that has been validated and fully applied to invoices.
Needs Revalidation	An invoice where validation has been run and has failed for one or more controls, creating holds on the invoice. Holds can be released either manually or by correcting the problem and revalidating the invoice (see "Hold and Releases" in Chapter 5).
Never Validated	An invoice has been entered but never validated. Never Validated invoices cannot be paid nor have accounting created for them, preventing them from being transferred to the General Ledger. Invoices entered and never validated will appear on the Aging Reports, but not on the Open Account AP Balances Listing report.
Permanent	A permanent prepayment that has been paid. Permanent prepayments cannot be applied to invoices.
Selected for Payment	Displays when an invoice has been selected for payment, but the payment batch has not yet been confirmed.
Unpaid	Denotes any invoice that has not yet been paid.
Unvalidated Prepayment	Any prepayment that has not yet been processed through the validation process.
Validated	An invoice has passed validation and can be accounted, paid, or routed for approval.

TABLE 6-2   *Invoice Statuses*

ACCOUNTED shows if an invoice has been selected by the accounting process, generating accounting entries for the distribution lines along with their offsetting liability accounts. APPROVAL is populated for every invoice, even when the invoice approvals are not being used. The approval statuses and their meanings are listed in Table 6-3.

Approval Status	Meaning
Initiated	The status of invoices that have started the approval process but have not yet been approved.
Manually Approved	Invoices that require approval can be force-approved by a user with the proper access and will display Manually Approved.
Needs Reapproval	An approved invoice that has changes to pertinent information, such as supplier or amount, will have a status of Needs Reapproval until it is reprocessed and reevaluated by the approval workflow.
Not Required	The status of all invoices when approvals are not turned on, or of invoices that have been processed by the invoice approval workflow and have been determined not to meet the criteria for approval.
Rejected	The status of invoices that were rejected by the approver during the approval process. Approval Manager can be set up either to allow invoices to be reprocessed when they are rejected, changing particular information, or to only allow rejected invoices to be canceled in the system. Use caution when setting it up to only allow cancellation, because if an invoice was valid except for an account number or the person it was sent to for approval, it can no longer be paid and will have to be canceled and reentered with a different invoice number, a practice that can lead to double payments.
Required	Used when Invoice Approval is turned on, reflecting the status of all invoices prior to their being evaluated with the invoice approval workflow to determined if they need to be approved or not.

TABLE 6-3 *Approval Statuses*

HOLDS will show the number of invoice holds that can be seen on the Holds tab, while SCHEDULED PAYMENT HOLDS displays the number of holds that are applied on the Scheduled Payments tab.

Invoice Lines

In EBS, invoices are entered using a hierarchy: headers, lines, and than distributions, as you can see in Figure 6-3. Headers, described earlier in this chapter, contain general or common information about an invoice, while lines contain detailed information specific to only a portion of the invoice. Distributions house the accounting-specific information, such as both the debit and credit accounts for an invoice.

While the distribution account can be entered on the line, the information is actually used to create the distribution. Entering the account on the Distribution form will also allow multiple accounts to be entered for each line. The detailed information exists on three screens, often repeating the same information. The Lines tab is where the data entry will take place, while both the DISTRIBUTIONS and ALL DISTRIBUTIONS buttons lead to much of the same information as SEND in the Lines section. Lines fields will first be described, and then any additional fields found on the distribution tabs will be considered. Just as on the invoice header region, Lines has a folder and contains both hidden and displayed fields. Hidden fields will be noted with an (H) after the field name.

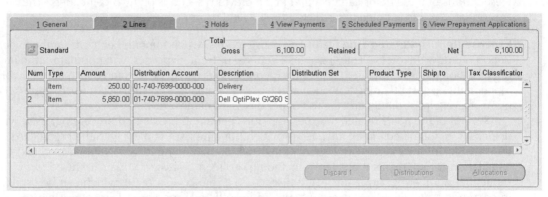

Payables Manager | Invoices | Entry | Invoices | Line tab

FIGURE 6-3 *Invoice lines*

Lines Invoice lines can be created in several different ways, the most basic being manual entry by the user entering the invoice. Additionally, they can be defaulted in with a Distribution Set that is associated with the supplier or manually added to the invoice, created when the invoice is matched to a purchase order or a receipt, or created by allocating system-created charges such as freight or tax.

Some of the information on a line will default in from the invoice header but can be overridden or added for each individual line. These fields include the following:

- Approval Status (Invoice)
- Award Number (Project)
- Business Category (Tax)
- Description (Invoice)
- Distribution Set (Processing)
- Expenditure Item Date (Project)
- Expenditure Organization (Project)
- Expenditure Type (Project)
- Fiscal Classification (Tax)
- GL Date (Processing)
- PO Number (Invoice)
- Project (Project)
- Task (Project)
- Type (Project)
- Withholding Tax Group (Tax)

Descriptions of these fields can be found in the previous sections on invoice headers. The appropriate section is noted in brackets after the field name.

Expense Report–Related Line Fields Expense reports, when imported either from the Expense Report window (Invoices | Entry | Expense Reports) or from iExpenses, will populate some data on the invoice lines for reference. While expense reports can also be entered as manual invoices, functionality is lost by doing this, such as the use of templates and employees to generate account numbers, receipt auditing, and the use of per diems, to name a few.

Several of the fields related to expense reports pertain to credit card processing, used when iExpenses is populated via an interface provided from the issuing bank with the credit card transactions for the employees. Merchant information pertaining to VAT (value-added tax) calculations or payments is available, including MERCHANT DOCUMENT NUMBER (H), used for sequential numbering, MERCHANT NAME (H), MERCHANT REFERENCE NUMBER (H), which can be used for internal notes, MERCHANT TAX PAYER ID (H), also called NIF in Europe or NIT in Latin America, and MERCHANT TAX REGISTRATION NUMBER (H).

When the auditing features are used for expense reports to track receipts, the audit status is also visible on the invoice line, showing whether the RECEIPT was REQUIRED, VERIFIED, or MISSING. Other basic information about the expense reports, such as START and END EXPENSE DATE (H), are available as well. The DAILY AMOUNT (H) is a calculated field based on the actual receipt amount for a line item divided by the number of days associated with the line. EXPENSE GROUP (H), which is assigned by iExpense, groups multiple types of expenses to one receipt. When a JUSTIFICATION (H) was given for an expense in both iExpenses and the Expense window in Payables, it will display on the associated invoice. The last hidden field relating to general expense report information is WEB PARAMETER ID (H), which will display the identification number for the application that originated the expense report, usually iExpenses.

Corporate credit cards can be integrated with iExpenses to prepopulate the expenses for employee approval and processing. When this happens, the invoice line is marked as a CREDIT CARD TRANSACTION. Some expense reports will be submitted for transactions that are prepaid with a corporate credit card, and this will be noted with the prepayment number in COMPANY PREPAID INVOICE.

Invoice-Related Fields Invoice-related fields include data that is entered directly from the invoice itself, or derived from information entered on the invoice. See Table 6-4 for descriptions of these fields.

Purchase Order–Related Fields One of the benefits of an integrated system is the ability to tie transactions entered in different subledgers to each other, using the data from one area to create and control data in another. A perfect example of this is the ability to match invoices to purchase orders, allowing the approval and receipt transactions in purchasing to determine when invoices are ready for payment as well as defaulting key information. To match an invoice to a purchase order, after an invoice header is entered, click the MATCH button, which allows the user to match the invoice to a receipt or a purchase order line (depending on the setups on the supplier and purchase order). This will accommodate 2-way (invoice to purchase order), 3-way (invoice, purchase order, and receipt) and 4-way (invoice, purchase order, receipt, and delivery) matching. When the invoice is matched to the purchase order, the lines details are created and purchase order–specific fields are populated.

How an invoice is matched to a purchase order is based on either quantity or cost and is tracked in the MATCH BASIS field. AMOUNT is used for service-type purchase orders, whereas QUANTITY is associated with orders for goods. MATCH TYPE identifies the type of matching transaction, such as

Field Name	Description
Amount	This represents the line amount, which can be classified as a general line item, freight, tax or miscellaneous charge, and to which accounting can be assigned. All the lines together must equal the INVOICE AMOUNT entered on the invoice header.
Distribution Total	This field is usually null, but after you click the DISTRIBUTIONS button for a specific line, it will show the distribution total for that line, which must be the same as the amount for the line.
Functional Amount (H)	Represents the amount of the line in the Ledger's functional currency.
Num (Number)	This is the line number for the line. Usually, these will be in successive (1, 2, 3) as opposed to 10, 20, 30.
Original Amount (H)	The initial entered value of a line is retained here if any changes are made to the amount or the invoice is canceled.
Original Functional Amount (H)	The initial entered value of a line in the functional currency of the Ledger is retained here if any changes are made to the amount or the invoice is canceled.
Quantity Invoiced	The amount of a line can be calculated automatically by entering a QUANTITY INVOICED and a UNIT PRICE.
Unit Price	The amount of a line can be calculated automatically by entering the QUANTITY INVOICED and a UNIT PRICE.
UOM (Unit of Measure)	When entering a QUANTITY INVOICED and UNIT PRICE, including a UOM will track the units that the price pertained to.

TABLE 6-4 *Line Fields Relating to Invoices*

Price or Quantity corrections, or if the line is matched to the PO or Receipt. EBS allows invoices to be finally matched to a purchase order, preventing changes to the invoices and their associated purchase orders after they are processed. Normally, this will default to NO or NULL in the FINAL MATCH field, but it can be set to YES if the Payables options for Purchasing (Setup | Options | Purchasing Options) are set to allow Final Matching. Remember, *final* is *final*—no changes will be allowed on these invoices and purchase orders when they are finally matched, including adjustments and corrections for mistakes. When the invoice is validated, the status of the match will be set to Done.

When an invoice line is created from the purchase order, the following fields will populate in if they are entered on the purchase order; they are for informational purposes only:

- INVENTORY ITEM

- ITEM DESCRIPTION

- MANUFACTURER

- MODEL

- PRODUCT TYPE

- PURCHASING CATEGORY (H)

- SERIAL NUMBER

- SHIP TO

- WARRANTY NUMBER

Invoices can be matched at different levels, starting at the highest, which is PO RELEASE (if there is more than one), and getting more detailed by matching to the PO LINE, PO SHIPMENT, and PO DISTRIBUTION. In the Payables Options setup under the Match tab (Setup | Options | Payables Options), PO Distribution must be allowed to match at the distribution level. Payables has the option of matching to a purchase order at the levels just named, or to the receipt itself.

It is important to understand that the receipt must first be made in EBS to match to it, whereas matching to a purchase order will place an invoice on hold if the receipt is not yet processed, and release the hold when the receipt is transacted and meets the tolerances set up in the system. When matched to a receipt, both the RECEIPT LINE and RECEIPT NUMBER are shown in the invoice line. Additional fields include the RECEIPT CONVERSION RATE (H), RECEIPT CURRENCY (H), and RECEIPT AMOUNT (H), all populated during the receiving process when the receipt is processed in a different currency than the Ledger default currency.

Retainage, or the withholding of payment during a long-term service contract, will reduce the amount of an invoice payment, tracking the retainage invoice information in the RETAINED AMOUNT (H), RETAINED INVOICE (H), and RETAINED INVOICE LINE (H) fields.

Processing Fields   Processing fields, or fields that control the current or future behavior of an invoice, are some of the most important fields on the invoice lines, often relating to the direct accounting of a line. When entering an invoice, the account number can be manually keyed or populated from a distribution set, but OVERLAY ACCOUNTS can override these account numbers. Overlay accounts will simply override a segment value, such as ACCOUNT SEGMENT, BALANCING SEGMENT, or COST CENTER SEGMENT, and happen when any or all of these fields are populated. When invoices are imported in via the Payables interface, the OVERLAY ACCOUNT field can be populated with specific segments that will overlay the distribution on an invoice, wherever it is created from, and allows for null segments. This feature cannot be used with a line that is matched to a purchase order.

The DISTRIBUTION ACCOUNT will always display the account that was entered on the transaction, while viewing the distributions will show the modified account, using the overlay information. DEFAULT ACCOUNT DESCRIPTION displays the description of the account shown in the distribution account field. GENERATE DISTRIBUTIONS (H) shows the status of the distribution lines. YES denotes that the distributions are ready to be generated because an account number or Distribution Set is entered on the line. NO is the status prior to entering any accounting information on a line; it prevents distributions from being generated when the invoice is validated or accounted for. DONE shows that the distributions are generated. The GENERATE DISTRIBUTIONS status is changed to DONE either when a line is matched to a purchase order, or when the invoice is validated and the line is successfully distributed.

Payables invoices can be integrated with Oracle Assets, sending lines that are marked as TRACK AS ASSET over to Assets' Mass Additions interface for processing. To speed up processing, an ASSET CATEGORY can also be populated, reducing the data that needs to be added in Assets to convert these transactions into actual assets.

Invoice lines can be either CANCELED or DISCARDED. As a general rule, invoice lines can be discarded when they are incorrect or not needed, but invoices themselves, along with any lines that have not yet been discarded, are canceled. To cancel an entire invoice, select the ACTIONS button and CANCEL INVOICES. The DISCARD button can be used for each individual line that needs to be discarded. Both of these actions will reverse any accounting entries associated with this invoice or line.

Invoice lines, like the headers, have to be validated and can be approved. The VALIDATION STATUS shows if the line has been validated, requires revalidation, or has never been validated. This can be helpful in determining why the validation status requires revalidation on an invoice by identifying the specific line requiring revalidation. While lines cannot be validated one at a time, the invoice validation does look at each line and evaluates if it passes, giving a status to each line. All lines must pass validation before the invoice will be fully validated.

During the approval process, invoices can be force-approved, and any line that was approved using this feature will be marked with a check in the FORCE LINE APPROVAL (H) field. LINE NEEDS REAPPROVAL (H) will display for any line that requires reapproval because of a change on the line. Not all changes will generate the need for a line to be reapproved; only changes relevant to accounting such as to the amount or account number will trigger the reapproval process. The REQUESTOR field is used for self-service invoices that are created from iSupplier, and that are matched to purchase orders, where the lines can be approved by different requestors, and the invoice will be approved when all the lines have been approved. Just like line validations, invoices can only be submitted for approval at the invoice level, but each line is evaluated for approval status.

When an invoice is created as part of an internal order in Payables, then the INTERCOMPANY INVOICE LINE NUMBER and INTERCOMPANY INVOICE NUMBER fields are populated on the corresponding Receivables transaction.

Additional miscellaneous fields on the invoice line are ENCUMBRANCE STATUS, showing if the line has been fully, partially, or not encumbered. LINE SOURCE displays the source that generated this invoice line, such as Manual or Open Interface. PERIOD NAME (H) will display the accounting period the General Ledger date falls into, based on the Ledger calendar. REFERENCE 1 and 2 fields can be populated with reference information for invoices imported from any third-party system via the Payables open interface. The final processing field is PRORATE ACROSS ALL ITEM LINES, which, when checked, will prorate any tax, interest, and freight charges automatically calculated across all the line items.

Settlement Fields   The settlement fields located on the lines relate to prepayments. When a prepayment is applied to an invoice, the PREPAYMENT LINE NUMBER and INVOICE NUMBER will populate, showing the invoices each line was used against. The INVOICE INCLUDES PREPAYMENT check box is used when an invoice that is received from a supplier is net of a prepayment amount, allowing lines to be entered for the total invoice amount, and a negative line to be entered for the prepayment amount. Using the check box, or applying a prepayment, both result in the same effect: the invoice amount that is available for payment is reduced by the amount of the prepayment applied or noted on the invoice.

Miscellaneous Fields   A few fields fall outside the groups mentioned. When invoices are imported from Oracle's Retail products, ADJUSTMENT REASON (H) will be populated with the reason code for the adjustment.

PROJECT QUANTITY will default in from the quantity invoiced on a project-related invoice, while the PROCESSED CODE (H) indicates if the invoice has been processed in Oracle Projects.

Tax information on an invoice line is extensive, to allow the proper calculation of taxes when using E-Business Tax or an integrated tax solution. They include:

- ASSESSABLE VALUE

- CONTROL AMOUNT

- COUNTRY OF SUPPLY (H)

- INCLUDED TAX AMOUNT

- INCOME TAX REGION

- INCOME TAX TYPE

- LINE GROUP NUMBER (H)

- NONRECOVERABLE TAX AMOUNT

- PRIMARY INTENDED USE

- PRODUCT CATEGORY

- PRODUCT FISCAL CLASSIFICATION

- RECOVERABLE TAX AMOUNT

- TAX

- TAX CLASSIFICATION CODE

- TAX JURISDICTION

- TAX RATE

- TAX RATE NAME

- TAX REGIME

- TAX STATUS

Invoice Distributions

At first glance, it looks like invoice lines and invoice distributions are the same, but they are not. The main difference to understand is that while there can be multiple lines related to each invoice, there can also be multiple distributions related to each line. It is the distribution-level transactions that are transferred to Oracle Assets and Oracle Project Costing. And it is the distributions that are validated, encumbranced, and accounted in the system, while lines are approved. Though much of the information belonging to a distribution can be entered in the Line window, the distributions are automatically created based on the data entered on a line during validation, and is actually tracked in the AP_INVOICE_DISTRIBUTIONS_ALL table.

Also found on the Distributions window, seen in Figure 6-4, are different statuses. These refer to each individual distribution, not the lines. STATUS refers to the validation status, showing the actual status of each distribution. It is not until all the distribution statuses are validated that the STATUS seen on the General tab of the invoice will show VALIDATED. Reviewing each distribution's status can help determine where a problem exists that is preventing invoice validation.

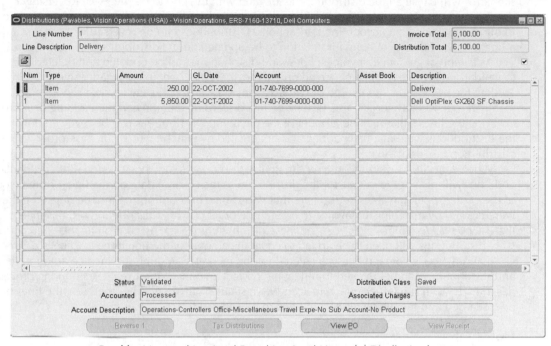

Payables Manager | Invoices | Entry | Invoices | Lines tab | Distribution button

FIGURE 6-4 *Invoice Distributions*

ACCOUNTED shows if a specific distribution has processed through the Subledger Accounting engine. Again, the ACCOUNTED status on the invoice's General tab reflects the statuses of all the distributions, only showing YES after all the distributions are accounted for without errors. There are two types of DISTRIBUTION CLASSES: PERMANENT and CANDIDATE. These are really just fancy words for the status of the distribution; PERMANENT means the distribution has been saved, and CANDIDATE means that the distribution is being previewed according to the information entered on the line but is not yet saved. Usually, a distribution class will update from CANDIDATE to PERMANENT when the distribution is validated.

The final field is ASSOCIATED CHARGES, which will show any freight or miscellaneous charges that have been allocated to these charges against this line.

The last feature that can be seen as a distribution on an invoice is the application and removal of prepayments. These will appear as a TYPE of PREPAYMENT on the distribution of the invoice it is applied to. These can be seen by clicking the ALL DISTRIBUTIONS button at the bottom of the Invoice Workbench window.

Canceling Distributions and Discarding Lines   Another difference between lines and distributions is how information can be updated after accounting or payment. Specific fields on both screens can only be updated when they have a certain status, usually unaccounted or unpaid, and after that point lines must be discarded whiie distributions require reversal.

Discarding a line will change the dollar amount associated with lines equal to zero. Lines are discarded when invoices are canceled or when a user selects the DISCARD button. Both of these scenarios will cause all the distributions associated with the line to be reversed. Reversing a distribution behaves slightly differently than discarding a line. It will generate a reversing transaction to offset any associated accounting transactions. Distributions can be reversed without discarding a line, allowing the accounting information to be updated on the distribution.

As a general guidance, invoices, lines, and distributions can be updated and deleted prior to validation. Invoices can be canceled only if they have not been paid, or after settlement by voiding the payment. Lines can be discarded at any time as long as the invoice is not finally matched to a purchase order. This is done by first discarding the line and then adding new lines, ensuring the lines still equal the amount of the payment. Distributions can be reversed only when the distributions were manually added and not created by matching to a purchase order, using a Distribution Set, or the like.

When canceling a distribution, you can update the GL DATE to any open period. Both distributions and lines will default the GL DATE on the distribution to the original date on the line, or the first day of the earliest open payables period after that date. Since distributions cannot be deleted if they were created by matching an invoice to a purchase order or with a distribution set, this means that there is no way to control the GL DATE on these distributions except by controlling the open periods. New distributions will need to be added to equal the amount of the line if the invoice is paid.

If an invoice is not paid but was entered for the incorrect amount, the invoice amount, lines, and distributions can be updated to reflect the correct amount. If the Create Accounting process has already been run (reflected by an ACCOUNTING status of anything other then NO), the lines must be discarded and the distributions will need to be canceled.

Holds Tab

EBS uses holds to control invoices and prevent either payment or accounting. Holds can be applied manually or by the system. Manual holds are holds that are added by users when invoices in the system should not be paid because of missing information or other valid business reasons. System holds are applied when an invoice does not meet a system setup, such as when a receipt is missing for a purchase order and 3-way matching is turned on, or when the invoice does not pass the system validation because the total of the invoice lines does not equal the amount of the invoice. System holds are evaluated during validation and applied or released based on the latest information in the system. Although additional manual hold and release reasons can be set up, the system holds come preseeded and ready for use.

Most holds can be released manually, but some of the system holds require the problem to be resolved. There is a report, the Invoice on Hold Report, that should be run on a regular basis to monitor invoices on hold in the system. An additional report, the Matching Hold Detail Report, shows additional details for invoices held for matching reasons to purchase orders or receipts. The Holds tab on any invoice will give information relating to each hold and allow the hold to be released (when manual release is allowed). When a hold is on an invoice, the number of holds will appear on the General tab in the HOLD field, alerting the user to look for additional information on the Hold tab. System holds are both applied and released by the system when the invoice is validated. Holds can be controlled on the Holds tab of the Invoice screen, shown in Figure 6-5.

HOLD NAME will denote the actual name of the hold on the invoice, while the HOLD REASON gives more information about the type of hold on the invoice. HOLD DATE is populated with the system date when the hold was applied, while the HELD BY field either shows the user who manually

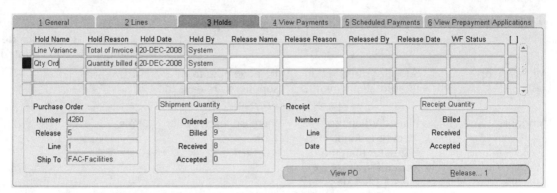

Payables Manager | Invoices | Entry | Invoices | Holds Tab

FIGURE 6-5   *Viewing holds on invoices*

placed the invoice on hold or displays SYSTEM to show that the hold was placed during validation based on the system setups. Once the hold is released, there are corresponding release fields. WF STATUS shows the status of any workflow where INITIATE WORKFLOW is checked, and the hold will send out notifications.

When an invoice matched to a purchase order is placed on hold by the system, information relating to the purchase order and receipts display on the Hold tab, to assist with resolving the hold. A listing of the system hold names can be found in Table 6-5. Some holds, noted in this table as well, will prevent the accounting from happening and must be resolved prior to sending this invoice to the General Ledger. If this type of hold is not resolved prior to month end, the invoice must be swept into the next accounting period (see the later section "Ensuring All Transactions Are Accounted and Transferred Prior to Closing the Period").

Notice that many holds can be released by fixing the invoice- or the purchase order–related information, or by changing a tolerance. If holds are being placed more often than is useful, adjusting the tolerance may be the best option to ensure that only valid holds are applied. This is especially true when the holds are being manually released without additional research. Removing the RELEASE button from the Invoice window for some users will prevent them from manually releasing any hold (manual or system) and ensure holds are managed properly.

Manually Releasing and Applying Holds   To add a manual hold, place the cursor in the HOLD NAME field, and select the appropriate hold from the list of values. Once saved, this invoice is now on hold.

Invoices on hold can be released manually either with a specific release name, or by performing a Quick Release. To use a specific release name, select the RELEASE NAME from the list of values and save the record. Releasing holds this way allows any manual release in the system to be selected, giving meaningful reasons for the release. Use the RELEASE button to perform what is called a Quick Release. The only RELEASE NAME that is allowed in the system is called Invoice Quick Release, giving no reason for the manual release.

Hold Name	Description	Action Required to Release	Can Be Released Manually?	Can Invoice Be Accounted?
All Payments	Supplier site is set up to hold all payments.	Remove hold from supplier to release the invoices.	Yes	Yes
Amount	Placed when the invoice amount is greater than the amount limit set on the supplier site.	Increase the supplier limit.	Yes	Yes
Amt Ord	The invoice amount is outside the tolerances set up for the purchase order.	Change the order amount, invoice amount, or tolerance.	Yes	Yes
Amt Rec	The invoice amount is outside the tolerances set up for the receipt.	Change the receipt amount, invoice amount, or tolerance.	Yes	Yes
Can not Execute Allocation	Invoice Allocations generated an invalid account number.	Correct the allocation so that it generates a valid account number, or ensure the account that is being generated is valid.	No	No
Can not Generated Distributions	Data entered on line is incomplete to generate distributions.	Add data on the line or manually create the distribution.	No	No
Can not Overlay Account	Account generated with the overlay data is invalid.	Correct the overlay data or ensure the account generated is a valid combination.	No	No
Can't Close PO	Receipts are accrued online, and the delivery does not equal the receipt.	Correct the receipt or delivery.	Yes	Yes
Can't Try PO Close	A hold is preventing the purchase order from being closed.	The hold causing the problem must be resolved.	Yes	Yes
Currency Difference	Invoice and Purchase Order are in different currencies.	Either change the currencies to agree or release the hold manually.	Yes	Yes

TABLE 6-5 *System Hold Names and Corrective Actions*

Hold Name	Description	Action Required to Release	Can Be Released Manually?	Can Invoice Be Accounted?
Dist Acct Invalid	Invalid distribution account.	Correct the distribution account to a valid account number, or make the account number or segments active.	No	No
Dist Variance	Invoice distributions do not equal the amount on the associated invoice line.	Adjust the amount on either the lines or the distribution so that they agree.	No	No
ERV Acct Invalid	Invalid Exchange Rate Variance account.	Correct the Exchange Rate Variance account to a valid account number, or make the account number or segments active.	No	No
Final Matching	An invoice cannot be matched to a purchase order that is already finally matched (this is usually a timing issue).	Reverse the invoice distribution and rematch the transaction to a purchase order that is not finally matched.	No	No
Funds Check	There are not enough funds to cover the invoice.	Used only with Encumbrances. Increase the budget or assign the invoice to a different budget account.	No	Yes
Inactive Distribution Set	Distribution Set assigned to a line is no longer active.	Reactivate the Distribution Set or remove it from the line.	No	No
Invalid Default Account	Account assigned on a line is invalid.	Update the account to a valid account or ensure the account assigned is valid in the system.	No	No

TABLE 6-5   *System Hold Names and Corrective Actions* (continued)

Hold Name	Description	Action Required to Release	Can Be Released Manually?	Can Invoice Be Accounted?
Insufficient Funds	The invoice is greater than funds available in Treasury.	Increase the cash in the bank account.	Yes	Yes
Line Variance	Invoice lines do not equal the amount on the invoice header.	Adjust the amount on either the lines or the header so they agree.	No	No
Matching Required	The supplier site is set up to hold all invoices not matched to a purchase order.	Match the distribution to a PO.	Yes	Yes
Max Amt Ord	The invoice amount is more than the amount ordered plus the maximum amount ordered tolerance.	Change the invoice, order, or tolerance amounts.	Yes	Yes
Max Amt Rec	The invoice amount is more than the amount received plus the maximum amount ordered tolerance.	Change the invoice, receipt, or tolerance amounts.	Yes	Yes
Max Qty Ord	The invoice quantity is greater than the purchase order quantity and the tolerance.	Adjust the invoice, order, or tolerance quantity.	Yes	Yes
Max Qty Rec	The invoice quantity is greater than the receipt quantity and the tolerance.	Adjust the invoice, receipt, or tolerance quantity.	Yes	Yes
Max Rate Amount	The exchange rate variance is greater than the setup tolerance.	Update the exchange rate on the purchase order or invoice, or else change the tolerance.	Yes	Yes
Max Ship Amount	The variance between a shipment and the invoice matched to it exceeds the tolerance.	Adjust the purchase order, invoice, or tolerance.	Yes	Yes

TABLE 6-5   *System Hold Names and Corrective Actions* (continued)

Hold Name	Description	Action Required to Release	Can Be Released Manually?	Can Invoice Be Accounted?
Max Total Amount	The invoice amount plus any exchange rate variance is larger than the tolerance.	Adjust the exchange rate or amount on an invoice or purchase order, or else increase the tolerance.	Yes	Yes
Milestone	Either the quantity or the invoice amount does not agree with the milestone on a purchase order.	Correct either the invoice or the PO so that they agree.	Yes	No
Natural Account Tax	The GL account associated with the tax code is invalid.	Correct the tax account to a valid account number, or make the account number or segments active.	Yes	No
No Rate	The exchange rate is missing for a foreign currency transaction.	Enter a rate or change the currency to the functional currency, or a currency where a rate exists.	No	No
Prepaid Amount	The prepayment applied is for more than the actual invoice.	Remove the prepayment and an amount equal to or less than the invoice amount.	Yes	No
Price	The average price (including corrections) is greater than the purchase order unit price by more than the tolerance.	Adjust the invoice, purchase order, or tolerance.	Yes	Yes
Qty Ord	The quantity on the invoice is greater than the quantity ordered plus the tolerance.	Adjust the quantity on the invoice or purchase order, or else the tolerance.	Yes	Yes
Qty Rec	The quantity on the invoice is greater than the quantity received plus the tolerance.	Adjust the quantity on the invoice or receipt, or else the tolerance.	Yes	Yes

TABLE 6-5 *System Hold Names and Corrective Actions* (continued)

Hold Name	Description	Action Required to Release	Can Be Released Manually?	Can Invoice Be Accounted?
Quantity	The invoice quantity is greater than the quantity accepted during delivery.	Adjust the invoice or accepted quantities.	Yes	Yes
Rec Exception	The receipt has an exception.	Can only be manually released.	Yes	Yes
Supplier	Placed when a supplier site is set up to hold all unvalidated invoices.	Manually remove the invoice hold, and remove the hold from supplier site to prevent future invoices from going on hold.	Yes	Yes
Tax Amount Range	The tax amount entered on an invoice does not fall within the tolerances for the calculated tax.	Adjust the rate, tax code, or group, or the tolerance.	Yes	Yes
Tax Difference	The tax code on the invoice is not the same as the code or taxable status on a purchase order.	Ensure the codes and status match.	Yes	Yes
Tax Variance	The tax amount entered on an invoice does not fall within the tolerances for the calculated tax.	Adjust the rate, tax code, or group, or the tolerance.	Yes	Yes
Withholding Tax	Unable to calculate invoice tax.	Requires the problem that is preventing the withholding from being calculated to be fixed.	No	No

TABLE 6-5   *System Hold Names and Corrective Actions* (continued)

View Payments

The View Payments tab, seen in Figure 6-6, is informational only and will populate after an invoice has been paid or partially paid. Voided payments will also appear here, along with any discounts that were taken. Place your cursor on one of the payments and click PAYMENT OVERVIEW to show additional information related to the selected payment.

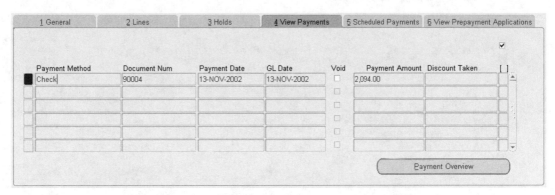

Payables Manager | Invoices | Entry | Invoices | Payment tab

FIGURE 6-6   *Viewing payments from an invoice*

Scheduled Payments

EBS utilizes a payment schedule to help determine when an invoice should be selected for payment, and allows multiple schedules to accommodate multiple payments for one invoice. Payment schedules are created automatically when invoices are saved in the system. When creating a settlement batch, note that two fields on the payment schedule window will affect if this invoice is considered for payment, as shown in Figure 6-7. The first is PRIORITY, used to limit the selection of invoices and group payments into batches, and the second is METHOD. METHOD tells EBS the manner that should be used to deliver this payment, such as a paper check or via electronic delivery such as ACH. When an electronic delivery method is selected, then the bank account name and number where the funds will be sent is displayed. This account number can be masked by setting the profile CE: Mask Internal Bank Account Number and AP: Mask Bank Account Numbers (System Administrator | Profile | System). GROSS AMOUNT and DISCOUNTS (first, second, and third, if applicable) can also be seen here, and payment holds can be manually applied and released.

Payment holds can be added by checking the HOLD box on the left of the screen, and optionally adding a HOLD REASON.

Payment schedules are assigned by EBS in accordance with the payment terms of the invoice, but additional schedules can be added by first changing the GROSS AMOUNT on the system-generated payment schedule to be less than the total invoice, and then clicking the SPLIT SCHEDULE button, which will create a new line for the remaining amount, allowing changes to due date or priorities to be made.

View Prepayment Applications

The View Prepayment Applications tab, seen in Figure 6-8, will show any prepayments applied to this invoice. AMOUNT APPLIED reflects the amount paid on this invoice with the prepayment, along with the GL DATE it was applied. PREPAYMENT NUMBER is the invoice number the prepayment was paid on, while PREPAYMENT LINE NUMBER reflects the actual line of the prepayment invoice. Both the SUPPLIER and the SITE for the prepayment invoice will also appear.

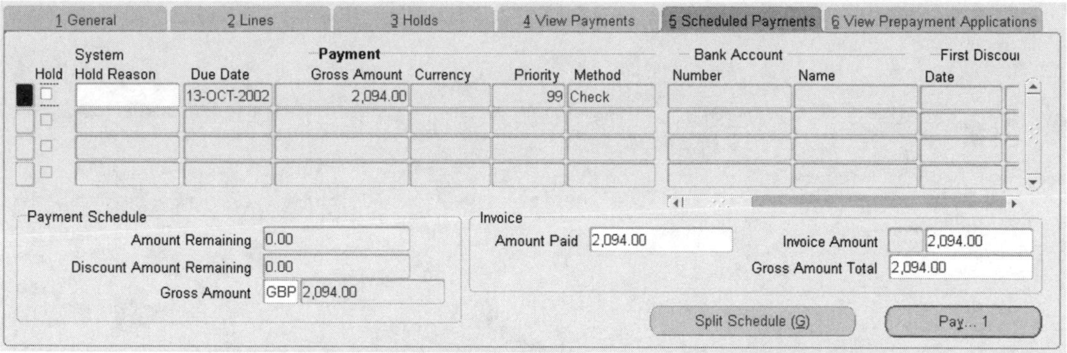

Payables Manager | Invoices | Entry | Invoices | Payment Schedule tab

FIGURE 6-7   *Invoice payment schedules*

Applying a Prepayment to an Invoice   Prepayments can be applied to one or more invoices that share the same supplier and site with the prepayment. Remember that only prepayments with a type of Temporary can be applied to an invoice. You do this with the ACTIONS button, on the invoice you want to apply the prepayment to. The top region of this screen, seen in Figure 6-9, is for the application of a prepayment. Any prepayment available to apply will appear, populating the PREPAYMENT NUMBER, LINE NUM, AMOUNT AVAILABLE, and SITE fields.

Checking the APPLY box will default in AMOUNT TO APPLY and GL DATE, both of which can be updated as needed. PREPAYMENT ON INVOICE can also be checked if the supplier invoice referenced the prepayment. If the prepayment is referenced on an invoice, the system will behave differently. When only PREPAYMENT is selected, the amount selected appears in the prepayment field on the General tab, and the amount paid will reflect the same amount, thus reducing the amount owed without reducing the invoice total. Selecting PREPAYMENT ON INVOICE actually reduces the amount of the invoice and shows no prepayment amount nor paid amount. This is because a Prepayment on Invoice assumes that the total invoice equals additional charges only, while a PREPAYMENT is just a previous payment against the total invoice.

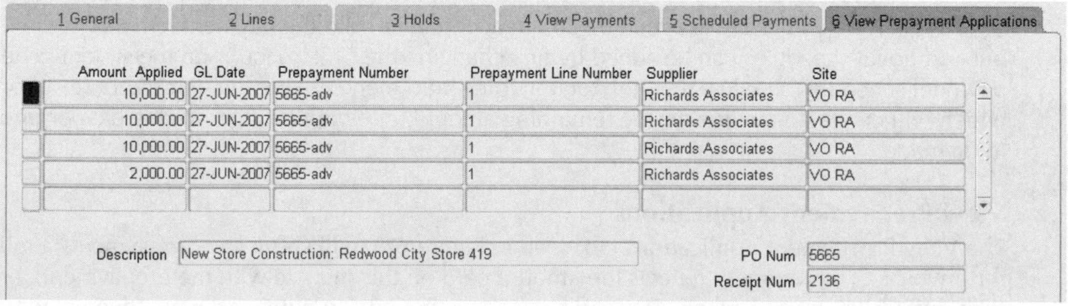

Payables Manager | Invoices | Entry | Invoices | View Prepayment Applications

FIGURE 6-8   *Viewing prepayment applications on an invoice*

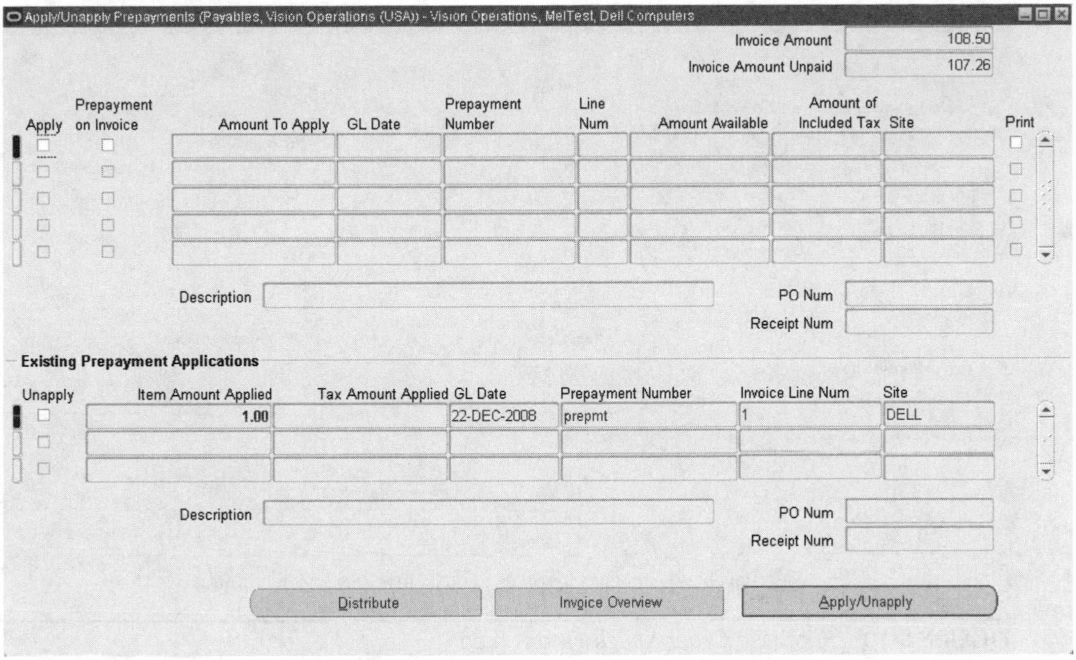

Payables Manager | Invoices | Entry | Invoices | Actions button | Apply/Unapply Prepayment

FIGURE 6-9 *Controlling prepayment applications*

As you can see, each tab is used for entering or reviewing different invoice-specific information. There are still additional buttons on the Invoice window, described next.

Match

When matching an invoice to a purchase order or receipt, enter the purchase order number in the PO NUMBER field on the invoice header, which will cause supplier name, number, and site to default in. Once you have entered the header information (the only fields that are required are the TRADING PARTNER, SUPPLIER NUMBER, and SUPPLIER SITE, which will default from the purchase order, and the INVOICE DATE, INVOICE NUM, and INVOICE AMOUNT), click MATCH and a Find screen will open with information from the invoice header populated, as shown in Figure 6-10. Notice that the purchase order number is populated for you; this is the minimum amount of information that is required on this Find screen and will return all rows on this purchase order, but additional fields can be added to decrease the rows returned, but they are not required to complete the match.

The most commonly used fields to limit the purchase order data are ITEM number or purchase order LINE number. Click FIND to continue with the match. The rows on the purchase order will populate for matching. If a purchase order was not entered on the invoice header, the MATCH button can still be used. The same screen will appear, but the Purchase Order NUM will not be populated, and you will have to add it or any other field to narrow the search. This is especially useful when the purchase order number is not known, as you can see all purchase orders available for the supplier and site.

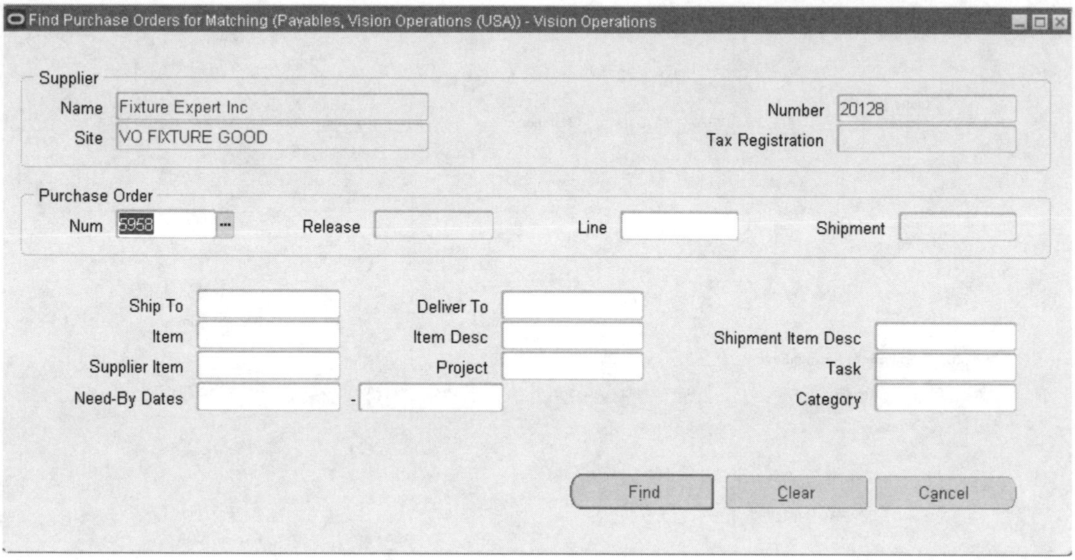

Payables Manager | Invoices | Entry | Invoices | Match button

FIGURE 6-10   *Purchase Order Match Find screen*

After the purchase order is found, select the line you want to match to by clicking the MATCH check box, and additional information for this line will populate in, as seen in Figure 6-11. This defaulted data includes any remaining quantities to be invoiced (QTY INVOICED), and a recap of the ORDERED and SHIPPED quantities pertaining to this line, as seen in the Shipment Quantity region at the lower-left of the Match screen. This section shows the total ORDERED, SHIPPED, RECEIVED, and previously BILLED quantities and is useful in ensuring this invoice is being validly matched to this purchase order line.

When matching to a purchase order, note that any tolerances that are not met will cause the invoice to be placed on a system hold. For example, you can match an invoice to a purchase order that is approved, but never received, and if the system is set up for a 3- or 4-way match, the invoice will be placed on a receiving hold until the receipt is made. This means a few things from a system standpoint: if the receiving tolerance is set to 0 percent, and an order is not received, the purchase order will stay open indefinitely unless someone manually closes it. On the flip side, if the receiving tolerance for invoices is set to 100 percent and the PO is not received, no hold will be placed, as the invoice was within the receiving tolerance.

There are three required fields on the Match window; QTY INVOICED, UNIT PRICE, and MATCH AMOUNT. Only two of the fields need to be entered; EBS will calculate the third. Quantity Invoiced times Unit Price must always equal the Match Amount. When any two of these fields are entered, the third field will be calculated to ensure accuracy. Only the quantity invoiced and the match amount have tolerances that control them, resulting in holds being placed on the invoices. There are also tolerances surrounding the closing of the invoices for these fields, where the workflow for the purchase order will change the statuses to closed when the amounts outstanding fall within the tolerances.

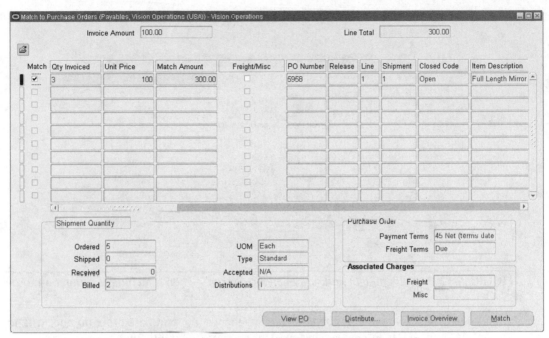

Payables Manager | Invoices | Entry | Invoices | Match button

FIGURE 6-11   *Entering purchase order matching information*

If an invoice includes freight or miscellaneous charges that were not included on the purchase order, they can be added by checking the FREIGHT/MISC box (refer to Figure 6-12). This will open up a window where Freight or Miscellaneous amounts can be added, and if you are using Advanced Pricing in purchase, you can add a COST FACTOR NAME to allocate the costs. Check the box the charges are associated with (FREIGHT or MISCELLANEOUS), and add the amount. This will add an additional line on the invoice for these amounts, allocating these charges over the distributions created on the invoice. EBS will create a separate line item for these, but the distribution account is the same as the line items on the purchase order.

If you are using Final Matching in your system, you can check the FINAL MATCH box. Use caution when using this feature, as once an invoice has been finally matched to a purchase order, no additional invoices can be matched to it.

In addition to matching to a purchase order or receipt (determined by how the Invoice Match Option on the purchase order was set up), you can match an invoice to a purchase order distribution instead of a line. Click the DISTRIBUTION button at the bottom of the Match page, and the invoice can be matched to a specific distribution line. From either screen, selecting MATCH will save the record and return you to the Invoice Entry window.

At the top of the Match screen, both the INVOICE AMOUNT and the LINE TOTAL will appear, allowing the user to see any variances in the matched transactions and balance the invoice header to the lines.

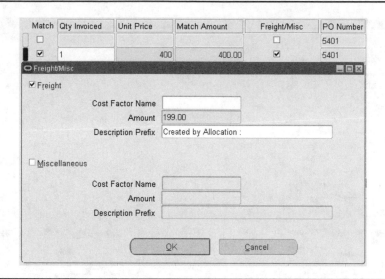

Match	Qty Invoiced	Unit Price	Match Amount	Freight/Misc	PO Number
☐				☐	5401
☑	1	400	400.00	☑	5401

○ Freight/Misc   ▬ ☐ ☒

☑ Freight

Cost Factor Name   [ ]

Amount   [199.00]

Description Prefix   [Created by Allocation :]

☐ Miscellaneous

Cost Factor Name   [ ]

Amount   [ ]

Description Prefix   [ ]

[OK]   [Cancel]

FIGURE 6-12   *Adding freight and miscellaneous charges when matching to a purchase order*

If this invoice is requeried for review or maintenance, the purchase order number will no longer be populated on the invoice header. This is normal, and the purchase order number can be found on the Lines section. This happens because one invoice can have lines matched to multiple purchase orders.

General Processing Guidelines for Matching Invoices to Purchase Orders   One of the biggest issues I tend to come across with clients is controlling the matching of invoices to purchase orders, and the ultimate closing of these orders. This is especially prevalent in organizations that are moving from a 2-way match process or manual matching process to a system-controlled 3- or 4-way match. Communication and system monitoring are key to understanding these holds and ensuring invoices are paid on time, holds are accurately removed, and perhaps the biggest issue I see, purchase orders are properly closed. No one wants to realize one or two years after go live that purchase orders are never closing and now they have a large manual cleanup effort on their hands. There are a few tips to ensure transactions are properly handled and that the system is set up to create meaningful and useful holds.

First, monitor the Invoice On Hold report. This is often done most effectively by one person who understands the policies for the organization. Having multiple users doing this review sometimes causes trends to be missed when system holds are applied and released, prolonging the problems and ultimate resolutions. The things you should monitor for are organization-wide holds that are being incorrectly placed and manually released on a regular basis, especially relating to tolerances. Holds are often incorrectly placed for a few main reasons besides incorrect tolerance setups: invoices incorrectly matched to purchase orders, invoices not matched to any purchase order, and purchase orders not properly received. These can be resolved with good communication between the payables department and suppliers, purchasing, and end users performing receipts.

Invoices are sometimes matched to an incorrect purchase order, or not matched at all when a purchase order exists. This can happen if the supplier provides no or inaccurate purchase order numbers, or when a previous invoice was incorrectly matched to the purchase order, leaving no open lines for matching an additional invoice. Communicating with the suppliers and ensuring they understand that any invoice received without a purchase order number will be delayed for payment processing helps to reduce the first problem, while training the Payables users how to research problems when purchase orders are already matched to invoices helps with the second. Research can be done by looking at all invoices already matched to the purchase order. In the Invoice Inquiry window (Invoices | Inquiry | Invoices), invoices can be queried up by Purchase Order number, finding all the invoices matched to that order, and allowing research to be done to determine the correct matching that should take place.

Sometimes the problem lies with the purchase order itself, where the order was canceled or closed in error prior to payment. Working with the purchasing department helps to resolve these issues. For new EBS implementations, or in established systems where problems exist with invoices and purchase order matching, I recommend weekly meetings to review matching problems and hold issues between purchasing and payables. Once both sides understand where the problems exist and are educated in the trickle-down effects of changes in an integrated processing system like EBS, then the problems tend to reduce and the frequency of these meetings can also be reduced.

Purchasing also needs to review the Open Purchase Orders Report to ensure that purchase orders are closing in a timely fashion. Purchase orders can remain open because they were not received, because they were not matched to an invoice, or because the tolerances were set incorrectly. Sometimes purchase orders do need to be manually closed when the final portions of the lines will not be received for whatever reason, but if a large percentage of orders are routinely being closed manually, the tolerances that control when the orders close are probably wrong and need to be adjusted.

All of the preceding problems will exist if Payables does not properly create corrections against a purchase order for any incorrectly matched invoice or correcting invoices and credit memos received from a supplier. If an invoice is incorrectly matched to a purchase order or has the incorrect coding associated with it, the line first needs to be discarded, which will open up the purchase order for the invoice matched quantities and amounts. Then, the invoice can be matched to the proper purchase order or line. Invoices should never be corrected by reversing the matched distribution or discarding the matched line, and then manually adding new lines or distributions without matching them to the correct purchase order. If the distribution on a purchase order is updated, payables must first discard the line and rematch the invoice to get the new accounting. Credit memos should be matched to the purchase order to offset the return to vendor (RTV) transaction performed when the item was returned.

In systems where end users outside of purchasing and manufacturing need to receive items, the receipt is sometimes not completed on a timely basis or at all, causing unwanted holds in Payables and leaving purchase orders open incorrectly for future receipts. Ensuring that users are properly trained in how to receive product, and that they understand the importance of performing this duty, is a key communication factor. Setting up the Oracle Receiving Workflow process to run on a regular interval with the timely escalations and reminders will assist in encouraging end users to receive product. Purchasing should also monitor the Expected Receipts Report along with invoices that are on hold for no receipt to help purchasing or payables ensure the users receive their orders.

The final problem typically found is usually in the General Ledger, due to improper journal entries created from an invoice. This happens when the distributions assigned to an invoice, and the Subledger Accounting's treatment of these distributions, are incorrect for some reason. First, it should be determined if a system setup is causing the problem, such as an expense account associated with an item, an incorrect account associated with the user, or an improper Subledger Accounting setup. If the system setups are correct, backtracking to the source of the problem and correcting it there is the best way to stop the issue from reoccurring. While these problems can be corrected with a journal entry in the General Ledger, they often repeat over and over unless they are stopped at the source.

In organizations where iProcurement is implemented, the end users need to be properly trained in the correct General Ledger codes for their orders. By taking the time to train the requestors and provide up-to-date procedures, you can often eliminate a majority of the problems. Since most users will refer to, or copy, a prior transaction when creating new ones, fixing the problems at the source prevents this type of repeat problem. For example, if a payables person always queries up the previous invoice to a supplier to get the accounting for it, and it is never fixed in Payables, then that person is always referring to the incorrect accounting and repeating the same problem over and over, when in reality he or she is trying to do it correctly. This goes for purchasing folks creating purchase orders, as well as end users creating requisitions. While it can be time consuming and sometimes cumbersome to coordinate these correcting entries, it is usually worth the effort to prevent repeat issues.

Quick Match

From the Invoice window, you can use the QUICK MATCH button to match an invoice to a purchase order, and the system will perform the match for you, allowing you to review the information on the Lines tab after the match is performed. Quick Match will match the invoice to the first open line/receipt on the purchase order, continuing to the next line until the entire amount is matched. Since the matching information cannot be updated, this feature is most useful when the purchase order has only one line, or the receipts are made in chronological order.

Corrections

You can perform corrections against purchase orders for both the quantity and the price to keep the purchase order reflecting the proper quantities or amounts still available for payment. Tolerances still apply when a price correction is made, putting the correction on hold if the adjustment makes the total amount matched to an invoice greater than the tolerance. After entering an invoice, credit memo, or debit memo, click CORRECTION, and a Find window appears, shown in Figure 6-13. Select PRICE CORRECTION, QUANTITY CORRECTION, or AMOUNT CORRECTION from the drop-down, and identify the purchase order or invoice matched to a purchase order that is being corrected. The window that will open up is very similar to the Match window for purchase orders but will also allow negative quantities and negative amounts. Quantities can only be entered when QUANTITY or PRICE CORRECTION is selected. AMOUNT CORRECTION allows just the total amount of the match to be corrected, and EBS automatically adjusts the unit price, based on the original quantity matched against the purchase order. This will not update the quantity that is matched against the purchase order, just the amount. Click CORRECT, and the correction will be saved and lines created on the invoice.

Corrections can be matched to either a purchase order or an invoice, depending on which is supplied. When matching a correction to an invoice, the correction will be related to the invoice and matched to the purchase order, creating a triangular relationship.

Tax Details

Detail Tax Lines, an informational screen seen in Figure 6-14, displays the tax drivers that are used at both the invoice and the individual line levels to calculate the tax when using Oracle's E-Tax solution. Information will display here only after you have had tax calculated automatically on an invoice by either validating the invoice or clicking CALCULATE TAX.

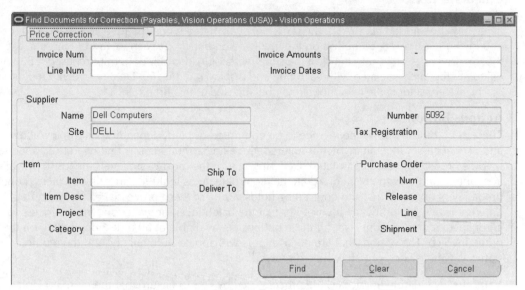

Payables Manager | Invoices | Entry | Invoices | Correction button

FIGURE 6-13 *Entering price or amount corrections*

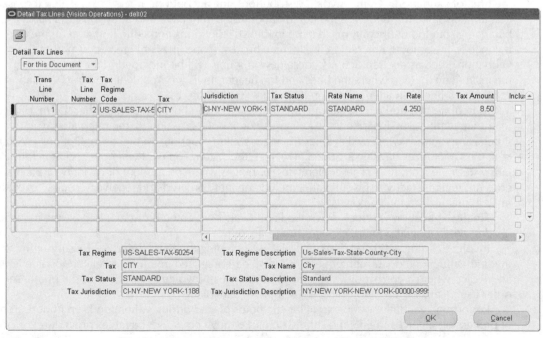

Payables Manager | Invoices | Entry | Invoices | Tax Details button

FIGURE 6-14 *Line-level tax details*

Calculate Tax

When EBS is set up to automatically calculate tax on an invoice (sales and use taxes, withholding taxes, or value-added tax [VAT]), the tax is only calculated when the invoice is validated, or when you click the CALCULATE TAX button on the invoice workbench, as seen in earlier Figure 6-2. Using the tax drivers, such as tax status on the supplier, tax jurisdiction, or item purchased, EBS will calculate the tax associated with each line and display it in the Tax Details screen. Depending on the system setups, the tax amount may be adjusted at this time.

Actions Button

The ACTIONS button allows the invoice to be controlled or paid, depending on the invoice status and user access. Once an invoice is entered, there are several actions that need to happen for the invoice processing to be completed. Every invoice, at the most basic levels, needs to be validated, accounted, and eventually paid. Additional control features include canceling invoices, controlling prepayment applications, and controlling holds. Many of these processes can be completed at different levels, including the invoice itself, at the batch level, or via a concurrent process to select all or specific transactions. Not all these options are available at all times, depending on the status of the invoice. The options that are not available will appear in light gray, and the required invoice status as well as each option will be discussed next.

Validate   Validating invoices is the process used by EBS to ensure that there are no violations not only to the system setups like matching and tolerances, but also to basic system rules, such as having the line total equal to the invoice or using a valid account combination. Validation also calculates any taxes associated with the invoice lines. System settings that are checked include the status of the period the invoice is entered against. The period must be Open or Future Entry at the time of validation. On the invoice distributions, the account numbers are checked to ensure that all the segments, as well as the combination itself, are active and allow posting. From a balancing standpoint, it confirms that the invoice distributions equal the line, and all the lines balance to the amount entered on the invoice header. If any lines are created as part of the validation, such as tax transactions, these new amounts will be included in the balancing. This means that an invoice where the lines and the header totals are in balance prior to validation may still go on a line hold after validation if tax lines were created.

Matching, tax, and exchange rate tolerances are also checked, using either the invoice tolerance template assigned to the supplier site or, if none is assigned, the template saved in the Purchasing Options window (Payables Manager | Setup | Options | Purchasing Options | Matching tab). If no tolerances have been added here, then the system approval will not check if a transaction falls within the tolerances. These tolerances, or ranges where an amount or quantity or percentage does not match exactly but is still valid, include quantity ordered and received, pricing, exchange rate, shipment, and total amounts.

Finally, validation will lock down the liability account entered or defaulted on the invoice header, preventing any future changes to this account.

Invoices can be validated in several places, including the Batch window, by submitting the Invoice Validation concurrent request, or by validating related invoices. A related invoice is an invoice where a correction was performed against an invoice as opposed to the purchase order itself, causing a relationship between the two invoices.

Performing validations and managing the holds placed during validation is an important part of processing invoices in EBS and should be part of any company's payables procedures.

Validate Related Invoices   Invoices become related when a credit or debit memo is matched to invoices during a price correction. Using the ACTIONS button, click the VALIDATE RELATED INVOICES button for an invoice or its related credit or debit memo to cause the invoice itself and its related credit memo/debit memo to be approved.

Cancel Invoices   Once an invoice has been validated, it can no longer be deleted from EBS, leaving canceling it the only option. Canceling an invoice will reverse all the accounting associated with an invoice by creating a distribution reversal, zeroing out all lines on the invoice, removing any payment schedules, and also removing this invoice from any invoice aging or trail balance in Payables. If an invoice has already been paid, the payment must first be voided in order to cancel the invoice. See Chapter 8 for more information on voiding payments.

Open periods in the system control the accounting date that is associated with a canceled invoice. The earliest open period *after* the original date on the invoice line will be assigned to the cancellation transactions and cannot be updated. For example, if an invoice has an accounting date as January 15, 2002, and is canceled on December 31, 2002, but November is still opened, the canceled transactions will have a General Ledger date of November 1, 2002. This date cannot be changed when the cancellation option is used. The only way to control the accounting date on a canceled invoice, besides controlling the actual period status, is by first reversing the invoice distributions and then discarding the lines to make them total zero prior to canceling the invoice. Use the reverse feature to control the accounting date. See the earlier section "Canceling Distributions and Discarding Lines."

Apply/Unapply Prepayment   Prepayments, or payments made in advance of the goods or services being rendered, are usually invoiced for at a later date, where an adjustment to the amount can be made by the supplier on the basis of the actual costs. There are two types of prepayments in EBS: Temporary and Permanent. Permanent prepayments represent such things as security deposits for leases, and cannot be later applied to an invoice as a reduction in payment. Temporary prepayments represent amounts that will later be reduced from an invoice received from the supplier. On either the prepayment itself or the applicable invoice, these applications can be controlled with the Apply/Unapply options, access from the actions button, either adding or removing the prepayment application. To create an actual prepayment in Payables, use the regular invoice window (Invoices | Entry | Invoices) and select a type of Prepayment. This should be entered for the supplier and site the invoice will be received for at a later date. After adding the invoice amount and a line, validate and pay the prepayment. The distributions for the invoice will be created based on the prepayment account setup on the Accounting tab of the supplier. Once the prepayment is entered and settled in EBS, the users will be reminded that it is available for application with every invoice or expense report entered into Payables.

Pay in Full   The PAY IN FULL option in Actions is really a shortcut to the Payments window, populating the invoice-specific data in for payment. The major difference between accessing the Payments window directly versus from the Invoice window is that multiple invoices can be paid when the Payments window is accessed directly, as opposed to through an invoice, which restricts the payment to the invoice it was accessed from. This feature is only available if the user actually has access to create payments as well as invoices in EBS. With the multitude of regulations governing accounting these days, including Sarbanes-Oxley's section on "Segregation of Duties," most companies no longer allow the ability to enter or change invoices and the ability to create payments to be assigned to the same user.

Create Accounting   The option to CREATE ACCOUNTING (from the ACTIONS button) will generate the accounting for the transaction based on the subledger accounting setups. Accounting can be generated in different modes. Draft will allow updates to the generated account numbers to be made prior to sending the accounting entries to the General Ledger. Final will create the accounting transactions, but these transactions will not be sent to the General Ledger interface tables until the Transfer Journal Entries to GL concurrent request is run. Accounting entries generated in Final mode cannot be modified. Final Post combines the accounting process and transfer to the General Ledger in one step, but it is important to understand that this will only transfer entries accounted as part of this run to the General Ledger, not all accounted transactions. CREATE ACCOUNTING will not only create the distribution and liability accounting entries, it also creates variance entries for such things as invoice price variances or exchange rate variances.

Invoices can be also be accounted at the individual level, for an entire batch, or for all transactions in the system by submitting the Create Accounting concurrent request.

Stop Approval   When an invoice has been submitted for approval, users with the proper authority can stop the approval process at any point in time, allowing changes to be made on the invoice, and then resubmitting it for approval, or canceling it all together. Invoices that have had STOP APPROVAL performed on them cannot be paid until the approval is reinitiated and the invoice is approved.

Force Approval   FORCE APPROVAL appears when an invoice has started the approval process and the user is set up to force the approval on an invoice. This process will approve the invoice, even when the user does not have the proper authority, and allow the invoice to be processed for payment. Use caution in adding this function to users, as it will bypass the system approval process and constraints that are built into it.

Release Holds   When a hold allows manual release, they can either be released on the Holds tab, one hold at a time, or by selecting RELEASE HOLDS in the ACTIONS button, which will release all holds that allow manual release at the same time. After clicking the RELEASE HOLDS option, you can enter a specific HOLD NAME, or ALL to release all holds. If ALL is selected, Holds Quick Released is the only HOLD REASON that can be selected.

Print Notice   Notices are used to inform suppliers of invoices, credit memos, or debit memos that have been entered in the system, and can be sent by selecting PRINT NOTICE from the ACTIONS button.

As you can see, the options on the Invoice Entry window are extensive, and allow detailed data to be tracked in the system, as well as be used for processing the transactions. Entering more information in the system reduces the need to refer to printed or backup information to complete analysis or answer questions.

Entering Quick Invoices

In addition to the data entry screens just reviewed, EBS also has a Quick Entry window for invoices. This window, seen in Figure 6-15, provides a faster way of entering invoices into Payables and is especially useful when detailed matching to purchase orders is not required, or invoices are not matched to purchase orders. The fields that exist on this window are the same as the fields on the Invoice Workbench, except that many of the informational fields are missing.

The main differences between the two different methods of entering invoices, from a functional standpoint, are that Quick Invoice cannot be used to enter Prepayments, Debit Memos, or Credit Memos, or to calculation taxes. Tax lines and distributions, invoice allocations, and sequential voucher numbering are not all visible on the Quick Invoice window. The Invoice Workbench has

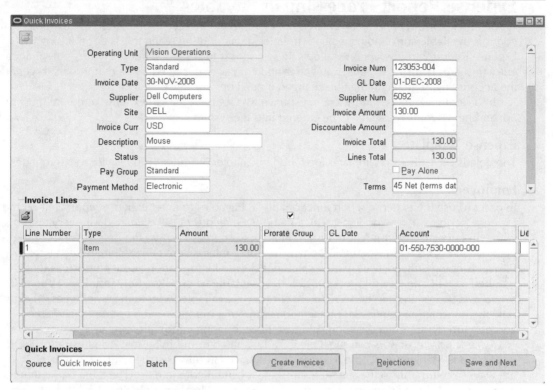

Payables Manager | Invoices | Entry | Quick Invoice

FIGURE 6-15 *Quick Invoice entry*

access to attachments and holds, and overrides can be made to payment priorities and terms dates, and you can create payments.

When invoices are entered using the Quick Entry window, they will need to be imported similarly to expense reports to appear on the Invoice Workbench for validation, approval, and payment processing. After you enter invoices in the Quick Entry window, you can import by either clicking on the CREATE INVOICES button or running the Payables Open Interface Import concurrent request. CREATE INVOICES will show the QUICK INVOICE BATCH name, which was entered when the Quick Invoice window was opened. You can add a HOLD NAME and a REASON for the entire batch, as well as a BATCH NAME. This BATCH NAME is required only when invoice batching is turned on in the system. Adding a GL DATE here will become the default for all the invoices in the batch; otherwise, the system will assign the GL date based on the system setups (Setup | Options | Payables Options | Invoice tab). Select PURGE to purge all processed invoices from the quick invoice tables once invoices are generated for them, and select SUMMARIZE REPORT to create a summary report as opposed to a detailed one for the processed batch. Once these processes are complete, the invoices are processed as normal invoices and appear in the Invoice Workbench for review and adjustments.

Expense Report Processing in Payables

While an expense report can be entered directly into the Invoice Workbench, there are no controls available surrounding expense policies or accounting when this is done. Using the Expense Report window not only allows these controls to be set up but decreases potential data entry mistakes by using expense categories and employee-assigned account numbers to generate the accounting, which can then be changed if need be.

In order to use this window, you must have two setups. First, an expense template must be set up, and next, employees have to be entered into the system.

Expense Template

The details on setting up templates are found in Chapter 5, under "Expense Report Templates."

Employees

In order to use the expense report functionality in Payables to enter expense reports (either the Expense Report window or iExpenses), an employee record must be created for every employee who will have an expense report. Oracle Human Resources has two different versions of the Employee/Persons window. The first one is for companies where either Human Resources or Payroll is being utilized. This window includes detailed information about employees that is required for HR and Payroll processing, and is available when HR is fully installed. When HR is set up as a Shared Install, then a different window is available for entering employees, tracking only the information required for integration with other modules, such as employee name, address, supervisor, office location, and default accounting information.

System Administrators can see if the install is shared or full in System Administration | Oracle Applications Manager | License Manager. If you have HR fully installed but are not using it, there are ways to return this to the shared install state if certain criteria exist. The table name that tracks the status of an installation is fnd_product_installations. MetaLink note 461063.1 outlines how to check for the type of installation and the conditions when it can be changed back to a shared install.

The fields that are used on the employee record when entering an expense report are employee name, MAIL designator under the personal information, employee address, locations, DEFAULT EXPENSE ACCOUNT, and possibly a supervisor for routing approvals. The MAIL designator can be set to either HOME, in which case the employee address is printed on the expense checks, or OFFICE, which prints their location address. The DEFAULT EXPENSE ACCOUNT is used to build the account number on the expense report, depending on how the template is set up.

Employee information is then used to create supplier records. With the new supplier structure for suppliers, employee addresses can now only be updated in the Employee window, and not on the supplier record. Employees are turned into suppliers when expense reports are exported, as well as updated for any changes. Employee changes such as terminations, and name changes, will also update the supplier record by running the Employee Update Program in Payables.

Entering Expense Reports in Payables

Expense reports can be entered into the Expense Report window in Payables by users who have the proper access. In general, it is used by the payables department to process expense reports as opposed to being used throughout the company for employees to enter their expense reports themselves. iExpenses is usually implemented for general, companywide access. The major difference between the two methods of entering requests for reimbursements is control. iExpenses limits the fields that employees have access to updating when entering expense reports as well as choosing the person an expense report is created for. It also has an audit capability that is accessible by Payables. It further integrates with Oracle Workflow for expense report approval processing prior to payment. Using the Expense Report window in Payables does not integrate with Oracle Workflow for approval process, but combines all the other functionality onto one window. Note that there are no limitations on the employee who can work in the Expense Report window, allowing all employees to enter expense reports for any person, as well as see any entered expense report.

To enter an expense report in Payables, refer to Figure 6-16. After entering the OPERATING UNIT, select the NAME of the employee the expense report is being processed for. Employees must be set up and not terminated in the Employee/Person window (Employees | Enter Employees) to be available here. The NUMBER will populate with the employee number. The GL ACCOUNT is the default expense account on the employee record, but this can be overridden. This account will be used to default in any account segments that are not populated on a line item on the Expense Report template. DESCRIPTION will default in from the GL ACCOUNT and represents the descriptions of each segment of the account number. SEND TO also defaults from the employee record but can be overridden here. This field will determine the actual address that prints on the checks. HOME will print the address on the Address tab of the employee record, while OFFICE will print the address associated with the Location assigned to the employee record. These addresses appear as Site Names on the supplier record, while the actual address is associated with the employee record.

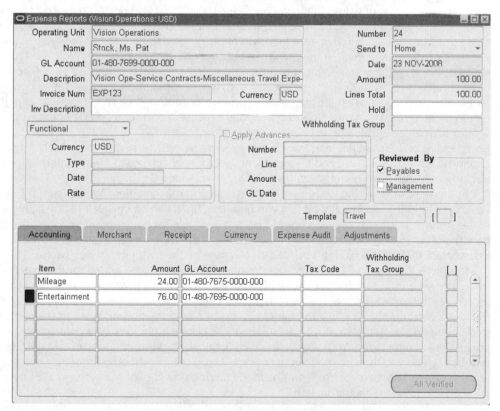

Payables Manager | Invoices | Entry | Expense Reports

FIGURE 6-16 *Entering expense reports in Payables*

The DATE field should be completed with the date on the expense report itself, often representing the last date the report covers. AMOUNT is the total of the expense report, and CURRENCY is the currency the expense report will be entered in. You can assign an INVOICE NUM, and your organization should adopt a numbering policy to distinguish expenses entered on this window from iExpenses or supplier invoices when querying information on the Invoice Workbench. An INV DESCRIPTION can be added as an explanation for the expenses. LINE TOTAL will populate as lines are added and will need to balance to the AMOUNT before the expense report can be processed. HOLD is used when this expense report is being entered but should not yet be paid for some reason. A hold will go on the invoice created from the expense report, preventing payment until it is released. If transactions on this expense report are subject to withholding tax, the WITHHOLD TAX GROUP can be added to calculate the taxes.

The FUNCTIONAL/PAYMENT section of the screen is used when invoices are either entered or paid in any currency other than the functional currency for the Ledger; it tracks exchange rate information.

When the employee name is first entered, a pop-up box will appear if there are any outstanding advances, entered as prepayments in Payables, for this employee. These will need to be manually applied to the expense report in the APPLY ADVANCES section. This area is only available for update when there are outstanding advances. Unchecking APPLY ADVANCES will leave the prepayment open for another expense report or invoice, and it will leave this expense report available for settlement.

To apply a specific prepayment, if more than one are available, select the prepayment invoice number from the list of values in the NUMBER field. The AMOUNT will default based on the expense report AMOUNT and the amount still available on the prepayment, but it can also be decreased to apply a lesser amount. Entering zero here will apply no prepayment to this expense report. The LINE only needs to be entered if the prepayment had more than one line and you want to apply a specific line from the prepayment. If neither a number nor a line is entered, EBS will apply the oldest prepayment to this expense report. A prepayment application reduces the amount owed on the expense report when it is imported as an invoice, and will close the invoice as paid if the prepayment applied is enough to satisfy the total expense report. Only prepayment types of Temporary can be applied to an expense report.

Check boxes are available to track if this expense report was reviewed by both the payables department for compliance, and management, but these check boxes are for informational tracking only and have no functionality or workflows behind them.

In the TEMPLATE field, the default template assigned in the Payables Options (Setup | Options | Payables Options | Expense Report tab) will populate, but it can be changed to any active template in the system. This template will control the ITEMS available for payment on an expense report, and how the GL ACCOUNT is built. Lines cannot be added to the expense report without selecting an ITEM to associate them to, so having a miscellaneous item on the template is often useful.

On the Accounting tab, specific accounting information can be added for the expense report. ITEM, AMOUNT, and GL ACCOUNT are the only required fields on this lower section of the screen. ITEM represents the expense categories available from the expense report template and determines how the GL ACCOUNT number is going to be built. EBS uses a combination of constant segments assigned to the template item, the employee default expense account, and any user-entered segments to create the account string. You must actually click the GL ACCOUNT field to generate this account number, which can then be modified if needed. The AMOUNTS entered on the lines must equal the AMOUNT entered on the expense report header. Entering TAX CODES or WITHHOLDING TAX GROUPS will record tax related to this transaction.

You can add merchant-specific information to each line item, referencing the NAME, DOCUMENT NUMBER, TAX REG NUMBER, and TAXPAYER ID. This is often required information in countries where VAT exists. Receipt-specific information, including a COUNTRY OF SUPPLY, can also be tracked on the Receipt tab.

Based on the functional currency information entered on the expense report header, currency information relating to the receipt (or specific line) appears on the Currency tab.

For auditing purposes, receipt information can be tracked and monitored as being VERIFIED, REQUIRED, or MISSING, and a JUSTIFICATION can be added. Clicking ALL VERIFIED will check the VERIFIED box for all the lines on this expense report. EBS allows an expense report to be either Verified or Reviewed by Payables. Both options are not available on the same expense report.

If an expense report is adjusted for any reason, an AUDIT EXCEPTION COMMENT can be added, and the line selected as POLICY NON-COMPLIANCE. Selecting this box will reduce the amount due on this expense report when the transaction is exported into Payables.

At this point, the expense report is ready to be exported into Payables to create an invoice that can be validated, approved if required, and processed for payment. The concurrent request Expense Report Export needs to be run, with the SOURCE set as Payables Expense Reports (the out-of-the-box default is Oracle Internet Expenses, which exports reports from iExpenses). After the invoice is created as an invoice, it still requires validation.

The Expense Report window can also be used to query up transactions that were entered here by clicking the FIND icon, which will open up a Find box. Enter a portion of the employee name to narrow down the selection, or the expense report number, prior to clicking FIND. In this Find window, all the way over to the right, the status of the report shows if it has been exported to Payables yet or not. Expense reports that have already been sent over are indicated with an asterisk (*) in the IMPORTED column. Unfortunately, there is still no seeded report to show unprocessed expense reports. Unlike in earlier releases, expense reports entered in iExpenses can no longer been seen in this form.

Netting Outstanding Receivables and Payables

At times, businesses agree to net outstanding Receivables and Payables transactions, as opposed to settling them separately, when a supplier is also your customer. This process has traditionally been performed with a combination of credit and debit memos in Receivables and Payables. The EBS AR/AP Netting feature helps to automate this process by storing predefined netting agreements that include business rules and transaction selection criteria, as well as a process that can be run to create, review, and approve these offsetting transactions. While this process is limited to Receivables and Payables transactions, it is not limited to third-party customers who are suppliers; when business requires that intercompany transactions be run through Payables and Receivables, but the companies are both in the same operating unit, the AR/AP Netting can be used to clear these transactions as well.

This netting process, as opposed to creating Credit or Debit memos to offset transactions, will create a netting receipt in Receivables and a netting payment in Payables.

Setting Up Netting in EBS

EBS has several setup steps required prior to using the netting feature. First, a bank account must be set up to allow netting transactions. This account must have NETTING ACCOUNT under General Controls set to YES, and it must also be set to be used in Payables and Receivables, as shown in Figure 6-17.

Next, ensure this bank account is added to the Receipt classes called AP/AR Netting in Receivables, as seen in Figure 6-18.

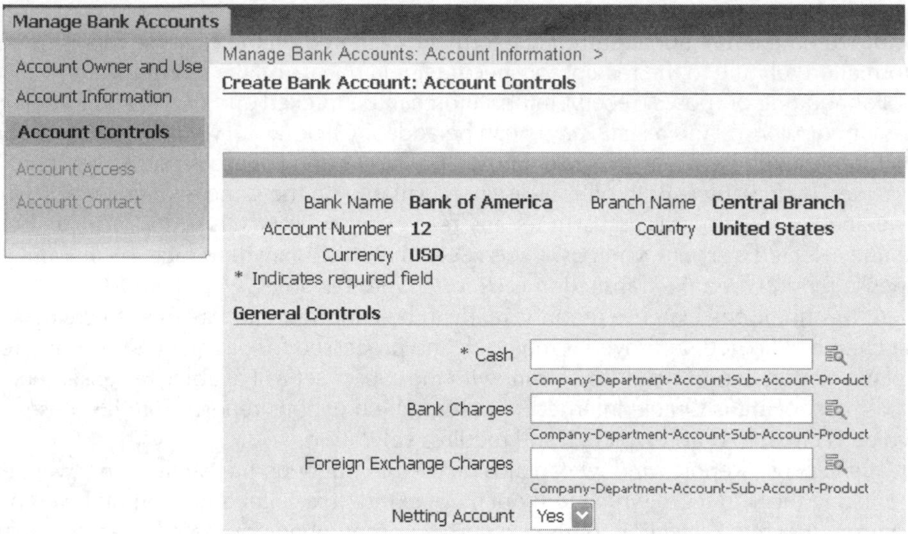

Payables Manager | Setup | Payment | Bank Accounts

FIGURE 6-17   *Making a bank account for netting*

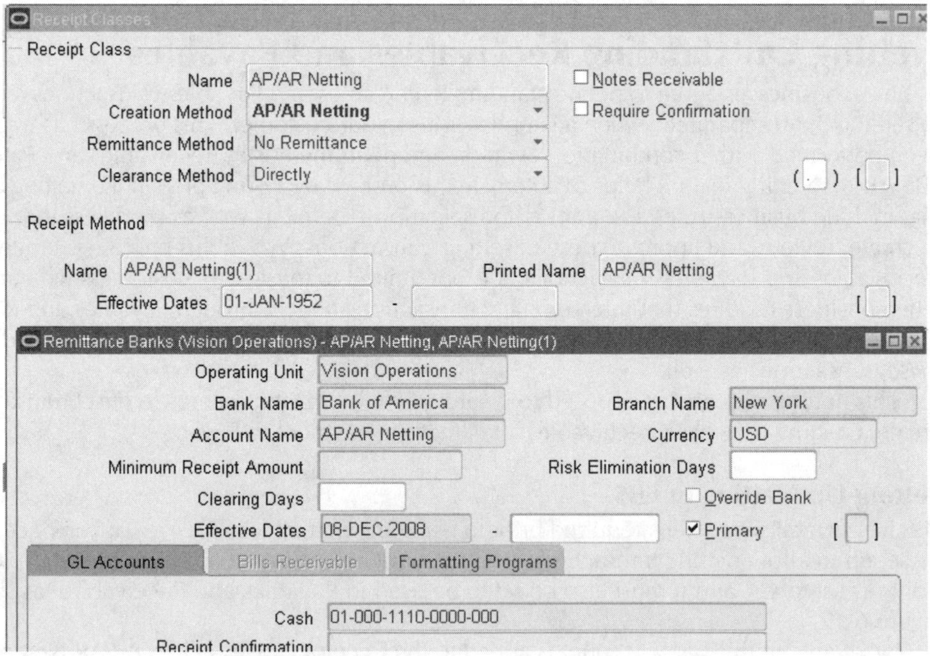

Receivables Manager | Setup | Receipts | Receipt Classes

FIGURE 6-18   *Adding the bank account to the Receipt class*

Receivables also needs to allow payment of unrelated transactions, as is determined in the Trans and Customer tab of the System Options (Receivables Manager | Setup | System | System Options).

EBS has the ability to require an approval from a contact at the customer/supplier prior to creating the transactions. In order to use this feature, the person who will be approving the transactions needs to be set up as a contact with an e-mail address and added to both the supplier and the customer.

Once the customer, supplier, and bank account are set up, a netting agreement needs to be created in the system. Besides creating the link by identifying the Receivables customers and Payables suppliers that will have their transactions considered for netting, the agreement also sets up the criteria that will be used to select the transactions. The Setup screen is show in Figure 6-19.

If you have access to more than one OPERATING UNIT, select the operating unit that the netting will occur for. EBS does not support netting transactions across different operating units. Assign a unique NETTING AGREEMENT NAME, and optionally add a TRADING PARTNER REFERENCE, which can be included on the e-mail to the approver for reference. This might be your supplier number or customer number in their system. Enter the START DATE for the earliest business day that can be assigned to any settlement transactions created with this agreement. Note that this is not the earliest transaction date that can

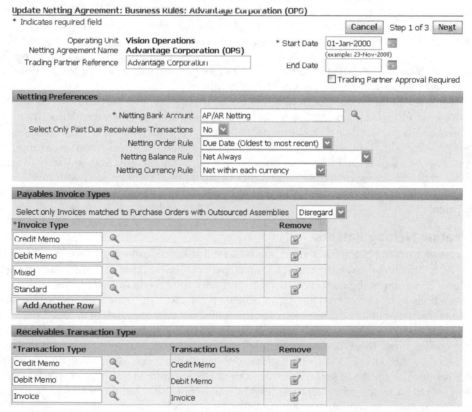

Payables Manager | Payments | Entry | Netting | Netting Agreement

FIGURE 6-19   *AR/AP netting agreement setups*

be selected for settlement, but the actual date that the settlement can be assigned. When this agreement is not longer in effect, enter an END DATE for the last day it can be used.

When TRADING PARTNER APPROVAL REQUIRED is checked, the proposed netting transactions will require an approval from the customer/supplier prior to processing. After it is checked, a box will appear to select an APPROVER NAME, which must have an e-mail address associated with it. Also, enter the results when there is NO RESPONSE ACTION from this person, choosing to approve the transactions or reject the batch that was generated.

Next, select the NETTING BANK ACCOUNT that was set up in the earlier step. To limit the invoices selected in receivables to only past due transactions, enter YES next to SELECT ONLY PAST DUE RECEIVABLES TRANSACTIONS. This will also show the field that allows the number of PAST DUE DAYS to be entered. You then assign NETTING ORDER RULES to determine how transactions are selected, based on due date, oldest to most recent or newest to oldest, transaction date, or ascending or descending amounts. Netting can occur either whenever there are transactions to net, or only when the Payables balance is greater than the Receivables balance, based on the setting for NETTING BALANCE RULE. Also, a NETTING CURRENCY RULE can be set to determine if netting occurs within a single currency and the currency is selected, for all currencies but only with transactions of like currencies, or for all currencies based on the functional currency value.

For Payables, you must determine how transactions are netted when the outstanding invoice is matched to a purchase order that has outsourced assemblies associated with it. Selecting YES for the option SELECT ONLY INVOICES MATCHED TO PURCHASE ORDERS WITH OUTSOURCED ASSEMBLIES only uses these invoices for netting, whereas NO will not use an invoice with outsourced assemblies for netting. The final option, DISREGARD, disregards if there is an outsourced assembly on the purchase orders and considers all invoices for netting. Next, assign the Invoice Types in Payables and Transaction Types in Receivables that should be considered for netting. If any type of transaction or invoice is not listed here, it will not be considered for netting.

After selecting the NEXT button, select both the supplier and the customer that will be considered for netting, and optionally select a specific address (SITE in payables, LOCATION in receivables) to be used. If no location or site is selected, all addresses will be considered. Note that you can add additional rows to accommodate multiple addresses as well as multiple customer or supplier accounts. EBS does not limit this netting feature in any way in terms of the name of the customer or supplier, but rather by their association created with this agreement.

Once the agreement is saved, it can be used to generate batches for both receipts and payments.

Creating Netting Batches

To create a netting batch for review, submit a netting batch request, as shown in Figure 6-20.

After selecting the OPERATING UNIT the agreement is for, select the NETTING AGREEMENT from the list of values. EBS will use the customer, supplier, and selection criteria from the agreement to propose any transactions to be considered for netting. Enter a SETTLEMENT DATE, which will determine the effective date of the netting transactions. Note that the settlement date must fall in an open period in both Payables and Receivables. Next assign a RESPONSE DATE if your customer will be approving the proposed netting. This will determine how long the customer has to respond, and if no response is received by this date, EBS will either process or cancel the batch, depending on how the agreement was set up. The option to SUBMIT BATCH WITHOUT REVIEW is available for uninterrupted processing, or select NO to allow the submitter to review the transactions selected for netting prior to processing the netting batch or sending it to the customer for approval.

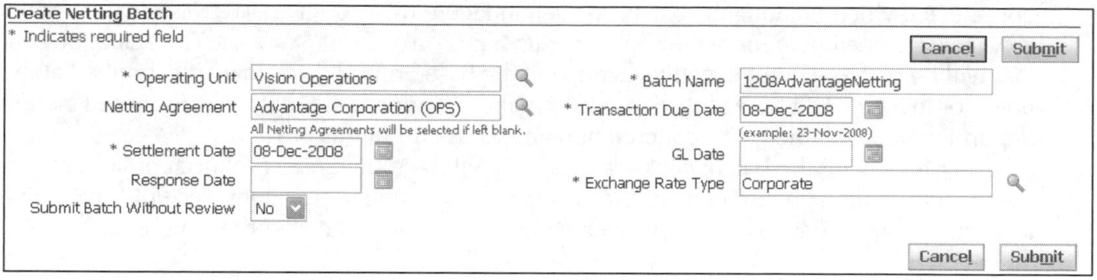

Payables Manager | Payments | Entry | Netting | Netting Batch

FIGURE 6-20 *Creating a netting batch*

The batch must be assigned a unique BATCH NAME, which can be used for querying the netting batch at a later date. The TRANSACTION DUE DATE determines which transactions in both Payables and Receivables are eligible for netting, based on the invoice or transaction date and terms assigned to the transaction. Finally, a GL DATE may be assigned to override the derived General Ledger date derived from the settlement date. This only needs to be filled in if the GL and settlement dates are not the same.

Enter the EXCHANGE RATE TYPE to determine how the rate is derived for foreign currency transactions, if they are being considered. Once the batch is submitted, a concurrent request will start the netting process. The batch can be queried in the Netting Batch screen where it was created, and monitored for the status before moving on to the next step, which is either review, approval, or creation. Table 6-6 explains the different statuses that exist for netting batches.

Status	Description
Clearing	Batch is being created.
Complete	Netting process complete, cash receipts and settlements created.
Error	Netting agreement and request found no eligible transactions in either Payables or Receivables.
Rejected	Status when batch is rejected by customer/supplier. Can be resubmitted for approval or deleted.
Running	Concurrent request is processing.
Selected	Transactions are selected and waiting for review.
Submitted	Batch is created and submitted for approval.
Suspended	Batch was not completed, and now the settlement date is *after* the current system date.

TABLE 6-6 *Netting Batch Statuses*

Once the transactions are selected, they can be reviewed if SUBMIT BATCH WITHOUT REVIEW was not selected when creating the batch. As seen in Figure 6-21, both the RECEIVABLES AMOUNT and PAYABLES AMOUNT eligible for netting appear, with a PROPOSED NETTING AMOUNT. The actual invoices that will be cleared with the netting action will be based on the agreement if submitted at this point, or invoices can be removed or added manually prior to submitting. A Proposed Netting Report is also available in the concurrent manager as part of this process.

After reviewing the batch, click SUBMIT, and it will be routed either to the supplier/customer for approval or to the concurrent manager to create the clearing transactions (receipts in Receivables and settlements in Payables). A Final Netting Report will print out after the transactions are created.

Recurring Invoices

Recurring invoices are set up and generated on a scheduled basis for expenses where invoices do not get received, such as when a coupon book is sent, or for contracted payments such as lease or rent. Use care when setting up a Recurring Invoice for expenditures where an invoice is received, because it can result in a double payment (once from the recurring invoice and once from the actual invoice received from the supplier).

There is one prerequisite setup to a recurring invoice, which is setting up a special calendar. This was covered in Chapter 5. Once the special calendar is set up for recurring invoices, the invoice itself can be defined, as seen in Figure 6-22.

First, the supplier and frequency of the invoice are defined. Enter a supplier NAME, NUMBER, and SITE from the list of values. Suppliers do not need any special setups to allow a recurring invoice to

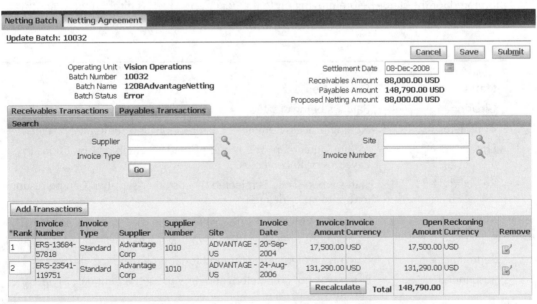

FIGURE 6-21 *Review netting transactions*

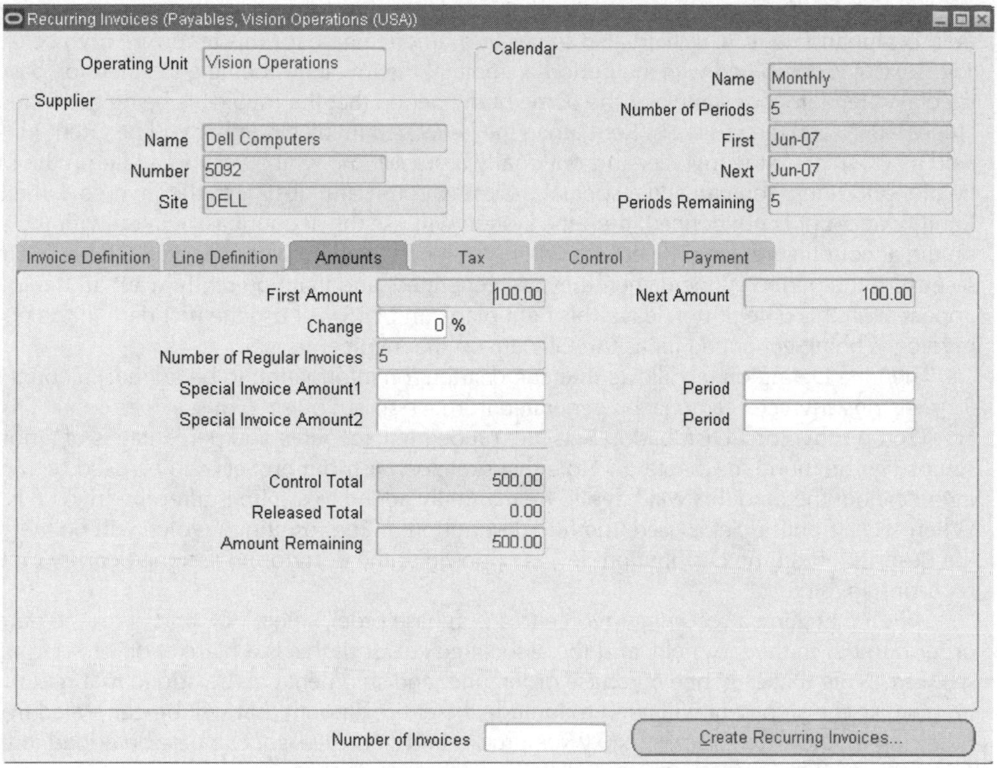

Payables Manager | Invoices | Entry | Recurring Invoices

FIGURE 6-22 *Setting up recurring invoices*

be defined for them, so any active supplier and pay site are available. In the Calendar section, select the special calendar that was set up in the NAME field. Special Calendars are used to determine the frequency of the payments, defined as periods, and what dates are covered in each period. Basically, if the FROM DATE on the special calendar is 01-JAN-06, and the TO DATE is 15-JAN-06 for the first period, then one invoice will be generated for the period January 1–January 15, making the frequency twice a month.

Enter the NUMBER OF PERIODS this recurring invoice is to be generated for. Entering **5** in the periods field will generate five invoices, based on the frequency set up in the special calendar. From the list of values, enter the FIRST period name that you want to generate an invoice for. The Calendar must have enough periods to accommodate the NUMBER OF PERIODS, based on the FIRST period selected, or you will receive an error message when entering the recurring invoice. In this case, change the number of periods, first period, or calendar to ensure there are enough periods. The NEXT period is maintained by the system, based on the last recurring invoice that was generated; if none have been generated, it will be the same as the FIRST period. PERIODS REMAINING, also maintained by the system, is the NUMBER OF PERIODS less the number of invoices that have already been generated.

Starting with the Invoice Definition tab, additional information can be set up for this invoice. NUMBER is the suffix that will appear on the invoice number when the invoice is generated; this field is alphanumeric. This field also serves as a unique name for this recurring invoice template. The NUMBER is combined with the Period Name that the invoice is being generated for, based on the special calendar. For example, if the name of the period that the invoice is being generated for is "Jun-01-06", and the NUMBER is 'Rent', then the generated invoice number will be "Rent-Jun-01-06". Add a CURRENCY for the invoice, and optionally a DESCRIPTION, which will populate on the invoice header and lines. You can add a special LIABILITY ACCOUNT and GL DATE to the invoice. When a liability account is not defined, then the system will use the account associated with the supplier on the accounting region. The GL DATE will be assigned to all invoices generated with this template, so ensure the period is open when they are generated, and that you really want all the invoices to appear with this date. If not, leave this field blank and EBS will use the first date in the period the invoice is being generated for as the GL date on the invoice.

The Line Definition tab allows line and distribution information to be added. Account numbers for recurring invoices can only be generated from a DISTRIBUTION SET or a PURCHASE ORDER. Distribution Sets (Setup | Invoice | Distribution Sets) are predefined accounts and percentages of amount, and setups can be found in Chapter 5. Note that skeleton Distribution Sets can be used on recurring invoices, but the amounts will have to be manually added to the lines after the invoice is created. When a Distribution Set is used, the line description on the resulting invoice will be the same as the description on the Distribution Set, as opposed to the description assigned earlier on the recurring invoice.

When matching a recurring invoice to a purchase order, select PO, and enter the purchase order number in the NUM field, and the associated RELEASE (if this is a blanket order), LINE, and SHIPMENT. Note that only one purchase order, line, and shipment can be added to a recurring invoice, so the shipment will need to include the entire amount that will be generated from this recurring invoice. ITEM DESCRIPTION, MANUFACTURER, and MODEL NUMBER can also be added in this tab and will populate their corresponding fields on the invoice line.

The Amounts tab is where the each invoice amount, control totals, and any special payments are set up. FIRST AMOUNT is the total amount of the invoice that is generated. This can be set up as a constant amount throughout the periods, or increased or decreased by adding a CHANGE percentage as either a positive or a negative. NEXT AMOUNT is populated by the system, letting the user know what the next amount of the invoice will be. NUMBER OF REGULAR INVOICES is populated by the system from the NUMBER OF PERIODS entered previously less any special amounts identified.

EBS allows for two special amounts to be included on recurring invoices; these are set up by using the SPECIAL INVOICE AMOUNT 1 and 2 fields. Add the dollar amounts in these fields, and select the PERIOD they should be paid. Note that when these are set up, the special amounts will be the only invoice generated for that period; they are not in addition to the regular invoices. CONTROL TOTAL, calculated by EBS from the NUMBER OF REGULAR PERIODS times FIRST AMOUNT, plus the two special amounts, is the maximum amount that will be paid out on this recurring invoice. This amount can be modified to prevent future invoices from being generated. RELEASED TOTAL, calculated by EBS, represents to total amount of invoices that have already been created, while the AMOUNT REMAINING is the difference between the CONTROL TOTAL and the RELEASED TOTAL.

Tax is not calculated on recurring invoice unless the Tax tab is set up. Add a TAX CONTROL AMOUNT if the tax is going to be manually added to the recurring invoice after it is created. This amount will place a hold in the invoice during validation if the total of the tax lines does not agree with the TAX CONTROL AMOUNT. Select the TAXATION COUNTRY, which can be added when the country where the tax is applicable should be tracked. To have EBS automatically calculate the tax on the invoices, you can add tax drivers for BUSINESS CATEGORY, PRODUCT FISCAL CLASSIFICATION, FISCAL CLASSIFICATION, and PRIMARY INTENDED USE.

The Control tab determines holds and approvals that are required for the created invoice. Selecting APPROVAL WORKFLOW REQUIRED will take the created invoice and route it through the Payables approval process. If the approval process is based on a REQUESTOR, it can be added here as well. The REQUESTOR field can also be populated for informational purposes when the approval process does not use it for routing purposes, or approvals are not required. Adding a HOLD here will prevent any recurring invoices from being created for this template (the CREATE RECURRING INVOICE button is grayed out and cannot be selected when a hold is entered). This HOLD will need to be removed prior to being able to create any invoices.

EXPIRATION DATE, when added, determines the last day an invoice can be created from this template. If the recurring invoice template is set up for a lease or contract with an expiration or renewal date, it can be populated here to ensure payments do not go out for expired agreements. There are a total of four controlling factors that restrict the creation of invoices. The first is NUMBER OF PERIODS, which determines the total number of invoices that can be created. The second is CONTROL TOTAL, which limits the actual total amount of the invoices that can be created, and third is the EXPIRATION DATE, determining the last day that an invoice can be generated. All three of these fields can be updated at any time to ensure that invoices are not created over the amounts owed to the supplier. Finally, the last controlling factor is that by adding a HOLD, you can prevent any invoices from being created as long as the hold remains on the recurring invoice.

The final tab, Payments, includes the defaults that control when and how the payment is going to be made. TERMS will default in from the supplier site but can updated for this recurring invoice. You can add a PAYMENT REASON and PAYMENT REASON COMMENTS for use when the PAYMENT METHOD is set to ELECTRONIC or ACH. You can define a DELIVERY CHANNEL for the payment as well. PAY GROUP, used to group invoices onto a payment selection, can be added to override the supplier or system defaults. Also, selecting PAY ALONE will create a single settlement document for the recurring invoice as opposed to combining it for payment with other invoices for this supplier. You can add up to three additional REMITTANCE MESSAGES as well. When using the bank charge feature in EBS, the SETTLEMENT PRIORITY and BANK CHARGE BEARER fields are available.

When a PAYMENT METHOD was set to ELECTRONIC or ACH, select a REMIT TO BANK ACCOUNT, REMIT TO BANK, and REMIT TO BRANCH where the funds will be sent to.

To generate a recurring invoice, optionally enter the NUMBER OF INVOICES before clicking on the CREATE RECURRING INVOICES button to generate more than one invoice at a time. When only generating one invoice, NUMBER OF INVOICES does not need to be populated. The CREATE button will open a window where the INVOICE NUMBER and AMOUNT can be seen, and the GL DATE can be modified if required. Remember, the Payables period corresponding to the GL DATE must be open in order to successfully generate a recurring invoice. When the Batch feature is turned on in Payables with the profile AP: Use Invoice Batch Controls, a BATCH NAME will be required. Tax Information will display if tax is on the invoice, and Exchange information can be added for foreign currency transactions. Click OK to generate the invoice. Once generated, the recurring invoice will update for the PERIODS REMAINING and the AMOUNT REMAINING, and the actual invoice will be created and can be found in the Invoice Entry screen, ready for validation, approval if required, and payment.

The Recurring Invoice Report can be used to monitor any open Recurring Invoice templates (open meaning there are still invoices to be generated with the template). It not only shows the template name, supplier, and any holds, it also displays Control Total, Released Total, Next Amount, Periods Remaining, and Next Period. Reviewing this report on a regular basis allows monitoring to ensure that the invoices are generated, and any templates where payments should no longer be generated are closed by controlling the Number of Payments, Control Amount, or Expiration Date.

Importing Invoices

Besides creating invoices within the Payable subledger, EBS has interfaces that can be used to import invoices created in other modules or in another system. While the main focus of this book is not a technical reference manual, these interfaces are important when importing transactions into Payables for payment, so a high-level overview is provided. Table 6-7 outlines where invoices can be imported from as well as the concurrent request that needs to be run to create them.

Source	Method Used to Load Interface Tables	Processes to Create Invoices
Oracle Payables	Quick Invoice	Payables Open Interface Import
Third-Party System	e-Commerce Gateway	Payables Open Interface Import
Third-Party System	XML Gateway	Payables Open Interface Import
Third-Party System	SQL*Loader	Payables Open Interface Import
Oracle Property Manager	Lease Invoices	Export Payments to Payables in Property Manager, Payables Open Interface Import in Payables
Oracle Assets	Lease Payment	Exported from Assets (Setup | Asset System | Lease | Lease Payments to Payables) to Payables Interface Import in Payables
Card Issuer	Procurement Card Transactions	Create Procurement Card Issuer Invoice
Card Issuer	Credit Card Transactions	Create Credit Card Issuer Invoice or imported with Expense Reports if card holder is responsible for payment
Oracle iSupplier	Self-Service Invoices	Create and Submit in iSupplier
Oracle Purchasing	Evaluated Receipt Settlement (ERS) or Pay on Receipt	Pay on Receipt AutoInvoice (found in Purchasing, not Payables)
Oracle Purchasing	Return to Supplier (RTS) Debit Memos	Pay on Receipt AutoCreate (found in Purchasing, not Payables)
Oracle Purchasing	Purchase Price Adjustments (PPA)	Pay on Receipt AutoCreate (found in Purchasing, not Payables)
Oracle Payables	Expense Reports	Expense Report Export
Oracle iExpense	Expense Reports	Expense Report Export
Oracle Inventory	Intercompany Transactions	Generated in Inventory (Create Intercompany AP Invoices) and then imported into Payables (Payables Open Interface Import)

TABLE 6-7   *Sources and Processes to Import and Create Invoices*

Payables Open Invoice Interface

The Payables Open Invoice Interface is the most commonly used interface for getting invoices into EBS. Besides bringing in lease payments from Assets, lease invoices from Property Manager, and Quick Invoices from Payables, data can be loaded from external companies or systems via the e-Commerce Gateway or the XML Gateway, or else by using SQL*LOADER. All of these options use the same import tables (AP_INOVICES_INTERFACE and AP_INVOICE_LINES_INTERFACE) and import process to create invoices in Payables.

The e-Commerce Gateway is used for importing EDI (Electronic Data Interchange) transactions. EBS supports the EDI 810 x12 Transactions for inbound invoices into Payables, but it requires the Oracle e-Commerce gateway to be implemented to process the transactions.

The XML Gateway, integrated in the EBS suite, allows transactions to be imported into the interfaces tables that have been created in XML.

SQL*LOADER is an Oracle-specific tool used to load data from a staging table into the import tables, using PL-SQL. Usually, data is FTP'd from the third-party system and then loaded into a staging table, where it is validated and additional default information is added to the transactions prior to creating records in the interface tables.

The Payables interface segregates data based on a source. It provides several sources out of the box, including Quick Invoice, Oracle e-Commerce Gateway, Oracle XML Gateway, Procurement Card, Oracle Property Manager, and Oracle Assets. Additional sources can be set up in the Payables lookup for Source (Payables Manager | Setup | Lookups | Payables). When importing data from any third-party system, it is a good idea to create a new source to segregate the data for not only importing, but also troubleshooting and purging.

Invoices that are staged to be imported via the Payables open interface can be updated in the Open Interface Invoices window, seen in Figure 6-23. This window is provided as a simple data fix alternative for transactions that are stuck in the interface due to invalid data. Care should be used when giving access to this feature, as it is not secured by organization and is not limited to transactions that have not yet been processed but also includes processed invoices that are not purged. The STATUS of the record can be used to determine which transactions are processed. Updates made here will not receive any validation until the Payable Invoice Interface is run. Updating a processed transaction here will have no effect on the actual invoice already created in Payables. The fields available in this window are the same fields that are available in the AP_INOVICES_ INTERFACE and AP_INVOICE_LINES_INTERFACE tables. While invoices created in the Quick Invoice window can be seen here, updates to these transactions should be made in the Quick Invoice window itself, which does include validations on the data.

Running the concurrent request Payables Open Interface Purge will remove processed transactions from this window as well as the interface tables.

Credit Card Transactions

EBS supports both credit card and procurement card (p-card) transaction processing in Payables. These two types of cards work a little bit differently.

Credit cards are defined as corporate-issued credit cards utilized by employees during travel or other approved expenditures, and transactions are loaded into the expense reports, allowing employees to approve, mark as personal, and add cash receipts prior to submitting an expense report for approval, verification, and processing. Credit cards can be set up to be paid either by the company or by an employee, where the employee is reimbursed for the expenses.

Procurement cards are company-issued cards typically used for low-dollar, high-frequency transactions, where the card usage is usually limited by type of purchase, type of store, and/or dollar amount. While p-card transactions can be classified and approved prior to payment, this

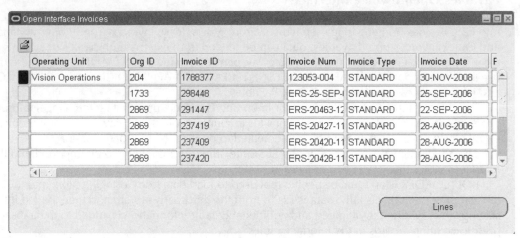

Payables Manager | Invoices | Entry | Open Interface Invoices

FIGURE 6-23 *Updating information on invoices in the Payables Open Invoice interface*

step can be bypassed and the imported charges can create an invoice to the issuing bank without employee intervention.

From a technical standpoint, the main difference between these two transactions is that credit cards are loaded into AP_CC_TRX_DETAILS. Once validated with the appropriate validation program (EBS provides existing validations for American Express, Diners Club, MasterCard, and Visa), these transactions are available for users to review and approve or to add to expense reports. When the transaction is added to an expense report, it is imported into Payables with the expense report. If the company is responsible for paying the credit card company directly, as determined by the setting PAYMENT DUE FROM being set to COMPANY or BOTH, then the Create Credit Card Issuer Invoice process needs to be run to move the transactions to the import tables (AP_INVOICES_INTERFACE and AP_INVOICE_LINES_INTERFACE) and imported for payment.

Procurement card transactions are loaded into the AP_EXPENSE_FEED_DISTS_ALL tables for review and approval, and are processed through the import tables (AP_INVOICES_INTERFACE and AP_INVOICE_LINES_INTERFACE) when Create Purchasing Card Issuer Invoice process is run.

Self-Service Invoices
When iSupplier is implemented, invoices can be submitted by suppliers for review, approval, and processing. These invoices are available in Payables after the supplier clicks SUBMIT, ready for review, approval, and processing.

Creating Invoices Directly from Purchasing
Purchase orders and purchasing transactions can be the source for the automatic creation of invoices when Pay on Receipt, or Evaluated Receipt Settlement (ERS), is turned on for a particular supplier. ERS, a type of self-billing, is an agreement between your company and your vendor that all transactions will be paid according to the actual purchase order and either receipt or usage of a product. ERS can be set up only when a supplier site is set up as both a Pay and a Purchasing Site, which makes the PAY ON field on the supplier Key Purchasing Setups available to be populated

with RECEIPT, RECEIPT AND USE, or USE. Once this is set up, running the concurrent request called Pay on Receipt AutoCreate from purchasing will create invoices for any purchase order transaction (receipt or usage) for the set up supplier.

Debit memos are also created for suppliers that are set up as ERS when a Return to Supplier (RTS) transaction is created for one of these purchase orders. These debit memos are transferred to Payables with the same program, Pay on Receipt AutoCreate.

Using this feature puts the controls of the invoice pricing solidly in the Purchasing subledger, which means that all adjustments to the invoices should come from there as well. When the amount is changed on a purchase order that was invoiced as an ERS, a Purchase Price Adjustment (PPA) transaction is created and, again, imported into Payables as a debit memo with the Pay on Receipt AutoCreate program.

Expense Reports

Expense reports, created in either iExpenses or the Expense Report window in Payables, are imported into Payables with the Expense Report Export program. Only submitted, approved, and validated expense reports are selected from iExpenses with this program. EBS determines which process it is importing expense reports for according to the SOURCE selected when the process is run.

1099 Processing

Form 1099 is a type of income reporting in the United States where companies making payments to individuals must report the payments to both the individuals and the Internal Revenue Service (IRS).

Prior to setting up suppliers to be 1099 entities, you must complete some system setups. First, if your organization is participating in the Combined Filing Program, select COMBINED FILING PROGRAM in the Payables Options (Setup | Options | Payables Option | Tax Reporting tab). Then decide if you USE PAY SITE TAX REGION, or if all transactions will fall under one specific INCOME TAX REGION. When a pay site is selected, the state on the site will become the region where the 1099 information is reported, whereas selecting a specific region for all transactions will ignore the pay site and report all the 1099 taxable income in this region.

Next, you must set up Tax Regions (Payables Manager | Setup | Tax | Regions). Here, you set up each state you are filing combined, adding a REPORTING LIMIT AMOUNT for any state where the reportable limits are over a set amount; when not populated, EBS uses zero as the lowest reportable limit. METHOD determines how transactions are evaluated against the REPORTING LIMIT AMOUNT. Comparing INDIVIDUALLY will treat each individual transaction when comparing against the reporting limit to determine if it should be included in the reporting, whereas COMPARE SUM will add up all the transactions before doing the comparison. Selecting SAME AS FEDERAL will ignore the region's reporting limit and use the federally defined limit of $600. There are EFFECTIVE DATES at the bottom of this window, which apply to the region your cursor is on, and determine the time period these setups are valid for.

REPORTING ENTITIES (Payables Manager | Setup | Tax | Reporting Entities) are required for both federal and state reporting and determine which balancing segments in the Chart of Accounts are reportable for a particular OPERATING UNIT and TAX ID NUMBER. Associated with the 1099 Forms concurrent request is a parameter called a Query Driver (System Administrator | Concurrent | Program | Define | Query up 1099 Form, select Parameters). This parameter determines if the reporting entity is determined from the cash account in the invoice payment (PAY) or the charge accounts on the invoice's distribution line (INV). With the system setting complete, you will next set up the suppliers as taxable.

The first setups are done in the Tax Details region of the supplier. The TAXPAYER ID is entered here. Entering **00000000** for the TAXPAYER ID is a trigger to EBS that you are still waiting for the number, while allowing all transactions to be tracked as 1099-able. Sometimes, a supplier will have one name that is used to cut checks to, but another on file with the IRS. The alternate name on file with the IRS can be stored on the Quick Update region of the supplier record in the ALTERNATE SUPPLIER NAME; this will be the name that prints on the actual 1099 forms and reports.

The supplier is next marked as REPORTABLE for FEDERAL or STATE reporting. FEDERAL is the designator that triggers a 1099 to be produced for this supplier for qualified payments, while STATE only needs to be checked if your company is enrolled in the IRS Combined Filing Program. This will add both the K and B records to the electronic filing to the IRS. A default INCOME TAX TYPE should also be added; it can be overridden for any transaction entered against this supplier. The different income tax types are listed in Table 6-8.

After the supplier is set up, all invoices entered in Payables will have the INCOME TAX TYPE associated with them for this supplier. This code can be changed or deleted, depending on the actual invoice being entered into the system.

When there are payments that exist in another system as well as EBS for a tax year, you can add the transactions into EBS by entering an invoice, with the INCOME TAX TYPE field populated, and then enter an offsetting credit/debit memo into EBS *without* a tax type. For example, enter an invoice in the system for $500 with the Tax Type of MISC7, and then an offsetting debit memo for ($500) with no tax type. A zero-dollar payment is then cut to the supplier for both of these transactions, causing the supplier to reflect the payment of $500 in EBS without creating an actual

Income Tax Type	Usage
Misc1	Rent
Misc2	Royalties
Misc3	Other income
Misc4	Federal income tax withheld
Misc5	Fishing boat proceeds
Misc6	Medical and health care payments
Misc7	Non-employee compensation
Misc8	Payments in lieu of dividend on interest
Misc9	Consumer products for resale
Misc10	Crop insurance proceeds not capitalized under sections 278, 263A, or 447
Misc13	Excess golden parachute payments
Misc14	Gross proceeds paid to an attorney

TABLE 6-8 *Income Tax Types as of 2008*

payment for $500. Adding the 1099 transactions in this manner will also prevent the transactions from having an impact on the General Ledger because the Credit Memo and Debit Memo will offset each other.

There are several reports available for 1099s in EBS. These not only include the 1099 forms themselves, but reports for auditing the accuracy of the data. The 1099 Supplier Exception Report is used to identify suppliers that are set up with inconsistent 1099 information, including suppliers with null or invalid state abbreviations, suppliers missing a Tax Identification Number or having a nonstandard one, or any supplier that will be flagged as foreign on the 1099 Electronic Media Report. This report can be run throughout the year to ensure accurate data.

EBS provides a Tax Verification Letter that can be sent out to all suppliers set up as 1099 reportable to validate the information in your system. Ensure you do this early enough in a tax year to mail out the letters and receive them back in prior to the IRS deadlines for reporting. October is often the latest you would want to do this for any year. Some organizations send these out for all new suppliers when tax information is set up or changed in EBS to confirm it is now accurate. If you entered inaccurate tax information, or if a supplier refused to provide tax information, the IRS may require you to withhold tax from all payments, so having the information validated is an important way to ensure this is not required.

The 1099 Invoice Exception Report, run for each Reporting Entity, identifies inconsistencies between supplier tax information and invoices entered for that supplier. Errors that appear on this report are shown in Table 6-9.

After running both the supplier and invoice exception reports, you can run the Update Income Tax Details Utility to assist with the updates. Once all the supplier records have been updated to reflect the correct tax status, running this process will update *all* invoices for a supplier to have the same status as the supplier. Since there are times when you may have some invoices as taxable and some not on the same supplier, use care when running this utility, because it may override adjustments to records that you do not want it to. An example of when the same supplier will have both taxable and non-taxable transactions is often the Board of Directors. While board meeting fees are taxable, travel expenses associated with the board meeting may not be. A solution to this problem is to set up two supplier sites for these suppliers, one taxable, and one not.

The 1099 Payments Report shows a listing of all supplier and payment information for review.

Concurrent processes available in EBS for reporting income taxes to the government include 1099 Electronic Media, used to upload 1099 to the IRS FIRE (File Information Returns Electronically) site—this is required for companies with more than 250 reportable suppliers to avoid potential fines. EBS also provides several 1099 layouts. The first is the 1099 Forms, used for printing 1099s on preprinted forms. 1099 Forms – Comma Delimited Format is used when a third-party company prints the 1099s for you, or when 1099 data needs to be combined from several systems. 1099 Forms PDF Format is also provided for printing the 1099 forms with XML Publisher. In order to use this, you must first sign into XML Publisher, call up the 1099 template, and make it active by end-dating the prior year and activating the latest version (XML Publisher Administrator | Home | Templates).

Oracle releases a patch every year around November to provide any changes in the 1099 reporting process as defined by the IRS. This patch includes changes to the 1099 forms, including the current year's 1099 PDF format, electronic media files, as well as any updates for the Income Tax Types.

Supplier	Invoice	Problem	Resolution
Set up as 1099	No income tax type	Payments for this invoice will not appear on 1099s (this may not be a problem if the supplier had both 1099 and non-1099 payments).	Update supplier record.
Set up as 1099	Incorrect or missing income tax regions	This is only a problem if you are participating in the Combined Filing Program.	If the supplier information is correct and the payment is to be reported as 1099 income, then update the invoice income tax type, or run the Update Income Tax Detail utility (see the next item). If you are filing with the Combined Reporting program, update the missing income tax regions.
Not set up as 1099	Has an income tax type	These invoices will not appear on any 1099 report to the government.	Remove the income tax type, or run the Update Income Tax Detail utility.
Set up as 1099	Net payments is a negative number for the tax year	All taxable transactions must result in a net positive number, or actual payments to the supplier.	Determine why the negative occurred. The most likely culprit is a voided check from the prior tax year, which should be reported as an adjustment to last year as opposed to a credit against this year's payments.
Set up as 1099	Income tax type of MISC4 resulting in a positive net number	MISC4 tax types are payments withheld from a supplier on behalf of the IRS, and are required only when the supplier does not provide correct W9 information. These should always result in a negative number, as it is withheld as opposed to paid.	Double-check the withholding calculations and make any corrections.

TABLE 6-9 *1099 Invoice Exception Errors*

Payables Processing Flow from Beginning to End

In order for invoices to be processed and ready for payment and accounting, whether they originate from expense reports, manually entered invoices, or imported invoices, they need to be validated and possibly approved prior to creating financial data or being paid.

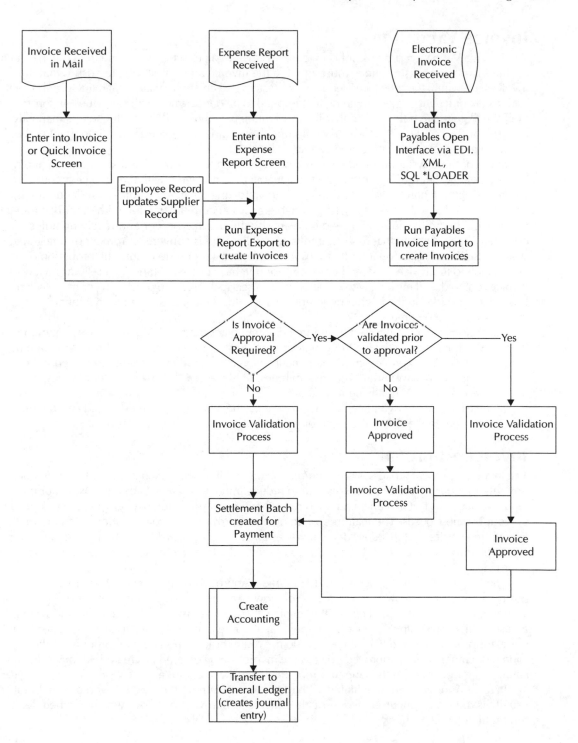

Invoice Validation

The Invoice Validation process not only confirms that invoices meet system-defined criteria, such as that invoice line distributions must agree to the invoice amount, it tests to ensure that the invoices are within the tolerances set up in the system and creates any automatic line distributions, such as tax or freight entries. Anything that is found to be out of synch with the setups or constraints in EBS will generate holds on the invoice, preventing payment until either the hold is manually released or the problem is resolved. Monitoring these holds and releases is an important part of processing invoices in an integrated system.

Some of these system holds are easily resolved within the accounting department, including invoices where the distributions entered or generated do not agree with the invoice amount, or where an account number was disabled prior to validating the invoice. Other validation holds, usually applied based on system setups and tolerances, require interaction with other departments to resolve. The holds most often seen here are usually purchase order and receiving holds, especially in a company that has just implemented EBS and is converting from a non-integrated system. It is not uncommon for tolerances to be tweaked after use to ensure the proper holds are being applied to invoices matched to receipts or purchase orders. Setting up a regular review of invoices on hold, and meeting with the appropriate users (payables and purchasing or manufacturing), is often a good idea in the beginning to ensure the holds are handled in a timely manner and invoices are paid on time.

Validations can be processed from three different places: by clicking the ACTIONS button on the Invoice Workbench, by clicking the ACTIONS button on the Invoice Batch window, or by running the Invoice Validation process from the concurrent manager. Often, this concurrent request is scheduled in the system to run every five minutes, or at the very least several times a day, so users do not have to manually perform this step.

Invoices that are not validated do not appear on the invoice aging reports and can not be accounted, sent to the General Ledger, or paid.

Invoice Approval

The Invoice Approval process is not required in EBS, but it is being used more and more frequently not only to reduce manual processes, but to reduce fraud and satisfy Sarbanes-Oxley audit requirements. This feature can be set up to run either prior to validation or after validation, depending on your business needs. The main reason to obtain approvals prior to validation is to confirm the accounting entries, but this does delay invoices that are not approved from being accounted for and appearing in the General Ledger. Accruals may need to be set up to account for in-process approvals.

The Invoice Approval processes utilizes Oracle Approvals Management (AME) to create the business rules for approvals, and Oracle Workflow to notify approvers. Often, customers set up a scanning process to attach a copy of the invoice to the actual Invoice Workbench window in EBS, and send this copy with the request for approval as a reference. Usually, invoices matched to a purchase order or created from iExpenses do not route through the approval process, as the source documents were approved prior to the invoice being entered or created. Invoices that are submitted for payment in the iSupplier module will always require approval prior to processing.

Invoice Approval can be initiated with the ACTIONS button on the Invoice Workbench, but it usually is run via a concurrent request called Invoice Approval Workflow, which is scheduled to run multiple times an hour.

Creating Accounting Entries

All invoices and payments will require accounting entries to be generated for them to create the final debit and credit accounts, and to route the entries to the General Ledger as a journal entry.

You can run the Create Accounting process from the ACTIONS button on either the Invoice Workbench or Batch Entry window, submit it as a concurrent request manually, or schedule it to run on a regular basis. Business needs will dictate how often this process needs to be run—at least once a month, prior to closing Payables, and many organizations run it multiple times a day. Once the Create Accounting process has been run in Final mode, updates cannot be made to the account numbers on invoice lines (unless the process found an error, in which case the accounting entries are not generated). Once the Create Accounting process is run for an invoice, this invoice can no longer be deleted from the system, only canceled. Distribution corrections, however, can be made using the REVERSE or DISCARD button for accounting mispostings.

In addition to creating accounting, the accounting entries must be transferred to the General Ledger. This can be accomplished either by creating the accounting in Final-Post mode for unaccounted transactions or by running the Transfer Journal Entries to GL concurrent request. All invoices and payments must be accounted and transferred to the General Ledger to close a period, or swept into the next period (which means the accounting date is changed to the first day of the next period).

The Create Accounting process not only generates account numbers for transactions, preparing them for journal entries, it also makes the invoices and payments eligible to be included on the Open Account AP Balances Listing (AP Trial Balance in prior releases). Invoices that have been accounted and transferred to the General Ledger appear on the report, and then they drop off the report when their corresponding settlement has been accounted and transferred to the General Ledger.

Accounting for Invoice Transactions

When most people think of accounting transactions for invoices, they usually think of Debit Expense and Credit Payables Liability when the invoice is entered, and Credit Cash and Debit Payables Liability when the invoice is settled. But in reality there are a large number of additional accounting entries that take place, especially when an invoice is matched to a purchase order for an inventory item. Purchasing actually starts the accounting process with the purchase order receipt. Purchasing creates Perpetual Accruals for inventory, and Reversing Accruals for expense receipts. The difference is very straightforward: perpetual accruals are created and remain on the General Ledger until they are relieved with a payment, whereas reversing accruals are created and reversed on a monthly basis. See Chapter 3 for more information on creating these accruals. This example will follow through a Purchase Order and Invoice for an Inventory Purchase.

    Receipt for Inventory Item (Perpetual Accrual).
        Dr Receiving (at standard cost)   105
            Cr Purchasing Accrual Account (amount of PO)   100
            Cr Purchase Price Variance (difference between standard cost and purchase
            order)   5
        Dr Inventory (at standard cost)   105
            Cr Receiving (at standard cost)   105

Purchase Prices Variances, defined as the differences between an inventory's standard cost and the cost on the purchase order, can be tracked by running the Purchase Price Variance Report in Payables.

Next, an invoice is entered against the Purchase Order created for an Inventory Item. This transaction will clear the accrual account and record any purchase price variance created for the difference between the purchase order and the actual invoice.

Dr Purchasing Accrual Account (amount of PO)   100
    Cr Payable Liability (amount of invoice)   95
    Cr Invoice Price Variance (difference between invoice and purchase order)   5

Invoice Price Variances are defined as the difference between the amounts on the purchase order and the amount on the invoice for the same line and quantity. There are two Invoice Price Variance reports, one sorting by purchase order and the other by vendor.

When the invoice is paid, the liability account is cleared.

Dr Payables Liability (amount of invoice)   95
    Cr Cash or Cash Clearing   95

Additional accounting entries would result for taxes, freight, or miscellaneous charges, as well as transactional gains and losses for foreign currency invoices or settlements. They are strictly guided by the actual EBS setups for these features, outlined in Chapter 5.

Inquiring on Payables Invoices

When researching questions for suppliers, you will use two main windows. The first is the Invoice Overview window, seen in Figure 6-24. This provides a one-page recap of an invoice, including any unpaid amounts, the purchase order or receipt it was matched to, the approval and validation status along with any holds, and the payment schedule. From here, you will find quick links not only to a one-page recap of any existing payments, but also to the receipt, purchase order, and supplier. Direct access to the Invoice Workbench inquiry is also provided. Via the Tools menu, you can view both the accounting and approval processes, as well as any currency details if the transaction is not in the Ledger currency.

The second option is to view the invoices directly in the Inquiry window of the Invoice Workbench. The Find screen here is much more robust, allowing you to perform more detailed finds. For example, on the Invoice Overview window, invoices can only be queried by Supplier information, Invoice or Voucher Number, and Type, whereas on the Invoice Workbench,

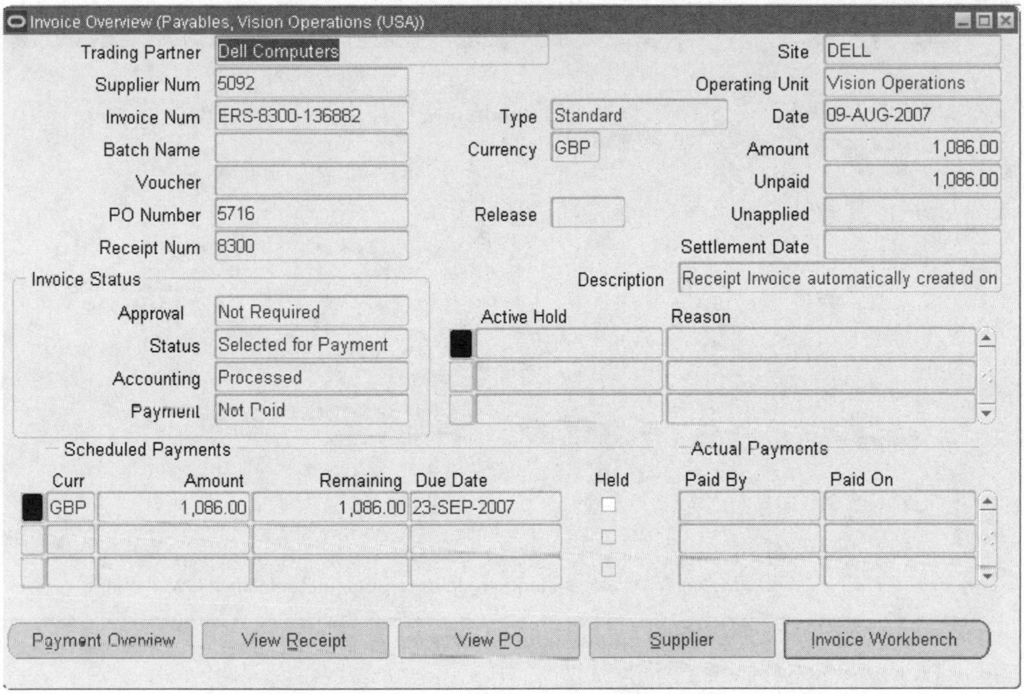

Payables Manager | Invoices | Inquiry | Invoice Overview

FIGURE 6-24 *Invoice Overview*

additional fields exist for narrowing down the search, such as the status of the payment, approval, and accounting. One additional button exists on the Invoice Workbench: CALCULATE BALANCE OWED. Selecting this option will open a form that recaps any outstanding invoices for the supplier, as seen in Figure 6-25. From here, clicking INVOICES will show the invoices that make up the outstanding balance due to the supplier.

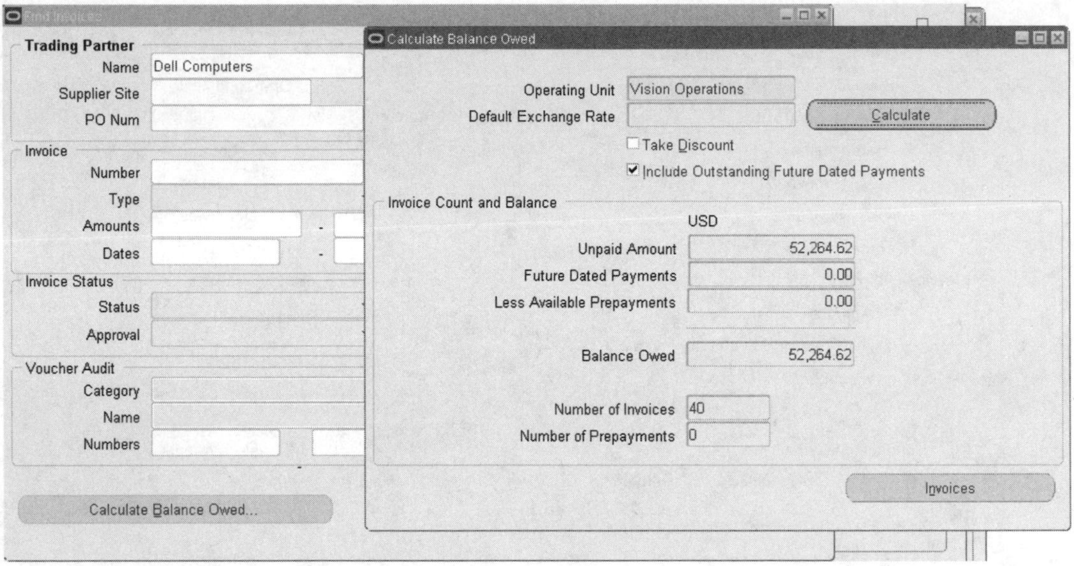

Payables Manager | Invoices | Inquiry | Invoice | Calculate Balance Owed button

FIGURE 6-25 *Calculating the balance due a supplier*

Closing and Reconciling Payables

The month-end close process in Payables, from a system standpoint, encompasses a few main steps, listed here. It is a good idea to suspend transactions during the actual month-end close process to prevent users from creating or updating transactions while trying to close the period.

- Validate all transactions
- Review the Invoice on Hold Report
- Create accounting
- Transfer data to the General Ledger
- Close the period
- Balance AP to GL

Validate All Transactions

Invoices must be validated prior to payment, and this process is usually performed multiple times throughout a day. Since validations are always based on the most up-to-date information in EBS, running one last validation during the close ensures that invoices and holds are updated with the most recent information.

Reviewing the Invoice on Hold Report

While this report should be reviewed on a regular basis throughout the month, it is important to confirm that there are no holds that will prevent EBS from accounting for a transaction. If these holds are not resolved prior to closing the period, they will have to be swept into the next period, changing the GL Date on the invoice transactions. System holds that cannot be accounted are listed earlier in this chapter, in Table 6-5.

Creating Accounting Entries

Next, accounting entries will need to be created for all unaccounted transactions in the system. There is an order, as defined in the Subledger Accounting setups, that transactions are accounted for. Usually, first the invoices are accounted, then a payment for the invoice, next any void transactions against the invoices payment, and finally the canceled check. Because of this, sometimes the Create Accounting process needs to be run more than one time at month end. Sometimes, running Create Accounting for a specific process category helps account for the transactions in the proper order. Table 6-10 shows the Process Categories in the recommended order they should be run to resolve accounting issues.

Transferring Data to the General Ledger

Creating Accounting in Final mode and selecting TRANSFER TO GENERAL LEDGER will automatically transfer journal entries to the General Ledger for any accounting entries created when the process is run, but it will not transfer any previously accounted transactions. Running the Transfer Journal Entries to GL concurrent request at month end will ensure all accounted transactions are moved to the General Ledger.

Ensuring All Transactions Are Accounted and Transferred Prior to Closing the Period

EBS provides an Unaccounted Transactions Report, which will list any transaction that is not accounted along with the reasons. Running and reviewing this report will show transactions that are still waiting for accounting, either because they have not been selected yet because a prior event needs to be accounted first, or because there is a problem with the transaction preventing

Process Category	Transactions Accounted
Invoices	All invoices associated with accounting, including currency transactions and canceled invoices
Payments	All payment-associated transactions
Third-Party Merge	All transactions moved with the Merge feature, including invoices and payments
Manual	Any manual transactions created in Subledger Accounting

TABLE 6-10   *Process Categories for Create Accounting, Listed in the Recommended Order for Accounting*

the accounting. To clear transactions off this report, you may sometimes have to repeat the previous steps multiple times (Validate, Reviewing Holds, Create Accounting, Transfer to General Ledger). Once the report is clean, or only contains invoices that you want to sweep into the next period, you are ready to close the period.

Controlling Payables Periods

EBS has four statuses available for the Payables periods: OPEN, FUTURE, NEVER OPENED, or CLOSED. While Payables uses the same calendar as the General Ledger, the periods are controlled separately. Both Open and Future statuses allow invoices to be entered and accounted; Future restricts any payments from being created or accounted. Never Opened prevents the period from being used, just as Closed will. Both these statuses include preventing both invoices and payments. Notice there is no Close Pending, which exists in some other subledgers, which allows unaccounted transactions to be reviewed and balancing to take place while preventing any additional data entry.

Payables can have multiple periods open at the same time, and there are many valid business reasons to do so. Understanding the implications of multiple open periods is important before making this decision. First, canceled invoices and voided checks will back-date to the period they were created or the first open period in EBS after the original GL date, and depending on how the GL Date is derived for invoices, prior periods may be assigned to new invoice entry as well. While the accounting date on the journal entry can be updated to a current period, it is a better business practice to close the Payables periods on a regular basis to prevent these prior period entries. Depending on your month-end close schedule, the period is usually closed within the first three days of the next month, and often on the evening of the last day of the month.

To close the period, go to the Control Payables Periods window, seen in Figure 6-26. After you select the PERIOD STATUS of CLOSED, Payables will confirm one last time that no unaccounted

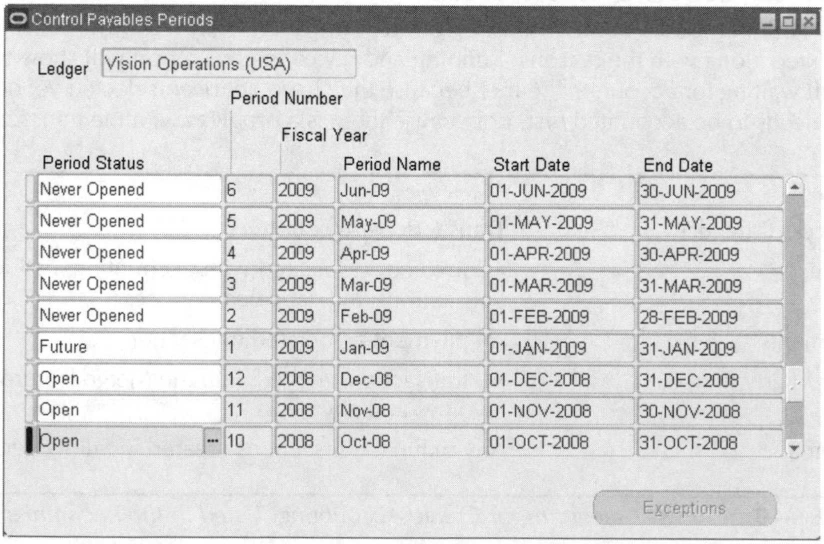

Period Status	Period Number	Fiscal Year	Period Name	Start Date	End Date
Never Opened	6	2009	Jun-09	01-JUN-2009	30-JUN-2009
Never Opened	5	2009	May-09	01-MAY-2009	31-MAY-2009
Never Opened	4	2009	Apr-09	01-APR-2009	30-APR-2009
Never Opened	3	2009	Mar-09	01-MAR-2009	31-MAR-2009
Never Opened	2	2009	Feb-09	01-FEB-2009	28-FEB-2009
Future	1	2009	Jan-09	01-JAN-2009	31-JAN-2009
Open	12	2008	Dec-08	01-DEC-2008	31-DEC-2008
Open	11	2008	Nov-08	01-NOV-2008	30-NOV-2008
Open	10	2008	Oct-08	01-OCT-2008	31-OCT-2008

Ledger Vision Operations (USA)

Payables Manager | Accounting | Control Payables Periods

FIGURE 6-26 *Controlling payables periods*

transactions exist in the system. If any do, a message will pop up stating that you cannot close the period because exceptions exist. This will make the EXCEPTIONS button available. This button performs two different tasks. First, if REVIEW is selected on the next screen, the Period Close Exception Report will run, showing any exceptions that are preventing the close from happening. This report lists any unaccounted invoice or payment and any open payment processing requests. If SWEEP is selected, then these transactions will be swept into the next period and the accounting date will be updated.

Once the transactions have been corrected or swept, the period can be updated to Closed. Payables periods can be reopened at any time after they are closed.

Balancing Payables to the General Ledger

It is important to balance subledgers to the General Ledger on at least a monthly basis to ensure the Payables liability account correctly reflects a company's commitments, and that all transactions are transferred without unnoticed errors somewhere. There are several reports that are used for balancing. Several reports and processes in Payables are outlined in Table 6-11.

During the closing process, ensuring the Invoice Aging Report balances to the Open Account AP Balances Listing is key to ensuring that all invoices entered into Payables are also considered transferred to the General Ledger. Ensuring the period is closed in Payables before starting to reconcile helps ensure these reports will stay in balance.

Once these two reports tie to each other, then their total can be balanced to the corresponding account(s) in the General Ledger. How Payables is set up determines how many liability accounts exist. While balancing the accounts in total provides a quick overview of how the subledger ties to the General Ledger, each individual liability account should be balanced as well to ensure invoices are clearing the correct liability in the General Ledger.

Differences between Payables and the General Ledger often result from a few select problems. First, depending on how transactions are transferred to the General Ledger, a journal may be stuck in the General Ledger interface tables. This can be verified by ensuring all transactions are imported with a source of Payables. Leaving the profile SLA: Disable Journal Import set to No will prevent transactions from getting stuck in the General Ledger interface tables. It is also possible that a

Process Name	Report or Update?	Purpose
Invoice Aging Report	Report	Reflects all outstanding invoices, credit memos, and debit memos entered into Payables, regardless of their status. This report always reflects the most recent information in Payables and cannot be backdated.
Open Account Balances Data Manager	Update	Normally this is run when data is transferred to the General Ledger from a subledger automatically, updating the open balance formats with the most recent information.
Open Account AP Balances Listing	Report	This Payables-specific subledger balance shows all transactions that create a specific General Ledger balance.

TABLE 6-11 *Payables Key Balancing Reports*

transaction was not accounted for or that a journal entry was not created for it in Payables, but closing the period prior to balancing usually eliminates these as potential problems.

Manual journal entries should never be made to the Payables liability account, and doing so will leave the subledger out of balance with the General Ledger. In general, if all is working correctly with Subledger Accounting, manual SLA transactions should also not be made. Review the liability account for manual transactions if there is an out-of-balance condition.

On a rare occasion, a journal entry from Payables may have been deleted in error. There are controls in the General Ledger that can prevent this, so ensure they are turned on (General Ledger Superuser | Setup | Journal | Sources). Also, ensure all the journal entries are posted prior to balancing.

The last problem may occur if SLA is not set up correctly and transactions are not creating the correct debits and credits to the liability account. This is perhaps the hardest problem to find. First, determine which subledger has the problem, General Ledger or Payables, by creating a roll forward. This is best done by taking the prior months Open Account AP Balances Listing, adding invoices entered during the period from the Invoice Register, and subtracting payments listed on the Payment Register. This balance should tie to the current month report as well as the General Ledger. If the General Ledger balances and Payables does not, an invoice or payment is probably reflected wrong on the reports. If the General Ledger does not balance, then either a transaction was accounted for in error or did not make it to the General Ledger. I wish I could tell you there was an easy way to find this, but there is not. I usually take the Open Account AP Balances Listing, run it in detail, and compare it in Excel to the detailed trial balance report in the General Ledger.

Ensuring Payables balances to the General Ledger on a monthly basis helps to ensure invoices are processed and accounted accurately in the financials.

CHAPTER
7

Payments Setups

racle Payments, new in R12, is a consolidated hub for grouping transactions for settlement, and creating the appropriate payment format for printing or transmission to the bank. More than just a way of generating checks and ACH (Automated Clearing House) settlements for invoices, Payments integrates with Payables for invoice settlements, Cash Management for bank transfers, and Receivables and iStore for credit card settlement. This chapter will focus on the Payables portion of the module.

Previously, payment batches were created based on user inputs, and settled as individual batches. The ability to generate custom payment formats required customizations to the Payment Format Programs. All this has changed. Invoices can be selected for payment according to predefined criteria, and the invoices validated by the users. Then these selections are aggregated into one centralized payment batch based on the required payment formats, printing requirements, and transmission instructions. A second approval can take place prior to being formatted and transmitted. What is most important, while the creation of payment batches can still be operation unit specific, batches can also cross operating units and legal entities for consolidated and centralized payment processing. Encompassed in the Payments process are payment instruction transmissions to the bank, complete with different transmission protocols and encryption methods. XML (eXtended Markup Language) is fully integrated into the payments module for creating custom formats and payment instructions, utilizing Oracle's BI Publisher.

While this enhanced functionality will greatly ease and streamline payment processing, it does come with a price. The setups just to generate a payment for a predefined check format are much more extensive than they were in previous releases of EBS, and any customizations created for payment formatting in previous releases will not upgrade but will need to be created using the new technology (XML).

Setups for Payments have two main steps: you complete setting up the Funds Capturing, Funds Disbursements, and Formatting rules in the Payment Setup Administrator, but you set up Templates for selection rules in the Payment Manager. There are two responsibilities in EBS for setting up disbursements: Setup Payments Administrator and Funds Disbursement Setup Administrator. These do not contain the same menu options, so ensure you are in the right place when attempting the setup for Payments.

Setting Up Payments

Payments setups are broken down into two main sections: first, setup system options that are shared by both Payables and Receivables, and second, Payables-specific setups. Both will be described here, but in the context of Payables and outbound payments.

Shared Setups

Shared setups between Payables and Receivables will be described next and relate to electronic settings and security.

System Security Options

Security Options control encryptions, masking, and credit card owner verification controls. They are utilized by both capturing (Receivable) and disbursing (Payables) funds.

Encryption   The first step in enabling encryptions is to set up the wallet. A *wallet,* or the file where the master key for encrypting data is stored, is created in the middle tier of the EBS install, keeping the data secured outside the Oracle database where all the payment information resides.

This added level of security helps reduce the risk of the wallet being compromised, as very few people in an organization (usually only one or two) have access to the middle tier. EBS uses a chained encryption approach for payment processing. This means that more than one level of encryptions and keys are utilized, ensuring that if one key is broken, a second level or more also would also have to be compromised. The system key will unlock the subkeys, or next level of encryption, allowing the system key to be rotated and changed more easily on a regular basis. Wallets also house the HTTP client authentication codes that are sometimes used with payment disbursement systems.

You can set up the wallet by clicking WALLET SETUP, as shown in Figure 7-1. You can next identify the WALLET FILE LOCATION, assign the wallet a PASSWORD, and determine how the SYSTEM KEY is generated. System Keys, which are the master keys for all encrypted data, should be kept secure at all times and can be changed periodically. Having the system generate a random key ensures no one knows the key, but the option to have the key defined by the system administrator is also available. Once this is completed, the locations assigned are confirmed, and the system key is set.

Encryption for Payment Instructions is available for both the payment instruction and credit card transmissions. Once this is enabled, the encryptions can be applied either immediately when a number is entered, or on a scheduled basis.

Masking and Confirming Sensitive Data   Masking payment instructions will ensure that bank account numbers and credit card information are secured not only in the system, but also on all printed documents. New in R12 is the added security that once the information is masked in the system, no responsibilities have access to the unmasked information, but there is an enhancement request to have this responsibility driven. For credit cards, the options for masking include to display the first or last digits, all digits, or none. The NUMBER OF DIGITS TO DISPLAY determines the number of digits when first or last is selected. External bank accounts have the same masking

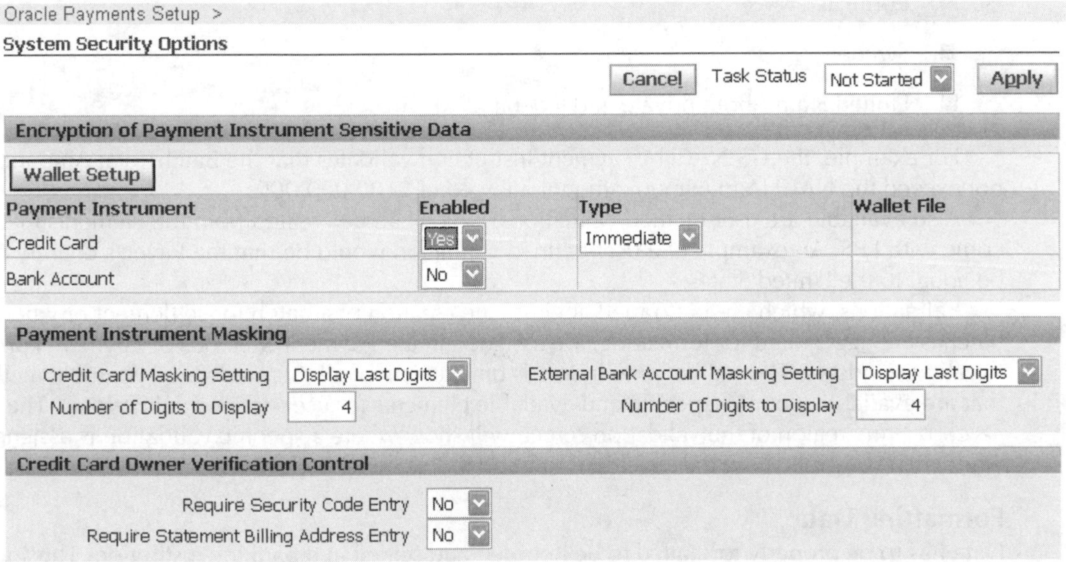

Oracle Payments Setup >

System Security Options

Cancel   Task Status   Not Started ▾   **Apply**

Encryption of Payment Instrument Sensitive Data

Wallet Setup			
Payment Instrument	**Enabled**	**Type**	**Wallet File**
Credit Card	Yes ▾	Immediate ▾	
Bank Account	No ▾		

Payment Instrument Masking

Credit Card Masking Setting	Display Last Digits ▾	External Bank Account Masking Setting	Display Last Digits ▾
Number of Digits to Display	4	Number of Digits to Display	4

Credit Card Owner Verification Control

Require Security Code Entry	No ▾
Require Statement Billing Address Entry	No ▾

Funds Disbursement Setup Administrator | Payments Setup | Shared Setup | System Security Options

---

FIGURE 7-1   *Security Options for both funds capture and disbursal*

options, and turning this on for external accounts (those associated with suppliers or employees) does not mask internal accounts used for disbursing or receiving funds.

When credit cards are accepted, users can validate the person providing the information either by validating the security code on the back of the card or by validating the billing address on the statement. You can require these validations by setting the Credit Card Owner Verification Control settings.

Once you are finished with the security options setups, change the TASK STATUS to COMPLETE and APPLY. Even though marked as complete, these can still be modified at a later date if needed.

Validation of Formats

Validations are used to ensure that the data being transmitted to a banking institution for both disbursement and capture of funds is not only formatted correctly but contains accurate information. EBS comes with predefined validations for payment formats, as shown in Figure 7-2, for the following countries:

- Austria
- Belgium
- Finland
- France
- Germany
- Japan
- Poland
- Portugal
- Sweden
- United States, both private and federal

For example, the US NACHA Payment Instruction validates that the Batch Total Amount does not exceed the NACHA maximum amount allowed of $100,000,000.

Also available are user-defined validations, which can be created from the elements that come with EBS. An example of a user-defined validation would be that the Payee's country must be equal to the United States.

Validations, which are performed at either the creation of a batch for settlement or when the batches are aggregated for formatting, are assigned in the Payment Methods or Payment Format Creation windows. The Validation window is only a view of all the predefined payment methods that are available (country specific and available elements for user-defined validations). The ASSIGNED ENTITY region of the validation screen will show where a specific validation is assigned, while the PARAMETERS show the specific validation that is being performed.

Formatting Data

Data has to be properly formatted to be honored and settled at a banking institution. This includes both electronic and printed settlements. There are two steps to setting up payment formats in EBS. First, a template needs to be created and uploaded into the system, and then additional information, such as validations, needs to be assigned to the template. R12 uses a new model for formatting

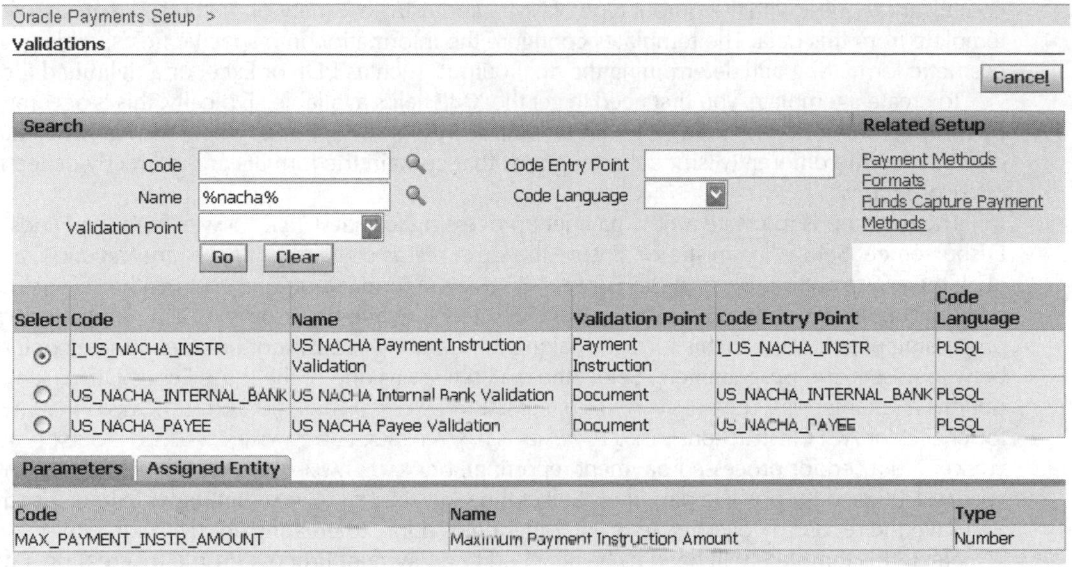

Funds Disbursement Setup Administrator | Payments Setup | Shared Setup | Validations

FIGURE 7-2 *Payment Validations*

payment instructions that is vastly different than previous releases. The concurrent request Format Payment Instructions (IBY_FD_PAYMENT_FORMAT) automatically runs when a user reaches this step in the invoice settlement cycle. This request has an embedded PL/SQL package IBY_FD_ EXTRACT_GEN_PVT, which calls the only XML extracts available in EBS, listed in Table 7-1.

These XML data extracts can have different templates associated with them, which will display the outputs in the specific format that you need to send to the bank or to print a document. Only the templates can be modified by Oracle, not the seeded extracts themselves nor the program calling them, without unsupported customizations.

Creating XML Output for Customizing Templates   While EBS comes with several predefined templates for formatting data, chances are that you will want to modify one to meet your individual company's needs. This modification uses Oracle's BI Publisher (previously called XML Publisher, and referred to as both in the latest EBS documentation). BI Publisher is widely used in R12, and

Instruction Name	System Name
Oracle Payments Funds Disbursement Payment Instruction Extract 1.0	IBY_FD_INSTRUCTION_1_0
Oracle Payments Funds Disbursement Payment Process Request Extract 1.0	IBY_FD_PMT_PROCESS_REQ_1_9
Oracle Funds Disbursement Positive Pay, Version 1.0	IBY_FD_POSITIVE_PAY_1_0

TABLE 7-1   *Disbursement Extracts Called by the Format Payments Program*

becoming familiar with the basics is important. Basically, it takes data that is created by running a concurrent request with the output type of XML, and using a variety of methods, creates an output template from this data. The templates configure the information into specific fields, adding cosmetic formatting and determining the final output, such as PDF or Excel or a delimited file.

To create a template, you first need to get the XML fields available. Typically, this is accomplished by running the concurrent request with an output type of XML, but payment format XML data is obtained a little differently, since the programs that contain the formats are indirectly called from other programs.

The first step is to create a new payment processing format. Click FORMATS from the Funds Disbursement Setup Administrator. Ensure the SELECT TYPE is DISBURSEMENT PAYMENT INSTRUCTION, and click the CREATE button. Referring to Figure 7-3, give the format a unique CODE, without spaces, and a NAME. The NAME is viewed by users in the EBS screens, while the CODE is used by programs when processing payments with this format. Making these settings consistent helps eliminate confusion between users and programmers. Select the DATA EXTRACT as one of the three Funds Disbursement options available: ORACLE PAYMENTS FUNDS DISBURSEMENT PAYMENT INSTRUCTION EXTRACT, VERSION 1.0 (used for checks or ACH Instructions), ORACLE PAYMENTS FUNDS DISBURSEMENT PAYMENT PROCESS REQUEST EXTRACT, VERSION 1.0 (used for processed payment reporting), or ORACLE PAYMENTS FUNDS DISBURSEMENT POSITIVE PAY, VERSION 1.0 (used for positive pay files). Select the XML PUBLISHER TEMPLATE setting of Extract Identity and save the record by clicking APPLY. No other fields apply to creating an XML extract file.

Next, this template will need to be attached to a Payment Process Profile by creating a new profile, as shown in Figure 7-4. Again, assign a CODE and a NAME to the profile. Adding a DESCRIPTION will help users know why this profile was created and when it should be used. Select the PAYMENT INSTRUCTION FORMAT that you created in the previous step, and save the new profile. No additional information is needed on a profile to create the XML extract file.

The final step is to associate this template to a bank account so that you can create a disbursement. Creating a physical disbursement is the only way to actually obtain the XML output, but since the format template being used is identified as Extract Identity, the disbursement document that can be settled by a financial institution is not created, just the raw XML. This should *always* be completed in a test instance.

Back in Payables, query up the Bank Account you want to associate this payment profile with (Payables Manager | Setup | Payments | Bank Accounts). Select the account, and select the Manage Payment Documents region. Assign the document a NAME, and select the FORMAT you just created. After assigning a FIRST AVAILABLE DOCUMENT NUMBER, save your work.

Now, you can enter an invoice and make a payment using the new Payment Process Profile and the output will be in XML, containing all the fields associated with the data extract. This can then be loaded into whatever tool you are using to create the template itself—there are many tools on the market, as well as a free BI Publisher add-in for Microsoft Word, that can be used

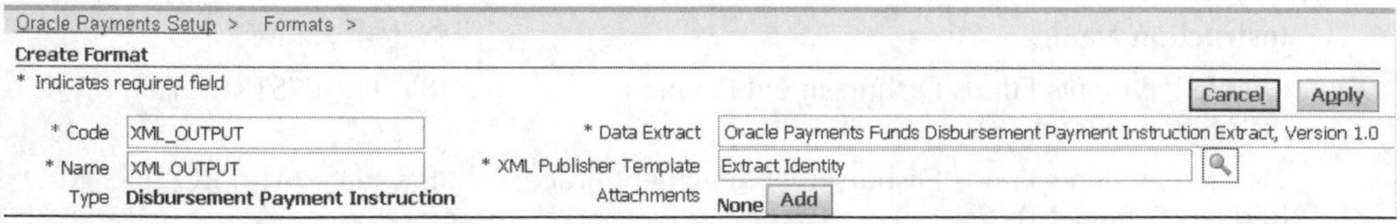

Funds Disbursement Setup Administrator | Payments Setup | Formats | Formats | Create

FIGURE 7-3 *Creating a format to load data into the Template Builder*

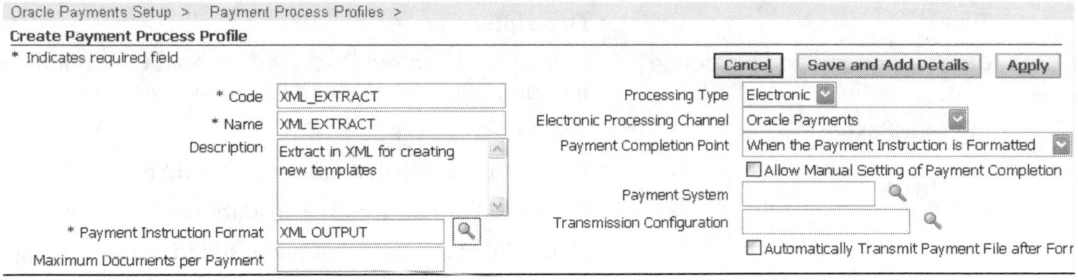

Oracle Payments Setup > Payment Process Profiles >
Create Payment Process Profile
* Indicates required field

* Code	XML_EXTRACT
* Name	XML EXTRACT
Description	Extract in XML for creating new templates
* Payment Instruction Format	XML OUTPUT
Maximum Documents per Payment	

Cancel | Save and Add Details | Apply

Processing Type: Electronic
Electronic Processing Channel: Oracle Payments
Payment Completion Point: When the Payment Instruction is Formatted
☐ Allow Manual Setting of Payment Completion
Payment System:
Transmission Configuration:
☐ Automatically Transmit Payment File after Form

Funds Disbursement Setup Administrator | Payments Setup | Payment Process Profiles

FIGURE 7-4 *Creating a profile to create data to load into the Template Builder*

(www.oracle.com/technology/software/products/publishing/index.html). If more information is needed on modifying templates, please refer to the BI Publisher manual on MetaLink.

Loading Custom Templates into Payments   Once the template is created or modified as needed, it is loaded back into EBS for use. This is done back in the Funds Disbursement Setup Administrator under XML Publisher Format Templates. As seen in Figure 7-5, both a NAME and a CODE are assigned to the template. The APPLICATION needs to be set to Payments for disbursement processing. Ensure you select the DATA DEFINITION that was used when creating the template, as not all the definitions have the same fields, potentially causing an error during payment processing.

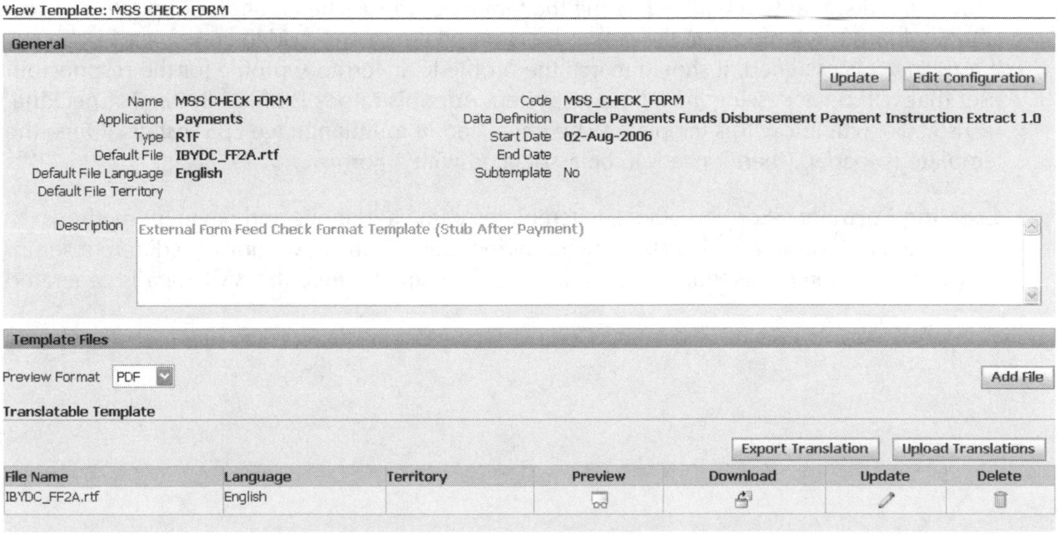

View Template: MSS CHECK FORM

General

Update | Edit Configuration

Name	**MSS CHECK FORM**	Code	**MSS_CHECK_FORM**
Application	**Payments**	Data Definition	**Oracle Payments Funds Disbursement Payment Instruction Extract 1.0**
Type	**RTF**	Start Date	**02-Aug-2006**
Default File	**IBYDC_FF2A.rtf**	End Date	
Default File Language	**English**	Subtemplate	No
Default File Territory			

Description: External Form Feed Check Format Template (Stub After Payment)

Template Files

Preview Format: PDF

Add File

Translatable Template

Export Translation | Upload Translations

File Name	Language	Territory	Preview	Download	Update	Delete
IBYDC_FF2A.rtf	English		🔍	📄	✏️	🗑️

Funds Disbursement Setup Administrator | Payments Setup | Formats | Open an existing template by clicking on the Name

FIGURE 7-5   *Loading a template into Payments for use*

Type	Description
eText – Inbound and Outbound	Output in Electronic Text, used for both Outbound and Inbound usage for EDI and EFT transfers
Microsoft Excel	Creates an .xls file
PDF	Creates a .pdf file that cannot be modified
RTF	Rich Text Format, which is readable in Microsoft Word
XSL (FO, HTML, Text, XML)	(Extensible Stylesheet Format) Used for easier styling of output

TABLE 7-2 *XML Output Options*

Templates can have different output types. These types will determine how the data is output when the payment is created. Oracle has had some troubles in R12 in which the output type assigned to a template overrides the output assigned to the concurrent request Format Payment Instructions. As of press time, there were unpublished patches to help resolve the problem. Table 7-2 explains each output type available.

The START DATE is the first date this template can be used, while the END DATE represents the last. Templates can be identified as Subtemplates, or templates that are called from another template, by selecting YES in the SUBTEMPLATE field. Adding a DESCRIPTION helps maintain reasons and usages for this template.

In the Template Files section, use the BROWSE button to identify the template location. To update a new template, first select the UPDATE button. This is the location on your local PC, not the Oracle servers, that you will be loading the templates from. The creation or update of a template actually loads the template to the proper location on the server. Add the LANGUAGE for the template. If a TERRITORY is assigned, it should match the profile ICX: Territory profile for the responsibility or user that will be accessing the template (System Administrator | Profile | System). Checking TRANSLATABLE will allow this template to be translated in multilanguage EBS installs. Once the template is loaded, then it needs to be associated with a Format.

Creating Formats   Formats associate templates with validations and payment methods (described later on in the chapter). The following illustration shows how the different setups flow and are interconnected. Formats combine the extract where the XML data is generated, the template the output will be displayed in, along with the disbursement type, which determines when the report will be generated (the process that will call them).

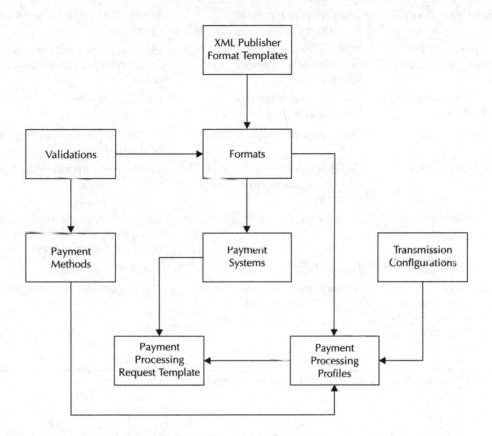

To create a Format, select the TYPE of format you are setting up and click CREATE. Format TYPES directly correspond to the reports or processes these formats will be used on. These processes are assigned in the payment process profile, while the report is a concurrent request. See Table 7-3 for the corresponding format TYPES and their corresponding payment process profile fields.

Payment Process Profile	Format Type	Purpose
Payment Instruction Format	Disbursement Payment Instructions	Instructions for disbursed funds, both check and electronic
Payment File Accompanying Letter Format	Accompanying Letter for Disbursement Payment Instructions	Electronic letter format that accompanies an electronic format to the bank
Payment Instruction Register Format	Disbursement Payment Instruction Register	Payment Register
Positive Pay Format	Disbursement Positive Pay File	Electronic Positive Pay file that is sent to the bank
Regulatory Reporting Format	Disbursement Federal Summary and Disbursement Regulatory Reporting	Government Reporting formats
Separate Remittance Advise	Disbursement Remittance Advise	Separate remittance created to send to supplier, used with either checks or electronic payments
Concurrent Request	**Format Type**	**Purpose**
Payment Process Request Status Report or as part of the Enterprise-wide Disbursement System Options	Disbursement Payment Process Request Status Report	Preliminary Payment Register

TABLE 7-3   *Format Types and Their Corresponding Purposes*

Referring to Figure 7-6, enter a CODE and a NAME to identify this Format. The TYPE will default in from the previous page, and will limit where this format can be used, as described in Table 7-3. Select the DATA EXTRACT that was used when creating the template and select the proper XML PUBLISHER TEMPLATE. EBS does come with a large number of Formats (the seeded United States formats are listed in Table 7-4), and reviewing them first can save development time. In addition to these formats, there are a large number of non-U.S. formats available.

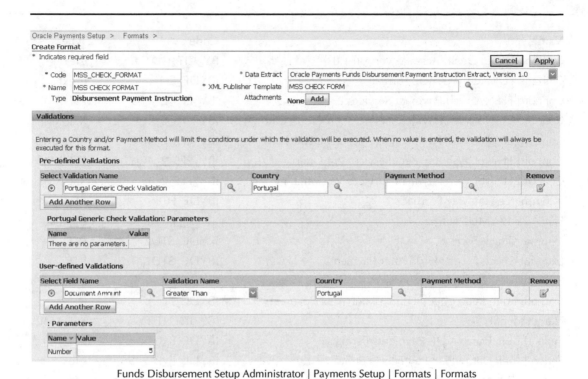

FIGURE 7-6   *Creating a format*

Name	Code	Type
ANSI X12 820 Format	IBYDE_820	eText
Bank Transfer Request	IBYDC_BTR	RTF
Citi Merchant Services Version 3.0 Batch	IBY_CIT_B_3_0	eText
Citi Merchant Services Version 3.0 On Line	IBY_CIT_O_3_0	eText

TABLE 7-4   *U.S.-Seeded Formats for Payments*

Name	Code	Type
Citibank Direct Debit Message Version 1.8	BY_CIT_DD1_8	eText
Citibank EDIFACT PAYMUL Format	IBYDE_CITI	eText
Concord EFSNet Web Payment Services 2.4	IBY_EFS_2_4TC	XSL-XML
Concord EFSNet Web Payment Services 2.4 Credit Card	IBY_EFS_2_4CC	XSL-XML
Concord EFSNet Web Payment Services 2.4 Debit Card	IBY_EFS_2_4DC	XSL-XML
Concord EFSNet Web Payment Services 2.4 Query	IBY_EFS_2_4QY	XSL-XML
Concord EFSNet Web Payment Services Version 2.4	IBY_EFS_2_4	XSL-XML
eCommerce Gateway Format	IBYDE_ECE	eText
EDIFACT PAYMUL Format	IBYDE_PYML	eText
External Check Format	IBYDC_STD2	RTF
External Check Format (Stub After Payment)	IBYDC_STD2A	RTF
External form Feed Check Format	IBYDC_FF2	RTF
External Form Feed Check Format (Stub After Payment)	IBYDC_FF2A	RTF
Extract Identity	IBY_IDENTITY	XSL-XML
Federal Bulk Data CCDP Payments Format	IBYDE_B_C	eText
Federal Bulk Data PPDP Payments Format	IBYDE_B_P	eText
Federal CTX ACH Vendor Format	IBYDE_CTX	eText
Federal ECS CCD Payments Format	IBYDE_E_CD	eText
Federal ECS CCDP Payments Format	IBYDE_E_C	eText
Federal ECS PPD Payments Format	IBYDE_E_PD	eText
Federal ECS PPDP Payments Format	IBYDE_E_P	eText
Federal ECS Summary Schedule	IBYDE_E_SS	eText
Federal SPS CCD Payments Format	IBYDE_S_CD	eText
Federal SPS PPD Payments Format	IBYDE_S_PD	eText
Federal SPS PPDP Payments Format	IBYDE_S_P	eText
Federal SPS Summary Schedule	IBYDE_S_SS	eText
First Data North Authorization Specification 2002/10/24	IBY_FDN_O2002	eText
First Data North Batch Specification Version 2003.1	IBY_FDN_B2003	eText
Laser Check Format	IBYDC_LSR	RTF

TABLE 7-4 *U.S.-Seeded Formats for Payments* (continued)

Name	Code	Type
Laser Check Format (Stub After Payment)	IBYDC_LSRA	RTF
Payment File Accompanying Letter-Funds Capture	IBYR_LTR2	RTF
Payment File Accompanying Letter-Funds Disbursement	IBYR_LTR1	RTF
Payment Instruction Register	IBYR_PI1	RTF
Payment Instruction Register with Document Details	IBYR_PI2	RTF
Payment Process Request Status Report	IBYR_PPR	RTF
Paymentech Batch Specification 2.1.1	IBY_PTK_B_2_1	eText
Paymentech Online 7.2	IBY_PTK_O_7_2	eText
Positive Pay File	IBYPOS_PAY	eText
Separate Remittance Advise	IBYR_SRA	RTF
Standard Check Format	IBYDC_STD	RTF
Standard Check Format (Stub After Payment)	IBYDC_STD1A	RTF
Standard Form Feed Check Format	IBYDC_FF1	RTF
Standard Form Feed Check Format (Stub After Payment)	IBYDC_FF1A	RTF
Swift MT 100 Format	IBYDE_S100	eText
Swift MT 103 Format	IBYDE_S103	eText
Transmit Bank Remittance Format	IBYCE	eText
US Bulk NCR Format	IBYDE_B_N1	eText
US Bulk Salary and Travel NCR Format	IBYDE_B_N2	eText
US CCDP Consolidated Format	IBYDE_C1	eText
US CTX Consolidated Format	IBYDE_C3	eText
US ECS NCR Format	IBYDE_E_N	eText
US NACHA CCD Format	IBYDE_N1US	eText
US NACHA CCDP Format	IBYDE_N2US	eText
US NACHA Generic Format	IBYDE_N_US	eText
US NACHA PPDP Format	IBYDE_N3US	eText
US PPDP Consolidated Format	IBYDE_C2	eText
US SPS NCR Format	IBYDE_S_N	eText
US Treasury Format	IBYDC_TRSY	RTF

TABLE 7-4   *U.S.-Seeded Formats for Payments* (continued)

Protocols and External Relationships Protocols, set up as transmission configurations, enable EBS to have electronic connectivity with payment systems. Protocols that are supported by EBS are listed here. The setups are unique for each payment system and should be coordinated with your payment processing company.

- HTTP(s) POST Request

- Oracle Payments Tunneling Protocol

- Paymentech Online Spec 7.2 Socket

- Paymentech Batch Specification 2.1.0 Acknowledgement FTP Get

- First Data North Authorization Spec 10/24/02 Socket

- First Data North Magnetic Media Specification 2003.1 Settlement Batch FTP Put

- First Data North Magnetic Media Specification 2003.1 Acknowledgement FTP Get

- Citi Merchant Services 3.0 Online Socket

- Citi Merchant Services Version 3.0 Batch Settlement FTP Put

- Citi Merchant Services Version 3.0 Batch Acknowledgement Get

- Citibank Direct Debit Message FTP Put

- File Transfer Protocol for Static File Names

- Secure File Transfer Protocol for Static File Names

- AS2 Send

- Local File System Delivery

Payment Systems is where external relationships with a bank or third-party settlement company is created, identifying not only the type of settlements, but also how EBS can communicate with this bank using the Transmission Protocols setup in the previous step. Referring to Figure 7-7, first add a system CODE and a NAME for the system, and then identify the type of PROCESSING MODEL this will be used for. GATEWAY refers to debit or credit card settlements, while PROCESSOR is used for Bank Transfers. For the Funds Disbursement section, only BANK ACCOUNT TRANSFERS are set up here. Associate a BANK with this system, and then optionally add a NETWORK COMMUNICATION CHARACTER SET to identify what alphabet/language the transmission will be performed in. If this is left blank, the default language for the system will be used. While the ADMINISTRATIVE URL is not required, the TRANSMISSION SERVLET BASE URL is for transfers, directing EBS where to send to transmission. The ADMINISTRATIVE URL is for reference only, showing where the administrative link for the bank or settlement company can be found.

Under Funds Disbursement, select BANK ACCOUNT TRANSFER for Payables, and add any Formats and Transmission Protocol that are required when sending this type of transfer. Settings Required by Payment System include any required fields for processing this transmission and will be populated when the Accounts are added in the next step. When utilizing Oracle's Treasury modules for cash forecasting, the BANK ACCOUNT LEAD DAYS will determine when these funds reduce

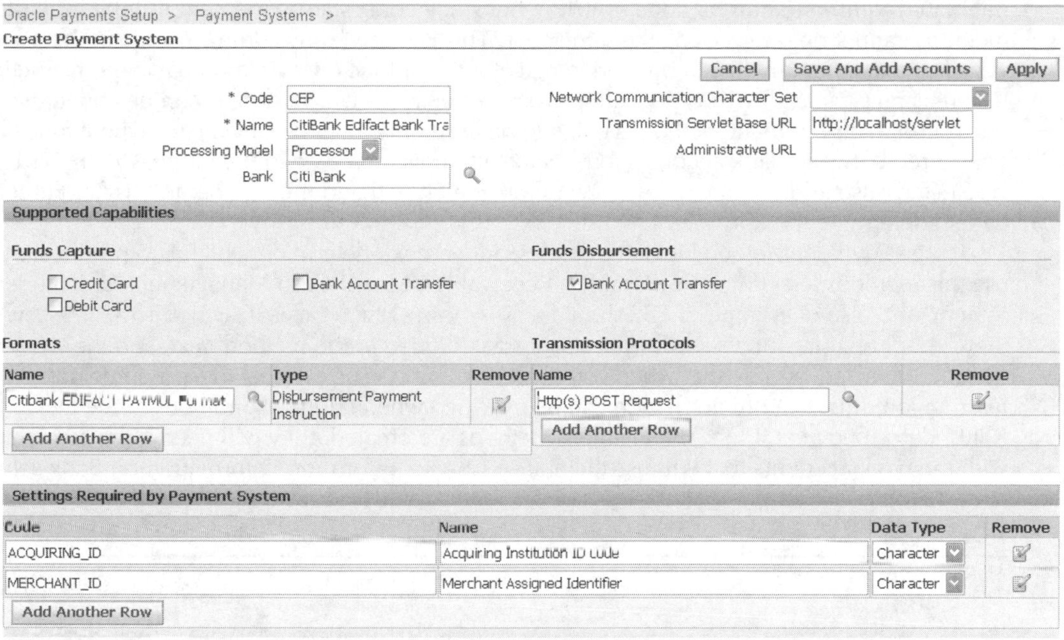

Funds Disbursement Setup Administrator | Payments Setup | Payment Systems | Payment Systems

FIGURE 7-7 *Payment System setups to send settlement transmissions to banks or third parties*

the cash balances. Once the payment systems are set up, accounts are added to provide values to the parameters added in the Settings Required by Payment Systems section. These parameters and values relate to general processing information as opposed to specific payment information unique to each payment. This ends the setups that are shared by both disbursed (Payables) and captured (Receivables) payments.

Disbursement-Specific Setups

The setups included in this section are Payables-specific and not used for other modules such as Receivables.

Payment Methods

Payment Methods are set up for each specific type of disbursement you want to make, such as Checks or Wires or Electronic Payments, and include required validations as well as determining which systems can use this method, such as Payables, Loans, Cash Management, Receivables, or Student System. Once the methods are saved, the order in which each method will default and be used by that system is added.

To create a payment method, as seen in Figure 7-8, assign a CODE and a NAME to the method. The CODE added here is seen when adding the payment method during the creation of payment instructions. Sometimes, it is necessary to set up multiple payment methods but use the same code to satisfy a government or bank requirement. For example, all payment instructions for wires might be required to carry a code of WIRE, but since CODE is a unique field in EBS, multiple methods cannot be set up using the same CODE. This is resolved by adding a value in the FORMAT VALUE MAPPING field, which can be used in place of the unique CODE field on payment instructions. When using Oracle's Treasury modules, ANTICIPATED DISBURSEMENT FLOAT days can be added. Next, determine if this payment method is going to be used only for Bills Payable, or where funds are transferred between bank accounts for specific amounts on a date in the future. When this option is selected, also add a MATURITY DATE CALCULATION, which will add the number in this field to today's date to determine the due date.

Usage Payment Method Defaulting Rules, added next, determine which EBS products can use this method, selecting from Payables, Receivables, Loans, Cash Management, and Student System, and also determines if EBS should AUTOMATICALLY ASSIGN PAYMENT METHOD TO ALL PAYEES when they are set up. PRE- and USER-DEFINED VALIDATIONS are added to the method next, and the work can then be reviewed. Notice that when you click SHOW DETAILS FOR PAYABLES, there is some default information; this default information can be modified when adding Conditions to the Defaulting Rules, described next. Once the Payment Methods are created, they will need to be associated with the bank accounts that will use them. (See Chapter 5 for more information on Bank setups).

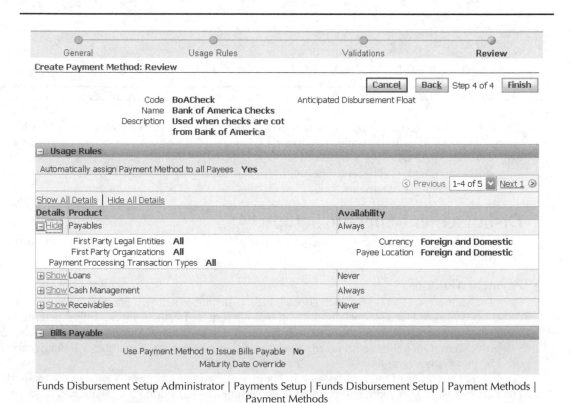

FIGURE 7-8 *Payment Methods Review page*

Once the Payment Methods are created, default rules and conditions can be added. In the Payment Method Defaulting Rules form, shown in Figure 7-9, click CREATE to add a rule to a specific product. After selecting the PAYMENT METHOD from the list that this rule is for, add a RULE NAME. Conditions determine if this payment method can be used in all or only specific Legal Entities or Operating Units, referred to as FIRST PARTY ORGANIZATIONS and FIRST PARTY LEGAL ENTITY. Payment Methods can also be restricted to PAYMENT PROCESSING TRANSACTION TYPE of Employee Expense or Payables Documents. Finally, both the CURRENCY of the transactions and the PAYEE LOCATION associated with them can be restricted to Foreign, Domestic, or both. Saving the rule adds it to the product, defaulting in the order rules were added. The priority order can be changed by clicking REORDER PRIORITY. Once these conditions are set up and the order defined, EBS will evaluate every Payables transaction document against each rule for the assigned conditions, and default the first payment method where the conditions are met. These payment methods can also be assigned to individual payment processing templates.

Bank Instructions, Delivery Channel, and Payment Reason Codes

Bank Instructions, Delivery Channels, and Payment Reason Codes are specific to each bank and can be added to payment instructions for electronic settlements. EBS comes with a set of seeded codes and also allows new codes to be created. All of these are segregated by the country they pertain to. When creating new entries, note that it is the CODE that will appear on the electronic payments, not the actual NAME assigned to it. Contact your banking institution to find out if there are required codes in your country. These are setup under Funds Disbursement Setup Administrator | Funds Disbursement Setup | Codes.

Disbursement System Options

Default system options for disbursements can be set either at the enterprise, or system, level or for a specific organization. On a new installation or an upgrade, these options will come predefined and should be reviewed to ensure they meet your business needs. Basically, these options determine where some of the setups will default in for the system during a payment run, as well as telling the system how to behave when an error is encountered.

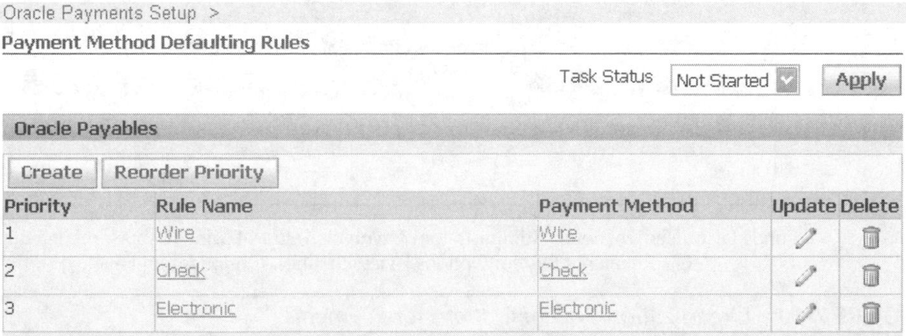

Oracle Payments Setup >
Payment Method Defaulting Rules

Task Status [Not Started] [Apply]

Oracle Payables

[Create] [Reorder Priority]

Priority	Rule Name	Payment Method	Update	Delete
1	Wire	Wire	✎	🗑
2	Check	Check	✎	🗑
3	Electronic	Electronic	✎	🗑

Funds Disbursement Setup Administrator | Payments Setup | Funds Disbursement Setup | Payment Methods | Payment Method Defaulting Rules

FIGURE 7-9 *Payment Method Defaulting Rules*

Organization-Level System Options   There are only two options that are organization-specific, as seen in Figure 7-10: where to default payment methods from, and if bank accounts can be overridden for a payee. The DEFAULT PAYMENT METHOD can come from either from the Payment Method Defaulting Rules, or from the Supplier (payee)–associated Payment Methods. For example, if the Payment Method Defaulting Rules have Wire set as priority 1, but a Supplier is set up for Check, EBS will bypass the rule hierarchies when OVERRIDE DEFAULTING RULES WHEN DEFAULT METHOD SET FOR PAYEE is checked, even when the criteria are met, and make all payments to this supplier as Check.

ALLOW PAYEE BANK ACCOUNT OVERRIDE ON PROPOSED PAYMENTS determines if the user creating a payment batch can change the bank account that a payment is being sent to. When this is not checked, the bank account would need to be updated on the supplier account, and the payment regenerated, thus ensuring segregation of duties.

Enterprise-Wide System Options   Enterprise-wide system options, shown in Figure 7-11, are also available. The organization option for DEFAULT PAYMENT METHOD is also available as an Enterprise option. If there are different settings for Organization and Enterprise, then the Organization setting will be used.

Once the payment processing begins, you have several options available for how to handle VALIDATION FAILURE RESULTS. Validation points happen for both Documents and Payments, and they would fail if any of the Payment Validations are not met for a particular Format or Payment Method. This validation is not the same validation the system performs after entering invoices, which applies and releases holds, but refers to the validation that ensures that documents meet specific payment criteria. When a document fails validation, EBS can reject only the documents with errors, reject all documents for a specific payee when an error exists, reject the entire batch, or stop the process and allow the batch to be reviewed. When a Payment itself does not pass the validation, the options are to reject all the payments with errors, stop all documents from being paid, or to stop the process and allow the payments to be reviewed.

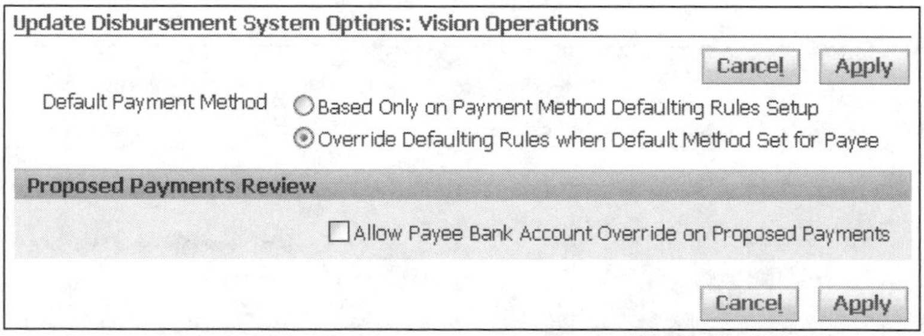

Update Disbursement System Options: Vision Operations

Cancel | Apply

Default Payment Method   ○ Based Only on Payment Method Defaulting Rules Setup
◉ Override Defaulting Rules when Default Method Set for Payee

Proposed Payments Review

☐ Allow Payee Bank Account Override on Proposed Payments

Cancel | Apply

Funds Disbursement Setup Administrator | Payments Setup | Funds Disbursement Setup |
Disbursement System Options | View Settings, Organization Level

---

FIGURE 7-10   *Organization System Options for Payments*

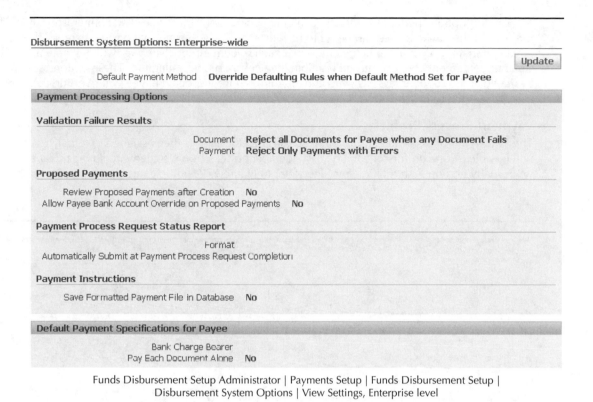

Disbursement System Options: Enterprise-wide

Update

Default Payment Method   **Override Defaulting Rules when Default Method Set for Payee**

Payment Processing Options

Validation Failure Results

Document   **Reject all Documents for Payee when any Document Fails**
Payment   **Reject Only Payments with Errors**

Proposed Payments

Review Proposed Payments after Creation   **No**
Allow Payee Bank Account Override on Proposed Payments   **No**

Payment Process Request Status Report

Format
Automatically Submit at Payment Process Request Completion

Payment Instructions

Save Formatted Payment File in Database   **No**

Default Payment Specifications for Payee

Bank Charge Bearer
Pay Each Document Alone   **No**

Funds Disbursement Setup Administrator | Payments Setup | Funds Disbursement Setup |
Disbursement System Options | View Settings, Enterprise level

FIGURE 7-11   *Enterprise System Options for Payments*

When a payment batch is created, EBS can be set up to allow straight-through processing, or to allow the user to REVIEW PROPOSED PAYMENTS AFTER CREATION. Again, the option to ALLOW PAYEE BANK ACCOUNT OVERRIDE ON PROPOSED PAYMENTS can be set, and when turned on, the person creating the batch will have access to change the banking information for any payee's payments in the batch.

If you wish the PAYMENT PROCESS REQUEST STATUS REPORT to have a default format, select it from the list of values. EBS comes with only one format, but additional ones can be created in XML Publisher. Selecting AUTOMATICALLY SUBMIT AT PAYMENT PROCESS REQUEST COMPLETION will print the report out with each batch. This report is the equivalent of a preliminary payment register for your batch.

Once created, the Payment Instructions can be saved by selecting SAVE FORMATTED PAYMENT FILE IN DATABASE. While this is good to have if there were transmission problems, it does also carry a risk, since this file would be available to people with the proper access to resubmit or change information and resend. These risks should be weighed carefully before deciding how to set this option.

The last options pertain to Default Payment Specifications for Payee. The entity responsible for bearing the bank charges can be set to be either the Payee, for normal or only express charges, Payer, or Shared. Also, it can be determined if each document for a supplier will generate a separate settlement check, or group multiple invoices onto one settlement. These options are available at the supplier level as well, and anything set for a specific payee will override these enterprise-wide settings.

Payment Process Profiles

The Payment Process Profile brings all the setups together and is then assigned to templates. There will be at least one profile for each type of document or electronic settlement, so organizations will usually end up with multiple profiles. Refer to Figure 7-12 while going through these setups.

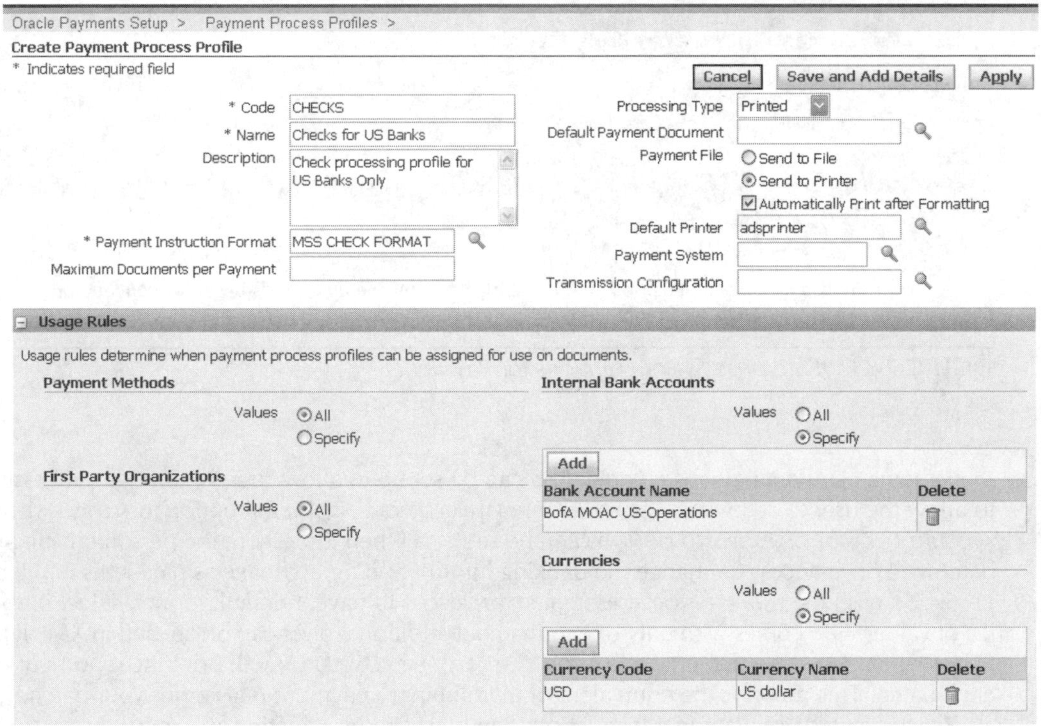

FIGURE 7-12 *Creating payment process profiles*

Add a CODE and a NAME for this profile, ensuring there are no spaces in the CODE, and add a DESCRIPTION for users to refer to when selecting it for use. Notice that only the fields with an asterisk are required throughout these setups—there are actually relatively few required fields. Select a PAYMENT INSTRUCTION FORMAT that will be used with this profile to produce the actual output for the payment. There should be at least one profile for each format used in your organization. Enter the number of invoices that can be paid on a single payment document in the MAXIMUM DOCUMENTS PER PAYMENT. EBS does have the ability to use overflow checks when printing to an overflow document. Such a document usually will not print a check associated with it if the check itself is part of the format.

Determine the PROCESSING TYPE for these payments, selecting from PRINTED to indicate the format will produce output to a printer, or ELECTRONIC when the output will be electronically sent to the processing institution. The next available fields will depend on which processing type is selected. For electronic, the ELECTRONIC PROCESSING CHANNEL can be selected, choosing from Oracle Payments or Oracle E-Commerce Gateway. Payment batches can be completed either manually, when the payment is transmitted, or when it is formatted, depending on how the PAYMENT COMPLETION POINT is set. Selecting ALLOW MANUAL SETTINGS FOR PAYMENT COMPLETION will allow a payment batch to be completed manually at any time without waiting for a bank confirmation.

For printed transactions, a DEFAULT PAYMENT DOCUMENT can be selected. This list is all the payment documents that are available for the PAYMENT INSTRUCTION FORMAT assigned earlier. Payment Methods are assigned to a specific Payment Instruction Format when the document is set up on a bank account (Payables Manager | Setup | Payment | Bank Accounts | Manage Payment Documents). Select if the PAYMENT FILE should be sent to a file or printer, and if it should AUTOMATICALLY PRINT AFTER FORMATTING, reducing the need for manual intervention to print the checks. Selecting this option will default the printer name from the system profile Printer (System Administrator | Profile | System). This can then be changed here or during printing if automatic printing after formatting was not selected. Both the PAYMENT SYSTEM and TRANSMISSION CONFIGURATION selections are limited to the payment systems that are associated with the Payment Instruction Format that was selected.

Usage Rules are added next to restrict which Payment Methods, Internal Bank Accounts, First Party Organizations, and Currencies can use this process profile. The default is ALL, allowing this profile to be used in all instances. Select SPECIFY under any area and an ADD button will appear to add Usage Rules.

Next, guidelines to determine how payments are grouped for inclusion on payment instructions are added. Under Payment Instruction Creation Rules, shown in Figure 7-13, Payment Groupings can be selected using Table 7-5 as a guide. Note that more than one grouping rule can be selected.

Payment Limits can also be added for processing, including AMOUNT CURRENCY, which limits the payments to a specific currency, EXCHANGE RATE TYPE, TOTAL AMOUNT, or total NUMBER OF PAYMENTS. Entering data here will restrict this profile to only consider transactions that call within these parameters. Payments can be sorted on the payment instructions using up to three PAYMENT ATTRIBUTES. You can select from the list of values, which includes FIRST PARTY ORGANIZATION, PAYEE BANK BRANCH NUMBER, PAYEE NAME, PAYEE NUMBER, PAYEE TAXPAYER IDENTIFIER, PAYMENT AMOUNT, PAYMENT DATE, PAYMENT FUNCTION, and POSTAL CODE. These can be sorted in ascending or descending order.

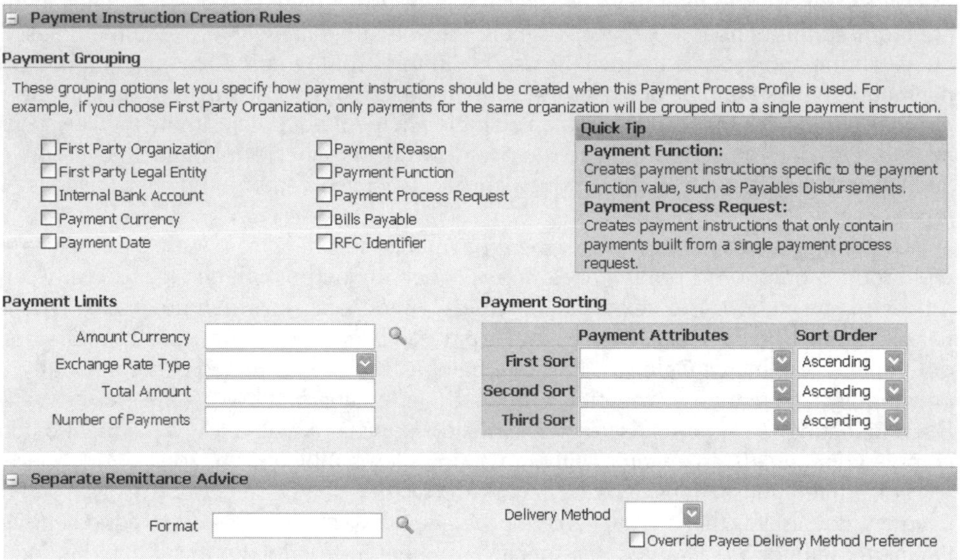

FIGURE 7-13 *Adding payment instruction creation rules in payment process profiles*

Grouping Rule Name	Meaning
Bills Payable	Groups all future-dated payments
First Party Legal Entity	Groups by Legal Entity associated with the Operating Unit on the invoice
First Party Organization	Uses Operating Unit assigned to the invoice
Internal Bank Account (for Electronic Only)	Based on the bank account where the settlement is being issued from
Payment Currency (for Electronic Only)	Based on the currency of the settlement
Payment Date	Based on the date of the payment
Payment Function	Type of payment, usually Supplier payment or Employee reimbursement
Payment Process Request	Allows only one payment process request to be grouped onto one settlement, as opposed to multiple
Payment Reason	Based on the Payment Reason, which can be associated with the supplier site
RFC Identifier	Used with payments created by a U.S. federal agency, groups payments by Regional Finance Center (RFC)

TABLE 7-5 *Payment Grouping Rules*

If a separate remittance advice is required, both the FORMAT and the DELIVERY METHOD are needed. Delivery Methods include Email, Fax, or Print. Since the delivery method can also be identified on a payee, the option to OVERRIDE PAYMENT DELIVERY METHOD PREFERENCE is available.

Selecting the SAVE AND ADD DETAILS button not only saves the payment process profile, but also allows details to be added. Many of the fields that were just entered will appear again, along with a few additional options. Under the Payment Creation tab, seen in Figure 7-14, additional criteria can be added for creating payments. While Payment Grouping rules, covered previously in Table 7-5, guide EBS on how to group payment formats, Payment Creation Rules – Document Groupings determine how the documents are grouped for payment. For example, two invoices can be selected into one payment because they both have the same Bank Charge Bearer, but remitted on separate payment instructions because they have different Payment Reasons. Table 7-6 lists the options for grouping documents.

Under the Document Limits region, you can add a PAYMENT DETAIL FORMULA and a MAXIMUM PAYMENT DETAIL LENGTH. You can populate the detail formula with a SQL statement to select document-specific information that can be added into a Payment template when the payment is created, while the maximum length will limit the data selected to under a specific size. This can be used with the seeded XML data definitions that come seeded with EBS to add an additional field without creating a new data definition, and it is commonly used in localizing payment formats for country-specific information. You can use MAXIMUM DOCUMENT PER PAYMENT to limit the invoices that will be grouped onto a single payment.

On the next tab, Payment Instruction Creation, there are a few additional options available now, such as Bank Instructions, which are bank-specific instructions that can be added to this payment process profile and will be referenced on every payment instruction in this batch. The fields BANK INSTRUCTION 1 and 2 include predefined bank instruction codes that are issued to a country's central bank. BANK INSTRUCTION DETAILS and PAYMENT TEXT MESSAGE 1 and 2 allow any information to be added to all the payments.

You add Payment Instruction Formats in the next tab, shown in Figure 7-15. When required, a PAYMENT FILE ACCOMPANYING LETTER FORMAT can be selected, which will produce a letter that will accompany any payment instructions to the bank. These letters are designed just like all other payment instructions are, by creating an XML template. For the payment files created using this

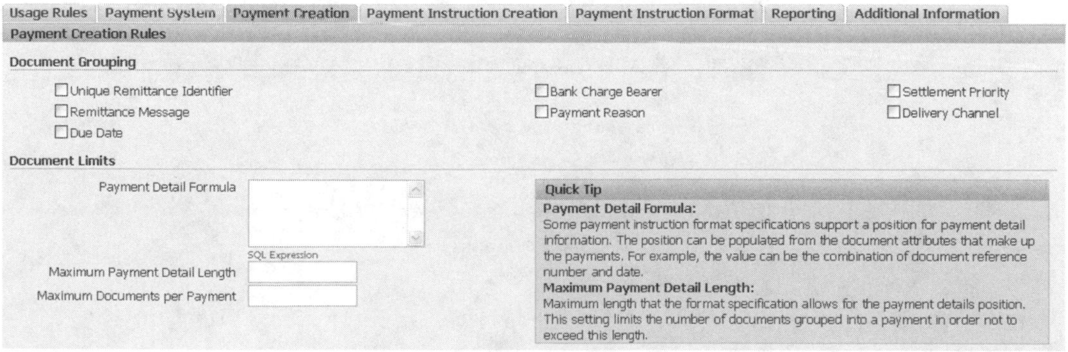

FIGURE 7-14   *Adding payment creation rules in payment process profiles*

Document Grouping Name	Meaning
Bank Charge Bearer	On the Invoice Header, and defaults in from the supplier's Payment Details
Delivery Channel	On the Invoice Header, and defaults in from the supplier's Payment Details
Due Date	Invoice Due Date
Payment Reason	On the Invoice Header, and defaults in from the supplier's Payment Details
Remittance Message	Based on the three Remittance Messages that were entered on the Invoice Header
Settlement Priority	On the Invoice Header, and defaults in from the supplier's Payment Details
Unique Remittance Identifier	Invoice Header, captures the IBLC code from the supplier site's Payment Reason Code

TABLE 7-6   *Document Grouping Options*

profile, you can assign a specific prefix for the file, file extension, and location/director where the outbound file should be saved. Some banks have specific requirements for sequentially numbering payments. EBS allows a specific sequence to be added and controlled for each payment process profile in the Period Sequences in Format section. Sequences should be added here when the sequential number must be unique for this type of payment only, or when the sequences are required to be reset on a regular basis; most commonly, these sequences are required for external reasons, as opposed to internally for tax reporting. Select the SET SCHEDULE icon to assign a frequency for EBS to automatically reset the sequence.

Finally, in the Reporting tab shown in Figure 7-16, additional formats can be added to the profile to create additional reports during the payment process without having to run them manually. First, a Payment Instruction Register format can be added, which will print a register

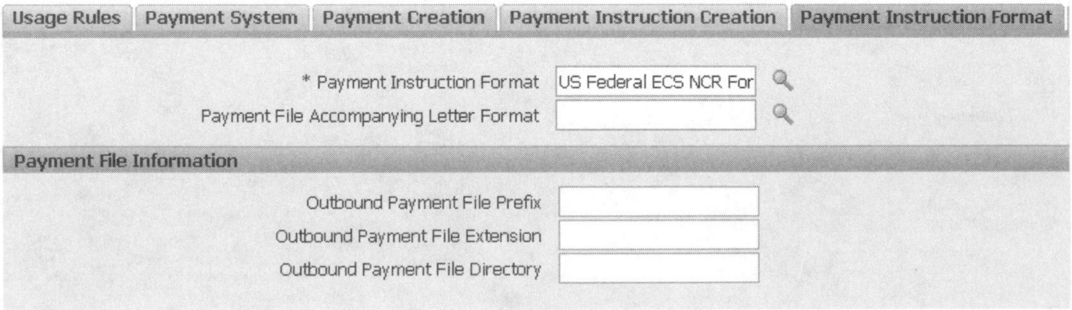

FIGURE 7-15   *Adding payment instruction formats to payment process profiles*

as part of the processing. Selecting AUTOMATICALLY SUBMIT AT PAYMENT COMPLETION POINT will cause the report to automatically print out without the user's advancing the process to print. When a Positive Pay file is required with the batch, the FORMAT is assigned here, as well as any prefixes for the file, file extensions, and an outbound directory for the file. Selecting AUTOMATICALLY TRANSMIT FILE will send the file out without the person processing the payment having to perform this task.

When a Separate Remittance Advice is being created, it can be automatically submitted after the payments are completed. Sometime, more than one copy of the remittance advice is required, and selecting ALLOW MULTIPLE COPIES FOR PAYMENT INSTRUCTION allows the number of copies to be specified. After selecting this, select NUMBER OF COPIES under the CONDITION field list of values, and a field for TOTAL NUMBER OF DOCUMENTS becomes available. Under the same CONDITION field, PAYMENT DETAIL LENGTH is available to identify that the separate remittance advice is to be printed only if the payment detail length is a specific length, identified in the PAYMENT DETAIL LENGTH field. These two fields (payment detail length and total number of documents) are only visible when their corresponding CONDITION is selected. Leaving the condition at the default of ALL DOCUMENTS will cause one remittance advice to be printed for every document in the batch.

When regulatory reporting is required for each payment created, EBS come with two main options: Report Directly to Central Bank, and Reporting Made by Bank. Both allow the OPTION TO REPORT ONLY FOREIGN CURRENCY PAYMENTS, and to assign a specific currency, exchange rate, and amount. When reporting directly to a central bank, a format can be added.

Now that the Funds Disbursement Manager is fully set up, Profiles should be evaluated and set, and a template created to combine the disbursement setups to be used to create payment batches.

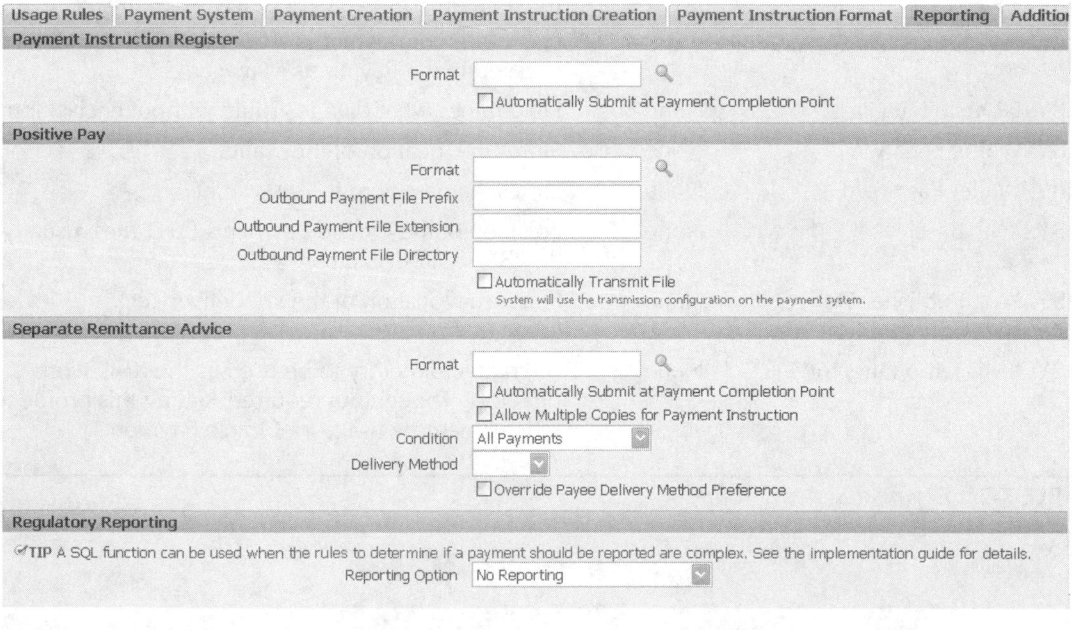

FIGURE 7-16 *Reporting Options for payment process profiles*

System Profiles for Payments

Profiles are set up under the System Administrator responsibility (Profile | System). The profiles relating to payment creation are outlined in Table 7-7.

Profile Name	Default	Usage
IBY: Default Payee for BR (Bills Receivable) Remittance	None	Set only at the site level, determines the responsible entity for creating the payment.
IBY: ECAPP URL	None	Must be set when using the PL/SQL API. Identifies the machine and port where the ECServlet is installed.
IBY: HTTP Proxy	None	Enter URL where the Proxy exists.
IBY: Java XML Long File	None	When set, this enables XML Logging, and identifies the location where the file will be written.
IBY: Network Timeout	None	Timeout for Payments.
IBY: No Proxy Domain	None	Identifies domain name where a proxy is not required.
IBY: Outbound Payment System Suffix	None	Three-letter suffix used to identify the system handling your outbound payment instructions.
IBY: Registered Instrument Encryption	No	When set to NO, encryption is not used for storing payment instruments. If changed to YES, then the encryption key must be provided.
IBY: System Security Key	None	Read-only profile for storing the system key for encryption for payment instructions. This can be updated in the Payments Manager.
IBY: UI Visibility Class	None	Determines what data is visible without encryption.
IBY: Wallet Location	None	Stores the location of the wallet.
IBY: Wallet Password	None	Stores the password for the wallet.
IBY: XML Base	None	Location of the Oracle Payments DTD files, usually in the IBY_TOP/XML directory.
IBY: XML Publisher Delivery Manager Configuration File	None	Stores the location of the xdodelivery.cfg configuration file.
IBY: XML Temp Directory	None	A writable directory to be used as the XML work directory. Though not required, setting this profile will reduce memory usage by Oracle Payments.

TABLE 7-7 *Payment System Profiles*

Creating Templates for Streamlined Payment Processing

Templates are used in Oracle Payments to process payment requests, including defining the invoice selection criteria, payment attributes and instructions, and how validation failures are going to be handled. Many of these criteria were created in the previous sections and can now be combined to create different options for processing payments, reducing the time a user has to spend creating and modifying payment batches. The selection criteria in templates can also be used to obtain cash required for all the payments selected with a specific template, prior to creating the payment batch.

Templates are created in the Payables Manager responsibility and not the Funds Disbursement Setup Administrator (Payments | Entry | Payments Manager | Template tab). Refer to Figure 7-17.

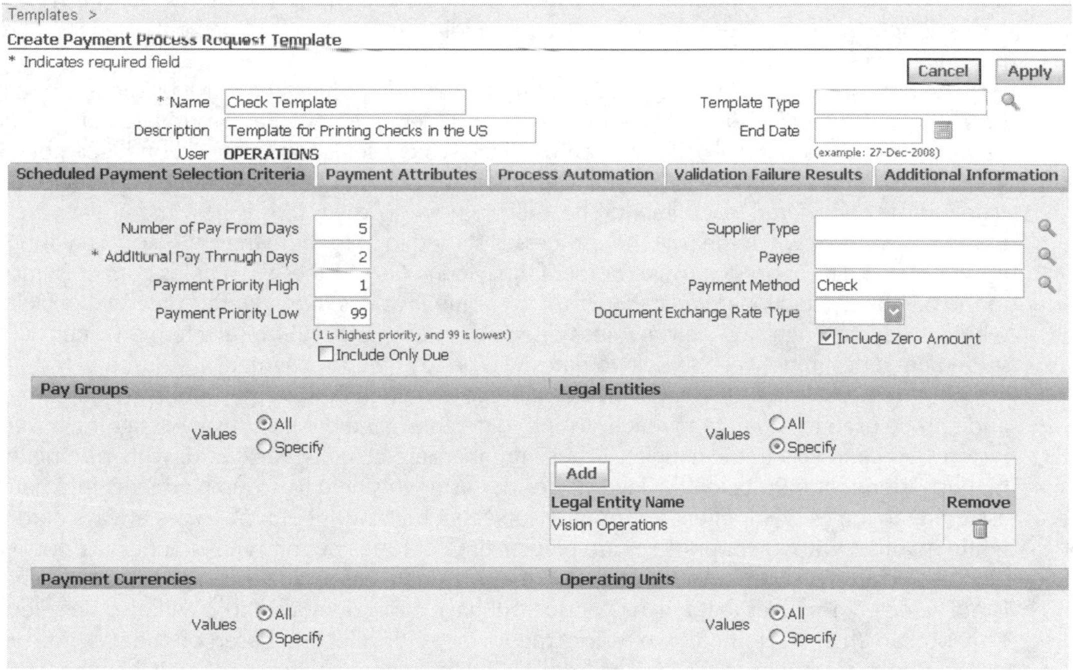

Payables Manager | Payments | Entry | Payments Manager | Template tab

FIGURE 7-17 *Creating payment process templates*

Templates, required for defaulting information on a payment batch, have only three required fields: NAME, EXCHANGE RATE, and ADDITIONAL PAY THROUGH DAYS. The default for the field CREATE PAYMENT INSTRUCTIONS is INITIATE WHEN PAYMENT PROCESS REQUEST IS COMPLETE, which will require a PAYMENT PROCESS PROFILE to be added as well, or this field can be changed to WAIT FOR STANDARD REQUEST SUBMISSION. Create this basic template and it can be used for any check run by modifying the selection criteria during the payment processing request. On the other hand, creating specific templates with different selection criteria or payment instructions can reduce the manual entries to create a single check run or to schedule weekly check runs. Templates are one of the setups that should be reviewed and modified on a regular basis and modified to meet changing business needs.

Ensure the NAME assigned to a template is unique and descriptive so that the users know what this template does, and add a DESCRIPTION to provide additional information. The USER will default to the user name for the person creating the template and cannot be changed. TEMPLATE TYPES can be added for template classification, making it easier to find templates when there are a large number of them in the system. For example, template types can include checks, wires, EDI, or Credit Card, depending on the payment process profile that is associated to them. The list of values for this field is a Payables Lookup; new options will need to be first added to the Lookup (Payables Manager | Setup | Lookups | Payables). The lookup type is PAYMENT_TEMPLATE_TYPE. If this template is no longer valid or being used, adding an END DATE will prevent users from creating payment requests using it.

The first tab, Scheduled Payment Selection Criteria, determines how the invoices are selected for payment processing. NUMBER OF PAY FROM DAYS will determine the Pay From date that will default in for the payment batch. If this is set to 5, and a payment selection is started on December 5, then the PAY FROM DATE that defaults in is December 10, and only payments due on or after to this date will be considered for payment. The ADDITIONAL PAY THROUGH DAYS is how many days are added to the system date when the payment process is started to determine the PAY THROUGH DATE, which is the last due date the system will consider for payment. Getting these two fields correct is important in the payment selection criteria: Pay From says only invoices due *after* this date will be selected, whereas Pay Through says only invoices due *prior* to this date will be selected; invoices with settlement dates in between these two dates will be selected for payment.

PAYMENT PRIORITYS are assigned to invoices, based on either the system, supplier, or batch defaults, and can be used to separate transactions into different settlement batches by assigning a PAYMENT PRIORITY HIGH and LOW to the template. These numbers are actually backward, with 1 being the highest priority and 99 being the lowest. Besides using this field to group payments into batches, assigning invoices or suppliers a priority ensures that high-priority invoices are always paid first, while invoices with lower priorities are paid as time or funds permit. The INCLUDE ONLY DUE option, when selected, will only select invoices on their due date based on the assigned terms. When this is not selected, invoices that are not yet due but have a discount available will also be selected.

You can enter a SUPPLIER TYPE to restrict the invoices for selection based on the SUPPLIER TYPE assigned to the Supplier, while PAYEE will restrict it to only one specific supplier. When the payment instructions are being created as part of the automated payments, adding PAYMENT METHOD as a selection criterion will ensure that only invoices assigned a specific payment method, such as Check or Wire, are considered and selected.

When foreign currencies are being used for documents (invoices entered in currencies other than the currency assigned to the Ledger), the payment selections can be narrowed down to either a user-defined exchange rate or one that is assigned by the system, based on the entry in DOCUMENT EXCHANGE RATE TYPE. Most often, settlements are not generated for suppliers where the amount due is zero, but sometimes this becomes necessary to clear transactions off the invoice aging. When an invoice is entered, and a credit or debit memo is applied to it, the net due supplier becomes zero, while leaving the invoice and credit memo open. These transactions will not normally be selected for payment until an additional invoice is entered in the system and becomes due. Checking INCLUDE ZERO AMOUNT will allow these transactions that net to zero to be included for payment. For suppliers you are no longer doing business with, or to clean up credits off the aging, you may decide to process zero payments as well. Using a template that has INCLUDE ZERO AMOUNT checked will select these transactions as well for payment. Ensure that there is also a bank account set up to allow zero dollar payments before using this option.

Invoices selection can further be narrowed down for a specific Pay Group, Payment Currency, Legal Entity, or Operating Unit. One or more selections can be added to each of these areas. This completes the options for Scheduled Payment Selection Criteria.

Additional Payment Attributes can be defined, such as the PAYMENT DATE, as seen in Figure 7-18. Typically, the date on the payment will be the SAME AS the REQUEST DATE, but future-dated payments can also be generated by defining the EXTRA DAYS to be added to the request date. As you may remember from setting up Payment Methods and Payment Process Profiles, bank accounts get assigned to Payment Methods, which are then in turn assigned to Payment Process Profiles. These next few fields are interactively linked. Selecting a DISBURSEMENT BANK ACCOUNT will limit the PAYMENT DOCUMENTS available to only documents assigned to that bank account, and the PAYMENT DOCUMENTS can only be entered when a bank account is already selected. If a PAYMENT DOCUMENT is selected, it will use the bank account associated with it and default the payment process profile that is linked to it in the setups. Since PAYMENT PROCESS PROFILES can be linked to a specific settlement currency, selecting the same currency on the selection criteria makes the selection process consistent. If no currency is entered on the selection criteria age, the currency from the profile will take precedence, but conversely, having these two currencies set differently will cause no payments to be generated. PAYMENT EXCHANGE RATE TYPE is a required field and will limit the invoices to be selected all to have the same payment exchange rate type associated with them.

If you want to assign a specific settlement priority for this entire template, an OVERRIDE SETTLEMENT PRIORITY can be added. If this is not added, the default in the bank setups will be used. BANK CHARGE BEARER can also be set for this entire batch, and will override this value from the invoices. When the bank charge bearer is set, then a TRANSFER PRIORITY is required and will determine which of the setup bank charges will be used. You can also assign a STARTING VOUCHER NUMBER, causing all vouchers to start with this number whenever this template is used. This is different than the actual settlement or check number, and is usually used in conjunction with sequential numbering requirements by a government.

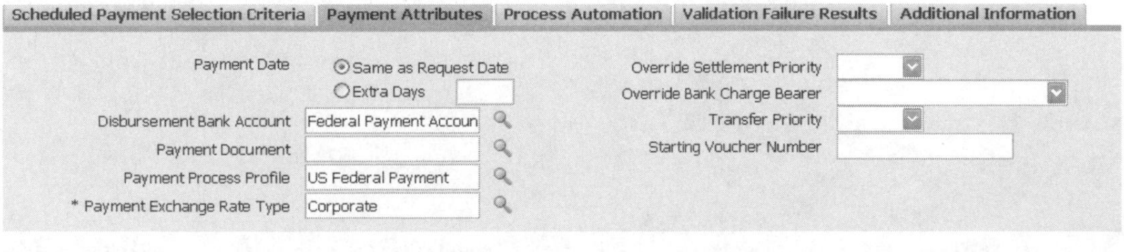

| Scheduled Payment Selection Criteria | Payment Attributes | Process Automation | Validation Failure Results | Additional Information |

Payment Date	◉ Same as Request Date	Override Settlement Priority	
	○ Extra Days	Override Bank Charge Bearer	
Disbursement Bank Account	Federal Payment Accoun	Transfer Priority	
Payment Document		Starting Voucher Number	
Payment Process Profile	US Federal Payment		
* Payment Exchange Rate Type	Corporate		

FIGURE 7-18 *Payment attributes on templates*

Under the Process Automation tab, you can check MAXIMIZE CREDITS to ensure that all credits and invoices are selected up to the credit amount and processed. When this is not selected and the total payment is less than zero, no transactions will be selected for payment. To use this feature, ensure that INCLUDE ZERO AMOUNT is also selected on the Payment Selection Criteria tab. If you want the ability to review the transactions selected for payment, check STOP PROCESS FOR REVIEW AFTER SCHEDULED PAYMENT SELECTION, causing the system to pause at the status of Invoices Pending Review, before being manually moved to the next step in the process.

CALCULATE PAYMENT WITHHOLDING AND INTEREST DURING SCHEDULED PAYMENT SELECTION will cause interest due on invoices as well as withholding taxes to be calculated after selection as opposed to after payment completion. An additional stopping point can be added here, which is to STOP PROCESS FOR REVIEW AFTER CREATION OF PROPOSED PAYMENTS, pausing the process after the Build Payments program runs to group the invoices onto payment instructions. The final review point is available with the CREATE PAYMENT INSTRUCTIONS; it determines if they are created after a review point, where a user needs to initiate the payment instructions, or by initiating it automatically after the payment process request is completed.

Even though Validation Failure Results were assigned on the Payment Methods, they can be overridden here for both the document and the payment. Document validation failures can be set to reject all documents, reject only the documents with a validation failure, reject all the documents for the payee where the failure occurred, or stop the process for review before proceeding. Payments failure options only have the option to reject payments with errors, to reject all payments, or again to stop for review.

At this point the template is ready for use.

CHAPTER
8

Payment Processing

ayment Processing has been reworked in R12, building on the concept of shared services and the old iPayments module. Previously, settling debt transactions was broken down into pieces, where EBS Payables would relieve and account for the settlement and print any settlement documents, iPayments would transmit any transactions to third parties, and any additional reporting was a separate step. Once a process was started, it was taken through to the end.

Now, settlements are broken down into stages, starting with invoice selection, then validations, aggregation of settlements, formatting, and finally, transmission, to create an integrated payment engine within EBS. Not only are documents created for settlement, they have built-in validations of the data as well as the ability to transmit this data to various institutions. EBS has several stopping points during this process that allow the users to confirm selections prior to moving on to the next step. With settlements being broken down into various steps and components, it supports both centralized and decentralized accounting models, or some combination of these models.

Introducing the Managers

EBS introduced two new managers in R12 to assist with payment processing: the Funds Disbursement Process Manager and the Payment Manager. The Payment Manager, shown in Figure 8-1, is all-inclusive and can be used to monitor payment requests, create and submit templates used for payment selection, and to create payment instructions, as well as inquire on confirmed payments. The Funds Disbursement Process Manager, seen in Figure 8-2, offers a different management view, and allows the creation of payment instructions only, while allowing inquiry into payment process requests and payments. This manager is not accessible from the Payables Manager responsibility as it installs from Oracle. Both can be used to manage void and stop payments. For purposes of this chapter, all navigation paths are for the Payment Manager.

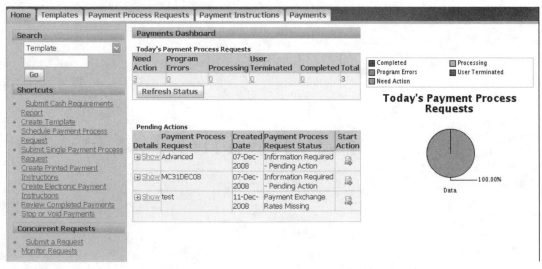

FIGURE 8-1 *Payment Manager Dashboard*

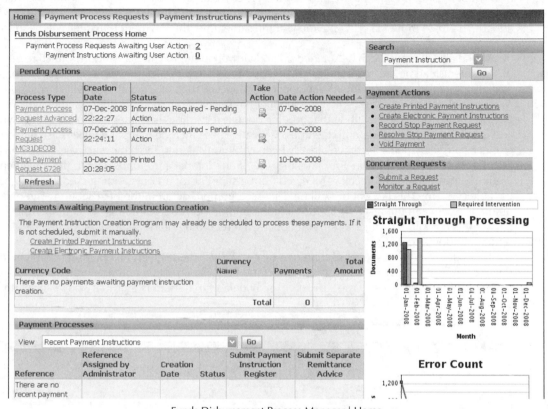

Funds Disbursement Process Manager | Home

FIGURE 8-2 *Funds Disbursement Process Manager Dashboard*

Payment Batches vs. Single Payments

EBS provides the ability to create a payment batch, based on specific selection criteria, or to pay a single invoice or supplier. While all payments can be created via the Payment Manager by submitting a payment request, there are other options for creating payments for a single invoice payment or paying several invoices for one supplier on a single settlement.

The single, manual invoice payment process can be started from the Invoice Entry screen (Payables Manager | Invoices | Entry | Invoices or Invoice Batches), if the proper access is granted. After querying up the invoice you want to pay (this must be done in Entry, not Inquiry), click ACTIONS and select PAY IN FULL. These days, with auditors emphasizing and insisting on strict segregation of duties, a person would not normally have access to both the Invoice Entry and Payment Creation screens, and this feature is not available on any seeded invoice inquiry window.

Generating Single Payments

Once you click the PAY IN FULL option, it takes you to the Payment window. You can also initiate a single payment directly from this window, shown in Figure 8-3. The main difference between creating manual payments these two different ways is that multiple invoices for the same supplier are manually added to the payment when the process starts from the Payments window, whereas only the invoice where PAY IN FULL was selected would be paid and additional invoices cannot be added. To create more than one payment at the same time, the Payment Manager will need to be used.

While all settlements can be queried up and viewed in the Payments window, only three TYPES of settlements can be created here: QUICK, MANUAL, and REFUND. *Quick* payments are created for a single supplier, where a settlement document is produced, such as a check or an electronic transfer. *Manual* payments are created when the supplier has been compensated with the settlement created outside of EBS, and the only thing that is being done is recording the settlement to close the invoice and create the payment accounting entries. Typically, these include manual checks, cash payments, or electronic settlements that have already been communicated to the bank, such as a wire transfer that was completed directly in your banking institution's interface. *Refunds* refer to the settlement of credit memos, whereas a check is received from a supplier for an outstanding credit memo in the Payables system. This last option will be discussed in more detail in the next section. The only difference between the first two options (MANUAL and QUICK) is output that is created after the payment is completed: either a report reflecting the recording of the settlement, or an actual settlement document.

If the user has access to more than one OPERATING UNIT, then select the operating unit where the invoices to be paid were entered. Next, select the TRADING PARTNER by entering either the supplier name or the SUPPLIER NUMBER. The SUPPLIER SITE may default in if there is a primary pay site set up on

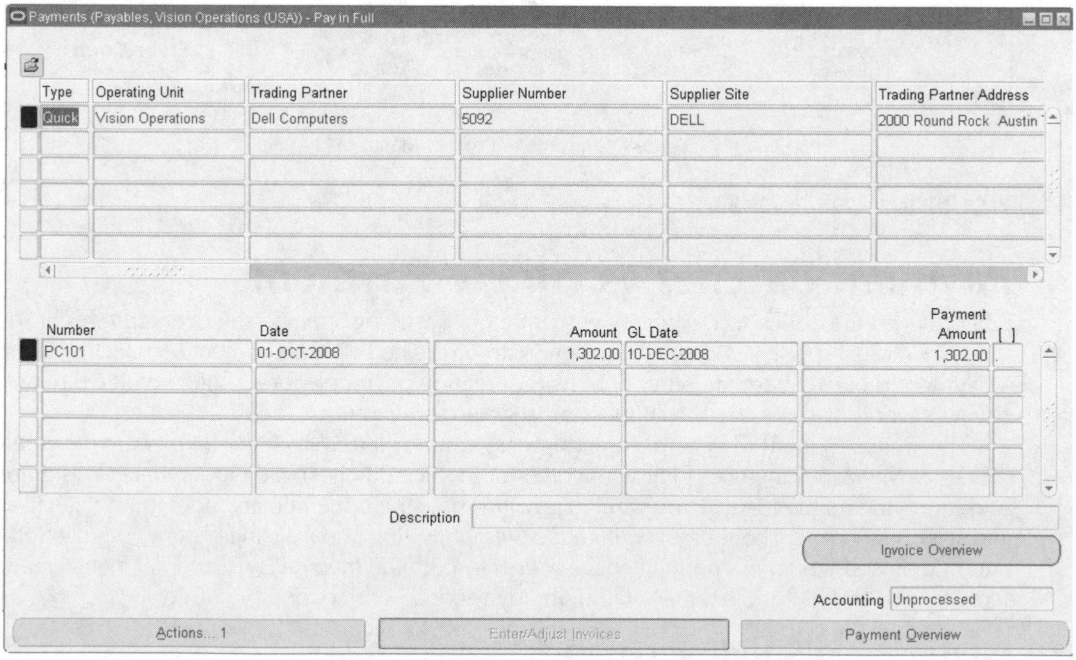

Payables Manager | Payments | Entry | Payments

FIGURE 8-3 *Single payment entry*

the supplier or only one pay site; otherwise, it can be selected from the list of values. Next, select a PAYMENT DATE for the settlement. If this is a manual settlement, this date can be backdated. Then fill in the BANK ACCOUNT to disburse the funds from, PAYMENT CURRENCY, PAYMENT METHOD, PAYMENT DOCUMENT, and PAYMENT PROCESSING PROFILE.

Just as when using the Payment Manager to create a payment, the PAYMENT PROCESSING PROFILE determines the payment instructions that will be created for this payment. The PAYMENT METHOD selected must match the payment method assigned to the invoices you want to pay. This can be found on the invoice screen under the Scheduled Payments tab (Payables Manager | Invoices | Entry | Invoices). Select the PAYMENT DOCUMENT from the settlement documents that are associated with the selected bank account, while the DOCUMENT NUMBER is the actual check or wire number that is being recorded. This will default in to the next available number from the bank setups and can be updated if necessary.

These are the only fields that are required to begin selecting the invoices that will be settled, but additional fields can be entered, as described in Table 8-1.

Field Name	Description
Trading Partner Address	If ALLOW ADDRESS CHANGE is enabled, an address can be entered here that is not on the supplier. (The controlling option to allow this is found in Payables Manager | Setup | Options | Payables Options | Payment tab | Allow Address Change).
Payee Country	Country associated with the payment address.
Payment Amount	EBS will calculate this based on the invoices selected for payment.
Account Currency	Base currency for the bank account selected.
Remit-to Account	Defaults in, and can be updated by the user if updating is allowed to the Remit-to Bank Account. (This option is controlled in Payables Manager | Setup | Options | Payables Options | Invoice tab, Allow Remit To Account Override).
Payment Address	Address on the Payment, usually associated with the supplier site.
Document Category	Determines the payment sequence, if sequential numbering is used.
Voucher Num	Assigned with the document category for sequential numbering.
Maturity Date	Required when this is a Bills Payable, or future-dated payment, and represents the settlement date for the payment.
Payment Processing Request	Payment Processing Request Name assigned when creating a batch, or "Quick Payment" followed by payment ID for Quick Checks.
Anticipated Value Date	Anticipated date the funds will be withdrawn from your bank account.

TABLE 8-1   *Informational, Optional, and Hidden Fields for Payments*

Field Name	Description
Status	Status of the payment: Cleared, Cleared but Unaccounted, Issued, Negotiable, Overflow, Reconciled, Set Up, Spoiled, Stop Initiated, Unconfirmed Set Up, Voided, or Reconciled but Unaccounted.
Rate Type	Exchange Rate Type used for foreign currency settlements.
Rate Date	Effective date of the rate for foreign currency payments.
Payment Rate	Actual rate for foreign currency payments.
Functional Amount	Amount of payment in the function currency.
Hidden Fields	
Actual Value Date	Date funds were withdrawn from bank account.
Bank Charge Bearer Override	Allows ability to override bearer of bank charge.
Cleared Amount	Actual amount disbursed for settlement, based on the bank statement.
Cleared Date	Assigned by Cash Management, date bank disbursed funds
Cleared Functional Amount	Amount recorded in Cash Management for functional currency.
Cleared Rate	Rate used by bank for foreign currency payments.
Cleared Rate Date	Effective date of the rate used.
Cleared Rate Type	Identifies exchange rate that was used by the bank for foreign currency funds.
Description	Payment description added during payment processing.
Employee Number	Populates with Oracle Human Resource employee number when payment is made to a supplier associated with an employee.
Functional Currency	Primary currency associated with the Ledger.
Maturity Rate	Associated only with bills payable, or future-dated payments, rate at the time of maturity for foreign currency payments.
Maturity Rate Date	Usually the same as the MATURITY DATE, is the date the maturity rate is based on.
Maturity Rate Type	Exchange rate used for bills payable, or future-dated payments, on the maturity date to calculate gains and losses.
Paid To Name	Actual recipient name on the payment document, and will be the supplier name at time of settlement. This field cannot be updated.
Sequence Number	Assigned by system when sequential number is turned on.

TABLE 8-1 *Informational, Optional, and Hidden Fields for Payments* (continued)

Field Name	Description
Hidden Fields	
Settlement Priority Override	Override assigned during payment process for the settlement priority.
Statement Line Num	Bank statement line number in Cash Management this payment was matched to.
Statement Num	Bank statement number in Cash Management this payment was matched to.
Status Date	Reflects the date of the last update to the payment.
Transfer Priority	Determines the bank charges associated with electronic settlements when this feature is turned on.
Treasury Date	Entered to record the treasury date from the US Treasury Agency Confirmation report.
Treasury Number	Entered to record the treasury issued number from the US Treasury Agency Confirmation report.

TABLE 8-1   *Informational, Optional, and Hidden Fields for Payments* (continued)

Once the required values, as well as any additional information, are entered for the payment, invoices can then be selected by with the ENTER/ADJUST INVOICES button at the bottom of the page. Using the list of values under INVOICE NUMBER, invoices can be selected for payment here. The invoices available will be restricted to the supplier and site entered on the previous screen, where the payment method on the invoice matches the payment method on the payment. Once the INVOICE NUMBER is selected, the PAYMENT AMOUNT will default in based on the amount remaining on the invoice, but can be reduced to make a partial payment that is less than the defaulted amount. The DISCOUNT AMOUNT can also be adjusted.

Multiple invoices can be added in this manner, but only for the trading partner specified on the previous page. For invoices to be available for payment, they must be validated without any holds, have the same payment method as was selected on the previous page, and have an outstanding amount still due on them. If more than one invoice is selected, then PAY ALONE must not be checked on the invoice. The last criterion for using this option for creating settlements is that the payment must be settled in the same currency as the invoice. While you can select multiple invoices for payment, the number of invoices selected is limited to the number of invoices allowed on the payment document (for printed checks, this is usually the number of invoices that will print on the check stub). Creating single payments in this manner does not allow for overflow transactions as payment batches do. After all the invoices are selected, saving the record will format and generate the payment document.

While the preceding text describes how to generate a quick or manual payment using this window, there are additional processes that can be performed on any payment in the system; they are accessible under the ACTIONS button (ensure you query up the payment you want to perform the action on first). These actions include such things as voiding and reissuing payments.

Each payment will need to have the accounting created for it, same as invoices, and this can be done either with the concurrent request Create Accounting, or using the ACTIONS button and selecting CREATE ACCOUNTING. The accounting transactions can be created in Draft, Final, or Final Post. For any payment, an additional Remittance Advice can be printed at any time by selecting PRINT REMITTANCE ADVISE and entering the format in the PROGRAM field.

Voiding, Stopping, and Reissuing Payments

At times, a check is either lost or destroyed or issued in error, and needs to be reversed from the system. This can be done as a Reissue, Stop Payment, or Voided payment. These processes are started by using the ACTIONS button on an invoice. *Reissue* will void the current payment while generating a new settlement. When this option is selected, the invoice will remain paid, but the initial document number will appear as voided, and the new document number as the active payment.

When a check has a *Stop Payment* associated with it at the bank, there is usually a waiting period while the bank confirms that the payment has not already been presented for settlement. EBS uses the process called Initiate Stop to reflect this time period, and the settlement still appears an active payment. Once the bank confirms the payment is not cashed and has been stopped, the payment can then be *Voided*. If the stop was issued in error or the payment was found to already be cashed, the option RELEASE STOP will remove this status and return the payment to a negotiable and issued status. The Stop Payments Report will show any payment with the status of Initiate Stop, allowing the transactions to be monitored and controlled.

To VOID a payment, either for a confirmed stop payment or a destroyed document, you have the options of leaving the invoice in the system available for another payment, placing the invoice on hold, or voiding the invoice at the same time. The actual void DATE and GL DATE are also assigned. When invoices are voided that had interest invoices associated with them, the interest invoices are also voided. Withholding invoices are also reversed if any were generated from the invoice being voided.

The Payment Manager offers a link to Stop or Void payments as well, but this link will take you to the same Payments window I've described here.

Refunds

Payables has the ability to record funds received for negative payables balances, allowing the transaction to be closed with a cash receipt. These balances usually occur when a credit is received on transactions already paid. EBS allows these negative balances to be cleared just as you would create a check, but instead they are for negative amounts and record a check number as opposed to generating a check payment. Refund transactions credit the liability account and debit cash, and close the negative balance transactions. Using the payment TYPE of Refund is the only time you can record a negative settlement. This feature should not be confused with the refund functionality that generates customer refunds in payables for an overpayment received in Receivables; these are settled the same as any Payables invoice.

Refunds are entered in the same window as manual payments or quick payments, but they have a TYPE of Refund. After selecting the TRADING PARTNER and SUPPLIER SITE, add the PAYMENT DATE. You must enter the PAYMENT AMOUNT as a negative number, and then you select the BANK ACCOUNT the payment will be deposited into. Instead of having EBS generate a DOCUMENT NUMBER, you can enter the actual check number received prior to selecting the ENTER/ADJUST INVOICES button. Here, the invoice numbers can be selected along with the amount being settled with the refund. Only invoices, credit and debit memos, and expense reports with negative balances will be available for refunds. Once this is saved, the transactions will be reduced by the amount applied, and closed if there is no longer an outstanding balance.

Using the Payment Manager

The Payment Manager is used to view outstanding request statuses, create templates, submit single and scheduled requests, and create payment instructions. Before submitting requests using the Payment Manager, a payment Template should be created. This template is really just default data that can be reused without having to reenter it each time a payment batch is requested. For more information on creating Templates, see Chapter 7.

Creating Requests for Payment

Payment requests can be submitted as a one-time request or as a scheduled, repeating request. With the introduction of payment Templates, you can create a definition for payment selection, which can then be scheduled to run on a regular basis. EBS will update the dates, such as payment date, based on the information in the template. This scheduling reduces the time a user needs to spend creating settlement batches, and allows him or her to focus on reviewing and modifying the selected invoices instead.

To create a one-time request for payment, you can start in one of three places, all of which will take you to the same window for submitting the request. In the Payment Manager, on the Home tab, select SUBMIT SINGLE PAYMENT PROCESS REQUEST from the Shortcuts area. From the Templates page, query up the desired template and click the SUBMIT SINGLE REQUEST icon next to the template you want to use. Finally, you can go to the Payment Process Requests tab and select SUBMIT SINGLE REQUEST. The window shown in Figure 8-4 will appear from all three paths.

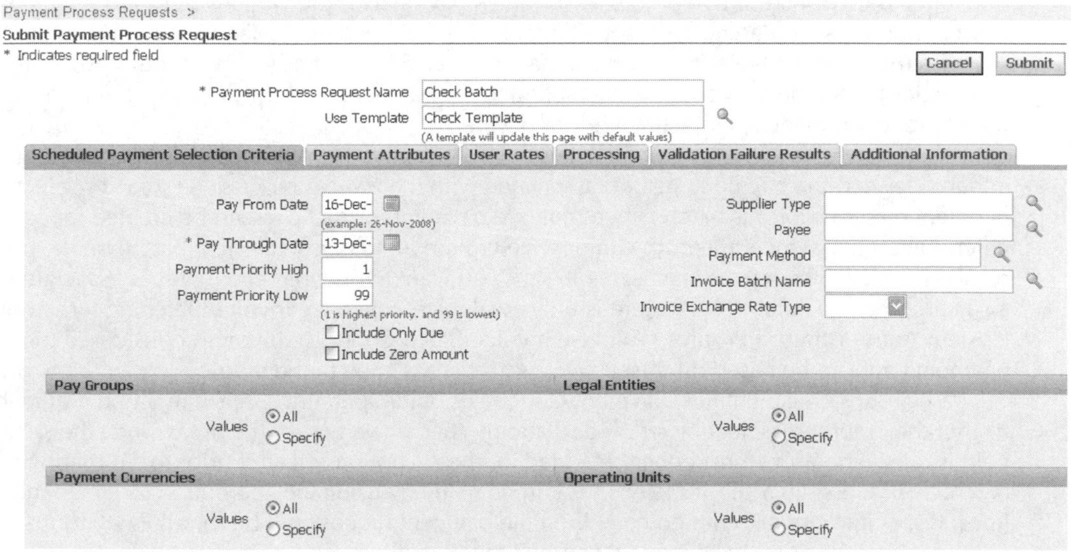

Payments Manager | Payment Process Requests tab | Submit Single Request

FIGURE 8-4   *Creating a single, non-repeating payment request*

Each request will need to be assigned a unique PAYMENT PROCESS REQUEST NAME. If you started from the Template tab, then the USE TEMPLATE will default in; if not, one can be added. While a template is not required, it will default specific values in for the payment request, which the users can then modify if need be.

On the Scheduled Payment Selection Criteria tab, specific information about the selection criteria for the payment can be modified or added. Many of these fields are on the template and can be defaulted in. PAY FROM DATE will determine the earliest due date that will be considered for payment, while PAY THROUGH DATE is the latest date. When the PAY FROM DATE is left blank, all payments due prior to the PAY THROUGH DATE will be considered. If this is always filled in, invoices that were due prior to this date may never be considered for payment. Placing invoices on payment hold is a better way to ensure that specific invoices are not paid in the system.

PAYMENT PRIORITIES are assigned to suppliers or batch headers and default on to the invoices themselves when they are entered; they help to ensure that most important payments are made prior to transactions that are less critical to the business. This feature can be helpful when cash flow is being monitored closely. Payment priorities can also be used to group invoices for payment at the same time, similar to PAY GROUPS. Both pay groups and payment priorities can be used together by the system as part of the selection criteria. Select INCLUDE ONLY DUE to ensure that no invoices with discounted terms are selected until their due date. If you want to create settlements for transactions where the net amount due is zero dollars, such as a supplier who has an invoice and a credit memo outstanding where the net amount due is zero dollars, select INCLUDE ZERO AMOUNT. Ensure that your bank account is set up to allow zero-dollar payments prior to selecting this option. (Payables Manager | Setup | Payment | Bank Accounts | Update Accounts | Account Controls | Payables Control).

You can limit payment selection to a specific SUPPLIER TYPE or PAYEE. Selecting a PAYEE will consider only outstanding invoices for a single payee; this setting can be used much in the same way a Quick Pay can be created in the Payment window (see the preceding section). The main difference between these two processes for quick payments is the way invoices are selected: the Payment Processing Manager will select the invoices for payment based on the selection criteria, whereas the Payment window (Payables Manager | Payments | Entry | Payments) allows any invoice for the supplier to be manually added to the payment, and does not use a selection criteria to recommend specific invoices for payment.

Select a specific PAYMENT METHOD for this batch. When no payment method is selected, it will either default to the payment method associated with the PAYMENT PROCESSING PROFILE or select all payment methods for this batch. Since multiple payment instructions can be created for each batch, different payment methods can now be grouped into one settlement batch, unlike previous releases of EBS. Select the INVOICE BATCH NAME if you want to only pay the invoices associated with a specific invoice batch. This feature is only available if you have Invoice Batching turned on (System Administrator | Profiles | AP: Use Invoice Batch Controls). Invoices considered for payment can also be based on the EXCHANGE RATE TYPE assigned to the invoice.

Pay Groups, Legal Entities, Payment Currencies, and Operating Units can all be modified to restrict the criteria by selecting SPECIFY and adding specific values for the area. Once the SPECIFY field is checked, a row must either be added, or the ALL option selected prior to submitting the batch for processing. Multiple selections can be made by using the ADD button to create more lines. If specifics are not entered here, then the payment request will be for all Pay Groups, Legal Entities, Payment Currencies, and Operating Units.

The Payment Attributes tab defines specifics about the payment, such as which bank account the funds will be disbursed from and the date that will appear on the settlement. There is one required field on this window that must be completed prior to submitting any payment batch, and one that is optionally required. PAYMENT EXCHANGE RATE TYPE is always required, even when the payments are going to be created in the same currency as the Ledger. If the batch is set up to automatically create the payment instructions on the Processing tab (which is the default), then a PAYMENT PROCESSING PROFILE must also be added. The PAYMENT DATE will be the settlement date that appears on the check or electronic settlement.

As you may remember from setting up payment documents and payment processing profiles, bank accounts get assigned to payment documents, which are then in turn assigned to payment processing profiles (see Chapter 7 for more details). These next few fields are interactively linked. Selecting a DISBURSEMENT BANK ACCOUNT will limit the PAYMENT DOCUMENTS available to only documents assigned to that bank account, whereas selecting a PAYMENT PROCESSING PROFILE will make the PAYMENT DOCUMENT field unavailable to select from. If a PAYMENT DOCUMENT is selected, it will use the bank account associated with it, and default the payment processing profile that is linked to it in the setups. Since PAYMENT PROCESSING PROFILES can be linked to a specific settlement currency, selecting the same currency on the selection criteria makes the selection process consistent. If no currency is entered on the selection criteria window, the currency from the profile will take precedence, but conversely, having these two currencies set differently will cause no payments to be generated. PAYMENT EXCHANGE RATE TYPE is a required field and will limit the invoices to be selected all to have the same payment exchange rate type associated with them.

OVERRIDE SETTLEMENT PRIORITY is used in some foreign countries for electronic payments, such as Norway's Urgency Called and Sweden's Express Payment. OVERRIDE BANK CHARGE BEARER will determine if the template default for bank charge bearer will override the setting on the supplier. TRANSFER PRIORITY, on the other hand, is used when creating bank charges. The system setups (Setup | Options | Payables Options | Payment tab) for the bank charge bearer can also be overridden for this batch only, no matter how the supplier or invoices were entered. STARTING VOUCHER NUMBER can be added for a run to start the voucher numbering at a specific number. This field should not be confused with the check numbers that are stored and assigned with the bank setups (Setup | Payment | Bank Accounts | Manage Payment Documents).

When processing foreign currency payments, user rates can be added for the settlements created in this batch; they will be used when the PAYMENT EXCHANGE RATE TYPE is set to USER on the Payments Attributes tab.

The Processing setups help to determine the specifics about how transactions are processed for batch. Select MAXIMIZE CREDITS when you want to generate zero-dollar payments for supplier who have credits that are greater than the outstanding invoices. This works by grouping all transactions for a supplier site, as opposed to grouping invoices for payment by some other criteria, such as due date. Ensure that the bank account and payment request were set up to allow zero-dollar payments when selecting this feature.

Payment creation has three main stopping points: after payment selection, after creation of payments, and prior to creating payment instructions. These can be set here by selecting STOP PROCESS FOR REVIEW AFTER SCHEDULE PAYMENT SELECTION, selecting STOP PROCESS FOR REVIEW AFTER CREATION OF PROPOSED PAYMENTS, or selecting HOW TO CREATE PAYMENT INSTRUCTIONS. Payment Instructions can be initiated either AUTOMATICALLY WHEN PAYMENT PROCESS REQUEST IS COMPLETE, or by WAITING FOR STANDARD REPORT SUBMISSION, which will require the user to Create either the Electronic or Printed Payment Instructions. Links to do this are available on the Home page of the Payment Manager.

Interest can be calculated on an invoice when it is paid past the due date, and interest invoices generated automatically by the EBS. These invoices are only generated when payments are processed using the Payment Manager. Withholding Tax invoices can be generated either when the invoice is entered or when it is paid, depending on the Payables Options (Payables Manager | Setup | Options | Payables Options | Withholding tab). Both Interest and Withholding Tax invoices are generated when the CALCULATE PAYMENT WITHHOLDING AND INTEREST DURING SCHEDULED PAYMENT SELECTION option is selected. This option must be selected to generate either type of invoice at the time of payment.

Even though Validation Failure Results were assigned on the Payment Methods as well as the template, you can override them here for both the document and the payment. You can choose settings to reject all documents, reject only the documents with a validation failure, or reject all the documents for the payee where the failure occurred, or else to stop the process for review before proceeding. Payments only have the option to reject payments with errors, reject all payments, or again stop for review.

Click SUBMIT at any time once the required fields have been entered to submit the payment request.

Scheduling Settlement Batches

Besides single payments created to only one supplier, or submitting a single payment request whenever needed, payment processing requests can also be scheduled to run at specific intervals. This is ideal when companies create payment batches on a set schedule with the same selection criteria. Adding in manual review points to the template allow invoices and payments to be reviewed and adjusted prior to completion.

To schedule a request, use the shortcut on the Home page of the Payment Manager by selecting SCHEDULE PAYMENT PROCESS REQUEST. This will take you through a series of windows. First, enter a REQUEST NAME for the payment request. The next page requires a TEMPLATE to be assigned, and allows a PAYMENT, PAY THROUGH, and PAY FROM DATES to be entered. These are the only processing options that will be available, so the TEMPLATE is always required for a scheduled request.

Two options exist for scheduling the request: the first is a basic option, which is shown in Figure 8-5 and contains a link to create an Advanced Schedule. A basic schedule will allow the START DATE for the request to be created for either AS SOON AS POSSIBLE or on a SPECIFIC DATE AND TIME. Ensure that the start date and time are in the future. Then determine if this request will run only once by selecting NEVER REPEAT, or on a scheduled RECURRENCE, by setting it to REPEAT every x number of days, hours, minutes, or months. To have this scheduled request stop after a set period of time, enter an END DATE. If you have previously defined a Schedule that meets your needs, it can alternatively be selected instead. Selecting INCREMENT DATE PARAMETERS will increase any dates defined in the template or request based on the REPEAT interval selected. (For instance, if the repeat interval is 1 day, then all the data parameters will be increased by one day for the next run.)

To create an Advanced Schedule, shown in Figure 8-6, enter a START DATE and TIME, and add an END DATE that represents the last day this request will run. Next, identify the Months this process should be run in, or select ALL MONTHS. Then select either specific DATES or DAYS of the week. Selecting LAST DAY OF MONTH will always run the request on the last calendar day of the month, no matter if it ends on the 28th, 29th, 30th, or 31st. Days can be set to run on the FIRST, SECOND, THIRD, FOURTH, EVERY, or LAST day for the days selected. The option to INCREMENT DATE PARAMETERS is also available here.

When creating a repeating, scheduled request, it is a good idea to add RECIPIENTS for NOTIFICATIONS when the request completes as NORMAL, with an ERROR, or with a WARNING. Last, select the PRINTER and NUMBER OF COPIES for any output for the request, and determine if EBS should SAVE OUTPUT FILES. Once the request is submitted, it will run according to the schedule entered.

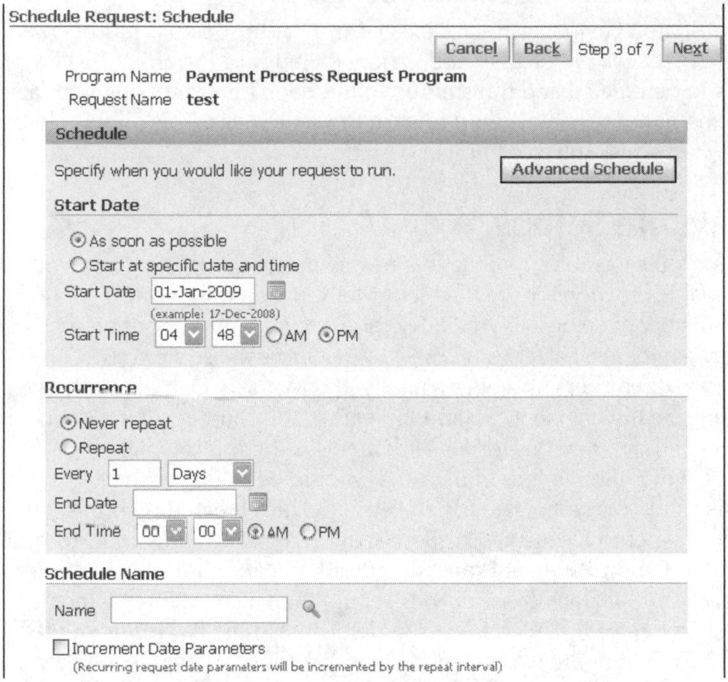

FIGURE 8-5 *Basic schedule options for scheduling payment requests*

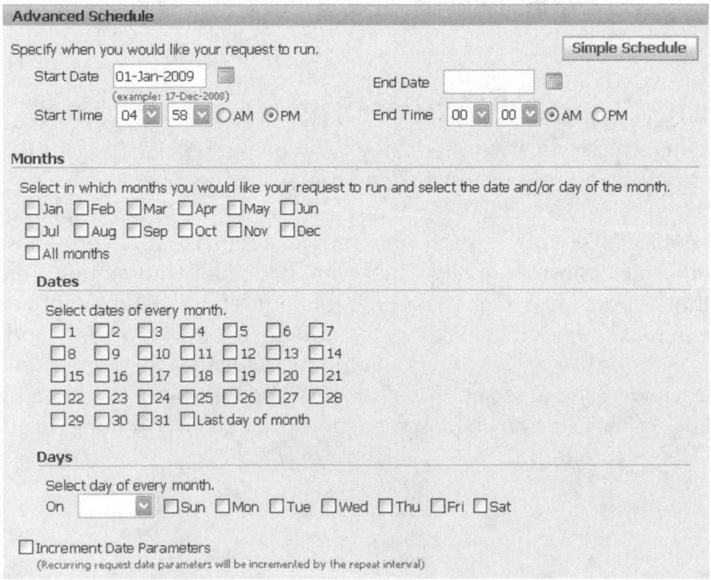

FIGURE 8-6 *Advanced Schedule options for scheduling payment requests*

Bills Payable Settlements

While future-dated payments always existed in EBS, this feature has been enhanced in R12 to improve the management of cash and is now called Bills Payable. Bills Payables allows electronic settlements to be created and transmitted to the bank for processing with a Maturity Date, which represents the date the bank should release the settlement. This allows fewer settlement batches to be generated while still maximizing cash flow.

Bills Payable Setups

Prior to using Bills Payables, you have a few setups to complete. First, you will need to complete the Bills Payables section for the Payment Method (Setup | Payment | Payment Administrator | Funds Disbursement Setup | Payment Method | Payment Method) being used to create these future-dated payments. Select USE PAYMENT METHOD TO ISSUE BILLS PAYABLE. Optionally, you can add a MATURITY DATE OVERRIDE here as well. Typically, the Maturity Date, literally meaning the date the bank will release the payment, will be the earliest discount or due date available on any given invoice. You can override this for all settlements using this payment method by adding a MATURITY DATE OVERRIDE. Enter the number of days that should be added to the batch's PAYMENT DATE, and EBS will use this as the Maturity Date for all Bills Payables created with this batch.

On the Payment Processing Profile (Setup | Payment | Payment Administrator | Funds Disbursement Setup | Payment Processing Profile), make sure PAYMENT GROUPINGS are set up for BILLS PAYABLE. If no Maturity Date Override was set up, then also set the payments to group by DUE DATE.

The final setup for Bills Payables is to determine if the Account Source will be from the Payment Document or the Supplier Site. This is set in the Payables Option (Setup | Options | Payables Options) on the Accounting Options tab under Bills Payable Account Source.

Once the setups are complete, a Bills Payable payment batch can be created using the Payment Method and Payment Processing Profile that are set up for Bills Payable. This will generate an electronic payment instruction to be sent to be bank that includes Maturity Dates, and the bank will release the settlements based on the Maturity Date as opposed to the Payment Dates.

Managing Payment Processing

Once payment requests are submitted, they will need to be managed for validation failures as well as any stopping points that were added to the submissions.

On the Home page, a recap of the requests submitted today is available along with the status they are in. Also seen are any requests that require actions to proceed. These include validation errors as well as any pauses for review that were added into the request (refer to Figure 8-7).

Under the section Today's Payment Process Requests, click the number in any section to drill down to the actual batches that make up the numbers, allowing review and actions. For example, click the 15 under NEED ACTION to drill down to the 15 batches requiring user intervention, allowing them to be reviewed and acted upon. This drill-down will show the same batches that are listed in the Pending Actions section of the screen, and you can take Actions on either screen by clicking START ACTION (see Figure 8-8).

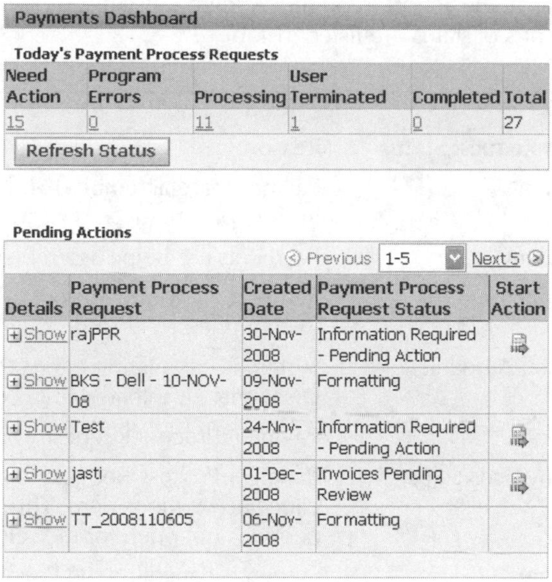

Payments Dashboard

Today's Payment Process Requests

Need Action	Program Errors	Processing	User Terminated	Completed	Total
15	0	11	1	0	27

Refresh Status

Pending Actions

⊙ Previous 1-5 Next 5 ⊛

Details	Payment Process Request	Created Date	Payment Process Request Status	Start Action
⊞ Show	rajPPR	30-Nov-2008	Information Required - Pending Action	▣
⊞ Show	BKS - Dell - 10-NOV-08	09-Nov-2008	Formatting	
⊞ Show	Test	24-Nov-2008	Information Required - Pending Action	▣
⊞ Show	jasti	01-Dec-2008	Invoices Pending Review	▣
⊞ Show	TT_2008110605	06-Nov-2008	Formatting	

FIGURE 8-7   *Dashboard for monitoring requests*

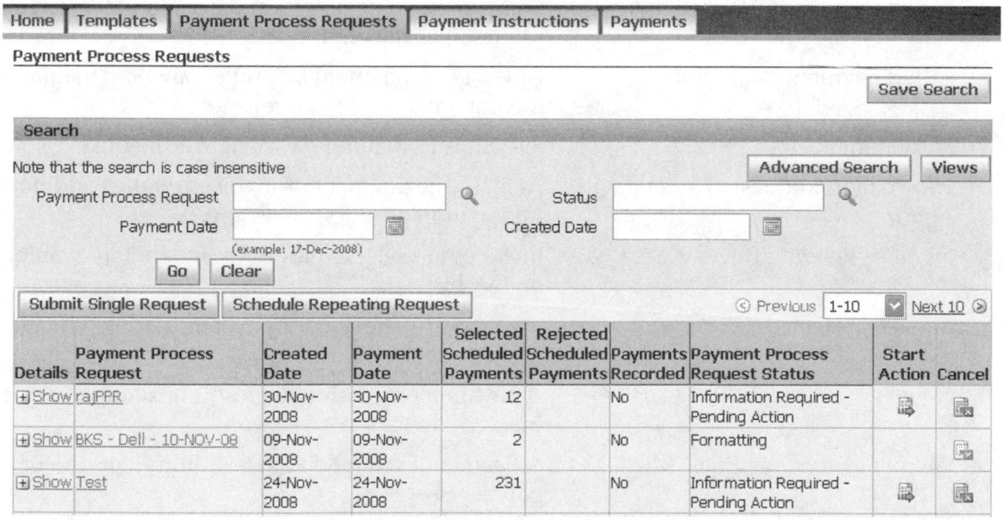

Home	Templates	Payment Process Requests	Payment Instructions	Payments

Payment Process Requests

Save Search

Search

Note that the search is case insensitive   Advanced Search   Views

Payment Process Request [   ] 🔍   Status [   ] 🔍

Payment Date [   ] 🖩   Created Date [   ] 🖩
(example: 17-Dec-2008)

Go   Clear

Submit Single Request   Schedule Repeating Request   ⊙ Previous 1-10 Next 10 ⊛

Details	Payment Process Request	Created Date	Payment Date	Selected Scheduled Payments	Rejected Scheduled Payments	Payments Recorded	Payment Process Request Status	Start Action	Cancel
⊞ Show	rajPPR	30-Nov-2008	30-Nov-2008	12		No	Information Required - Pending Action	▣	▣
⊞ Show	BKS - Dell - 10-NOV-08	09-Nov-2008	09-Nov-2008	2		No	Formatting		▣
⊞ Show	Test	24-Nov-2008	24-Nov-2008	231		No	Information Required - Pending Action	▣	▣

FIGURE 8-8   *Payment process requests needing actions*

The Payment Process Requests Status window shows the status of the request and provides some information as to the actions required. Additional statuses exist for formatting payment instructions. Both sorts of status are listed in Table 8-2.

Payment Process Request Status	Reason
Assembled Payments	Payments are assembled and ready for Payment Instruction Creation.
Assembling Payments	Payments are being assembled.
Assignment Complete	Requested information provided and payment is ready to continue processing.
Calculating Special Amounts	System is calculating Interest, Withholding, and Discounts on selected invoices.
Canceled Payment	Payment Process Request was canceled.
Canceled – No Invoices Selected	Payment Process Request selected no invoices and was canceled by the system. This is also the status when the period is not open for the selected PAYMENT DATE.
Canceling Payment	System is canceling the Payment Process Request.
Confirmed Payment	All payments are confirmed.
Document Validation Errors – Pending Action	Some invoices selected failed validation and are pending review and correction.
Failed Document Validation	Some documents failed validation, and the entire request was rejected.
Failed Payment Validation	At least one payment failed the payment validation, and the documents were all rejected.
Formatting	System is formatting payment instructions.
Information Requested – Pending Action	At least one payment or invoice requires additional information prior to processing.
Invoices Pending Review	Invoices are selected for payment and are waiting for review by user.
Invoices Selected	Invoices are selected for payment and will be advanced to the next step by EBS.
New	A payment processing request is unstarted for selecting invoices.
Payment Exchange Rates Missing	A Payment Exchange Rate is required for one of the payments.
Payment Validation Errors – Pending Action	Some payments failed validation and are pending review and correction.
Pending Proposed Payment Review	Payments are created and manual review is required.

TABLE 8-2 *Payment Process and Payment Instruction Status Codes*

Payment Process Request Status	Reason
Selecting Scheduled Payments	Invoices are being selected for a scheduled payment processing request.
Terminated	The payment processing request was terminated in the concurrent manager.

Payment Instruction Status	Reason
Created	Instructions are created.
Created – Ready for Formatting	Instructions are ready to be formatted.
Created – Ready for Printing	Checks are ready to be printed.
Failed Validation – Pending Action	One or more documents failed validation and is waiting for review and action.
Formatted	Instructions have been formatted, printed, recorded, and transmitted.
Formatted – Ready for Printing	Instructions are ready to be printed.
Formatted – Ready for Recording	Instructions are ready for recording as payments against the invoices.
Formatted – Ready for Transmission	Electronic payments are ready to be transmitted to the bank.
Printed	Checks are Printed.
Retry Payment Instruction Validation	The Payment Instructions were missing information. The status will become Retry Payment Instruction Validation after the information is provided.
Submitted for Printing	Status when the instructions were submitted for printing but not yet processed by the print queues.
Terminated	The Payment Instruction, and payment batch, was terminated by the user.
Transmission Failed	Transmission to the bank failed.
Transmitted	Transmission to the bank completed successfully.

TABLE 8-2 *Payment Process and Payment Instruction Status Codes* (continued)

Processing Review Points

EBS allows the following review points to be set up when creating a Payment Processing Profile, Enterprise-Wide Disbursement System Options, or Template:

- After Payment Selection
- After Creation of Proposed Payments
- Payment Process Request Status Report (Preliminary Payment register)

- Validation Failures

- For Payment Instruction Creation, Electronic and Printed

- For Transmission of Payment Instructions

- For Transmission of Positive Payment File

- For Transmission of Remittance Advice

After Payment Selection   The first review point is after invoices have been selected for payment (Status = Invoice Pending Review), as shown in Figure 8-9. Use the START ACTION link to view a recap of the selected invoices, by payment currency, and to add or remove invoices from the payment run (see Figure 8-10). To remove an invoice from the payment selection, check SELECT and click REMOVE FROM REQUEST. To add additional payments not selected as part of the request, click ADD SCHEDULED PAYMENTS. Invoices can be searched for by Payee, Document (or invoice) Number, Payment Currency, Discount Date, and Due Date.

You have several options once the payment selection is completed. CANCEL will discard the changes you have made. TERMINATE REQUEST will cancel the request and release the selected invoices to be processed by another request. Normally, interest and withholding amounts are not calculated till after the payment processing is submitted for the next step, but selecting CALCULATE will perform these calculations now, as well as applying any new exchange rates that were entered by clicking UPDATE RATE. SAVE will save any changes you have made but not proceed on to the next step in the process, while SUBMIT will move the process on to the next step in the payment process. You can review invoices removed from the batch as well as invoices not selected by clicking VIEW UNSELECTED.

Resolving Pending Actions   A payment process can be stopped at any point during the process with a status of Information Requested – Pending Action. Here, EBS is missing some information it requires to move on in the process, such as an exchange rate or payment process profile. Complete

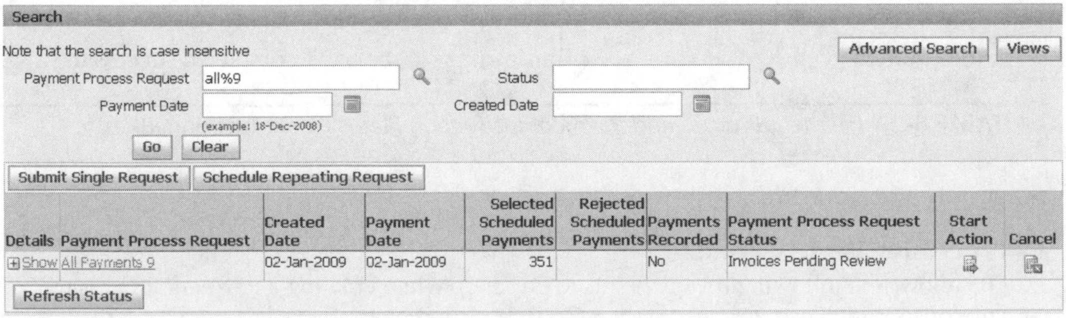

Search									
Note that the search is case insensitive								Advanced Search	Views
Payment Process Request	all%9			Status					
Payment Date				Created Date					
	(example: 18-Dec-2008)								
Go	Clear								
Submit Single Request	Schedule Repeating Request								
Details	Payment Process Request	Created Date	Payment Date	Selected Scheduled Payments	Rejected Scheduled Payments	Payments Recorded	Payment Process Request Status	Start Action	Cancel
⊞Show All Payments 9		02-Jan-2009	02-Jan-2009	351		No	Invoices Pending Review		
Refresh Status									

FIGURE 8-9   *Invoice selection ready for review*

Payment Process Request: Selected Scheduled Payments

Click the Calculate button to see new calculations and totals.

Cancel	Terminate Request	Calculate	Save	Submit	Save Search

Payment Process Request **All Payments 9**
Payment Date **02-Jan-2009**
User **CBROWN**

Selected Scheduled Payments **351**
Scheduled Payments Missing Rates **0**

View Unselected
Update Rates

Current Estimated Currency Totals

Payment Currency	Selected Scheduled Payments	Amounts Remaining	Withheld Amounts	Discounts	Payment Amounts	Interest Due	Total Amounts Payable
NLG	4	51,906.15	0.00	1,018.12	50,888.03		50,888.03
GBP	14	17,609.00	0.00	0.00	17,609.00		17,609.00
JPY	2	26,991	0	0	26,991		26,991
SGD	2	36,887.42	0.00	737.74	36,149.68		36,149.68
FRF	2	60,630.00	0.00	0.00	60,630.00		60,630.00
USD	325	178,685,847.94	0.00	7,153.44	178,678,694.50		178,678,694.50
MXP	1	100,000	0	0	100,000		100,000
CAD	1	6,977.62	0.00	0.00	6,977.62		6,977.62

Search Selected Scheduled Payments

Note that the search is case insensitive

Advanced Search

Payee [   ] 🔍   Document Number [   ]
Pay Curr [   ] 🔍   Amount Remaining [   ]

Go   Clear

Select Scheduled Payments: Remove from Request | Add Scheduled Payments   ⊙ Previous 1-10 ▾ Next 10 ⊙

Select All | Select None

Select	Details	Payee	Document Number	Due Date	Payment Currency	Amount Remaining	Withheld Amount	Discount Taken	Payment Amount	Interest Due	Total Amount Payable
☐	⊞ Show	CDS, Inc	23-MAY-2007	07-Jul-2007	USD	2,229.00		0.00	2,229.00		2,229.00
☐	⊞ Show	CDS, Inc	25-AUG-2007	08-Oct-2007	USD	2,160.00		0.00	2,160.00		2,160.00

FIGURE 8-10   *Adjusting invoices selected for payment*

the missing information, as seen in Figure 8-11, and determine the next ACTIONS for the request. Actions include SAVE FOR LATER, allowing the batch to be worked on later, ensuring the selected invoices have the status of SELECTED FOR PAYMENT, preventing other payment requests from selecting them, or SAVE AND REFRESH, which will update the screen with the latest information entered. Requests can also be Terminated or Run, moving them on to the next step in the process.

Reviewing Rejected Scheduled Payments   Once the payment process begins to build the scheduled payments, some items may be rejected. These items will be removed when the validation failures were set to Reject only Documents with Errors. These rejections require no action for this payment run and can be reviewed by clicking REJECTED SCHEDULED PAYMENTS. The reasons for errors, available at the bottom of the screen after clicking REFERENCE NUMBER, will need to be corrected prior to selecting these for another payment run. Figure 8-12 is an example of these errors.

Proposed Payment Review   Once the payments are prepared when the Build Payments program runs, they can be reviewed one final time before they are created and submitted for transmission or printing. The payments can be removed, the entire batch terminated, or the process submitted for the next step.

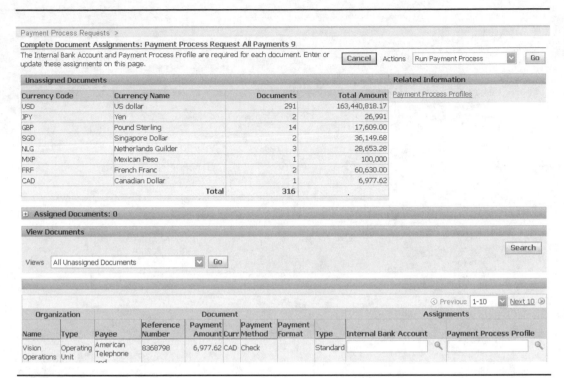

FIGURE 8-11 *Resolving pending actions*

Creating Payment Instructions   At this point, the payment instructions will be created if the process was set to create them automatically. If not, you must submit the request Create Printed Payment Instructions or Create Electronic Payment Instructions manually. The link for this process is on the Home tab under Shortcuts. When payment instructions are submitted manually, they are not specific to any single batch but will be created for all outstanding batches that meet the Payment Processing Profile. Ensure you select the same Payment Processing Profile that was assigned to the batch when it was created.

Transmitting Electronic Payments to the Bank   Once electronic payments are created, they can be transmitted to the bank as a separate step. This can be done by Taking Action in the Payment Instruction window when a batch has the status of Formatted – Ready for Transmission, and selecting TRANSMIT.

Recording Check Number   For manual checks, the outcome of the printing will need to be recorded to complete the batch. The Payment Instruction Status will now be Submitted for

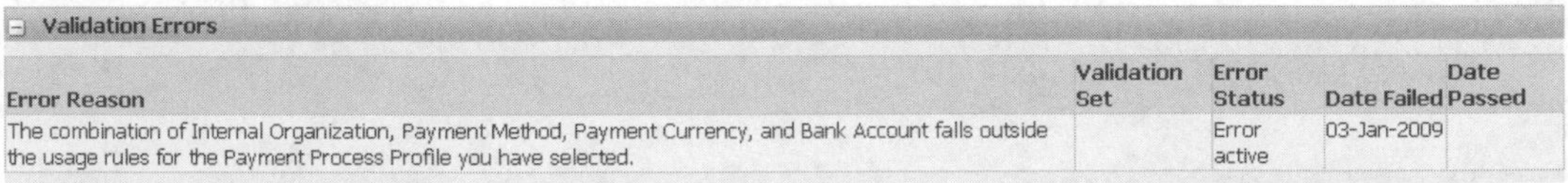

Validation Errors				
Error Reason	Validation Set	Error Status	Date Failed	Date Passed
The combination of Internal Organization, Payment Method, Payment Currency, and Bank Account falls outside the usage rules for the Payment Process Profile you have selected.		Error active	03-Jan-2009	

FIGURE 8-12 *Errors during payment assembly*

Printing. Select TAKE ACTION next to the payment batch; record any Printed, Spoiled, or Skipped checks; and select Update Print Status. If for some reason the entire batch of payments needs to be voided after they were created, query up the batch in the Payment Instruction form and select Void All Payments. This will void the entire batch, not an individual payment. Assign the DATE for the void transaction, and optionally add a REASON for voiding the transactions. To void a single payment, use the Payments form (Payables Manager | Payments | Entry | Payments) and select Actions | Void.

Positive Pay Files   At this point, EBS will transmit the Positive Pay files for any check that was recorded as Printed.

Determining Cash Requirements

Templates can also be used to create a cash requirements report, based on the selection criteria on the template. From the Home page under Shortcuts, select SUBMIT CASH REQUIREMENTS REPORT. After entering the REQUEST NAME and selecting the OPERATING UNIT if you have access to more than one, set the parameters for the report. These will decide the transactions that will be considered for the report. First, determine if Unvalidated and Unapproved invoices will be included. Then decide when the PAY THROUGH date will be for the cash requirements. The date entered here is used by EBS to select invoices that are due on or before this date. Enter a PAYMENT DATE, which is used with the INCLUDE ONLY DUE option on the template, and the discounted amount will be used to calculate the cash requirements, as opposed to the total invoice amount.

Next, select the TEMPLATE you want to use to select the transactions for payment. These templates are the same ones that are used to create a payment process request, ensuring that your cash requirement will agree to an actual payment batch. If the SUMMARY OPTION is set to NO, the EBS will print all invoices on this report; when set to YES, only a total for each supplier will display. INCLUDE SELECTED INVOICE, when set to YES, will include any invoices selected in a payment batch but not yet confirmed. This report can either be run immediately or scheduled to run on a regular basis, such as the morning of the day payments are cut. See Figure 8-13 for a sample of this report.

```
                              Cash Requirement Report              Report Date: 03-JAN-2009 14:20
                                                                                   Page:         1

                    Template:AP_PAYMENT_TEST                    Include Unvalidated Invoices:Yes
              Pay Through Date:03-JAN-09                         Include Unapproved Invoices:Yes
                 Payment Date:03-JAN-09                                   Summary Option:No


              Vision Operations
                    Currency:AED


           Trading          Invoice       Invoice              Pay                                    Cumulative
  Date     Partner          Number        Date         Amount  Group        Validated   Approved           Total
 --------- ---------------- ------------- --------- ----------- ----------   ---------   --------   ---------------
 13-DEC-08 RAMESH LLC       01            13-DEC-08    1,000.00 Standard     Holds:  1   Yes
           RAMESH LLC       02            13-DEC-08    1,500.00 Standard     Holds:  2   No
           RAMESH LLC       06            13-DEC-08   <200.00>  Standard            No   No
           RAMESH LLC       07            13-DEC-08    5,000.00 Standard            No   No
                                                     -----------
                       Total for RAMESH LLC:          7,300.00

                                                     ===========
              Total for 13-DEC-08                     7,300.00                                          7,300.00

 16-DEC-08 Abbott Laboratories, xxxx1234  01-NOV-08 295,000.00 Standard            Yes   No
                                                     -----------
                 Total for Abbott Laboratories, :   295,000.00

                                                     ===========
              Total for 16-DEC-08                   295,000.00                                        302,300.00
```

FIGURE 8-13   *Cash Requirement Report*

Bank Reconciliations

Embedded in EBS is a basic bank reconciliations process. While the Cash Management or Treasury modules can be set up with tight bank integration, the bank reconciliations feature can be used without creating these interfaces. This process will allow checks to be cleared, and an outstanding check register generated, which is usually the most time-consuming process during a bank reconciliation. While this next section is not intended to be a complete cash management setup and user tutorial, it will describe how an outstanding check register can be achieved without a large implementation or coding for interfaces.

To set up Cash Management to allow manual bank reconciliations, you only need to carry out one additional setup. In Cash Management, set up the System Parameters for the Legal Entity you want to use bank reconciliation for (Cash Management | Setup | System | System Parameters). When completing these setups, it is the BEGIN DATE that controls the first payables transaction that will appear in cash management for clearing, and this is the most important setup for manual check clearing. Once this is set, all checks after this date will be available for clearing.

Updating Transactions

To clear transactions in cash management manually, enter the bank you want to see the transactions for in the Find Transactions window, as shown in Figure 8-14, and select FIND. This will display all uncleared transactions for this bank account. The option to FIND AND MARK also exists, which will display all the uncleared transactions but mark them for clearing when it brings them up. EBS will not actually clear them until CLEAR TRANSACTION is selected on the next page (shown in Figure 8-15),

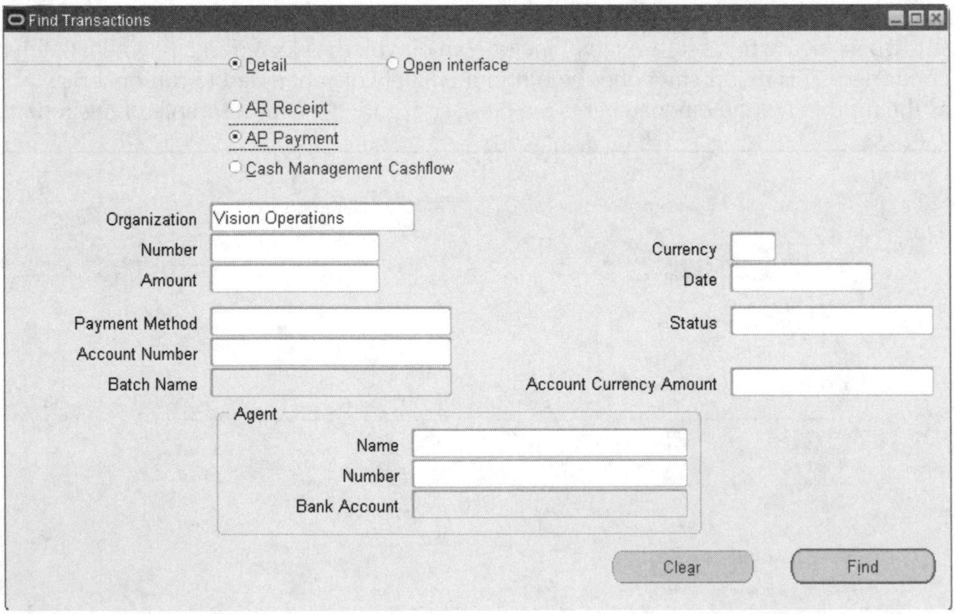

Cash Management | Bank Statements | Manual Clearing | Clear Transactions

FIGURE 8-14 *Finding transactions to clear manually in cash management*

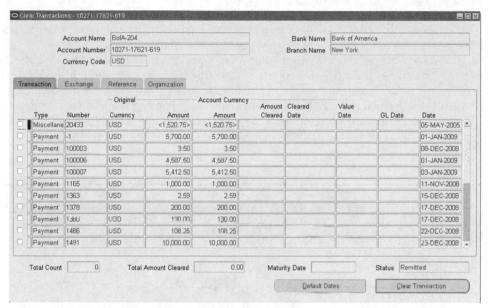

Cash Management | Bank Statements | Manual Clearing | Clear Transactions | Find

FIGURE 8-15 *Clearing transactions in cash management*

allowing a review of the transactions prior to clearing. This option works well when a majority of the checks are cleared, with only a few outstanding.

If a transaction is cleared in error, it can be uncleared in the Unclear Transaction window. On the Find screen, enter information to find only the transaction you want to clear, such as Payment Number or Amount, and then select FIND. As in the Clear screen, check the transaction(s) and click UNCLEAR TRANSACTION, and they will now appear as uncleared again.

Bank Reconciliation Reports

There are two main reports that assist with this process. The Transactions Available for Reconciliation Report, which lists the outstanding checks and transactions that have not been cleared, is basically an outstanding check register. The Cleared Transactions Report lists all the transactions that were cleared for a set time period.

Since the setups are very minimal to use this feature, it is worth looking at and deciding if it can be used to assist with bank reconciliations.

Calculating Balances Owed to Suppliers

While an Invoice Aging report can always be run to determine how much is due to a specific dealer and the invoices included in that balance, EBS provides an easier way to determine the amount due for a specific supplier. From the Invoice window, click on the flashlight icon to bring up the Find window (if you are using Invoice Batches, the Find window will come up automatically). Alternatively, you can use View | Find to bring up the Find screen as well. Narrow down the selection of invoices by entering at least the supplier's NAME or NUMBER. Additional fields can be entered to narrow down the information. Then click the CALCULATE BALANCE OWED button, shown in Figure 8-16.

If you have access to multiple operating units, enter the OPERATING UNIT. Decide if the calculated balance should be reduced by Discounts by selecting TAKE DISCOUNT, and if it should INCLUDE OUTSTANDING FUTURE DATED PAYMENTS. Then click CALCULATE. EBS will calculate the total amount due to the supplier, which is the total unpaid invoices, including credit and debit memos, plus future-dated payments, less any outstanding prepayments. Counts are available at the bottom, as seen in Figure 8-17. You can see the invoices that make up the balance by clicking INVOICES.

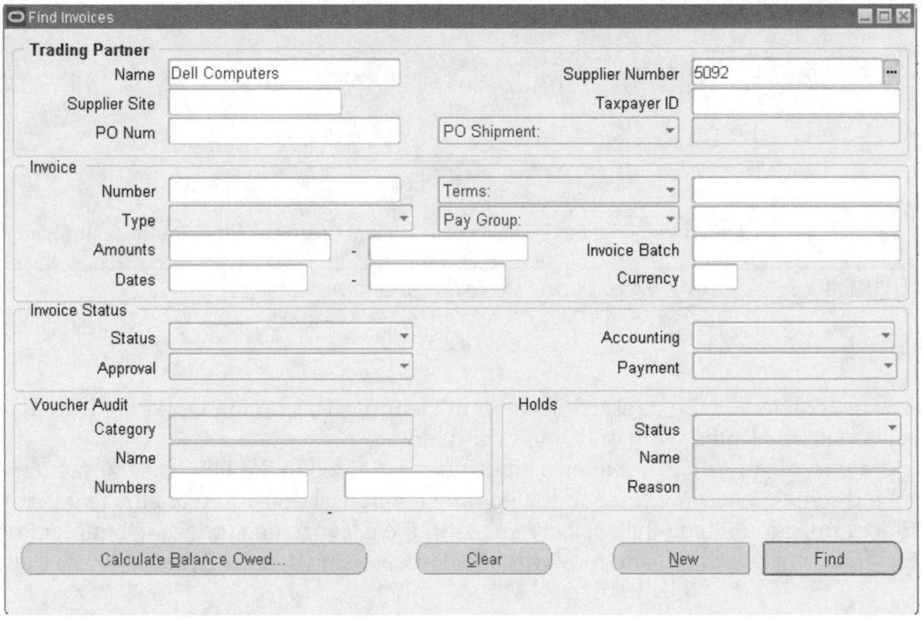

Payables Manager | Invoices | Entry | Invoices | Find

FIGURE 8-16   *Calculating a balance due a supplier*

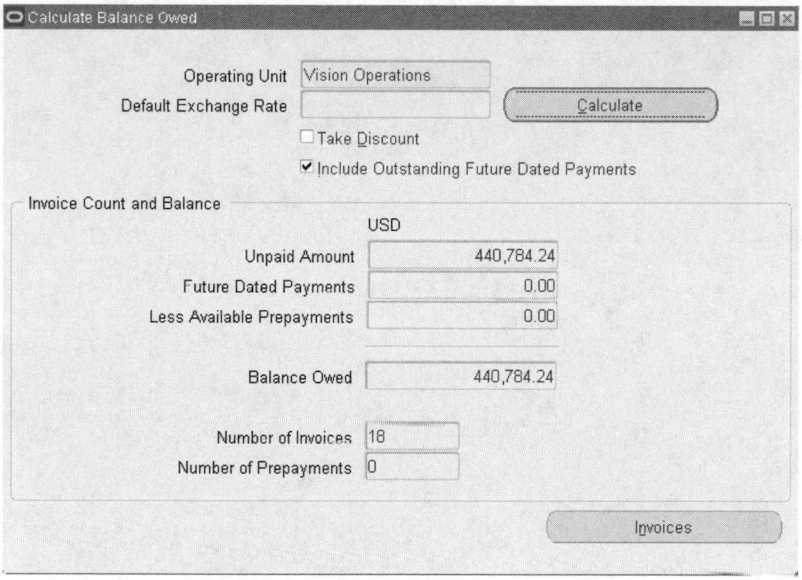

FIGURE 8-17 *Balance owed a supplier*

Glossary

BS has its own set of terms and language, which I call Oracle-ese. The most commonly used terms in this text can be found here.

Accounting Flexfield   The definition of the individual segments that make up an account number.

Accounting Methods   Also known as Subledger Accounting, provides rules for how subledger transactions are accounted and represented in the General Ledger.

Advance Shipment Notice (ASN)   A notification from a supplier containing shipping information when the product is sent out from the supplier site. Can be used to reduce receiving steps in EBS.

Attachments   A feature in EBS that allows files or comments to be attached to specific documents, such as purchase orders and invoices.

AutoCreate   The ability to turn Requisitions into other documents, such as Requests for Quote or Purchase Orders.

Balancing Segment   Segment in the account number where debits must always equal credits, often referred to as Company or Entity.

budgetary controls   Controls put in place surrounding a budget, presenting either a warning or a hard prevention on any transactions created over the budget limits. Usually used with encumbrances, they can be set up on all or specific accounts.

Business Group   A grouping of employees in EBS.

Concurrent (Processing) Manager   A method used in EBS to run reports and processes.

Cross-Validation Rules (CVRs)   A set of defined rules in EBS that control the account combinations that can be created.

Descriptive Flexfields   Also called DFF, these are fields denoted with [] on different windows that can be enabled to track data specific to your company and the screen.

Distribution Set   Predefined account numbers and percentages that can be assigned to a supplier or selected when entering an invoice to reduce data entry.

Dynamic Insertion   The ability to create Flexfield value combinations on the fly in EBS, based on rules defined in the Cross-Validation Rules.

EDI (Electronic Data Interchange)   A standard format for exchanging business data, such as Invoices and Advance Shipment Notices, with other companies.

encumbrance   The recording of obligations prior to paying them out. An encumbrance will be recorded for all purchase orders, whereas accrual accounting will usually record this obligation when the product is received. Encumbrances are usually used in federal governments.

Enterprise Performance Foundation   A set of predefined tables and dimensions used by Management and Planning applications in EBS such as the Consolidation Hub. The data and tables are tightly integrated with EBS data but also allow data from other systems to be loaded and used.

Flexfield   A definable and flexible field in the Oracle database for storing data.

General Ledger Key Flexfields   The EBS name for the segment definitions in a Chart of Accounts.

Inventory Organization   Groupings of locations within a warehouse for processing inventory transactions.

iExpense (also called Internet Expenses)   A web-based interface for submitting, approving, and monitoring expense reports and settlements. Can be integrated with credit card feeds from your bank

iProcurement   A web-based interface for buying or requesting items or receiving orders that integrates to Purchasing.

iSupplier Portal   A module offered by Oracle that integrates with Purchasing and Payables, allowing suppliers to see invoice and purchase order statuses, request updates, and see statistics about specific supplier information.

Key Flexfield (KFF)   A required but flexible field in EBS. Key Flexfields include such things as General Ledger account numbers (Accounting Flexfield), Item Numbers, and Item Categories.

Ledger   Defined by the 4 C's—Chart of accounts, Calendar, Currency, and aCcounting Methods—where transactions are segregated based on this commonality.

Legal Entities   Literally, the entities responsible for paying obligations, including invoices and payroll, or performing any transaction.

Lot Control   Used on items in inventory to track lot numbers as they move through the system. Lots have assigned quantities associated with each number.

MOAC (Multi-Org Access Control)   Allows multiple operating units to be accessed from one responsibility.

Oracle Approvals Management (AME)   An EBS module that integrates with other modules to create hierarchies and rules for approval. While it can be used for most approval processes, AME still does not integrate with Journal Entry approvals.

operating unit   Also known as an Org in EBS, segregates data in submodules like Receivables and Payables. MOAC allows operating units to be grouped for centralized access. This is not to be confused with an Inventory Org, which is one level lower and only pertains to inventory transactions.

Order Management   An EBS subledger for tracking internal and external sales orders along with their shipment and billing information.

outside processing   Items and services sourced to a third-party supplier, that are used in a manufacturing process.

perpetual accrual   Refers to an accrual that is created when an item is received and that is relieved when the invoice is entered.

Pay on Receipt   A feature that allows invoices to be automatically created in Payables when a purchased item is received in purchasing. Also called Self-Billing.

Party   Both customers and suppliers are part of the Trading Community Architecture (TCA) in R12, and are called Parties. These Parties represent entities (corporations and individuals) your organization legally does business with.

Processing (Concurrent) Manager   A method used in EBS to run reports and processes.

Profile Option   A variable that is set in System Administration for any of the system levels as well as the user level. The system profiles can be set for Site, Application, Responsibility, or User, controlling certain features of the system.

Report Manager   A repository to share and store reports.

Responsibility   A grouping of forms (functions) and reports that can be assigned to specific users or roles (which then get assigned to users). Also, many system profiles are set at the Responsibility level, changing data that is accessed (such as when a Ledger is assigned) or how the system behaves (such as when Sequential Numbering is set).

Return Material Authorization (RMA)   Items authorized for return from customers against a previously shipped order.

seeded   Data that gets installed with the base EBS database and is accessible for all companies to use is referred to as seeded. Some seed data can be disabled if it is not going to be used, while other data is required to stay active for the system to function properly.

segment qualifier   Additional attributes added to a Flexfield to provide additional functionality.

Self Billing   A feature that allows invoices to be automatically created in Payables when a purchased item is received in purchasing. Also called Pay on Receipt.

site   An address associated to a specific supplier or customer.

subledger Subledgers refer to non–General Ledger modules that are available from EBS, such as Payables and Receivables.

Subledger Accounting (SLA) Also known as Accounting Methods, provides rules for how subledger transactions are accounted and represented in the General Ledger.

Value Set Value Sets are lists of data that are both used by EBS's programs and selected and entered by users. They can be as important as valid General Ledger account numbers, and as trivial as a designation for a supplier. Value Sets can be added not only for custom data, like your Accounting Flexfield, but also to restrict data allowed in Descriptive Flexfields. These are also a good way to track data that may change for custom reporting so that users, not just programmers, will have access to make updates. When multiple languages are installed, EBS also uses Value Sets to store translated data.

VAT (Value-Added Tax) Tax-related reporting fields, and tax calculations, often found in European or Latin American countries.

Workflow Workflow is a service used by certain EBS functions either to process a transaction, based on a set of rules, or to send a notification to a specific person or group of people for information or to request an action or approval.

XML (Extended Markup Language) A programming language used by Oracle to create reports using Excel, Word, or PDF templates.

Index

A

Account Generators, 37
accounting
 categories creating
  Payables, 215
 creating for invoices,
  187–188
 effect of canceled invoice
  on, 187
 Purchasing month-end
  and accruals, 77–80
 setting up calendar for, 8
Accounting Options tab
 (Payable Options screen),
 114–116
Accounting tab (Financial
 Options screen),
 108–109, 110
accounts. *See also* bank
 accounts
 available for receiving
  transactions, 33
 detailing supplier's bank,
  95–97
 distributing requisition
  costs to, 47–48
 overlay, 166
 prepayment, 116
 Receiving Inspection, 29
 setting up inventory
  organization, 12–13
Accrual Reconciliation Load
 Run program, 78
accruals
 defining inventory and
  expense item, 29

period end, 79
 types of, 77–78
Actions button (Invoice
 Workbench), 186–188
Address Details page
 (Location screen), 8–9
addresses for suppliers, 90–93
Advanced Schedule options
 (Payment Manager), 260, 261
aging
 configuring periods for, 124
 Invoice Aging Report, 217
Agreement tab (Purchase
 Orders), 64
AME. *See* Approval
 Management
AO and PO Accrual
 Reconciliation Report, 78
Approval Groups, 20–22
Approval Management (AME).
 See also approvals
 about, 50, 210
 creating approvals with, 20
 function of, 3
Approval Options screen, 21
Approval tab (Payables
 Options screen), 118–119
approvals
 applying to invoices,
  118–119, 188, 210
 approving related credit/
  debit memos when
  validating invoices,
  186–187
 configuring rules for, 20, 50
 defining Approval Groups,
  20–22

requiring for purchase
 order changes, 61
 using for purchasing
  documents, 50, 68
 validated invoice
  lines, 167
Approve Document screen,
 51–52
auditing
 invoice expenses, 164
 Sarbanes-Oxley
  requirements for, 210
 Supplier Audit Report, 105
AutoCreate
 Document Builder vs., 54
 fully automating, 59–60
 turning requisitions into
  purchase orders, 54–59
automatic offset methods, 116

B

balances
 loading into accrual
  tables, 78
 owed to suppliers,
  271–273
bank accounts
 adding instructions to
  electronic transfers, 235
 adding organization
  access to, 132–133
 assigning to payment
  methods, 247
 associating payment
  profiles with, 224
 changing for payment
  batches, 236

choosing for
 payments, 253
 configuring branches
  for, 127
 controls for, 130–132
 designating transferring
  and receiving banks, 145
 exporting Payment data
  to, 232–233
 modifying XML output for,
  223–225
 netting, 193–194, 196
 protecting data in, 221–222
 reconciling payments in,
  270, 271
 setting up, 125–127,
  128–129
 sorting reports with
  alternate, 121
 suppliers details for,
  95–97
 transmitting electronic
  payments to, 268
bank charges
 deducting from payment,
  120
 setting up transactions for,
  144–145
 settling with suppliers,
  158–159
banks. *See* bank accounts
Base Units of Measure, 13–14
batches
 creating netting, 196–197
 designing templates for
  payment, 246
 invoices, 150, 152–153
 payments, 251

batches *(continued)*
processing payment, 237
scheduling settlement, 260–261
BI Publisher, 223–224
Bills Payables, 262–269
configuring, 262
payment processing with, 262–265
processing review points for, 265–266
blanket agreements
adding for purchase orders and releases, 64, 65
auto-creating purchase orders with, 59–60
changing prices on, 69
branches for banks, 127
business classifications for supplier, 93–94
buyers
creating for Purchasing, 22, 23
entering detailed information about, 43–44
Buyers Work Center
AutoCreate vs. Document Builder, 54
Demand Workbench in, 72–73
overview, 71, 72–73

C

Calculate Tax button (Invoice Workbench), 186
calendars
setting up accounting, 8
special Payables, 123–124
Workday, 12
canceling
distributions, 169–170
invoices, 187
purchasing documents, 69
Cash Management module
banking features in, 125, 126
finding and clearing transactions, 270–271
manual bank reconciliations in, 270
cash receipts, 256
Cash Requirement reports, 269
categories
creating Purchasing, 16–19
Payables process, 215

checks
recording number for manual payments, 268–269
transferring Positive Pay files for, 269
voiding, stopping, and reissuing, 256
classes
adding Units of Measure to, 14–15
Receipt, 193–194
Clearing account, 33
clearing transactions, 270–271
closing
purchasing orders, 69–70
Purchasing periods, 80
reviewing invoice holds before Payables, 215
steps for Payables month-end, 214
codes
adding to category sets, 17, 18
Invoice Workbench color coded fields, 153
Standard Industry Code, 86
comments for requisition items, 43–44
Company Profile window, 86–87
confirming
sensitive Payments data, 221–222
verbal purchase orders, 65
contacts for suppliers, 93
contract terms, 64, 65
Control Payables Period window, 216
controls
bank account, 130–132
setting up Purchasing document, 24–27
converting
active purchase orders, 5
open transactions, 4
options for open invoices, 4
suppliers, 4
Units of Measure, 15
correcting
invoice distributions, 170
purchase orders in Invoice Workbench, 184
system holds on invoices, 171–176
credit cards
creating invoices from transactions, 203–204

Invoice Workbench fields for, 164
protecting data, 221–222
credit memos, 186–187
currency selection
configuring, 8
invoice, 104, 113, 157
netting batches, 197
options for foreign, 116–117
purchasing documents, 57–58, 64
requisitions, 44, 56
using in payment process templates, 245, 246–247

D

data. *See also* electronic data transfers; XML data
adding supplier accounting, 97–98
changes affecting supplier reports, 82
converting to Procure-to-Pay, 4–5
creating supplier, 82–83
encrypting, 220–221
entering requisition, 43–45
modifying XML output for Payment templates, 223–225
new bank tables, 125
Payment format types for XML template, 226–231
protecting sensitive, 221–222
protocols for exporting Payment, 232–233
transferring from Payables to General Ledger, 215–216
updating supplier, 83–84
U.S.-seeded Payment formats for, 229–231
using historical, 45, 70–71
validating format of Payment, 222
data entry. *See* fields
dates
invoice term, 158
options for invoice due, 118
debit memos, 186–187
deducting bank charges, 120
defaults
category set, 17–19
defining Purchasing Options screen, 27–29

providing supplier's operating unit information, 84–85
setting purchase order session, 67
setting up requisition, 49
sources of invoice, 151–152
supplier invoice, 104–105
Demand Workbench, 72–73
Descriptive Flexfields (DFFs), 119
Detail Tax Lines screen, 184, 185
disbursements, 233–243.
See also Funds Disbursement Setup Administrator; payments
configuring system defaults for, 235
formats associated with Payment, 226–228
instructions for electronic, 235
organization-specific rules for, 236
payment methods for, 233–238
setting up payment, 220
discounts, 116, 123
distribution
canceling invoice, 169–170
distributing requisition costs to accounts, 47–48
invoice distribution sets, 143–144
Distribution account, 166
distribution sets
generating recurring invoices numbers from, 200
invoice, 143–144
Distributions window, 168–170
Document Builder
AutoCreate vs., 54
opening and using, 58–59
documents. *See also* invoices; processing purchasing documents; purchase orders; requisitions
approvals associated with, 22, 23
creating payment profiles for, 238
numbering payment, 253
numbering Purchasing, 30
payment grouping options for, 239, 240
referencing contracts on purchase orders, 64

selecting types for purchasing, 35–37
setting rules and limits for Purchasing, 24–27
types of purchasing, 40
duplicate suppliers, 105

E

E-Business Tax, 3, 99, 159, 160
e-Commerce Gateway, 202, 203, 239
EDI (Electronic Data Interchange)
  configuring supplier data for, 103
  importing invoice transactions in, 203
EFT (Electronic Funds Transfer), 102
electronic data transfers
  adding bank instructions to, 235
  configuring supplier for EDI, 103
  creating payment profiles for, 238
  importing invoice transactions in EDI, 203
  protocols for, 232
electronic payments. *See also* disbursements
  protocols for, 232
  supplier payments as EFTs, 102
  transmitting to bank, 268
employees
  creating in Purchasing, 19–20
  processing expense reimbursements for, 151
  setting up expense reports for, 190
  using hierarchies for document approvals, 50
encrypting payment data, 220–221
encumbrances, 51, 111
errors
  reviewing rejected payments for, 267, 268
  viewing on 1099 Invoice Exception report, 207, 208
Evaluated Receipt Settlement (ERS), 202, 204–205
Excel, 5
exchange rates, calculating, 117
Expense Report tab (Payables Options screen), 120

Expense Report window, 151, 190–193
expense reports
  importing into Payables, 205
  methods for entering, 120
  setting up Payables for, 151, 190–193
  templates for, 142–143
expenses
  auditing invoice, 164
  reimbursing to employees, 151

F

fields
  Accounting tab (Financial Options screen), 110
  approving changes to purchase order, 61
  bank account information, 129
  color coding of, 60, 153
  configuring Receiving Options screen, 30–32
  created from Invoice Workbench purchase order, 164–166
  defining Purchasing control, 24–27
  Descriptive Flexfields, 119
  entering for Lines tab (Invoice Workbench), 162–168
  finding receipts with, 74
  hidden Invoice Workbench, 162
  hidden Payments module, 254–255
  invoice-related Invoice Workbench, 154–157, 164, 165
  payment, 253–255
  project-related Invoice Workbench, 158
  settlement-related Invoice Workbench, 158–159, 167
  supplier address, 90–91
  tax-related Invoice Workbench, 159–160, 168
  types of Invoice Workbench invoice processing, 166–167
  used to find purchase orders and receipts, 179
files
  data protocols for exported Payment, 232–233
  Positive Pay, 269

Final Matching option, 181
final payment review, 267
financial institutions. *See* bank accounts
Financial Options screen
  Accounting tab, 108–109, 110
  Encumbrance tab, 111
  Human Resource tab, 111
  Supplier-Purchasing tab, 109, 110
  Tax tab, 111
Find Documents for Correction screen, 162
Find Requisition Lines screen, 54
Find window (Supplier Item Catalog screen), 46–47
finding
  and clearing transactions, 270–271
  documents for correction, 162
  and grouping requisition requests, 54–56
  purchase orders, 179
  receipts, 74, 179
  requisition items, 46–47
Folders Menu Options for Payables, 146–148
Format Payment Instructions program, 222–223
freezing purchasing orders, 70
freight terms
  adding to invoices, 181
  setting for supplier, 100
fully distributed sets, 143
Funds Disbursement Process Manager, 250, 251
Funds Disbursement Setup Administrator
  about, 220
  configuring Payment Process Profile, 238–243
  creating payment formats in, 228–229
  loading custom XML data templates, 225–226
  selecting template formats in, 224
  setting up payment method rules, 235
funds transfers. *See* electronic payments

G

gain/loss transactions, 115
General Ledger. *See also* subledgers; *and specific subledgers by name*
  balancing Payables subledger to, 217–218
  functions setup by, 8
  transferring invoice accounting entries to, 211
  transferring Payables data to, 215–216
General tab (Invoice Workbench), 160–162
global agreements, 55, 57
glossary, 276–279
government regulations. *See also* taxes
  tracking supplier business classifications, 93–94
grouping
  categories into sets, 17–18
  payment grouping rules, 239, 240
  requisition requests, 54–56
groups, defining Approval, 20–22

H

headers
  Invoice Workbench invoice, 162
  purchase order, 60–61
  receipt, 74
hidden fields
  Invoice Workbench, 162
  Payments module, 254–255
hierarchies for document approval, 35–37, 50
historical data
  tracking purchasing order changes, 70–71
  using for requisition templates, 45
holds
  placing supplier orders on, 100
  putting purchasing orders on, 70
  reviewing invoice holds before closing Payables, 215
  setting up and releasing, 135–141
  supplier, 83, 92
  supplier payment, 97

holds *(continued)*
    unmet tolerances
        creating, 180
Holds tab (Invoice
    Workbench), 170–176
Human Resource tab (Financial
    Options screen), 111

I

iExpenses module, 3, 120, 205
importing invoices, 202–205
income taxes, 88, 206
interest
    calculating during
        scheduled payments, 248
    configuring payment, 116,
        119, 259
Interest tab (Payables Options
    screen), 119
internal requisitions, 42
inventory
    accounting options for
        receiving transactions, 33
    adding detailed information
        on requisitions, 45
    creating organization unit
        for, 11–12
    defining Base Units of
        Measure, 13–14
    entering account numbers
        for transaction processing,
        12–13
    handling accruals in, 29
Invoice Aging Report, 217
Invoice Batches window,
    150–151, 152–153
Invoice Hold and Release
    Names screen, 141
Invoice Overview window,
    212–213
Invoice tab (Payables Options
    screen), 117–118
Invoice Tolerances Template
    screen, 113–114
Invoice Workbench, 153–187
    about, 153–154
    Calculate Balance Owed
        button, 213–214
    Calculate Tax button, 186
    color coded fields for, 153
    correcting purchase
        orders, 184
    entering data for Lines tab,
        162–168
    General tab of, 160–162
    hidden fields on, 162
    Holds tab, 170–176
    illustrated, 154

invoice inquiries from,
    212–214
invoice-related fields,
    154–157, 164, 165
making invoice
    distributions from,
    168–170
matching invoices to POs
    or receipts, 156, 179–184
options with Actions button
    of, 186–188
processing-related fields,
    157, 166–167
project-related fields, 158
purchase order-related
    fields on, 164–166
Quick Invoices window
    vs., 188–189
Quick Match button in, 184
Scheduled Payments
    tab, 177
selecting invoice
    currency, 157
setting up expense
    reporting for, 190
settlement-related fields,
    158–159, 167
Tax Details button in,
    184, 185
tax-related fields,
    159–160, 168
types of invoices, 155–156
View Payments tab,
    176–177
View Prepayment
    Applications tab, 177–179
invoices
    accounting transactions for,
        187–188, 211–212
    adding interest for past due
        payments, 119
    aging periods for, 124
    approving, 118–119,
        188, 210
    assigning payment
        priorities to, 246
    batching, 150, 152–153
    calculating remaining
        supplier balance, 271–273
    canceling, 187
    charging to specific
        projects, 48–49
    choosing payment methods
        for, 158–159, 258
    configuring terms and
        discounts for, 121–123
    converting open, 4
    correcting purchase
        orders, 184

creating accounting entries
    for, 215
credit/debit memo
    approval when validating,
    186–187
data entry in, 162–168
determining default
    currency for, 113
distribution sets for, 143–144
distributions from, 168–170
entering employee expense
    reimbursements as, 151
features of Invoice
    Workbench, 153–160
folders options for, 146–148
holds on, 97, 170–176
importing, 202–205
Invoice Workbench
    processing fields, 166–167
looking up, 160–162
making inquiries on,
    212–214
managing supplier, 104
matching, 112–113, 119,
    156, 166, 179–184
multiple payments
    processing for,
    251–252, 255
Payable options for,
    117–118
paying, 187, 251–256
payment grouping options
    for, 239, 240
prepaying, 159, 167, 187
printing notices about, 188
processing steps for, 150
project-related data fields
    in, 158
purchase orders as source
    of, 204–205
Quick Invoices, 188–189
recurring, 151, 198–202
rejected for payment,
    267, 268
releasing holds on, 188
reviewing, 215, 248
scheduling payments, 177,
    246–247
settlement-related fields for,
    158–159, 167
sources of default
    information for, 151–152
statuses for, 160–162
stopping or forcing
    approval for, 188
supplier purchases as
    source of, 84–85
tax calculations for, 184,
    185, 186

tax-related fields on,
    159–160, 168
tolerances for, 113–114
validating, 150,
    186–187, 210
viewing applied
    prepayments, 177–179
viewing payments
    from, 176
windows used to create,
    150–151
iPayments module, 250
iProcurement module, 2
iSupplier module
    function of, 3
    importing invoice
        transactions from
        suppliers, 204
    supplier surveys with, 97

J

journal entries for Payables,
    217–218

K

Key Flexfields (KFF), 8, 16
keystroke mimickers, 5

L

Ledgers, 8
liability accounts, 116
lines
    adding to receipts, 75–76
    purchase order, 33–34,
        62–63
    requisitions, 33–34, 42,
        43, 54
Lines tab
    Invoice Workbench,
        162–168
    Purchase Orders, 62–63
    Receipts, 75
    Requisitions, 42, 43
loading balances into accrual
    tables, 78
locations
    creating supplier
        shipping, 84
    defining purchasing-
        specific information for, 9
    information for
        requisitions, 45
    inventory- and payables-
        specific information
        for, 9–10
lookups for Payables, 146

M

manual processing
bank reconciliations, 270
holds and releases,
135–141, 170, 171–176
manual payments, 252,
268–269
requisitions, 41–42
Match button (Invoice
Workbench), 179–184
matching invoices
guidelines for, 182–184
Payables options for,
112–113
to purchase orders or
receipts, 119, 166,
179–184
Quick Match button, 184
using Invoice Workbench,
156, 179–184
merging suppliers, 105–106
Microsoft Excel, 5
Miscellaneous Accrual
Reconciliation Report, 78–79
modules. *See specific modules
by name*
month-end processing
accruals and Purchasing,
77–80
closing Payables, 214
More tab (Purchase Orders), 64
multiple payments
batching invoices as,
251–252, 255
for one invoice, 177

N

Negotiated Sources tab
(Supplier Item Catalog
screen), 45, 46
netting outstanding
transactions, 193–198
creating netting batches,
196–197
reviewing transactions, 198
setting up netting bank
accounts, 193–194, 196
statuses for netting
batches, 197
number, supplier's customer, 93
numbering
payment documents, 253
purchase orders, 57
Purchasing documents, 30
recurring invoices, 200
supplier invoices, 85
suppliers for Payables, 112

O

offsets for Payables module, 116
one-time payments, 257
Open Account AP Balances
Listing, 217
opening
first Payables period, 133
Purchasing periods, 80
Operating Unit Information
screen, 10, 11
operating units
adding Purchasing, 10–12
choosing for Payables, 108,
114, 115
overriding supplier sites
with, 92
providing defaults for
supplier's, 84–85
selecting for payments, 252
Oracle Approval Management.
See Approval Management
Oracle E-Business Suite. *See
also* R12 version; *specific
modules by name*
about Payments, 220
about Procure-to-Pay, 2
accrual process in, 77–78
Bills Payables
enhancements in, 262
converting closed
subledger transactions
in, 5
determining approval path
in, 50
E-Business Tax, 99
employee and position
hierarchies in, 50
features of Buyers Work
Center, 71–73
glossary for, 276–279
interfaces for importing
invoices, 202–205
receiving in, 73–74
setting up netting for,
193–198
tracking supplier business
classifications, 93–94
upgrading suppliers to
R12, 82
organizations
adding bank account
access to, 132–133
configuring payments from,
235–238
rules for disbursements
by, 236
Other Details page (Location
screen), 9–10

outside processing, 49
Overlay accounts, 166

P

Parent Suppliers, 86–87
password for wallet, 221
past due payments, 119
Payable Options screen,
114–121
Payables Lookups window,
146
Payables Manager, 271–273
Payables module. *See also* Bills
Payables; invoices;
processing payables
aging periods for, 124
approving invoices,
118–119, 210
automatic offset and
discount methods, 116
balancing subledger to
General Ledger, 217–218
bank charges in, 120,
144–145
banking information in,
125–133
closing and reconciling,
214–218
configuring Payables
Options screen, 114–121
controlling periods for,
216–217
controls for bank accounts,
130–132
currency and tax options
for, 116–117
defaults and options for
payments, 113
determining when
transactions accounted,
114–116
distribution sets for
invoices, 143–144
enabling bank account
access, 132–133
entering expense
reports, 120
expense report templates
for, 142–143
expense reporting setup,
151, 190–193
financial option setup for,
108–111
Folders Menu Options for,
146–148
function of, 3
importing credit/p-card
transactions, 203–204

inquiring on invoices,
212–214
interest on payments,
116, 119
invoice options in, 117–118
invoice tolerances for,
113–114
Lookups for, 146
matching invoices for,
112–113, 119, 166,
179–184
netting outstanding
transactions for, 193–198
new supplier tables in, 82
numbering suppliers for, 112
opening first period for, 133
operating units for, 108
options shared with
Receivables and
Payments, 220–233
payment options for, 120
payment term configuration
for, 121–123
Payments module vs., 108
placing holds and releases
on, 135–141
prepayments in, 116, 159,
167, 187
profile options for, 133–134
selecting operating unit for,
114, 115
sorting reports with
Alternate Names field, 121
special calendars for,
123–124
1099 processing for
suppliers, 205–208
troubleshooting journal
entries for, 217–218
updated payment
processing in R12, 250
validating all
transactions, 214
withholding tax
configurations in,
120–121
workflow for processing,
208–209
Payables Open Invoice
Interface, 203, 204
Payables Options screen
Approval tab, 118–119
Currency tab for, 116–117
Expense Report tab, 120
Interest tab, 119
Invoice tab, 117–118
Payment tab, 120
Reports tab, 121
Tax Reporting tab, 117

Payables Options screen
(continued)
  Withholding Tax tab,
    120–121
Payables System Setup screen,
  112–113
payment instructions
  adding to electronic
    transfers, 235
  formatting, 222–223
  including in payment
    process profiles, 241–242,
    253, 268
  saving, 237
  statuses for, 265
Payment Manager
  about, 250
  creating payment requests,
    257–260
  illustrated, 250
  invoice interest
    calculations in, 259
  scheduling settlement
    batches, 260–261
  setting up selection rule
    templates in, 245–248
  setting up templates for,
    220, 257
payment methods
  assigning bank accounts
    to, 247
  creating disbursement,
    233–235
  payment discount
    methods, 116
  selecting invoice,
    158–159, 258
  setting enterprise-wide,
    236–238
payment process profiles,
  238–243
  adding instructions for
    payments to, 241–242,
    253, 268
  assigning to templates, 238
  associating with bank
    accounts, 224
  choosing Bills
    Payable, 262
  creating for each
    document, 238
  reporting options for,
    242–243
  request statuses for,
    264–265
  rules for, 239–241
  saving, 241
  setting review points in,
    265–266

using payment instruction
  formulas with, 241–242
payment process templates,
  238, 245–248
Payment Setup
  Administrator, 220
Payment tab (Payables Options
  screen), 120
payment terms
  configuring invoice,
    121–123
  entering invoice, 158
  including on purchase
    order, 64–65
  setting supplier, 104
Payment Terms screen, 121–123
payments. *See also* payment
  methods; prepayments;
  settlements
  batching, 251
  calculating balances owed
    to suppliers, 271–273
  configuring schedules for,
    121–123
  creating templates for
    batching, 246
  deducting bank charges
    from, 120
  determining cash
    requirements for, 269
  electronic, 102, 232,
    235, 268
  encryption, 220–221
  entering default options for
    Payables, 120
  enterprise-wide methods
    for, 236–238
  final review of, 267
  generating single, 251–256
  grouping options for
    documents, 239, 240
  including terms on
    purchase orders, 64–65
  instructions accompanying,
    235, 241–242, 253, 268
  interest for, 116, 119
  items rejected for, 267, 268
  making Bills Payable
    settlements, 262–269
  making multiple invoice,
    251–252, 255
  paying invoices in full, 187
  processing rules for,
    239–241
  reconciling, 270
  recording check number
    for manual, 268–269
  recurring invoices, 201
  refunds, 252, 256–257

regulatory reports for, 243
requesting, 257–260
resolving pending, 262–263,
  266–267, 268
rules for methods of,
  234–235
scheduling invoice, 177,
  246–247
scheduling settlement
  batches, 260–261
setting up disbursements
  for, 233–243
setting up supplier, 85–86,
  102–103
stopping points for
  reviewing, 259
supplier terms for, 104
term setups for, 121–123
updated features for
  processing, 250–251
viewing from invoice, 176
voiding, stopping, and
  reissuing, 256
Payments module. *See also*
  Payment Manager; payments;
  prepayments
  about, 220
  adding instructions to
    electronic transfers, 235
  batching payments, 251
  configuring Payment
    Process Profile, 238–243
  configuring system,
    organization, and
    enterprise system
    payments, 235–238
  creating payment methods,
    233–235
  data export protocols for,
    232–233
  data format types for
    templates in, 226–231
  data validation in,
    222, 223
  encrypting data, 220–221
  enterprise-wide payment
    methods in, 236–238
  function of, 4
  generating single
    payments, 251–256
  loading custom templates,
    225–226
  making Bills Payable
    settlements, 262–269
  masking and confirming
    sensitive data, 221–222
  modifying XML output for
    custom data templates,
    223–225

organization-specific rules
  for disbursements, 236
output options for, 226
Payables vs., 108
reconciling payments, 270
refunds from, 252, 256–257
scheduling settlement
  batches, 260–261
setting up disbursements
  for, 233–243
setup options for, 220–233
streamlining payments with
  templates, 245–248
system profiles for, 244
U.S.-seeded formats for,
  229–231
voiding, stopping, and
  reissuing payments, 256
periods
  assigned to canceled
    invoices, 187
  controlling purchasing, 80
  generating recurring
    invoices for, 199
  Payables, 133, 216–217
  period end accruals, 79
permanent prepayments, 187
perpetual accruals, 77, 78
Personal Information screen, 20
position hierarchies, 50
Positive Pay files, 269
preferences, setting purchase
  order, 67
prepayments
  making invoice, 159,
    167, 187
  options for Payables
    invoices, 118
  unapplying, 187
  using prepayment
    accounts, 116
  viewing applied, 177–179
Price Reference tab (Purchase
  Orders), 63–64
prices
  adding price breaks to
    purchase orders, 65
  changing on blanket
    agreements, 69
  retroactive adjustments
    for, 33
printing
  invoice notices, 188
  purchasing documents, 68
Prior Purchases tab (Supplier
  Item Catalog screen), 45, 46
priorities
  assigning to invoices, 246
  payment, 258, 259

process categories for Payables accounting, 215
processing payables, 150–218
  accounting transactions for invoices, 211–212
  approving invoices, 118–119, 210
  balancing subledger in General Ledger, 217–218
  closing and reconciling Payables, 214–218
  controlling Payables periods, 216–217
  expense report imports in, 205
  importing invoices, 202–205
  inquiring on invoices, 212–214
  netting outstanding Receivables and Payables transactions, 193–198
  recurring invoices, 151, 198–202
  reviewing invoice holds before closing, 215
  setting up expense reporting, 190–193
  1099 processing, 205–208
  transferring data to General Ledger, 215–216
  validating all transactions, 214
  validating invoices, 150, 186–187, 210
  viewing payments from invoices, 176
  windows used for invoices, 150–151
  workflow for, 208–209
processing payments
  assigning priorities to invoices, 246
  bank reconciliations, 270
  batching payments, 237, 251
  calculating balances owed to suppliers, 271–273
  creating payment requests, 257–260
  determining cash requirements, 269
  generating single payments, 251–256
  including instructions for, 241–242, 253, 268
  making Bills Payables settlements, 262–269
  making multiple invoice payments, 251–252, 255

R12 features for, 250
recording check number for manual payments, 268–269
refunds, 252, 256–257
resolving pending requests, 262–263, 266–267, 268
reviewing pending invoices, 248, 266
reviewing rejected payments, 267, 268
scheduling settlement batches, 260–261
setting payment process profiles for, 239–241
stopping points when, 259
using payment process templates, 245–248
voiding, stopping, and reissuing payments, 256
processing purchasing documents. See also purchase orders; requisitions
  approving documents, 50, 68
  canceling documents, 69
  changing prices on blanket agreements, 69
  closing orders, 69–70
  handling returns, 76
  managing supplier invoices, 104
  opening and closing Purchasing periods, 80
  period end accruals, 79
  printing approved documents, 68
  processing returns, 76
  purchase orders, 53–54, 60–67
  releasing shipments, 71–72
  requisitions, 41–49, 51–53
  tracking changes to documents, 70–71
  types of documents, 40
  writing off accrual transactions, 79
Procure-to-Pay cycle
  about, 2
  data conversions for, 4–5
  modules contributing to, 2–4
Procurement Contracts module, 3
procurement (p-cards) cards, 203–204
products
  defining Base Units of Measure, 13–14
  listing supplier's, 94–95

profiles. See also payment process profiles
  configuring payment process, 238–243
  creating custom payments, 224–225
  Payables, 133–134
  Payments system, 244
Project Costing module, 48–49
protocols for exporting Payment data, 232–233
purchase agreements, 40, 41
purchase orders
  adding price breaks for, 65
  approving changes to fields, 61
  canceling, 69
  changing prices on blanket agreements, 69
  charging to specific projects, 48–49
  closing, 69–70
  configuring item number format for, 13
  confirming verbal, 65
  converting active, 5
  correcting in Invoice Workbench, 184
  creating invoices from, 204–205
  defined, 40, 41
  defining Approval Groups for, 20–22
  headers for, 60–61
  Invoice Workbench fields created from, 164–166
  line-related information on, 62–64
  line types for, 33–34
  matching invoices to, 112–113, 119, 166, 179–184
  numbering, 57
  payment terms on, 64–65
  placing supplier orders on hold, 100
  requisitions vs., 53–54
  setting preferences for, 67
  shipping details for, 66–67
  tracking changes to, 70–71
Purchase Orders screen
  Agreement tab, 64
  Lines tab, 62–63
  More tab, 64
  Price Reference tab, 63–64
  Reference Documents tab, 63
  Temporary Labor tab, 63

purchase requisitions, 42. See also requisitions
purchasing. See also processing purchasing documents
  Account Generator's use in, 37
  accounting options for receiving transactions, 33
  adding Operating Units, 10–11
  approval path for documents, 50
  approval rules and groups for, 20–22, 23
  assigning categories for, 16–19
  configuring Receiving Options fields, 30–32
  creating requisitions in, 41
  defining inventory organizations, 11–13
  defining Purchasing Options screen default settings, 27–29
  document controls for, 24–27
  employee assignments in, 19–20
  features of Buyers Work Center, 71–73
  Financial Options for, 33
  handling inventory and expense item accruals, 29
  including cost factors on receipts, 33
  Inventory Units of Measure for, 13–14
  line types for requisitions and purchase orders, 33–34
  location information for, 8–10
  module's function, 2
  numbering documents for, 30
  opening and closing periods for, 80
  receiving, 73–77
  selecting document types for, 35–37
  setting up Buyers for, 22, 23
  setup shared with other EBS modules, 8
  templates for requisitions, 34–35
  using Payables invoice tolerances with, 113

purchasing documents
  color coding fields in, 60
  creating approval rules
    for, 50
  currency designations for,
    57–58
  numbering, 57
  types of, 40
Purchasing Options screen,
  24–29

Q

Quick Invoices window, 151,
  188–189
Quick Match button (Invoice
  Workbench), 184
quick payments, 252
Quick Update window
  Key Payment setups for,
    85–86
  Key Purchasing setups for,
    84–85
  updating supplier
    information in, 83–84

R

R12 version
  banking information in,
    125
  formatting payment data in,
    222–223
  payment processing in, 250
  security options in, 221–222
recalculating payment
  schedules, 121
Receipt class, 193–194
receipts
  about, 73–74
  adding cost factors to, 33
  creating headers for, 74
  matching invoices to,
    112–113, 119, 166,
    179–184
  period end accruals for
    expense, 79
Receivables module
  netting outstanding
    transactions for, 193–198
  shared setup options with
    Payables and Payments,
    220–233
receiving, 73–77
  about receipts, 73–75
  accounts available for
    transactions, 33
  correcting transactions for,
    76–77

function of, 73–74
  supplier options for,
    101–102
Receiving Inspection
  accounts, 29
Receiving Inventory
  account, 33
Receiving Options screen,
  30–32
recurring invoices, 151,
  198–202
Reference Documents tab
  (Purchase Orders), 63
refunds, 252, 256–257
regulatory reports for
  payments, 243
reissuing payments, 256
releases
  defined, 40
  invoice holds and,
    135–141, 188
releasing shipments, 71–72
remittance advice, 243
reports
  Cash Requirement, 269
  changes to suppliers
    affecting, 82
  entering expense, 120
  key Payables balancing,
    217–218
  Recurring Invoice, 201
  regulatory reports for
    payments, 243
  sorting with Alternate
    Names field, 121
  Supplier Audit, 105
  templates for expense,
    142–143
  1099 Invoice Exception,
    207, 208
  tracking supplier
    information for, 86–87
  types of bank
    reconciliation, 270, 271
Reports tab (Payables Options
  screen), 121
requester information for
  requisitions, 45
requests for quote, 40
Requisition Templates
  creating, 34–35
  using, 45, 46
requisitions, 41–49, 51–53
  adding information at
    bottom of, 44–45
  Approval Groups for, 20–22
  approving, 51–52
  charging to projects, 48–49
  converting in-process, 5

creating purchase orders
    from, 53–54
  currency setup for, 44
  defaults for, 49
  defined, 40
  Demand Workbench
    features for, 72–73
  distributing cost to
    accounts, 47–48
  finding and grouping items
    for, 54–56
  including outside
    processing on, 49
  item number format for, 13
  line types for, 33–34
  lines for, 42, 43, 54
  locating in Supplier Item
    Catalog, 46–47
  manual, 41–42
  providing detailed
    information about, 43–44
  purchase orders vs., 53–54
  reserving funds for, 51
  statuses for, 42, 52–53
  templates for, 34–35, 45, 46
  types of, 42
Requisitions screen
  about, 41–42
  Lines tab, 42, 43
  Source Details tab, 43–44
reserving funds for
  requisitions, 51
resolving pending payment
  requests, 262–263,
  266–267, 268
retainage, 166
Retroactive Price Adjustment
  account, 33
returns, 76–77
reversing accruals, 77, 78
reviewing
  Bills Payables processing,
    265–266
  invoice holds, 215
  payment creation, 259
  pending invoices before
    payment, 248, 266
  rejected payments for
    errors, 267, 268
  setting up for payment
    process profiles, 265–266
  settlements, 250
rules. See also approvals
  payment method, 234–235
  purchasing document
    approval, 50
  setting payment profile
    usage, 239–241
  supplier sourcing, 45, 46, 55

S

Sarbanes-Oxley audit
  requirements, 210
saving
  payment instructions, 237
  payment process
    profile, 241
Scheduled Payments tab
  (Invoice Workbench), 177
scheduling
  configuring payment,
    121–123
  invoice payments, 177,
    246–247
  settlement batches, 260–261
security
  encrypting data, 220–221
  masking and confirming
    sensitive data, 221–222
serial numbers, 12
Services Procurement module, 3
services, supplier, 94–95
settlements
  Bills Payables, 262–269
  Invoice Workbench fields
    for, 158–159, 167
  scheduling batches of,
    260–261
  transaction workflow for
    Payment, 250
Setup Payments
  Administrator, 220
shipments
  freight terms for
    supplier, 100
  locations for, 9, 84
  purchase order details for,
    66–67
  sending items to alternate
    supplier address, 93
Shipping Details page
  (Location screen), 9
SIC (Standard Industry
  Code), 86
sites
  adding supplier, 97–98
  adding supplier URLs for, 87
  skeleton distribution sets, 143
SLA. See Subledger Accounting
Source Details tab
  (Requisitions screen), 43–44
Sourcing Purchasing module, 3
sourcing rules, 45, 46, 55
special calendars for Payables,
  123–124
SQL*Loader, 202, 203
statuses
  invoices, 160–162

netting batch, 197
payment process and
information, 264–265
requisition, 42, 52–53
stopping payments, 256
Subledger Accounting (SLA)
about, 4
Account Generators vs., 37
subledgers
balancing Payables in
General Ledger, 217–218
conversion of closed
transactions, 5
creating requisitions in
purchasing, 41
Summary Accrual
Reconciliation Report, 78
Supplier Audit Report, 105
Supplier Item Catalog
finding items in, 46–47
illustrated, 46, 47
using with requisitions,
45–47
Supplier-Purchasing tab
(Financial Options screen),
109, 110
suppliers, 82–106
adding customer data
for, 93
adding sites and
accounting data for,
97–98
banking details for, 95–97
calculating balances owed
to, 271–273
changes affecting reports
for, 82
choosing for payments,
252–253
configuring payment data
for, 85–86
contacts for, 93
converting, 4
creating, 82–104
entering addresses for,
90–93
identifying duplicate, 105
importing invoice
transactions from, 204
invoicing purchases from,
84–85
iSupplier and surveys
for, 97
listing products and
services for, 94–95
maintaining, 104–106
merging, 105–106
numbering in Payables, 112
operating unit setup for, 92

payment options for,
102–103
processing invoices
from, 104
purchasing options for, 100
receiving options for,
101–102
researching invoice
questions for, 212–214
settling invoice bank
charges for, 158–159
sorting reports with
alternate name for, 121
sourcing rules for
requisition, 55
tax detail setup for, 88–90
tax and reporting setup
for, 99
1099 processing for,
205–208
tracking business
classifications for, 93–94
tracking specific
information about,
86–87
updating in Quick Update
window, 83–84
upgrading to R12, 82
surveying suppliers, 97
system holds, 135–141
System Keys, 221
system security options,
220–223

T

Tax Details button (Invoice
Workbench), 184, 185
Tax Reporting tab (Payables
Options screen), 117
Tax tab (Financial Options
screen), 111
taxes. See also income taxes;
1099s; withholding taxes
adding to requisitions, 48
calculating for invoices,
184, 185, 186
filing 1099s with
K-records, 117
income, 88, 206
Invoice Workbench fields
related to, 159–160, 168
processing 1099s for
suppliers, 205–208
setting for recurring
invoices, 200–201
1099 reporting for
suppliers, 87,
88–89, 99

tracking details on
suppliers, 88–90, 99
VAT, 88, 99, 111
Template Builder, 224–225
templates
assigning payment profiles
to, 238
creating Cash Requirement
reports from, 269
expense report, 142–143
modifying XML output for
custom Payment, 223–225
payment process, 245–248
Payments formats
associated with, 226–231
requisition, 34–35, 45, 46
setting up for Payment
Manager, 220, 257
Temporary Labor tab (Purchase
Orders), 64
temporary prepayments, 187
1099s
configuring suppliers for,
87, 88–89, 99
filing with K-records, 117
processing for Payables
suppliers, 205–208
1099 Invoice Exception
report, 207, 208
terms. See also payment terms
contract, 64, 65
freight, 100, 181
third-party settlement
companies, 232–233
tolerances
applying to PO price
corrections, 184
configuring for Payables,
113–114
holds on POs with
unmet, 180
setting invoice tax, 118
tracking
changes to purchasing
documents, 70–71
supplier business
classifications, 93–94
supplier information, 86–87
training new Procure-to-Pay
users, 5
transactional taxes for
suppliers, 88, 89–90
transactions
accounting for invoice,
211–212
accounting options for
receiving, 33
bank charge, 120,
144–145

conversion of closed
subledger, 5
converting open, 4
correcting receiving and
return, 76–77
determining when
payments are accounted,
114–116
finding and clearing,
270–271
gain/loss, 115
netting outstanding
Receivables and
Payables, 193–198
setting up taxes for
suppliers, 88, 89–90
validating all Payables, 214
workflow for
settlements, 250
writing off accrual, 79
Transactions Available for
Reconciliation Report, 271
transfers. See electronic data
transfers
transportation. See also
shipments
adding to receipts, 33
Treasury module, 270

U

unclearing transactions, 271
Units of Measure (UOM),
13–14, 15
upgrading, suppliers to R12
version, 82
U.S.-seeded Payment formats,
229–231

V

validating
all Payables
transactions, 214
handling unvalidated
disbursements, 236
invoice lines, 167
invoices, 150,
186–187, 210
Payment data format,
222, 223
VAT taxes, 88, 99, 111
View Payments tab (Invoice
Workbench), 176–177
View Prepayment Applications
tab (Invoice Workbench),
177–179
voiding payments, 256

W

W9s for suppliers, 99
wallets, 220–221
wires. *See* electronic payments
Withholding Tax tab (Payables
  Options screen), 120–121
withholding taxes
  calculating during
    scheduled payments, 248
  configuring for Payables
    module, 120–121
  defined, 88
  generating invoices in
    Payment Manager with,
    259–260
  reporting supplier, 89

Work in Process module, 49
Workday calendar, 12
workflow. *See also* processing
  payables; processing
  payments; processing
  purchasing documents
  Payments setup, 220
  processing payables,
    208–209
  quick invoice entry,
    188–189
  requiring invoice
    approvals, 118–119
  setting up document's
    approval, 36

settlement transaction, 250
  using payment process
    profiles, 239–241
writing off accrual
  transactions, 79

X

XML data
  loading Payments
    templates for, 225–226
  modifying Payment
    templates output,
    223–225

output options in
  Payments, 226
Payments format types for,
  226–231
using payment instruction
  formulas for, 241–242
XML Publisher, 223–224

GET YOUR FREE SUBSCRIPTION
TO *ORACLE MAGAZINE*

Oracle Magazine is essential gear for today's information technology professionals.
Stay informed and increase your productivity with every issue of *Oracle Magazine*.
Inside each free bimonthly issue you'll get:

- Up-to-date information on Oracle Database, Oracle Application Server, Web development, enterprise grid computing, database technology, and business trends
- Third-party news and announcements
- Technical articles on Oracle and partner products, technologies, and operating environments
- Development and administration tips
- Real-world customer stories

If there are other Oracle users at your location who would like to receive their own subscription to *Oracle Magazine*, please photocopy this form and pass it along.

Three easy ways to subscribe:

① Web
Visit our Web site at **oracle.com/oraclemagazine**
You'll find a subscription form there, plus much more

② Fax
Complete the questionnaire on the back of this card
and fax the questionnaire side only to **+1.847.763.9638**

③ Mail
Complete the questionnaire on the back of this card
and mail it to **P.O. Box 1263, Skokie, IL 60076-8263**

Want your own FREE subscription?

To receive a free subscription to *Oracle Magazine*, you must fill out the entire card, sign it, and date it (incomplete cards cannot be processed or acknowledged). You can also fax your application to +1.847.763.9638. **Or subscribe at our Web site at oracle.com/oraclemagazine**

○ **Yes, please send me a FREE subscription *Oracle Magazine*.**   ○ No.

○ From time to time, Oracle Publishing allows our partners exclusive access to our e-mail addresses for special promotions and announcements. To be included in this program, please check this circle. If you do not wish to be included, you will only receive notices about your subscription via e-mail.

○ Oracle Publishing allows sharing of our postal mailing list with selected third parties. If you prefer your mailing address not to be included in this program, please check this circle.

If at any time you would like to be removed from either mailing list, please contact Customer Service at +1.847.763.9635 or send an e-mail to oracle@halldata.com. If you opt in to the sharing of information, Oracle may also provide you with e-mail related to Oracle products, services, and events. If you want to completely unsubscribe from any e-mail communication from Oracle, please send an e-mail to: unsubscribe@oracle-mail.com with the following in the subject line: REMOVE [your e-mail address]. For complete information on Oracle Publishing's privacy practices, please visit oracle.com/html/privacy/html

X _____
signature (required)   date

name   title

company   e-mail address

street/p.o. box

city/state/zip or postal code   telephone

country   fax

Would you like to receive your free subscription in digital format instead of print if it becomes available? ○ Yes ○ No

---

YOU MUST ANSWER ALL 10 QUESTIONS BELOW.

① WHAT IS THE PRIMARY BUSINESS ACTIVITY OF YOUR FIRM AT THIS LOCATION? (check one only)

- ☐ 01 Aerospace and Defense Manufacturing
- ☐ 02 Application Service Provider
- ☐ 03 Automotive Manufacturing
- ☐ 04 Chemicals
- ☐ 05 Media and Entertainment
- ☐ 06 Construction/Engineering
- ☐ 07 Consumer Sector/Consumer Packaged Goods
- ☐ 08 Education
- ☐ 09 Financial Services/Insurance
- ☐ 10 Health Care
- ☐ 11 High Technology Manufacturing, OEM
- ☐ 12 Industrial Manufacturing
- ☐ 13 Independent Software Vendor
- ☐ 14 Life Sciences (biotech, pharmaceuticals)
- ☐ 15 Natural Resources
- ☐ 16 Oil and Gas
- ☐ 17 Professional Services
- ☐ 18 Public Sector (government)
- ☐ 19 Research
- ☐ 20 Retail/Wholesale/Distribution
- ☐ 21 Systems Integrator, VAR/VAD
- ☐ 22 Telecommunications
- ☐ 23 Travel and Transportation
- ☐ 24 Utilities (electric, gas, sanitation, water)
- ☐ 98 Other Business and Services _____

② WHICH OF THE FOLLOWING BEST DESCRIBES YOUR PRIMARY JOB FUNCTION? (check one only)

CORPORATE MANAGEMENT/STAFF
- ☐ 01 Executive Management (President, Chair, CEO, CFO, Owner, Partner, Principal)
- ☐ 02 Finance/Administrative Management (VP/Director/ Manager/Controller, Purchasing, Administration)
- ☐ 03 Sales/Marketing Management (VP/Director/Manager)
- ☐ 04 Computer Systems/Operations Management (CIO/VP/Director/Manager MIS/IS/IT, Ops)

IS/IT STAFF
- ☐ 05 Application Development/Programming Management
- ☐ 06 Application Development/Programming Staff
- ☐ 07 Consulting
- ☐ 08 DBA/Systems Administrator
- ☐ 09 Education/Training
- ☐ 10 Technical Support Director/Manager
- ☐ 11 Other Technical Management/Staff
- ☐ 98 Other

③ WHAT IS YOUR CURRENT PRIMARY OPERATING PLATFORM (check all that apply)

- ☐ 01 Digital Equipment Corp UNIX/VAX/VMS
- ☐ 02 HP UNIX
- ☐ 03 IBM AIX
- ☐ 04 IBM UNIX
- ☐ 05 Linux (Red Hat)
- ☐ 06 Linux (SUSE)
- ☐ 07 Linux (Oracle Enterprise)
- ☐ 08 Linux (other)
- ☐ 09 Macintosh
- ☐ 10 MVS
- ☐ 11 Netware
- ☐ 12 Network Computing
- ☐ 13 SCO UNIX
- ☐ 14 Sun Solaris/SunOS
- ☐ 15 Windows
- ☐ 16 Other UNIX
- ☐ 98 Other
- ☐ 99 None of the Above

- ☐ 18 Minicomputer
- ☐ 19 Intel x86(32)
- ☐ 20 Intel x86(64)
- ☐ 21 Network Computer
- ☐ 22 Symmetric Multiprocessing
- ☐ 23 Workstation Services

SERVICES
- ☐ 24 Consulting
- ☐ 25 Education/Training
- ☐ 26 Maintenance
- ☐ 27 Online Database
- ☐ 28 Support
- ☐ 29 Technology-Based Training
- ☐ 30 Other
- ☐ 99 None of the Above

④ DO YOU EVALUATE, SPECIFY, RECOMMEND, OR AUTHORIZE THE PURCHASE OF ANY OF THE FOLLOWING? (check all that apply)

- ☐ 01 Hardware
- ☐ 02 Business Applications (ERP, CRM, etc.)
- ☐ 03 Application Development Tools
- ☐ 04 Database Products
- ☐ 05 Internet or Intranet Products
- ☐ 06 Other Software
- ☐ 07 Middleware Products
- ☐ 99 None of the Above

⑤ IN YOUR JOB, DO YOU USE OR PLAN TO PURCHASE ANY OF THE FOLLOWING PRODUCTS? (check all that apply)

SOFTWARE
- ☐ 01 CAD/CAE/CAM
- ☐ 02 Collaboration Software
- ☐ 03 Communications
- ☐ 04 Database Management
- ☐ 05 File Management
- ☐ 06 Finance
- ☐ 07 Java
- ☐ 08 Multimedia Authoring
- ☐ 09 Networking
- ☐ 10 Programming
- ☐ 11 Project Management
- ☐ 12 Scientific and Engineering
- ☐ 13 Systems Management
- ☐ 14 Workflow

HARDWARE
- ☐ 15 Macintosh
- ☐ 16 Mainframe
- ☐ 17 Massively Parallel Processing

⑥ WHAT IS YOUR COMPANY'S SIZE? (check one only)

- ☐ 01 More than 25,000 Employees
- ☐ 02 10,001 to 25,000 Employees
- ☐ 03 5,001 to 10,000 Employees
- ☐ 04 1,001 to 5,000 Employees
- ☐ 05 101 to 1,000 Employees
- ☐ 06 Fewer than 100 Employees

⑦ DURING THE NEXT 12 MONTHS, HOW MUCH DO YOU ANTICIPATE YOUR ORGANIZATION WILL SPEND ON COMPUTER HARDWARE, SOFTWARE, PERIPHERALS, AND SERVICES FOR YOUR LOCATION? (check one only)

- ☐ 01 Less than $10,000
- ☐ 02 $10,000 to $49,999
- ☐ 03 $50,000 to $99,999
- ☐ 04 $100,000 to $499,999
- ☐ 05 $500,000 to $999,999
- ☐ 06 $1,000,000 and Over

⑧ WHAT IS YOUR COMPANY'S YEARLY SALES REVENUE? (check one only)

- ☐ 01 $500, 000, 000 and above
- ☐ 02 $100, 000, 000 to $500, 000, 000
- ☐ 03 $50, 000, 000 to $100, 000, 000
- ☐ 04 $5, 000, 000 to $50, 000, 000
- ☐ 05 $1, 000, 000 to $5, 000, 000

⑨ WHAT LANGUAGES AND FRAMEWORKS DO YOU USE? (check all that apply)

- ☐ 01 Ajax
- ☐ 02 C
- ☐ 03 C++
- ☐ 04 C#
- ☐ 13 Python
- ☐ 14 Ruby/Rails
- ☐ 15 Spring
- ☐ 16 Struts
- ☐ 05 Hibernate
- ☐ 06 J++/J#
- ☐ 07 Java
- ☐ 08 JSP
- ☐ 09 .NET
- ☐ 10 Perl
- ☐ 11 PHP
- ☐ 12 PL/SQL
- ☐ 17 SQL
- ☐ 18 Visual Basic
- ☐ 98 Other

⑩ WHAT ORACLE PRODUCTS ARE IN USE AT YOUR SITE? (check all that apply)

ORACLE DATABASE
- ☐ 01 Oracle Database 11*g*
- ☐ 02 Oracle Database 10*g*
- ☐ 03 Oracle9*i* Database
- ☐ 04 Oracle Embedded Database (Oracle Lite, Times Ten, Berkeley DB)
- ☐ 05 Other Oracle Database Release

ORACLE FUSION MIDDLEWARE
- ☐ 06 Oracle Application Server
- ☐ 07 Oracle Portal
- ☐ 08 Oracle Enterprise Manager
- ☐ 09 Oracle BPEL Process Manager
- ☐ 10 Oracle Identity Management
- ☐ 11 Oracle SOA Suite
- ☐ 12 Oracle Data Hubs

ORACLE DEVELOPMENT TOOLS
- ☐ 13 Oracle JDeveloper
- ☐ 14 Oracle Forms
- ☐ 15 Oracle Reports
- ☐ 16 Oracle Designer
- ☐ 17 Oracle Discoverer
- ☐ 18 Oracle BI Beans
- ☐ 19 Oracle Warehouse Builder
- ☐ 20 Oracle WebCenter
- ☐ 21 Oracle Application Express

ORACLE APPLICATIONS
- ☐ 22 Oracle E-Business Suite
- ☐ 23 PeopleSoft Enterprise
- ☐ 24 JD Edwards EnterpriseOne
- ☐ 25 JD Edwards World
- ☐ 26 Oracle Fusion
- ☐ 27 Hyperion
- ☐ 28 Siebel CRM

ORACLE SERVICES
- ☐ 28 Oracle E-Business Suite On Demand
- ☐ 29 Oracle Technology On Demand
- ☐ 30 Siebel CRM On Demand
- ☐ 31 Oracle Consulting
- ☐ 32 Oracle Education
- ☐ 33 Oracle Support
- ☐ 98 Other
- ☐ 99 None of the Above